FIVE PLAYS
for stage, radio, and television

PORTABLE AUSTRALIAN AUTHORS

This series provides carefully selected volumes introducing major Australian writers and movements. The format is designed for compactness and for pleasurable reading. Each volume is intended to meet a need not hitherto met by any single book. Each is edited by an authority distinguished in his field, who adds an introductory essay and other helpful material.

General Editor: L.T. Hergenhan

Also in this series:

Marcus Clarke edited by Michael Wilding
Henry Lawson edited by Brian Kiernan

In Preparation:

The 1890s: Selected Stories, Verse, Essays edited by Leon Cantrell
Joseph Furphy edited by John Barnes
The Jindyworobaks edited by Brian Elliott
Rolf Boldrewood edited by Alan Brissenden

Portable Australian Authors

FIVE PLAYS

for stage, radio, and television

LOUIS ESSON:
The Drovers

ALAN SEYMOUR:
The One Day of the Year

DAVID WILLIAMSON:
What If You Died Tomorrow

DOUGLAS STEWART:
The Golden Lover

TED ROBERTS:
Lindsay's Boy

Edited with an Introduction by
ALRENE SYKES

University of Queensland Press

Published by University of Queensland Press
St. Lucia, Queensland, 1977

Introduction © Alrene Sykes, 1977
This compilation © University of Queensland Press, 1977

The Drovers © Louis Esson, 1920
Performing rights enquiries should be addressed to
Currency Methuen Drama Pty. Ltd., 87 Jersey Road,
Woollahra, New South Wales, 2025

The One Day of the Year © Alan Seymour, 1962
Performing rights enquiries should be addressed to
Laurence Fitch Ltd., 113–117 Wardour Street,
London, WIV 4EH, England

What If You Died Tomorrow © David Williamson, 1974
Performing rights enquiries should be addressed to
Curtis Brown (Aust.) Pty. Ltd., PO Box 19, Paddington,
New South Wales, 2021

The Golden Lover © Douglas Stewart, 1944
Performing rights enquiries should be addressed to
Curtis Brown (Aust.) Pty. Ltd., PO Box 19, Paddington,
New South Wales, 2021

Lindsay's Boy © Ted Roberts, 1977
Performing rights enquiries should be addressed to
Ted Roberts, 5 Tower Street, Vaucluse, New South Wales, 2030

This book is copyright. Apart from any fair dealing for the
purposes of private study, research, criticism, or review,
as permitted under the Copyright Act, no part may be reproduced
by any process without written permission. Enquiries should
be addressed to the publishers.

Typeset, printed and bound by Academy Press Pty. Ltd., Brisbane.

Distributed in the United Kingdom, Europe, the Middle East, Africa, and the
Caribbean by Prentice-Hall International, International Book Distributors
Ltd., 66 Wood Lane End, Hemel Hempstead, Herts., England

National Library of Australia
Cataloguing-in-Publication data
Five plays for stage, radio and television.

(Portable Australian authors).
Bibliography.
ISBN 0 7022 1444 2.
ISBN 0 7022 1450 7 Paperback.

1. Australian drama. I. Sykes, Alrene Maude, ed.

822.008

Contents

Acknowledgments   vii

Introduction: Australian Drama Since 1920   ix

for STAGE

Louis Esson *The Drovers*   3
  Letters from Esson to Vance Palmer   12
  From Hilda Esson's Introduction to *The Southern Cross and Other Plays*   25

Alan Seymour *The One Day of the Year*   29
  Seymour on *The One Day of the Year*   83
  Seymour as A.B.C. "Guest of Honour"   84
  Autobiographical Article   85

David Williamson *What If You Died Tomorrow*   93
  Williamson on *What If You Died Tomorrow*   141
  From a *Cinema Papers* Interview   143
  From a *Cleo* Interview   147

for RADIO

Douglas Stewart *The Golden Lover*   151
  Glossary   212
  Introduction to *The Golden Lover*   214
  The Playwright in Australia   218

for TELEVISION

Ted Roberts *Lindsay's Boy*   223
  Roberts on *Lindsay's Boy*   274
  Roberts on Writing for Television   275

Select Bibliography   277

Acknowledgments

Acknowledgment is made to: Currency Methuen Drama Pty. Ltd. for permission to include *The Drovers* (reprinted from Louis Esson, *Dead Timber and Other Plays*, London: Hendersons, 1920); Angus & Robertson Publishers for permission to include *The One Day of the Year* (reprinted from *Three Australian Plays*, Harmondsworth, Penguin, 1963); Currency Methuen Drama Pty. Ltd. for permission to include *What If You Died Tomorrow* (reprinted from David Williamson, *Three Plays*, Sydney: Currency Methuen, 1974); Curtis Brown (Aust.) Pty. Ltd. and Angus & Robertson Publishers for permission to include *The Golden Lover* (reprinted from the A & R edition, 1962); Ted Roberts for permission to include *Lindsay's Boy* (previously unpublished).

Acknowledgment is also made to Hugh Esson for permission to include letters from Louis Esson to Vance Palmer and Hilda Esson's introduction to *The Southern Cross and Other Plays*; to the Australian Broadcasting Commission for permission to include Alan Seymour's "Guest of Honour" broadcast; to *Meanjin Quarterly* for permission to include Alan Seymour's "Encounters with the Great" article; to *Cinema Papers* and Dave Jones for permission to include an extract from an interview with David Williamson; to *Cleo* for permission to include an extract from an interview with David Williamson; and to Douglas Stewart for permission to include his introduction to *The Golden Lover* and his article "The Playwright in Australia".

Introduction: Australian Drama Since 1920

THE STAGE

Australian drama in the twentieth century, as has been more than once observed, is extraordinarily violent; in fact, it is quite difficult to think of plays which do not at some point explode into physical violence, normally by way of one character knocking down another. (In this collection of plays, blows are struck in *The One Day of the Year*, *What If You Died Tomorrow*, and *Lindsay's Boy*; Ruarangi in *The Golden Lover* half-strangles Tiki; there are no fights in *The Drovers*, but the central character has just been fatally injured, off stage, in a stampede of cattle.) But violence is not the only obsession in Australian drama: another which seems even more deeply rooted is, simply, Australianness. Fortunately for the continuing interest and vitality of the drama, the concept of what Australianness is, and the modes of exploring it, have changed from decade to decade.

The earliest play concerned with Australia was apparently the French drama, *Les Emigrés aux Terres Australes*, produced in Paris in 1792, four years after the foundation of Australia;[1] but it was not until the late nineteen sixties and early seventies that Australian plays suddenly became a normal part of the average theatregoer's fare, rather than a minority interest for a few fervently partisan supporters. Some of the smaller Australian theatres, particularly in Melbourne and Adelaide, began to show a tentative sympathy towards local playwrights quite early in this century, but the driving force which every new movement needs to get it off the ground did not materialize until the advent of the playwright Louis Esson and the Pioneer Players (a Melbourne amateur theatre group organized by Esson, Vance Palmer, and Stewart Macky) in the 1920s. Ironically, the plays normally regarded as Esson's best (*The Woman Tamer*, *The Drovers*, *The Time Is Not Yet Ripe*) were actually written before the Pioneer Players came into being, but the Players, who opened in 1922 with Esson's "The Battler", were important in that they produced at least some creditable plays (by Louis Esson, Vance Palmer and others) and because they demanded to be taken seriously: Esson, writing in 1921, described how he had earlier "refused to be played one season, in a cellar, while Bennett* was being done, seriously, in the theatre."[2] Another reason of course for the considerable attention the Esson movement has received is that it is much better documented than other early attempts, particularly since the publication in 1948 of Vance Palmer's fascinating book, *Louis Esson and the Australian Theatre*.[3] The Pioneer Players had as their inspiration and model the famous Abbey Theatre in Dublin; the story is often told of how Esson met Yeats and Synge when he visited the theatre in 1905, and was advised by both of them to seek inspiration in his own country. As Synge told Esson, "You ought to have plenty of material for drama in Australia. All those outback stations with shepherds going mad in lonely huts."[4] Esson hoped that like their predecessors in Ireland the Pioneer Players would ultimately develop into a national theatre.

Esson's vision of what Australian drama should be was less complex than that of today's playwrights—but a good deal more difficult to put into practice. He wanted plays by Australian playwrights, on Australian subjects, produced in proper theatres, and taken seriously by audiences and critics. Dreaming of such a theatre in 1921, when he and his family were about to leave London and return to Melbourne after several years abroad, Esson wrote to Vance Palmer: "We have admirable material for all kinds of plays, even historical and fantastic. We could give the critics some real work to do. What they have to say about Bennett and Galsworthy is of no importance to anybody; but they could be right or wrong about us."[5] In the cause of an Australian drama he was, apparently, prepared to sacrifice quality, and wrote to Stewart Macky, " ... personally I'd have nothing but local and original works, however inadequate they were, a kind of Folk Theatre."[6] Perhaps the plays were not good enough, perhaps the productions were too amateurish, the audiences not ready, or the group too unbusiness-like; whatever the reason, the Pioneer Players ceased to be in June 1926, their last production being Esson's *The Bride of Gospel Place*. Nearly thirty years were to go by before there was a second serious assault by Australian playwrights on the theatres of their land.

Without doubt, *The Drovers* is Esson's best play. It was written in London in 1919. Vance Palmer recalls that at the time there was a fad in London theatres for seasons of short plays, particularly plays with exotic foreign settings, and William Moore suggested to Esson, Palmer, and others that this might be an admirable opportunity to launch a season of short Australian plays.[7] The Australian season did not eventuate, but hopes for it had inspired *The Drovers*. Esson based the play on a story told to him by his half-brother, Frank Brown, a skilled horseman with experience of the outback.

The Drovers is an extraordinary play, the more so if one compares it

---

* Arnold Bennett, remembered today as a novelist rather than as a playwright, though his plays were highly popular in their day. Among the most successful were *The Great Adventure* (1913), *Milestones* (with Edward Knoblock, 1912), and *The Love Match* (1922).

with other dramas of the period. The impression it leaves is partly reflected in Esson's entry in his diary, "I find I have little interest in events. I like the lurid and dramatic, a vivid impression, a twist of thought, a scene, a crisis, a glimpse of beauty."[8] The play has no real plot, no real conflict, and the characters are sketched simply, for the most part characterized by their obsessions: Bob with his passion for horses, Mick with his admiration for the Boss, the Cook (Albert) with his cooking skills and the money he is going to make at the Brunette races; the Jackeroo (the only character with no name except the one indicating the job he does) is the conventional ignorant new chum, and Pidgeon, the then familiar (and no longer acceptable) slightly comic Aborigine. The Boss and Briglow Bill are similarly lightly outlined, but the sense of their controlled, almost-concealed suffering, gives their characterization depth.

In the 1970s, more than fifty years after *The Drovers* was written, the characters still seem realistic and credible; their dialogue does not. Until very recently, any playwright bringing on stage characters who in real life would swear freely and naturally, needed to write with exceptional care and tact. It would be ludicrous to "blame" an author for failing to provide his characters with dialogue that would in fact have kept the play right off the stage; nevertheless, in our era of uninhibited speech in the theatre, the expletives used by Esson's tough drovers fall quaintly on the ear. The word that occurs most frequently is "blanky"; others are "'struth", "my oath", "blarst them"; and the hard-bitten Boss, in the moment when his pain and anger break through, cries out "Curse the Jackeroo!" However, what really dates the dialogue of *The Drovers*, if one is looking to it for realism, is the speech rhythm. Clearly Esson was attempting to reproduce authentic Australian speech rhythms; equally clearly, he did not quite succeed. (Eunice Hanger suggested that the real breakthrough in presenting truly Australian speech came with *Summer of the Seventeenth Doll.*)[9] The dialogue of *The Drovers* may, on the printed page, deceive the eye; read aloud, much of it suddenly becomes "written", faintly literary. The Cook, for instance, saying "You'll be as right as rain then," or Briglow Bill, in what is probably the best-known and most moving speech in the play:

> It don't matter. It had to come sooner or later. I've lived my life, careless and free, looking after my work when I was at it, and splashing my cheque up like a good one when I struck civilisation. I've lived hard, droving and horse-breaking, station work, and over-landing, the hard life of the bush, but there's nothing better, and death's come quick, before I'm played out—it's the way I wanted.

With its short, unfinished sentences, the speech looks like spoken Australian; but it does not—quite—sound like it.

Presumably the most negative way possible to approach a play is to list all the things that it is not—except perhaps in the case of *The Drovers*, which derives part of its fascination from not being like most other plays. There has always been debate whether Synge's *Riders to the Sea*, the play with which *The Drovers* is almost automatically compared as a depiction of man's stoicism in the face of malignant nature, is or is not a tragedy. It is possible to see in *The Drovers* the "tragic inevitability" of the way of life in the bush, claimed for a good deal of early outback-Australian literature; but there is very little of the sense of waste (the waste of one young life after another; the hardship of the women left behind) which permeates *Riders to the Sea*. I would suggest that *The Drovers* is in the end almost aggressively non-tragic. The audience, and presumably the other characters, are deeply moved by Briglow's death; but he makes it very clear that this is the death he would have chosen (quick, and before he's played out) after the life he has chosen, the best of all possible lives, the life of the bush. If the play enacts the familiar conflict between man and country, it also takes for granted the old Australian cult of the superiority of the man on the land: is it then only city sentimentality to read tragedy into the play?

Equally, *The Drovers* is not, as one might well have expected given the situation, a problem play. Bill will risk his life to save Briglow, the Boss will mourn for him; but it does not occur to any of them, except of course the Jackeroo, that they can do anything but leave him to die, cared for by a convenient Aborigine. The cattle unquestionably must go through. But: what if Briglow Bill had only been injured, and had a chance of recovery if he were looked after? What if the situation had presented a conflict of values, a man's life against a mob of cattle? What if there had been no one to leave behind, and the Boss had had the choice of abandoning Briglow to die alone, or pushing on? Given such premises, the play would have been, one assumes, a three-act drama of human conflict; as Esson wrote it, it is a one-act impression of the stoicism of a group of true men of the bush, contrasted with the noisy, superficial softness of the outsider.

The outstanding quality of *The Drovers* is its consistent understatement. Esson was apparently very anxious that this understatement should be preserved in production, and not sentimentalized into strong, silent suffering. In 1921 Esson wrote from London to Vance Palmer in Melbourne, saying he had heard of a proposed production of the play, and asking Palmer to visit the producer, and "tell her that you know my intentions about the play, to avoid American 'suppressed emotion', 'strong silent men' atmosphere, false stresses etc. It needs to be played simply to make any effect. 'Briglow' is a hard part to get across, the others are easy enough. I should be grateful (if it is not too inconvenient for you), if you would keep an eye on the performance—that is, if there is a performance—and curse the actors freely."[10] *The Drovers* evokes for the audience a sense of the understanding, the teamwork among the men, their common obsession with getting the cattle through; it evokes the harshness and the beauty of the land; tension is kept high by the constant threat of a stampede among the cattle off stage. And if it is not too prosaic a conclusion, I would like to suggest, rather apologetically, that for a city audience at least, *The Drovers* has the fascination of allowing one to watch and listen to people who are doing an unfamiliar job—a fascination currently exploited by dramatists such as David Storey, in plays like *The Contractor* and *Changing Room.*

In the years following the demise of the Pioneer Players, Australian plays continued to be written, and occasionally performed, mostly by little theatre groups; a very few playwrights such as Max Afford became widely known and their plays received successful commercial production. It would probably be true to say, however, that Australian playwriting, from the thirties to the fifties, was kept alive not by theatres but by radio. Both the A.B.C. and the commercial stations had, fortunately, voracious appetites for plays and serials, serials which often ran on year after year and became an important part of family life. Occasionally too there were play competitions, conducted by bodies like the Playwrights' Advisory Board in Sydney. In 1955, this board awarded a co-first prize in a drama competition to a play by an unknown Melbourne author, one Ray Lawler. The play was *Summer of the Seventeenth Doll.* If *Look Back in Anger* (1956) marked a turning point in the history of modern British drama, *Summer of the Seventeenth Doll* marked a turning point in the history of Australian drama. It was played successfully all over Australia, taken to London where it was again successful, and to New York, where it was not. Quite suddenly there was a new, encouraging climate for an Australian playwright; he need no longer take for granted that the drama he had laboured over would finish up in the drawer or at best with an amateur production. *Summer of the Seventeenth Doll* was followed by a wave of Australian plays, not carbon copies of *The Doll* but palpably Lawler-influenced: *The Shifting Heart, The Slaughter of Saint Theresa's Day,* "The Multi-Coloured Umbrella", *The Bastard Country, The One Day of the Year.* Generalizations are made to be disproved, but it would be broadly true to say of the plays of the fifties that they moved decisively away from the bush to the cities; that their settings were rarely the middle class suburbia with whom the bulk of the audience could identify, but dealt instead with people whose lives, emotions, and language the playwrights apparently felt to be more "colourful" than those of suburbia (significantly, Jan from Sydney's North Shore is usually singled out as the only character in *The One Day of the Year* who is not wholly credible); and finally, the plays of the fifties became critical, not only of individuals, but more broadly critical of Australian society, Australian myths, Australian institutions. *Summer of the Seventeenth Doll* is about a great many things, including illusion, pride, the cycles of growing older and one generation giving way to the next; it also casts a sceptical eye on the Australian myths of mateship (or what the tradition of mateship has become) and the superiority of the outback over city life.[11]

One of the most interesting of the Australian plays from this period is Alan Seymour's *The One Day of the Year.* Now that Australian attitudes towards Anzac Day have become rather less emotionally charged, it is difficult to understand the uproar which greeted a play now frequently set as a school text. *The One Day of the Year* was initially turned down for the Adelaide Festival by the Board of Governors, on the grounds, apparently, that it might offend the R.S.L.; it was put on by an amateur group in Adelaide, and finally, on 26 April 1961, given professional production in Sydney, after a bomb threat to the theatre. After that there was no real trouble, though the play became widely known—particularly to those who had not seen it—as "the play attacking Anzac Day". Alan Seymour denied at the time that *The One Day of the Year* was intended to be anti-Anzac Day, insisted that it was in fact about the clash of father and son; many years later, he pointed out that the conflict of generations is a constantly recurring theme in his work, and is found in almost every play he has written.[12] The clash of generations gives *The One Day of the Year* breadth, universality—but it is also one of the most thoroughly explored themes in all literature; a good part of the interest of the play for Australian audiences does surely lie in the fact that the catalyst of the clash in this case was indeed one of our more sacrosanct national institutions. *The One Day of the Year* preserves a delicate balance of sympathies. For many people, Hughie wins his argument intellectually all along the line, and proves conclusively that for a good number of the men who celebrate Anzac Day, what matters is not the patriotism but the booze; emotionally, Hughie is not quite such a clear winner. Hughie is something of a prig, and fails to understand his father as dismally as his father fails to understand him; Hughie fails to understand that for a man who lives a nondescript, frustrated life, Anzac Day can be the one day when he ceases briefly to be "nothin' much". In fact the author has, perhaps unintentionally, loaded the dice against Hughie. Real life Alfs are very difficult to live with, but on stage they can have for an audience an almost Falstaffian richness and life; and Alan Seymour's Hughie is, as a stage character, pallid by contrast to Alf, Mum, and Wacka.

"What happened afterwards" has no legitimate place in one's assessment of a play, but Alan Seymour has himself provided a sequel to *The One Day of the Year* and this sequel is perhaps relevant to his initial conception of the characters. Seymour was commissioned to write a novel based on his play, and the result was the novel *The One Day of the Year*,[13] in which Hughie (now Hugh, and an adult) finally visits Gallipoli, and recalls the events of the play in flashbacks. Hugh, like Alf, now sees himself as a failure.

> Walking along the cobbled street, he thought briefly of the years between. His father's stricken eyes and disbelief: "Failed?" Failed. He left his University ingloriously after all, and bummed about in useless jobs before getting a job as a photographer for a morning paper and finding his joy in a camera turn sour in his mouth. Society weddings, first nights, car accidents ... Jan was married now, he'd heard, a sharp young solicitor from Wahroonga, only a suburb or so away. Doing very well.[14]

The guide gives Hugh a brochure quoting figures which make it quite clear that the landing at Gallipoli was indeed pointless. Hugh puts the brochure into an envelope, addresses it to his father; then tears up envelope and brochure, and drops the pieces into the waters of the

Dardanelles. Hugh has at least learnt compassion. His failure and frustration, so like that of his father, inevitably leaves the reader wondering, "Why?" Alan Seymour does not say.

The area of the play which has come under greatest critical fire is the ending, which has been variously accused of being sentimental, inconclusive, dramatically weak, and so on. The fall of the curtain, with Hughie deciding to stay, and Alf determinedly continuing to be a bloody Australian, is not dramatically strong, but it is a truthful ending, in character for both of them. (Many of Seymour's plays end with the hero being trapped in some unwelcome situation.) One could well contrast the ending of *The One Day of the Year* with that of *Summer of the Seventeenth Doll*. The ending of *The Doll*, I believe, sacrifices credibility of character to the demands of working out of theme and of a strong curtain; Olive would certainly reject Roo's clumsy proposal in disillusioned fury, but it is hard to believe that after sixteen years, given their characters and relationship, the illusion is indeed all and the man counts for nothing. For all its sticky sentimentality, the film (which had Roo coming some time later into the bar and Olive, of course, smiling through her tears) was rather more true to life, if not to the carefully built up themes of the play. Alan Seymour has taken exactly the opposite path: his ending is impeccably credible; theatrically it is something of a whimper. Seymour too has had some problems with sentimentalized interpretations. In 1966, for instance, there was a French production of the play, under the title of "L'unique jour de l'année", and Catherine Duncan wrote an article about it for *Meanjin*.[15] She suggested that French audiences had no difficulty in identifying with what was happening on the stage: "Australians, on the contrary, might have found it a good deal more difficult to recognise themselves in their effervescent Gallic counterparts, who were emphatic where we would be laconic, talked at machine-gun speed where we would drawl, and seemed totally unembarrassed by their emotions."[16] Alan Seymour read the article, wrote to the director of the play, and as a result the cast set to work, "to bring out the difficulty and irony of the final curtain instead of letting shy conciliatory smiles gleam through blinked-back tears."[17]

After hopeful beginnings, the drama wave of the fifties in its turn flattened and died. Some of the best writers, including Ray Lawler and Alan Seymour, left to live abroad, and certainly the opportunities for playwrights in Australia, outside radio and television, were limited in their rewards. The whole blame cannot however be laid on unresponsive Australian audiences, the traditional scapegoats who are supposed to prefer any imported success, however mediocre, to the home product; in a sense, in the fifties, the reverse was true. So eager were we to have an indigenous theatre that some managements who normally would not consider Australian plays put on dramas which were not ready for full-scale professional production—in some cases, the relative professionalism of the production showed up the amateurism of the writing; audiences came, saw, and had their prejudices confirmed that they really did not care for Australian drama.

The third wave began to form in the late sixties; once again, it started in Melbourne. The apparent catalyst was a tiny experimental theatre, La Mama. In 1967, Betty Burstall returned from a visit to America, fired with enthusiasm for the off-beat theatres of Off Off-Broadway. She rented a small disused factory in Carlton, and turned it into a simple theatre, where writers, actors, and producers who were frustrated by the confines of the established Melbourne theatre structure could try out their ideas; the theatre was called, after its American inspiration, the La Mama. In the beginning, La Mama was used mostly for folk-singing sessions and poetry readings, but these soon developed into play productions, the first play performed being Jack Hibberd's short drama, "Three Old Friends"—this was later made into a film. An exploratory actors' workshop developed in 1968, and the rest is one of the most important chapters in the history of Australian drama. La Mama is still alive and well, but in the intervening years a good many of her first offspring have moved out into broader areas of Australian theatre. The Australian Performing Group was formed from the original members of La Mama, and established itself in yet another disused factory quite close to La Mama; this new theatre took the name of the Pram Factory. Some of Australia's best-known actors have been associated with La Mama, including Graeme Blundell, Bruce Spence, and Peter Cummins; equally, most of our best-known dramatists have either sprung from La Mama and the Australian Performing Group or have at least been performed by them: Jack Hibberd, Barry Oakley, John Romeril, David Williamson, and, to a lesser extent, Alexander Buzo and Dorothy Hewett. In other cities, other theatres gave their enthusiastic support to the new Australian writers; in Sydney, for instance, the Jane Street and Nimrod Street (now Nimrod) theatres. Suddenly, it was no longer a novelty to go to the theatre and see an Australian play; and the sheer number of young Australian playwrights is hopefully a guarantee that this situation will continue, that this wave will not, like its predecessors, slowly recede from sight. We are at last achieving a situation where Australian playwrights are taken seriously; where Australian audiences do not draw back nervously at an unflattering image of themselves on stage; and, what really matters, where more good plays are being written than ever before.

A mark of the increased seriousness with which Australian drama is currently treated (as well as an indication that more high-quality plays are being written) is the increase in the number of plays being published, both by the established presses (Angus and Robertson, Heinemann, Penguin, and University of Queensland Press have all, over the years, published a number of Australian plays) and by a newcomer, the Currency Press, now Currency Methuen, which publishes only Australian plays, and which, since its first publication (Alexander Buzo's *Macquarie*, in 1971) has put out about half a dozen plays a year. Naturally enough, this proliferation of publication makes it very difficult to represent the new drama as fully as one might like in an anthology such as this. David Williamson, author of *What If You Died Tomorrow*, is without doubt the best known of the new playwrights; and a list of suggested further reading for those interested in contemporary Australian drama is included in the bibliography.

The new wave Australian drama of the late sixties and early seventies has, like drama all round the world, been characterized by a break from traditional naturalism, by playwrights such as Buzo, Hewett, Hibberd, Romeril, and an attitude to society that is even more critical than that of the fifties. Playwrights have worked through caricatures, stereotypes, cartoon figures, rituals, to analyze and objectify Australian life styles. The attack has been witty, savage, outspoken; the few relatively gentle plays such as Jim McNeil's *How Does Your Garden Grow* are an almost startling contrast.

There is no doubt that David Williamson is Australian drama's great success story. He estimates that approximately four hundred people saw the first production of his early play, *The Removalists*, at the La Mama theatre in 1971.[18] Four years later, his plays are being performed, to packed houses, all round Australia; *What If You Died Tomorrow* was commissioned for the opening of the Drama Theatre in Sydney's new Opera House (9 October 1973); *The Removalists*, *Don's Party*, and *What If You Died Tomorrow* have had full scale London productions; and Williamson has written the scripts for several successful films, including *Stork* (from an early play), *The Family Man* (one of the segments of *Libido*), *Peterson*, and *The Removalists*. In style, David Williamson stands outside current fashion, with plays that are almost traditional in their naturalism; however, like the rest he is fascinated by the patterns and pressures of our society. In an interview in London the week before *The Removalists* opened at the Royal Court, he said:

> What brought us together, apart from Betty Burstall at La Mama, was a desire to write about this Australia we all grew up in. No one had got it right before. And it's a weird place. Take the surface of mateship which rules the country: everyone plays the role of ebullient friendship, but underneath there is an undercurrent of violence. Go back a hundred years or so and you'll find that the crime rate in Australia was eight times that of England. Where's the violence gone? It's been suppressed by the mateship, but it's only just beneath the surface and it simply needs a touch on the trigger to fire it off.[19]

David Williamson was talking about *The Removalists*, a play in which the touch is applied to the trigger, and a man is beaten to death; violence in other Williamson plays to date has stopped short of manslaughter, but characters and situations are frequently taut with aggression, aggression which explodes into humour, words, blows. Williamson described *What If You Died Tomorrow* as "a social documentary somewhat compressed", and added "All my plays are social documentaries to some extent."[20]

Though David Williamson's plays are indeed social documentaries, he does not moralize; he does not take open attitudes of praise or blame towards his characters, but says rather "This is how they are"; he does not provide poetic justice, or indeed any other kind of tidy conclusion—the ending of *What If You Died Tomorrow* is very typical, Andrew thinks he has done the right thing, but he cannot be sure, his block structure is chaotic but not randomly so, and the author reassures us that it is "*quite aesthetically pleasing*". David Williamson seems to be more interested in relationships than in individual psychology; the interreactions between his characters seem always to have been observed with the same devastating accuracy as their speech. (The shock of recognition of self, even though it is self in heightened form, is a major reason for David Williamson's popularity with Australian audiences.) He is acutely aware of Australian manners and mores as a conscious *style* of self-expression. One of Williamson's difficulties with British audiences and critics is that for the most part they take for granted that his plays (and those of other Australian playwrights performed in England, such as Alexander Buzo's *The Front Room Boys* and *Rooted*) are in fact literal transcripts of life in Australia, about which in fact they know very little; and it is often assumed that Williamson and the rest are dissecting their countrymen for the particular amusement of sophisticated London audiences. Commenting on London's rather bemused reaction to *Don's Party*, Williamson said:

> There seemed to be no realisation that the play presented a heightened distillation of the social manners of a particular Australian sub-culture—that a line such as "G'day gorgeous, care for a screw?" wasn't a bestial assault on delicate sensibilities but the logical extension of certain Australian male attitudes and styles of approach towards women, summed up and used by Cooley with an element of engaging self-mockery. The fact that most of the characters in the play are patently *aware* of the un-English bluntness of their social manners and are using this bluntness as a *style* is quite clear, even in the text. The scene in which Don and Mal shout abuse at each other in apparent fury, dissolves into laughter. They have been using an archetypal Australian style. Belligerence without real resentment. Real resentment in this country tends to be wreathed in polite smiles.[21]

A charge sometimes laid against David Williamson is that his plays, though amusing and realistic, in the end lack depth, reverberation. It is very possible that Williamson has been writing too much and too fast; it is also possible that those who accuse him of superficiality are influenced at least in part by his refusal to imply how things ought to be, instead of simply how they are; and perhaps by a sardonic and peculiarly Australian irony that permeates the plays. It has been said more than once, for instance, that *What If You Died Tomorrow* sells out, betrays its characters for the easy laugh. It is perfectly true that many of the characters in this play have serious personal problems, and that these problems are the fount of the comedy; a comic mode not of course unique to Williamson. Irene, the frigid, nagging wife and possessive mother, is very funny indeed; Gunter's attempted suicide does not spare him from being both "comic" European and catalyst of a good deal of satiric comedy directed against the Australian characters ("It's his Australian name"). One could almost make out a formula demonstrating that the more serious the problem, the more comic the character, but the pattern probably breaks down with Harry Bustle, an entertaining character who keeps his personal problems, if any, hidden behind his own thick skin. Is this necessarily a betrayal of the characters? I do not think so. In the London interview quoted earlier, David Williamson said:

> ... for all my criticism I still have affection for the Australian society. I like the terrible, sardonic sense of humour that develops in the worst situations. The archetypal Australian joke, I suppose, is the one about the drunk sitting on a park bench who watches a man come in with a length of rope, tie a noose and hang himself from a tree; the drunk takes a look at the result and says "Silly bastard, made the rope too long and only broke a leg."[22]

There is a good deal of this sardonic, and not necessarily superficial, humour in *What If You Died Tomorrow*; there is also—to borrow one of David Williamson's own phrases—"heavily disguised compassion".[23] When the play opened in Sydney, Ruth Cracknell played Irene as an almost straight comedy role; when the production (with an almost identical cast) moved to London some months later, the same actress brought out the fear and pain of the character as well in a really splendid performance which gave depth to the play as a whole. Perhaps one ought to give David Williamson himself the last word on the subject, in the passage from Act I of *What If You Died Tomorrow* where Kirsty imitates one of Andrew's interviewers:

> KIRSTY: (*imitating interviewer*) "Some critics have said that your work has a crackling surface but on closer analysis veers towards the superficial." (*Imitating* ANDREW) "Yes, they have!" "Can you answer that charge?" "No". "You agree that your work does veer towards the superficial?" "No." (*Searching for another question*) "I believe you cook a fair Stroganoff?"

RADIO AND TELEVISION

In Australia, as in most other developed countries, the form of theatre preferred by the bulk of the population is the theatre they can experience in their own homes. From the thirties to the early fifties, millions of Australians gathered each night round their radio sets, absorbed in the hour-long plays and countless serials that flowed from the A.B.C. and the commercial stations. Serials like "Hagen's Circus", "First Light Frazer", and "Stranger Come In" became part of family life.[24] Since the advent of television in the mid-fifties, most home audiences have switched their allegiance to the box, with its stream of serials, series, and the occasional self-contained play.

On the face of it, it would seem that television had badly undermined, if not completely killed, radio drama. Certainly the numbers listening to radio plays have dropped quite drastically; the commercial radio stations have largely given drama away, apart from repeats of old soap operas from some country stations, and in the cities, capsule serials (with episodes of about five minutes) and, at the time of writing, the Macquarie Network's "Theatre of the Mind". The A.B.C. has kept on broadcasting dramas, for a varied though diminished audience. But is this quite the defeat that it sounds? In fact, the advent of television provided radio drama with its greatest challenge and opportunity since the early days of Norman Corwin and Arch Oboler, and there are signs that radio is in fact taking up this challenge—primarily through the expanding radio drama programmes of the A.B.C. and Radio 2 on Sunday nights. Any programme which must entertain a large number of people is likely to end up as conservative, non-challenging; and now that radio no longer has to carry the responsibility of catering for wide audiences, it can in some programmes at least afford to take risks, to broadcast the way-out, the experimental, the kind of play which will interest a minority group only; though ratings suggest that this minority audience is rather larger than expected. At the same time, television (though admittedly fostering some sessions so mindless that they seem cynically contemptuous of their audiences) has developed from fumbling beginnings to produce many thoughtful and highly sophisticated programmes, both from the A.B.C. and commercial channels.

Douglas Stewart's *The Golden Lover* and Ted Roberts' *Lindsay's Boy* are very good plays; they also demonstrate clearly how wide is the gulf between the techniques of radio and television. It is possible to lay down certain suggestions, if not rules, for the writing of radio plays; but the one commandment of radio which cannot be broken is, simply: "Thou shalt not forget that the radio audience is unable to see what is happening." Radio is made up of sounds only, the chief sound being that of the human voice, and these sounds must somehow suggest to the listener all that he needs to "see" in his mind's eye: what the characters look like, for instance, and the setting, if these happen to be important; any physical action necessary to the plot, even if it happens silently. In television, on the other hand, the audience has no need of visual imagination, the pictures are presented ready made, and are at least as important as the dialogue in conveying information; there are normally far fewer words in a television play than in a radio play, and the playwright must in fact be careful not to repeat in words what is already patently obvious from the picture.

Douglas Stewart, a New Zealander who came to live in Australia in 1938, is not only one of our major playwrights, but also known as poet, short-story writer, critic, and for many years editor of the famous "Red Page" of the *Bulletin*. In a burst of dramatic creativity, between 1939 and 1947, he wrote five verse plays, three of them for radio (*The Fire on the Snow, The Golden Lover* and *The Earthquake Shakes the Land*) and two for the stage, *Ned Kelly* and *Shipwreck*.

Since *Shipwreck*, he seems to have turned his back on play writing, his only subsequent drama being *Fisher's Ghost*, a light and amusing dramatic entertainment, published in 1960. *The Golden Lover* was first broadcast by the A.B.C. on 24 January 1943.

Like many verse playwrights, Douglas Stewart has looked always to the romantic past for the subjects of his plays, but not necessarily as an escape. He said once, "The playwright, I think, creates the myths by which the people live: the heroic, gigantic, legendary figures, fathers of the race, ancestors spiritual or actual, to which the living man can point and say, 'This is what I am made of; that is what makes us different from other people; that is what I believe in; those are my gods and my devils.'"[25] Several themes recur in Stewart's plays, but the major informing theme is his vision of man as a heroic dreamer who risks everything, and suffers greatly, for a dream that is doomed to fail. *The Fire on the Snow* presented this vision in its simplest form, and in telling the story of Scott's disastrous expedition to the Pole, accepts uncritically the intrinsic worth of endurance for its own sake, even when this endurance accomplishes very little of practical worth. In *Ned Kelly* the approach was more complex and more critical; this time the dreamer (or dreamers, if one includes Joe Byrne as a dreamer along with Ned Kelly) was also an anti-hero, and the dream, exhilarating and attractive though it might be, did involve hurt to at least some decent ordinary citizens who had had no share in it. The moral boundaries in *Ned Kelly* are a good deal less clearly defined than those of *The Fire on the Snow*.

Perhaps one reason why *The Golden Lover* (which I believe to be the best of Stewart's plays) is normally taken rather less seriously than either *The Fire on the Snow* or *Ned Kelly* is that in *The Golden Lover* the dream is on the face of it less heroic and less destructive; this is the domestic version of the dream. The dreamer is Tawhai, a young and beautiful Maori woman, married to the unromantic Ruarangi, who is fat, lazy and far from brave; her dream is of a lover,

the golden hawk,
Who hangs in the sky of my dreams.

If the dream seems less heroic than that of *The Fire on the Snow* and *Ned Kelly*, it is probably because Tawhai is herself less heroic, more practical, less inclined to risk all for a dream which may destroy her; the only female protagonist in Stewart's plays, she is also the only one to deliberately reject the dream, rather than see it torn from her grasp; the only one to opt for the safe, the comfortable, the familiar. Tawhai is a delightful character but she is not one of the great lovers of literature. Douglas Stewart says in his introduction to the play, "It is a play about the acceptance of life." While *The Golden Lover* is by far the most erotic of Stewart's plays, it is in a sense the least romantic, primarily because Tawhai retains an unromantic grain of what is known as practical common sense; it is also noticeable that the genuinely passionate and beautiful love scenes between her and her golden lover Whana can slide very easily into witty exchange, no less erotic but a good deal less romantic.

TAWHAI: Although, Whana, you are certainly my golden lover
And of faery blood, and handsome as the sun to look at,
You behave at times surprisingly like a husband.
WHANA: Although, Tawhai, I could not doubt for one moment
That you are my crimson blossom and the song of a tui,
You argue at times disconcertingly like a woman.

The Golden Lover is witty, amusing, and contains a good deal of very beautiful verse. Some of the best poetry is descriptive; Douglas Stewart slips very easily into the radio convention that what cannot be seen should be suggested in words, and by the end of play, one has a clear though no doubt highly individual vision of what it all looked like; the characters, the young and beautiful and the old and bent; the setting, from the comfortable village and hut to the dark mystery of the forest. Certain images recur: warmth and light is associated with the village, cold, mist and darkness with the forest and the haunts of the patu-pairehe. Fire is interestingly associated with both; it is part of the comfort of the village, and the faery people are known to be afraid of it; but fire is also intrinsic to Whana, with his "body strong and golden and his hair like flames", and "his hands are fire"; Whana himself says of Tawhai, "your body under my hand is all one flame." There is a good deal of bird and animal imagery; Whana is the hawk, Tawhai the white heron, though for Ruarangi she is like other women " a plump brown bird/That tempts the hawk to strike". Most of the villagers are associated with far more domesticated animals than either hawks or herons; they are crayfish, dogs, worms, ducks; the menacing Te Kawau is the cormorant, the black shag.

Harold Oliver, writing about Douglas Stewart's radio plays, once pointed out that "The radio play has one great defect, that the characters in it must talk."[26] He was primarily making the point that the simple description of the death of Oates in the original, Scott's Journal, was probably more moving than Stewart's dramatization of it in *The Fire on the Snow*, and went on to suggest that very occasionally in *The Golden Lover* the poet takes over from the character speaking, as in Ruarangi's beautiful but uncharacteristic description of Tawhai at the end of scene three. A problem in producing Douglas Stewart's plays is that he does tend to write a little too much; *The Golden Lover* is normally broadcast in a slightly abbreviated form (its length is not likely to be a problem to the reader) and the length and unconventional structure of *Ned Kelly* set up immediate difficulties in the theatre. *The Golden Lover* is not a technically challenging radio play, there are no fireworks of sound, and its modest demands would not strain the production facilities of any studio; but it is, deeply, a radio play. It adapts easily enough to the stage; but loses a great deal in the process. An obvious problem is the difficulty of finding an actor to play the golden lover, someone who can stand on stage during the extravagant descriptions of his beauty, and not seem to be derided by the verse; but there is an even more fundamental difficulty. As we have seen, *The Golden Lover*, like most good radio plays, constantly paints pictures in the mind. When "real" pictures

Radio and Television

are added, either these real pictures seem irrelevant, or the dialogue itself suddenly appears—most unfairly—to be over-written.

The A.B.C. has (at the time of writing this) a televised music programme called, wittily enough, "Radio with Pictures". In the early days of television, this was a description sometimes applied to television drama; it could hardly be less accurate, as the most superficial glance at *Lindsay's Boy* makes clear. More than half the script of *Lindsay's Boy* consists of "stage directions", outlining what the characters do, how they look, what emotions are expressed on their faces, and these pictures convey a good deal of information that is not available from the dialogue. It would be just possible to follow the story line of *Lindsay's Boy* from the dialogue alone (quite often in a television play this is not a possibility) but without pictures the dialogue would seem scrappy, the rhythms disturbing and unsatisfying, and finally, one would miss a great deal of the interplay between characters, an often wordless interaction. The opening of the play is as good an example as any of this silent "body language". Kevin stands a little apart from his father at the graveside, kicks a pebble along the path, stares at his father, "*If the boy is showing any expression at all, it could be regarded as almost hostile. He looks away from his father.*" As his father says good-bye, tears come into Kevin's eyes, and as he watches Jim leave, he rocks gently back and forward, in the rain. Throughout this scene Kevin does not speak, but the audience has learnt volumes about the tensions between father and son; and as the play progresses, Kevin, and to a lesser extent the other characters, constantly express in wordless involuntary gesture or reaction what they very deliberately do not put into speech.

Television has the reputation of being rather conservative, both technically and in subject matter. One good reason for this conservatism is the nature of the audience, which is traditionally the family audience, viewing in their own homes, and often cynically assumed to ask, for the most part, only to be amused, soothed, titillated but not shocked, and never for a moment bored. Stage drama in recent years has frequently grated upon the sensibilities of its audiences; television rarely does this, if only because the "off" switch is so near at hand. Family audiences are apparently excited by violence, but they are also interested in "ordinary people", in plays and serials about people basically like themselves who happen to lead more eventful and traumatic lives. Television's traditional naturalism is very suitable for such plays. It has always been recognized that the small, intimate screen is the perfect vehicle for the revealing close-up, be it of the real-life politician or the actor expressing wordless emotion through the tightening of the lip, the twitching of a cheek muscle; this is one reason why television is so good at giving us the impression that we have special insight into character. It is equally good at convincing an audience that what they are viewing on the screen is really happening—in fact, the division between television documentary and television drama can be very fine indeed, as shown by one of the best know television programmes of recent years, the B.B.C.'s *Cathy Come Home*. Even in dramas which are unequivocally drama and not documentary, filmed shots of places known to the audience reinforce the sense of realism and give a pleasurable feeling of familiarity; for instance, the streets and suburbs of Melbourne in the highly popular "Homicide" series. The restrictions of television are apparent, but a number of writers have worked within these restrictions to produce fine and memorable dramas. One of these is *Lindsay's Boy*, written by Ted Roberts, and first broadcast on 4 July 1974, on A.B.C. Channel 2.

Ted Roberts is one of Australia's most prolific television writers, producing mostly plays, trilogies, and short series for the A.B.C. He describes his career thus: "Spent twelve discouraging years in business, threw it in on realising instead of a part-time professional writer, had become full-time professional Sales Manager. Went freelance, thereby abandoning all claims to sanity." He writes exclusively for film and television, and says that his ambition is "to be a craftsman writer in those media, and to remain one."[27] In 1974 he won two of the Australian Writers' Guild Awards: one for a Serial Episode (an episode in the A.B.C.'s "Certain Women") and one for Original T.V. Drama, awarded for his trilogy, "Three Men of the City". *Lindsay's Boy*, which Ted Roberts describes as "the play I like best of all that I've written",[28] was also awarded an Awgie, as "Best Original Television Drama, 1975".

Lindsay's Boy belongs to the "family genre", with a touch of violence thrown in when Jim Lindsay is beaten up because he cannot pay his gambling debts—a very ancient Australian tradition. The action is securely anchored in Sydney in the forties (Jim's kitchen has, nostalgically, a Silent Knight refrigerator) and because the period, post-war, has great influence on the actions and motivations of the characters, we are frequently reminded of it: scene 9, newsreels showing celebrations of the end of the Pacific War; scene 11, people dancing in the streets; scene 13, more celebrations; and scene 15, the aftermath of the celebrations in Martin Place, with dirty streamers, balloons, and drunks sleeping in the arches of the G.P.O. The celebratory news clips serve a second function by providing an ironic reminder that when the problems of a world war are over, the problems of family peace may just be starting.

Lindsay's Boy moves along at leisurely pace and with a deceptively casual structure. Like *The One Day of the Year* and *What If You Died Tomorrow*, *Lindsay's Boy* is concerned with the misunderstandings and collisions of values between generations, and one of the main structural props, unobtrusively suggested, is the parallel in character and experience between father and son. Both are capable of emotional explosion; both are learning to cope with an unfamiliar situation. Only once does the author openly underline the similarities between father and son, and that is in scene 4, when Kevin is accused of theft by Brother Ernest, and we are told that "*his hand rubs up and down the leg of his pants, in a gesture reminiscent of his father's at the graveside*". Though the play is primarily about Jim Lindsay and his son Kevin, it is sympathetic in its treatment of the women in their lives, Denise and the girl Karen; on occasion, Denise and Karen show far greater maturity than either man or boy. The beginning and the ending of the play are marked by visual and symbolic contrast: the play begins in pouring rain at a graveside, and ends with Kevin and his friend Mick lazily sunbaking on sun-drenched Coogee Beach— the familiar, unchanging image of Australian well-being.

NOTES TO INTRODUCTION

1. Leslie Rees, *The Making of Australian Drama* (Sydney: Angus and Robertson, 1973), p. 1.
2. Vance Palmer, *Louis Esson and the Australian Theatre* (Melbourne: Georgian House, 1948), p. 40.
3. See footnote above.
4. Palmer, *Louis Esson and the Australian Theatre*, p. 3.
5. Ibid., p. 42.
6. Ibid., p. 40.
7. Ibid., p. 16-19.
8. Quoted by Hilda Esson in her Introduction to *The Southern Cross and Other Plays* (Melbourne: Robertson and Mullens, 1946), p. xvi.
9. "Australian Drama", *The Literature of Australia*, ed. G. Dutton (Harmondsworth: Penguin, 1972), p. 453.
10. Palmer, p. 34. The Pioneer Players produced *The Drovers* in 1923. See review, *Argus*, 4 December 1923, p. 12.
11. For a discussion of the attack on myth in *Summer of the Seventeenth Doll, The Shifting Heart*, and *The One Day of the Year*, see P.H. Davison, "Three Australian Plays: National Myths Under Criticism", *Southerly*, 23 (1963): 110-27.
12. Alrene Sykes, "Alan Seymour", *Australian Literary Studies* 6 (1974): 286-87.
13. *The One Day of the Year* (London: Souvenir Press, 1967).
14. Ibid., p. 253.
15. Catherine Duncan, "A French Production of Alan Seymour's *The One Day of the Year*", *Meanjin Quarterly* 25 (1966): 229-37.
16. Ibid, p. 233.
17. Alan Seymour, "One Image of Australia", *Meanjin Quarterly* 26 (1967): 227.
18. David Williamson, "*The Removalists*: A Conjunction of Limitations", *Meanjin Quarterly* 33 (1974): 414.
19. John Higgins, "David Williamson on Australian Rituals", *The Times*, 14 July 1973.
20. Leonard Radic, "David Williamson Goes Bush", *The Age*, 6 October 1973.
21. Letter from David Williamson to Alrene Sykes.
22. *The Times*, 14 July 1973.
23. David Williamson, introduction, *Three Plays* (Sydney: Currency Methuen, 1974), p. v.
24. Three of the many serials written by Max Afford and broadcast by A.B.C. and commercial stations.
25. Douglas Stewart, "The Playwright in Australia", *Australian Theatre Year*, I, 1955-56 (issued by The Australian Elizabethan Theatre Trust as *The First Year*), p. 9.
26. Harold J. Oliver, "Douglas Stewart and the Art of the Radio Play", *The Texas Quarterly* 5 (1962): 199.
27. Letter from Ted Roberts to Alrene Sykes.
28. See "Roberts on *Lindsay's Boy*", p. 274 of this volume.

Louis Esson

Emblem used on the programmes of the Pioneer Players, a Melbourne amateur theatre group organized by Louis Esson, Vance Palmer, and Stewart Macky in the 1920s. Photograph by courtesy of the La Trobe Collection, State Library of Victoria.

The Drovers

A Play in One Act

Characters

ALEC. McKAY, the Boss
"BRIGLOW" BILL
BOB
MICK
ALBERT, the Cook
A JACKEROO
PIDGEON, a black boy

Scene—A droving camp, on the edge of the Barklay Tableland. The camp is made on a little muddied water-hole fringed with a few gydgea trees; the plains, unbroken by timber, stretching to the horizon.
Time—Early morning.

A Camp-fire. Pack saddles strewn about. ALBERT, *the* COOK, *is busy at the fire. He is a little fat man, fussy but cheerful. A shot rings out. The* COOK *drops the frying pan, and watches.*
COOK: They're off again.
(*Sound of hoofs, stockwhips cracking—a stampede of cattle.* COOK *picks up billy of water, and puts it on fire. Two drovers,* BOB *and* MICK, *carry in* "BRIGLOW" BILL. "BRIGLOW" BILL *is a square built, determined looking man, with steely grey eyes. He is about forty-five, and has lived all his life in the bush.* BOB *and* MICK *are young men.* BOB *is tall, wiry, and sandy-haired. He is burnt brick-red, and heavily freckled. He is good-natured, and has a fanatical love of horses.* MICK *is a little dark man, mild and rather silent, with perfect faith in the* BOSS.)
COOK: What's wrong?
BOB: A stampede.
MICK: They've got Bill.
BOB (*as they put him down*): How's that, Bill?
BRIGLOW: Easy, boys, easy.
MICK: How's that now, Briglow?
BRIGLOW: Let me sit up. It hurts to lie back. Prop me up a bit.

BOB: Is that better?
BRIGLOW: Yes. It catches me here.
COOK (*giving him water*): Here's a drink.
BRIGLOW: I'm done.
BOB: Nothing like it.
BRIGLOW: They've got me at last.
DROVERS: It's hard luck.
COOK: How did it happen?
BOB: The jackeroo fired his revolver at a dingo, and rushed the mob off camp.
COOK: God's truth, and them been ringing these two hours!
MICK: The Boss is as mad as a snake—he was flourishing his greenhide and cursing thunder and lightning till we got 'em together again.
COOK: It's hard luck, hard luck for us all.
BOB: It's no good growling. It's done now, and we've got to make the best of a bad job.
MICK: You should have seen the boss——
BOB: He takes it worse than Briglow.
MICK: Can you blame him! Fancy the Jackeroo firing his revolver and rushing the mob like that—it's the dead finish—Briglow's horse smashed to bits, Bob's horse with a broken neck, and Briglow here laid out—
COOK: And nothing in front of us but the long dry plains.
MICK: We'll have a lively time from now on.
BOB: My oath, we will!
COOK: What's up, Briglow?
BRIGLOW: Gimme a drink.
COOK: Right-o!
  (*Gives him pannikin of water.*)
  Sorry we haven't a drop o' grog left.
BOB (*examining him*): One thing—nothing's broken.
BRIGLOW: It's here—inside.
MICK (*to* BOB): Any hope?
BOB: It'll be a long time before he's in the saddle again.
BRIGLOW: Bob!
BOB: I'm here.
BRIGLOW: Thanks for pulling me out.
BOB: That's nothing.
BRIGLOW: You risked your life to save me.
BOB: Give it a bone, Briglow.
BRIGLOW: It's rotten bad luck for Alec.
MICK: It is that.
BRIGLOW: He's responsible for them cattle.
BOB: We're a man short now. I dunno what we can do about Briglow.
MICK: The Boss'll think o' something.
COOK: He's quieter now.
MICK: The old man gave eighteen pounds for the gelding Briglow rode. He was going to run it at the Brunette races.

COOK: Wish we were there now! I'm going to get a tenner for two days' cooking.
BRIGLOW: Are the cattle steadying?
MICK: They were ringing when I left.
BRIGLOW: They'll give some trouble yet.
MICK: The Boss is with them, they'll never get away from him.
BRIGLOW: I can't do no more. It's the dead finish.
(*Enter* JACKEROO, *an athletic young man, city-bred, out for experience. It is his first trip in the Never Never.*)
JACKEROO: Where's Briglow?
COOK: There he is.
JACKEROO: Don't say he's done for! It was all my fault, firing at that dingo. The cattle rushed like mad, trampling him into the ground. My horse bolted. I couldn't pull him up in time to help.
MICK: Run away, you make me tired.
BOB: You've too much talk, young fellow.
JACKEROO: How are you now, Briglow? What can I do?
BRIGLOW: You can't do anything ... it's all over.
JACKEROO: Don't say that!
BRIGLOW: Part o' the game, lad.
JACKEROO: If I only had that medicine chest! The Boss wouldn't let me bring it.
COOK: It's all we can do to carry the tucker.
BOB: Pain-killer's all right, though.
COOK: Where can it be! Any of you blokes seen the Pain-killer? There's some kicking about somewhere.
BOB: It's hard luck. Here we are, camped on a muddy water-hole, where there's not enough water to fill your hat, and five hundred cattle mad for a drink!
MICK: The old bloke'll think o' something, and pull us through. D'you remember when he took those steers from the yellow water-hole at Murrimji, the short cut through the devil-devil country, where the ground broke under your feet, and the ants would eat you alive—only three of us and a Myall nigger! We got one drink for the mob in a hundred miles. He's a marvel, the old man is, and delivered only six short of his number.
(*Thunder of hoofs heard.*)
BOB: They're off again.
MICK: Blarst them!
BOB: Come on Mick!
(BOB *and* MICK *dash off. A pause.*)
COOK (*to* BRIGLOW): By gum, that Bob can ride. ... See him jump on that brumby brute! ... By gum, tho', look at the old bloke putting a bend on them. ... He's got 'em. ... Wheeled 'em a treat. Bob's up now, so's Mick. ... They've got 'em all right. ... Got 'em rounded up, and fetchin 'em back to camp. ... Say, Briglow, ain't old Alec a bird! You should have seen him bending that mob, right on the shoulder o' the lead, swooping round 'em like a hawk.
BRIGLOW: The old man's a tiger, you can't beat him.
COOK: They're steadied now. ... On camp again. ... but they're on

the prod all right, and looking for trouble.... Here's the Boss coming in, Briglow. He knows where the Pain-killer is. You'll be as right as rain then.
BRIGLOW: He's a hard case, ain't he?
COOK: My oath!
(*Enter* ALEC, *the* BOSS. *He is a man about fifty, tanned, wrinkled, with thick bristling eyebrows, and grey hair and beard. He is bandy legged, but sturdily built. In his younger days he was champion horseman of three states, and is now a famous bushman and drover.*)
BOSS: The cattle's steadied.
(*To* JACKEROO.)
What the devil are you doing here?
JACKEROO: I wanted to see Briglow.
COOK: We're looking for the Pain-killer.
BOSS: It's in the pack-bag.... In the black bottle.
(*To* BRIGLOW.)
We've got them steadied.
BRIGLOW: Well done.
BOSS: But the trouble is they're still pegging for a drink.
COOK (*with bottle*): I've found it.
BOSS: Give it to me. (*Reads directions.*)
"Twenty drops maximum dose".
(*Pours half the bottle into the pannikin.*)
JACKEROO: It's too much.... Three times too much!
BOSS: I know the dose for Briglow. Here, drink this.
BRIGLOW (*drinking*): That's good.
BOSS: That'll fix you, eh?
(*To* COOK.)
Get a move on, Albert.
(*Enter* PIDGEON, *a black boy, behind tree. He is tall and thin, and dressed in ragged trousers and shirt. He is quite young, but a little black growth of whiskers gives him a comical appearance.*)
PIDGEON (*poking head round tree, with a grin*): Gibbit tobacco.
COOK: Get out o' this.
PIDGEON: Gibbit tobacco, Boss.
COOK: I'll give you a cracked skull....
(*Exit* PIDGEON.)
BOSS: Here's the Pain-killer, Briglow. Here, stick my swag under you. (*He fixes him up.*)
BRIGLOW: Right.
JACKEROO: My God! It's terrible!
BOSS: What's done is done. You get out to the cattle now.
JACKEROO: All through an accident.
BOSS: You make things worse, jawing away like a blasted cockatoo. Get out, and mind you stay with them.
(*Exit* JACKEROO.)
BOSS (*to* BRIGLOW): How are you feeling?
BRIGLOW: Numb and comfortable now.
BOSS: Good.... We must get water for the mob. Not half of them

had a drink at this mud-hole. That's the real trouble.
BRIGLOW: Yes, that's the trouble all right.
(*Enter* BOB *and* MICK.)
BOB: Cattle's steady as a rock.
BOSS: What's the time?
COOK: Quarter past four.
BOSS: How's the breakfast, Albert?
COOK (*taking up a comically pugilistic attitude*): Right, whenever you're ready. Stew on the left, damper on the right, and me in the blanky centre if you don't like it.
BOSS: Hurry up, boys.
(DROVERS *take quick breakfasts.*)
COOK (*to* BRIGLOW): Here's some stew, and a drink o' tea. That stew's made o' roast beef gravy. I reckon I can knock up a better stew than any man in this blarsted country.
BRIGLOW: My oath, you can, Albert. Leave it there, I'll have a cut at it directly.
COOK: When we get through to Urandangy, me and Bob's going to the Brunette races. I've got the offer of the cooking there—my oath, there'll be a jamboree. Avon, and Eadingly, and Alexandra, and Alroy, and the O.T., and all the stations are sending horses. What o' the two-up then, eh? And they're getting a waggon load o' grog from Townsville. Paddy Lenny told me.
BRIGLOW: Remember me to the boys.
COOK: But what do you think o' this, Briglow? They're going to give me a blanky Chow for an offsider.
BRIGLOW: That's murder, Albert.
COOK: I'll make the yellow heathen move. Chows—Brunette's got one cooking now ... they can't cook ... Now, I can make pastry out o' weevily flour as good as you'll buy in the Brisbane shops. And I can cook a ragout——
(*Sees* PIDGEON *breaking a piece of brownie.*)
Here, you blanky black thief, I'll skin you alive——
(*Exit* COOK *after* PIDGEON. *The* DROVERS *take pannikins of tea.*)
MICK (*to* BOSS): What are we going to do?
BOSS: There's only one thing to do, get going.
MICK: What about Briglow?
BOSS: We'll see.
MICK: When are we starting?
BOSS: Right away ... picaninny daylight.
BOB (*coming over*): Without Briglow?
BOSS: How the Hell can we travel with an injured man?
MICK: It's hard luck.
(COOK *and* PIDGEON *enter.*)
COOK: Pack the horses, Pidgeon.
(*Goes over to* BRIGLOW.)
Can't you do a bit o' stew, Briglow?
BRIGLOW: I don't feel like eating.
COOK: How about a drink o' tea?

BRIGLOW: Gimme a drop o' water.
COOK: Right you are, lad.
(*Gets water.*)
BRIGLOW (*to* BOB *and* MICK): Look here. I've got a few pounds on me, you blokes can divvy that, and my cheque.
BOB: You'll be all right, Briglow.
BRIGLOW: But send a fiver to Joe Duggan. I owe him that.
MICK: We won't forget.
BOB: ... I think I'll buy that little mare—down at Banka Banka. (*To* BOSS.) Briglow says we can divvy his cheque.
BOSS: What about it?
BOB: I'm thinking o' buying that little Banka Banka mare, you know her—bay wi' black points.
BOSS: Yes.
BOB: And there's that roan gelding at Alroy. What do you think o' him—think he'd be better than the mare?
BOSS: Give it a rest, Bob.
(BOB *and* MICK *finish breakfast. The* BOSS *goes to* BRIGLOW, *and fixes him up carefully.*)
BOSS: How are you feeling, mate?
BRIGLOW: I'm settled, Alec.
BOSS: By God, man, I'd rather it was me!
BRIGLOW: I ain't growling.
(*The* BOSS *fills a pipe, and holds a match over it, while* BRIGLOW *puffs till the tobacco glows.*)
BOSS: Have a quiet smoke.
BRIGLOW: We've had good times together.
BOSS: My oath, they've been good times.
BRIGLOW: Alec!
BOSS: Yes.
BRIGLOW: You'll be a man short now.
BOSS: We'll work it somehow. Albert will have to do a watch; and Bob will take your place on the tail of the cattle.
BRIGLOW: You might tell Bob if that bald-faced piker gets slewing out on the left wing, not to lay the whip into him. He's blind in one eye. I just found out, last night ... Just sing out, and he'll go back himself.
BOSS: How's it now, Briglow?
BRIGLOW: Easier. The pain's gone.
BOSS: That's something. Why should it end like this?
(*He looks across the plains.*)
The cattle are uneasy, and bellowing with thirst.
BRIGLOW: What are you going to do, Alec?
BOSS: We can't stay here, and we can't take you, Briglow. It's the devil's own luck—but there—what's the use of magging like an old crow?
BRIGLOW: Who's grumbling? We know the bush, me and you. We're old at the game.
BOSS: We've got to get on. I'm in charge, and I'd push them through if every blanky man in camp snuffed his candle.

The Drovers

BRIGLOW: You don't have to tell me that mate.
BOSS: I've got to deliver the damned cattle.
BRIGLOW: I'd like to be going with you. ... but ... there's no chance ...
BOSS: There's no bones broken. Lets see ...
BRIGLOW: It's inside ... something's crushed in the fall.
BOSS: I've seen such cases.
BRIGLOW: Haemorrhage.
BOSS: You might get better yet.
BRIGLOW: It's no use pretending. I'm settled, Alec.
BOSS: Curse the Jackeroo!
BRIGLOW: Let the lad off light if you can. He didn't know what he was doing when he fired that shot. He's new to the bush.
BOSS: ... And it's all a damned accident. ...
BRIGLOW: It don't matter. It had to come sooner or later. I've lived my life, careless and free, looking after my work when I was at it, and splashing my cheque up like a good one when I struck civilization. I've lived hard, droving and horse-breaking, station work, and overlanding, the hard life of the bush, but there's nothing better, and death's comes quick, before I'm played out—it's the way I wanted.
BOSS: Maybe I'll finish like you, Briglow, out in a bush, I hope so anyway.
BRIGLOW: I've got no family to leave behind. Maybe the bush'll miss me a bit ... the tracks I've travelled, and a star or two, and the old mulga.
BOSS: And I'll miss you. I've never travelled with a better man.
BRIGLOW: I hope you get the mob through safe. I'm real sorry I ain't no use, but it ain't my fault.
BOSS: Don't I know it! You've always done your share, Briglow, and a lot extra. I'll never find another mate like you. The others are good lads, but they're young yet.
BRIGLOW: They'll soon get over it, and forget all about me.
BOSS: But I'll never forget, Briglow. It's part of my life.
BRIGLOW: Well, it's been a good life. I'm satisfied.
BOSS: That's the way to look at it, Briglow.
BRIGLOW: It's fate.
BOSS: That's right. It's fate.
BRIGLOW: No man can dodge his fate.
BOSS: We've had some good times together.
BRIGLOW: Yes ... they were good times.
(COOK *comes over to* BRIGLOW.)
BOSS: I'll just have a drink o' tea, and get them started.
(*He goes to camp fire and fills pannikin. The* DROVERS *come over.*)
BOB: How's it now, Briglow?
BRIGLOW: The pain's gone.
BOB: I'll be taking your place on the tail of the cattle now.
BRIGLOW: Yes.
BOB: ... I think I'll buy the mare, Briglow.

BRIGLOW: The mare's the best.
BOB: Well, so long Bill.
BRIGLOW: So long, Bob.
(Exit BOB, singing:
"Give me a horse wi' a bit o' pace
And a saddle that's made by Uhl.")
COOK: I've packed up and started the horses.
MICK: So long, Briglow.
BRIGLOW: So long, Mick.
(Enter JACKEROO.)
JACKEROO: Good God, we're not leaving him, are we?
COOK: You're as bad as a kerosene tin in a yard full of colts.
MICK: We're in for a rocky time, but I think the old man'll get through. He a marvel, ain't he? So long, Briglow!
(Exit MICK.)
JACKEROO: How can I leave you, Briglow!
BOSS *(coming over)*: Why ain't you with the cattle?
JACKEROO: I can't leave Briglow like this.
BOSS: You're a drover, ain't you?
JACKEROO: Yes.
BOSS: Your place is with the cattle. We've got to push that mob along, and we're a man short now. Get out to them. I'll see to Briglow.
BRIGLOW: You ought to be with the cattle, lad.
JACKEROO: What can I do? So long, Bill.
BOSS: Hurry up. Come on.
(Exit BOSS with JACKEROO.)
COOK: The cattle's started.
BRIGLOW: Fill my pipe, Albert.
COOK: Right O! A smoke'll do you good.
(Gives him pipe.)
All right now, Briglow?
BRIGLOW: Yes.
COOK: Well, so long. I'll tell the boys about it at Brunette.
BRIGLOW: So long, Albert.
(Exit COOK. A pause. Then enter BOSS.)
BOSS *(calling)*: Here Pidgeon.
(Enter PIDGEON.)
BOSS: You look out, Briglow. Supposin' him want tucker, water-bag, you gibbit!
PIDGEON: Poor fellow! Bullocky bin kill him dead all right.
BOSS: Bye'n'bye, me come back quick-fellow, and by God, if you no more bin good fellow, I'll murder you, you black devil.
PIDGEON: Me good fellow watch.
BOSS: You can't run away from me. Supposing you run, me track him up, track him up, bye'n'bye catch-im you, shoot-him Pidgeon full with bullet, leave-him Pidgeon alonga little fellow black ant. ... Here, tobacco.
(Throws a plug. To BRIGLOW.)
I'll come back myself when we get the cattle to water.
BRIGLOW: I'll be gone then.

The Drovers

(They shake hands.)
BOSS: So long, old mate.
BRIGLOW: So long, Alec.
BOSS *(to PIDGEON)*: You good-fellow watch.

(Exit BOSS. A pause. The sun rises. From the edge of the Barklay Tableland the great plains stretch away, unbroken by timber, except the few gydgea trees that fringe the muddy water-hole. The Drovers have disappeared on their journey across the long, dry stage. BRIGLOW BILL is lying on the ground, his head resting on a swag. Albert's stew, and a bottle of Pain-killer are both untouched.)

BRIGLOW: The sun's rising. It'll be hot for the cattle. And here I am, lying in the shade, instead of eating dust on the tail of the mob.
PIDGEON: See, hawk and crow, hawk and crow, they fly alonga mob. Plenty bullocky die before they catch-him water.
BRIGLOW: The old bloke'll pull them through. He's the big gun drover of the North, and I've been his right hand man these twelve years. He's got good lads with him, but he'll miss me.

(PIDGEON throws some sticks on the fire, and blows up the dying embers. Then he sits down, his legs crossed under him, and starts clicking two sticks together, and murmuring a kind of chant.)

PIDGEON: You, Briglow, and old man Boss, you savee bush all-the-same blackfellow ... I think first time you blackfellow, Briglow. You die, then jump up white fellow. Now you die, and bye'n'bye ... next time, you jump up blackfellow, alonga new fellow country—good country—plenty water, plenty fish, plenty tucker ... You die all right.
BRIGLOW: That's right Pidgeon, I'm going.
PIDGEON: Oh, you poor fellow Briglow, me big-fellow sorry alonga you ... Bye'n'bye me go back alonga my country, alonga camp fire, alonga tribe ... Me tell-im father, mother, brother, sister—me tell-im blackfellow all alonga camp—me tell-im poor fellow Briglow, he bin dead now. ... Then all blackfellow alonga camp make-im big-fellow corroboree alonga you ... all day, all night, we sing in corroboree, cut-im head, cut-im arm, alonga sharp-fellow stone.

(BRIGLOW BILL falls back exhausted. His pipe rolls along the ground. PIDGEON rises stealthily, and goes across to the drover. He looks down at him carefully, shakes his head, and mutters.)

PIDGEON: Poor fellow! Me sit down, wait along Boss. Old man soon come back alonga shovel ... put him deep in ground ... dingo can't catch-im bone.

(BRIGLOW makes no stir. PIDGEON peers round camp.)

PIDGEON: Me make little-fellow hill; me build up little mound, grass, bushes, stones, keep off bad spirits alonga bush. That one frighten-im debbil-debbil ... debbil-debbil can't catch-im Briglow now.

(PIDGEON picks up the pipe, and then sits smoking, again chanting to himself, and clicking the sticks together.)

CURTAIN

Letters from Esson to Vance Palmer*

November 1920

15 Waverley House,
Kenton Street,
London, W.C.1.

I have just returned from Oxford, where I have had some long, elaborate and stimulating conversations with W. B. Yeats. I'm sending you a few notes that I hope you'll find suggestive. They are meant to hearten you, to give you confidence; and they have a moral—production. I would like to be able to talk things over with you; I have material for a number of important discussions, but you'll have to put up with a few hints. I think you'll understand, and know how to expand them, though I doubt if many people in Melbourne would. Certain principles, that you really hold, you can take for granted. I'm sure you'll be in complete agreement with what is said—I want you to feel that Yeats' authority would be behind your nationalism, and that you can hit the barren 'intellectuals' (who are as intellectual, usually, as rabbits) on the head hard.

I must get my boasting over, though it is necessary to state it. Yeats asked me up to see him and put me up for the night. I landed late afternoon, and he talked for an hour on my plays, theories, etc., before dinner. At dinner he told good stories. After that we talked till past midnight. Next morning he took me into his study, and he was very sympathetic. I then took a walk round the town, had lunch with them, and returned.

He thought more of my little plays than I could possibly have dared to hope. He thought the dialogue excellent, the 'atmosphere' as suggestive as could be. I told him I didn't think much of myself as a 'plotter', but he said the four little plots were perfect. The only adverse criticism made was that near the end of *The Woman-Tamer* the woman might have pretended to relax to make the end more surprising. He said he thought the element of surprise was necessary in comedy, but not in tragedy. (He doesn't mean 'surprise' in the American

---

* Written from London and Melbourne and reprinted from Vance Palmer, *Louis Esson and the Australian Theatre* (Melbourne: Georgian House, 1948).

magazine-editor's sense.) On the whole, he thought, I might do my best things in tragedy. There it doesn't matter if the end is foreseen, the emotion should carry the interest through. He thought success would come to me some day, though I don't believe that. I mention this not to skite, but to indicate the principle of sound literature.

Plays on really national themes, he said (not 'popular plays', in the ordinary sense—and this is his important principle—help to *build a nation* in the spiritual sense; while the other type of play, so-called intellectual drama, abstract and cosmopolitan—Galsworthy, Bennett, etc., and the husband, wife, lover triangle (not on moral, but artistic grounds) will 'shatter a nation'. That is what our scholars fail to realise. Their arguments look good on the surface, rather difficult to meet sometimes, though they are quite unsound. We are on the side of life, and they ('they' means too many people in Melbourne) are on the side of death and desolation. And yet most people would be against us.

He thought we ought to get the theatre going, no matter how small. A good 50 enthusiasts are better than 500 indifferents. You must see Stewart Macky about this. He has a sympathetic philosophical personality. He will feel what is right. The plays we give should all be national. Academics will say we haven't got them. Well, we've got to get them: they'll never get them or anything else. At the beginning of the Abbey Theatre Miss Horniman wanted to do, with the local plays, the European masterpieces. That is what our repertory theatres have tried to do. Yeats said he wavered, but that 'inquiring man,' Mr. Synge, objected, and Irish drama was saved. '*A theatre like that,*' said Synge, '*never creates anything.*' Isn't that true? What did MacMahon create? What did Hilda's University Society that did Shaw, Galsworthy, etc., create? They should have discovered me for a start, but they didn't! What has Adelaide ever done, with all its list of plays?

The same applies to the writing of novels.

Stewart's English plays, if he does them, are all in vain. The local play, he [Yeats] says, will also produce a better type of acting; there are no bad models to imitate.

If Stewart's show is still going he'd better get a definite policy to begin with. A small sheet, stating some definite aims, needs to be drawn up. I would anticipate a startling success, not a failure, if some energy were put into the movement. But there must be no bloody lectures about it. They darken counsel. Also B. or people like that mustn't say anything until they're asked.

Yeats said they had to kill the pompous literary humbugs for a start. Their idiom was objected to as not being English; they retorted by showing that the professors couldn't write at all. It is really the same battle; it always is.

I wish I could give you the faintest suggestion of his intellectual power, the strongest I've ever met, even apart from his imaginative insight, vast erudition, and wonderful humour. In the midst of some elaborate discussion he'll drop in an outrageous story, but it always has an application and is not given for its own sake.

Among subjects touched on were early Egyptian art, Blake, Shelley, Browning and Balzac, whom he regarded as great medieval minds, all comprehensive and wise, as artists, though they were futile, especially Balzac, in life; professional poets, George Moore's art criticism (which I told him taught me a lot, and he thought they were Moore's best written books), sayings of Oscar Wilde, memories of William Morris, Mrs. Besant, some gorgeous stories of Dr. Gogarty, the great wit, Shakespeare, Ben Jonson's plays (when I mentioned the dialogue of Bartholomew Fair, Billingsgate made classic, he said that play influenced Synge. Curiously enough, I did think of Synge as I read some of Ben's speeches), a continuation of the Canterbury Tales, a remark on the phases of Henry James (James the first, James the second, and the Old Pretender), modern English poets, Tolstoi and the Saints, Japan, the distinctive nationality of Australia—everything deep, interesting, and all linked to his general philosophy of art and life. That is only a meagre list. His chief theme, on which he is writing a book (the book they told you about in Dublin. What they said was true in one sense, but comically exaggerated) is on unity of personality. He divides writers into different classes—subjective, objective, half and half, etc., the self—and the antithetical self—the writer usually expressing his opposite, to realize the self. I could explain all this fairly clearly, but it would take too long. Just take it as a suggestion of something! Yeats seems to me to have a mind as clear and penetrating as that of an old schoolman. There are a lot of things I'd like to tell you. Here are the last two.

(1) Why, in a Catholic country like Ireland, have most of the writers been Protestant? He said it was simply education. In the age of Huxley, etc., the Catholic Church had to be on the defensive. But now that age is passed; and probably in the future the Catholic education will be better than the Protestant, and the Catholics produce the best writers.

(2) Is Australia a race yet? Could it develop a nationality in a hundred years? He said yes. It was so in Iceland. Iceland produced its heroes, conscious of their nationality, though they had been on the island for a less time than we have been in Australia.

I'll drop Sinclaire a note next mail on some other topics suggested. Do you think we could convert him to a national view? His classicism is not unsound, but I don't think it is fruitful, that is all. He is regarding literature from an absolute standpoint. My point would be simply that absolute truth doesn't matter; our job is to do something, however poor it is, but something ... and classical rules won't help production. Also in his theology I want to suggest the possibility of a new colouring in new conditions. It may come to the same thing at the end, of course.

I have some good ammunition in the locker now. Yeats will read anything I like now, and he is quite interested in me. He isn't interested in many people nowadays. He sees nobody in Oxford, professors or undergraduates. His old castle in the south of Ireland has been wantonly raided by the Black and Tans. He writes every morning regularly, and is doing some big works and some slighter pieces, like memories of his first years in London, with impressions of Morris, Ernest Dowson and Oscar Wilde.

I hope to get back when I can. I'm dreaming of a three or six months' break with the Bradys at Mallacoota. It looks a good place on the map.

December 1, 1920

15 Waverley House,
Kenton Street,
London, W.C.1.

I have just finished *Such Is Life*. I am sorry I can't regard it as a literary work. I admit it was well worth preserving for its matter, which is excellent, but Furphy has done all he could to spoil it. The general form, I think, is good, but what I object to is his vicious style. He writes in the usual style of the badly educated man who has taken as models the articles in the Rationalist press and the penny encyclopedia: 'in arrogant assertion of parental authority, yet glancing apprehensively', 'escort', 'receptacle', 'ensued', 'belying', 'elicited', 'replenished', 'incoherent', 'vicinity', 'subdued suavity', 'earnest entreaty', 'cheap complaisance', 'sudden reticence', 'exigency of his errand', 'adverted to', 'established efficiency', 'endeavour to palliate it', and hundreds and thousands of other dreadful words. This style gets between him and his subject, a character, an anecdote, a bit of landscape, like a fog.

What has damned him is his 'ideas' which are poor: he gives an opinion on music, Shakespearian criticism, theology, history, metaphysics, natural science and other subjects that are quite beyond the range of his special training. That is the secret of it all, I feel sure. He can't see anything simply and he won't let well alone. His cheap science was popular at the time; A.G.S. often wrote the same jargon. It is bad luck. If he hadn't such a false idea of literature, he would have written a wonderful book. The material is gorgeous, and I like the type of book. I fancy it has to be taken as raw material, and used again in a better form. I think you are right in holding it a valuable work; it is a first-class document, but I'm sorry for Furphy's sake. Nobody seems to have told him how badly he was writing. Literature, finally, never exists for its matter. Form, which must be the spiritual element, alone remains. Byron had admirable matter, but he is passing rapidly; we even underestimate him nowadays. Keats or Coleridge seemingly had no matter at all; they stand higher every year. It is as great a mystery as the mass.

I wanted to say the worst I could, for despite everything I enjoyed the book. Some of the stories could not be bettered: I hope I am not doing him injustice, for I should be delighted to learn that the style is only a superficial blemish. But I'm afraid it is fundamental, the expression of a mind that has become sophisticated by cheap science.

I wanted to thank you for your suggestion of changing the phonetics in my dialogue. It was meant for the actor or speaker, but it does no good even in that way, and, of course, is always an eyesore. If the idiom isn't good, impossible spelling won't make it so.

You say Furphy's second book is in some ways better than his first. Is there no way of dredging him? I could read a series of them with pleasure mixed with damns.

January 22, 1921

15 Waverley House,
Kenton Street,
London, W.C.1.

Just a line to thank you for the book. I read it with pleasure for the descriptions of the life; and I was surprised, even a little disappointed, at not being able to get a good laugh. It is not a Viva Dubova. Some of the material is so good that I hope you haven't wasted it.

By the same mail Gerald Byrne sent me *The Camp, The Australian Poetry Annual* and *Fellowship*. I had quite an exciting night reading. Some of your pieces gripped me painfully; I wanted to chuck everything and return, for these are my people, too. Your patriotic poems are good. I wonder only why you selected the proletariat instead of your own cattlemen. 'There'll be little care for beauty ... ' I think your own cattlemen would be more truly your own people. My only other criticism is that I think you wilfully spoilt 'The Dandenongs' with the suggestion of future 'fumes' and 'smoke,' which was not a happy thought then, and only spoilt something that was quite charming. So it seems to me. It was a very pleasant book indeed; and I read slowly and dreamed, and wondered why I wasn't there.

The *Annual* cheered me greatly. It is a sign of life; that is the great thing. Many of the verses are poor enough, naturally, especially the mild fluting of the ladies; and, on the whole, there isn't much originality. There are no strong ballads, no songs, no simplicity. That wasn't the point, of course, that struck me first, but the fact of the existence of a Melbourne literary group. Don't you think a more definite aim among the best writers would produce better results? Macartney seems to be an intellectual poet, an interesting personality, though, unfortunately, I haven't got his books. He may be really good. O'Leary was quaint and strong, though I can't judge what he can do from one piece. I liked Byrne's sonnet also, *The Road to Marysville*. The whole show was a good performance for Melbourne. I think it would be a good policy for Melbourne to become a definite centre, distinct from, and in friendly rivalry to, Sydney. I hope *Birth* continues, and that the next *Annual* will be fresher and more original.

I was surprised at 'Og's' article in the December *Fellowship*, on the need for buying Australian books which were said to be up to contemporary English standards. It is hardly necessary to go as far as that. I would have been satisfied if 'Og' had admitted the possibility of an Australian work justifying its existence simply because it was a genuine thing, however small. I've been firing away at Sinclaire; and he is replying more hotly than I ever expected. If he really believed, he could have a powerful influence in the literary sphere. He could kill off all the academics, for he is a better scholar than any of them.

Could you give me a brief account of the Melbourne Literary Club? What is its activity, if any? Who edits *Birth* and the *Annual*?

I hope you are keeping well and happy. I think I must return before next winter. I'm very interested in the new developments. Books must keep on getting printed. It's a pity there's no rich bloke, with some sporting instinct, who would found a good review or monthly magazine. I want a bush house, say at Emerald, within reach of Melbourne. Whatever forces we have need bringing together. In the early days *The Bulletin* had a definite aim. That was its strength. It is time for a newer movement now. But it must be just as national. There's too much rushing about. I go to London, Allen seeks Araby, and Miss Derham goes to Eden—there's too much travel altogether.

March 21, 1921

15 Waverley House,
Kenton Street,
London, W.C.1.

I was very pleased to get your last letter. You will excuse me for being amused at your innocent surprise at the want of criticism in Australia. I had ten years of it. Did you think you would get a serious notice for your book in the *Age* or *Argus*, or from Bert Stevens? I once got a two-line notice in the *Age*, which is still the delight of my frivolous cousins. The expert said the pieces had appeared in papers, and he couldn't see the necessity why they were brought into a book, which was probably true and sound criticism. For my own part I don't believe in criticism. I take the position of Whistler, who challenged the competence of all his critics, except artists. Every art has an elaborate technique, and only the performers can possibly understand it. There is far too much criticism in London. It is an easy job for journalists; that's all that can be said for it.

I have finished two long Australian plays that I feel pretty sure are far beyond the little plays. Both are in three acts. One is a comedy set in an old deserted gold-field; and the other is a primitive tragedy, in the Wimmera district, with a suggestion of bees, duck-lakes, the desert, etc. It is a very beautiful district, strange and shimmering, remote for Victoria, where, at least in my time, you came on emus and kangaroos. I don't think I can be mistaken about these plays. Page by page the dialogue is much richer; and I think the construction is sound. I've done all I can to them, and won't touch them again.

I am never anxious to get plays published. A play is meant to be acted, not read. I regard the text only as a musical score. That is why I avoid comment as far as possible. Directions should be purely practical; anything else is, strictly speaking, illegitimate. Shaw tried to make a play compete with the novel as a book, but it can't be done. The forms are quite different.

As you suggest, I may have to use some modern or cosmopolitan themes. I wouldn't do them as well. But this year I'll try a comedy. It will be a rest, for I've worked very hard lately. I feel pleased that I've finished two plays that I wanted to write, and I need a spell.

I am sorry Australia is still so provincial. You did the heroic thing in returning; but I don't think it would be unpatriotic if you came over here again, to establish your reputation. You could return later in a stronger position. Three or four years' serious work in London could do you no harm. You must have more raw material than you need. Every year you'll get to hate journalism more and more. There's no escape in Australia from useless drudgery. I don't want you to desert your post: I would like everybody to return to Australia. But at present you can do no more there than here. In fact it seems you can do less. London, after all, is not England. It is a great centre, like ancient Rome. You want to talk it over quietly with Nettie. You'll get out of touch with London and New York very quickly, for things are always changing. There is no reason why Australia should always be a generation behind. I don't want you to leave, but I don't want you to ruin yourself by attempting what can not yet be done. You'll have to get your novels and stories done. I think you'll be able to do them better here, at least till you're properly established.

I see Kattie's* *Black Opal* is announced for publication by Heinemann. I read it in m.s. I think it is a decided advance on *The Pioneers*.

Harrison Owen is doing well in journalism. He is really worthy of a better fate, for he has a wonderful instinct for the right things. He surprises me by the way he always backs the right horse. He is the only journalist I've met who had taste, and knew one thing from another.

Squire, editor of the *Mercury*, does a causerie every week for the *Observer*. They are rather dull. I used to think Squire pretty good, or fairly good, but he is only the Gosse of the younger generation, and not so good as the old man. He wrote a review of Moore's latest book, *Heloise and Abelard*, mild but inadequate. Moore wrote an amusing letter saying Squire had suggested that there were anachronisms, 'which he was kind enough to say, did not matter.' Moore challenges him to find any, and if he can't, to apologise. Squire can't know anything about it, though like most critics, he pretends to a knowledge he doesn't possess. Whatever he says, I know he's in for a bad time. Squire has been a bit of a bubble lately, it is time he was burst. He isn't good enough to take a lofty position, and Moore at present seems to be in a fighting mood.

March 29, 1926

73 Rathdown Street,
Carlton.

We have had a dreadful season, terrible fires, a heavy atmosphere and no rain. I just found out that some of the worst fires were in the district where I did *Dead Timber*. The family I stayed with are still there, and the old man said that they had now been burned out four times. The life there is just as epical as that described in the *Growth of the Soil*.

* Katherine Susannah Prichard.

The last few days have been fresher, so we are feeling livelier, though the expected rain hasn't come yet. But the oppressive period is over. I have been very lethargic and unable to write a line without pain and difficulty. But I'm feeling all right now.

Kattie arrived safely back and found a contract waiting from Jonathan Cape, who admired *Working Bullocks* very much. To my judgment it is a real piece of work, though it is doubtful what kind of popular appeal it will have. It's good for everybody, as well as the country, that an Australian novel can be a serious literary work.

The Meldrums are off to Paris soon and later they will go to America. It's a pity he is leaving just when he has got a small group of admirers. We went out to see his work at his studio one night. His landscapes are marvellous, and he would rather stay here than go abroad. From our point of view he has not done badly, but painters nowadays expect a good deal or maybe their expenses are heavy. If a writer made £300 or £400 out of a book, as a painter does from an exhibition, he would think he was a millionaire.

Stewart is working again on his play which, I trust, will turn out all right this time.

And how is the work getting on? I hope you find conditions favourable. Brisbane ought to be a young and virorous centre of a new culture, but I don't suppose it is. I got a note from Stable of Queensland University asking for a couple of verses for a new anthology. He had selected an imbecile piece, so I sent him something else. I find I haven't written more than six or seven, if that, tolerable pieces of verse. We needed a Whitman thirty years ago, to give a lead. Most Australian verse belongs to the crinoline age. Each new anthology makes us look still more ridiculous. How does it come about that such unlikely people are asked to edit anthologies! There's a subject for Nettie, though I fancy it would be more politic not to mention it.

June 15, 1926

73 Rathdown Street,
Carlton.

At last our troubles are over. On the whole we did very well. It was a fairly smooth performance with less prompting than usual, and by good luck we had a satisfactory audience. From 7 to 9, after a week's perfect weather, there was an unexpected and heavy downpour of rain. It must have made a tenner difference to the house. But the booking had been good, much better than ever before, so we did very well after all. The house was almost full, except the balcony, and the show went over not so badly. It was a slow start as usual, not a laugh coming till page 5. We had only two breaks, Joe going out for a plate and not returning, but Frank as Smithy covered it up cleverly, and even Rowe didn't notice it. The second was that the curtain in Act III fell on the screen.

The first act, that on paper seemed the liveliest, made the least effect. But I was lucky in most of the characters. The outstanding successes were Frank as Smithy and Irene Appleton as the Charwoman. But equally good in character were Ruby May, Hilda and Reg., O'Connell as the policeman, and Bryce Dunning and Violet Groves (doctor and nurse). The beautiful Ivy did quite well in a difficult and artificial part. We had decent programmes and good music, but we hadn't made proper arrangements for the front of the house, and the ushering was poor. Still it was a decent show.

At the finish we had everything to do. Nobody did a solitary thing. Entertainment tax, rehearsals, printing (programmes, tickets and dodgers), scenery, Glen's, props (hundreds of them) and furniture, carting to and from the Playhouse, music, publicity—Hilda and I, especially Hilda, did the lot. The Playhouse people were decent, and the men behind were really expert on scenes and props. When we started, vaguely and tentatively, the company wanted to get busy, and before we knew where we were everything was to be all right. Leo proposed a business meeting of a few men, but we never had it, so we were left with the business. We had to pay every bill and were made responsible for everything. There was never time to get things sorted out. The last few weeks were a whirl and placed as we were we had to go through. Hilda managed everything in the most marvellous way. We did everything well, and yet expenses were kept in reason. When the ticket-sellers weigh in, the expenses will be practically covered.

When it's all over I expect we'll be about a fiver down, which is not worth mentioning in the circumstances. Without the rain, we would have been a fiver up. A second performance might have been successful, but the risk wasn't worth while. We have been extraordinarily lucky. If things had gone wrong, as they might have, we could have been £40 out. Stewart came to the house twice at private rehearsals, and got down to the show after the second act. That was the beginning and end of his effort. He looks worried and I don't blame him, for he has a rough road to travel (I mean spiritually).

I learned a lot from rehearsals and the performance. Better strategy in Act 1 will make all the difference. The fact that the actors showed up the weak spots (good playing sometimes can disguise a weakness) was to my advantage. Acts II, III and IV all went well, I believe, and require only slight alterations.

But next time it won't be my play. I don't want the company to bust, for it is getting better. Leo certainly did good work in getting a good company together. He and Frank will be along tomorrow night to discuss future plans. I propose we should do a bill of short plays for two or three nights at the Queen's Hall. I don't think expenses should be more than £20. About five of us could put up a fiver each and I don't see there would be much chance of a loss. My conditions are that I'll have nothing to do with finance or props, or carting. Otherwise I don't mind seeing to the publicity, printing, rehearsals, etc. It's up to some of the players to take some of the responsibility. After the short plays it might be possible to do Stewart's play, either at the Playhouse or the Queen's Hall. As it has a small cast the Queen's Hall would probably be best. For the short play evening this is all I can see at the moment:

> Comedy by Gerald Byrne.
> Something by Woollacott.
> *Black Horse*, by Vance Palmer.
> *The Ruling Passion*, by J. V. Duhig.

Gerald's and Duhig's plays are the sort of thing we want. They are not very strong, but with a bit of fixing they could be made pleasant enough. We would need *The Black Horse*. A revival is good in itself to show we are getting a repertoire and that we keep going on.

I'll try to fix up Gerald's little play. Do you think you could go over *The Ruling Passion* with Duhig? It is good in idea, character and atmosphere. But it is badly put and the points are not made clear. It seems to me like this:

> 1st scene. Wife complaining to husband about his gambling. *That's the point.* All her troubles come from this vice. No sob stuff. Keep the life of the trainer. Too wordy and confused at present.
> Work up excitement of the race.
> Result. Celebrations.
> Jim in the dumps.
> On the Newmarket. Barney opens book.
> Jim refuses the bet.
> Why? ... *the big surprise*: he hasn't backed his own horse.
> Instead of the row—surprise of the others.
> Jim's explanation: the wife was right and I don't blame her. See what it's done to us ... etc. A good scene.
> Then the wife enters jubilant: trained a winner at last ... I always like that mare, etc. Finds he hasn't backed her.
> Jim tries to explain he took her advice.
> She turns on him: You fool! Call yourself a sport, etc.
> For curtain I suggest Jim goes over to Barney: 'I'll have a fiver on ...'

That seems the play to me. I think it could be simplified and made quite amusing. It would be good if we could do a Queensland sketch. The atmosphere is good. Will you fix it up with Duhig and send it back? I'll do my best for Gerald.

July 15, 1926

73 Rathdown Street,
Carlton.

I've been waiting for 'news' to send you but I'm afraid nothing important has turned up. We're getting more or less used to the city. There are not the long quiet days and dreamy nights of Emerald, and there is a certain nervous tension, but we are trying to find compensations. We have been out in society a few times. We were at Esther's on two Sunday nights, at Fritz Hart's and at the Mortills.

I had lunch with a young American scientist from Chicago who is interested in our art and literature. I have him a little information, not much, and suggested two or three books. I fancy he is going to write a book about Australia.

Mrs. Mortill is interesting, a true Russian. I'm quite satisfied they are the straightest and most sincere people in the world. We've been to hear Chaliapin—it is truly an event in one's life. You feel this is great art, an art that comes out of life itself. He is sympathetic and can render any shade of emotion—he has an extraordinary range—and yet, somehow, you feel he stands above the storm. He seems to understand. Hilda is more eloquent about him than I can be, and she may tell you what he has made out of his songs. With his delightful exuberance Fritz saw us and came up breathless and dishevelled, shouting along the passage: 'Marvellous! His dissipated life seems to have given him a Shakespearean serenity.'

It seems we are becoming social people. Next Monday Mrs. Pitt and Bernard O'Dowd are coming along for a yarn. Hilda saw Bernard in the street, and he was looking very well. I'll be delighted to see them. There is a possibility that I might meet Leonard Merrick. Fritz Hart has met him, and I believe Merrick would be pleased to see me, God knows why. I've never had any reputation to speak of, but every year it seems to dwindle a little. Ten years hence I shall be in an absolute blaze of obscurity.

I do hope you'll soon pull off a good solid narrative that will do you justice. Kattie is lucky in being able to get a good publisher and do exactly what she likes. It would make all the difference to you. You've got a good few years yet, and plenty of fight left, but it is wearisome at times always having to struggle up hill. Success may be a stimulus. You've got to go harder than ever till it comes. If what you've done won't do the trick, you've simply got to do something bigger next time. There are chances open, but it wants a bit of luck to get them. I hope you are all well and enjoying your good fortune in being in such a splendid place. We miss you all very much.

November 15, 1926

73 Rathdown Street,
Carlton.

Your play seems to have made a hit in Brisbane. The press notices Nettie sent give the impression that it was taken seriously and recognised as a new departure. But from what you say I gather the Brisbane Repertory Theatre is content to follow the example of the Melbourne and Adelaide societies instead of trying to strike out for itself. Australia is perhaps the only country in the world that is not ashamed of its provincialism. I received a letter from Leon from New York in which he says that Dallas, Texas, which has nothing like the population of Melbourne, has one of the best Little Theatres in America.

It is strange that Australia has no interest in seeing its own life depicted on the stage. It is different in painting, for even the best people will pay a good price for a picture of the Australian scene, which twenty years ago they would have thought an impossible subject. Percy Grainger thinks the time will come when Australia will have a distinctive music of its own. He points out that certain forms, say the minuet and scherzo, arose out of a definite social order that has no existence here. Australian music will come out of nature rather than out of a salon, and, if it is true, it will have something big and simple and democratic about it.

Grainger's ideas, I thought, were good and stimulating. In literature and drama there must inevitably be an Australian note that is neither American nor English. I received from Barnett Clark the first book devoted to O'Neill. Clark has done the job well, for he shows what O'Neill is striving to express. There is no doubt O'Neill is an absolutely sincere writer. He does his best every time.

I don't know what Hilda said about my historical play, but Nettie guessed right when she thought it must have been about Eureka. I woke one morning, and found I was interested in the subject, though I had thought little about it before then. I don't think I was influenced by Mrs. Davidson's effort, which I had quite forgotten. Maybe the subject may have influenced me subconsciously. Anyway, the theme dropped into scenes of its own accord. I don't see how the main scenes could be altered. I read Ross and Turner, and they give a good deal. Many sidelights came from the histories of Victoria.

But the source book, my Plutarch or Holinshed, is Raffaelo's book, *The Eureka Stockade*, published in 1855. It is rare, but Blackburn got a copy for me from the Commonwealth Library. It's a little gem of a book in its own way. I would defy anyone to do Eureka without him. He will be my chief character, and about half of the play will be taken direct from his account. He is a Roman, a man of 40, a little red-headed man (not our usual idea of an Italian), a teacher of languages, and a gentle, quaintly humorous character. I don't think he was a revolutionary, with definite political ideas. I think he was more a man who thought life should be better but knew by experience that it was always the same story of oppressors and oppressed. He is the sole authority for the most vital scene. In his quaint style, using many languages, he gives the characters, the scenes, and many verbatim speeches and sayings.

I've arranged the story in three acts, divided into about fifteen scenes. I open on the gold-fields with the arrival of the new Governor Hotham. The first act ends with the great meeting on Battery Hill, with Raffaelo's speech, resolutions by Lalor and Vern, and the first burning of the licences in a bonfire. The Australian flag is here hoisted for the first time.

Act II is a block of actual happenings. It opens next day with a digger hunt, the last on record. There is a scene in a store where Lalor is elected commander-in-chief. Follows on the same day a kind of fragment, the oath to the flag. And that night an interview in the Government Camp. Then come three Eureka scenes, Friday, Saturday, and the attack on Sunday morning, which ends the act.

I practically finished the first two acts in a few weeks; but journalistic necessity prevented me from starting Act III, which I would easily have finished by now. It may be a few weeks now before I can tackle it. I want to give the atmosphere as well as the ideas of the time. It ought to be a picturesque thing. I want to be fair to everybody, including Hotham, who is not uninteresting; there will be a dozen chief characters, but the most important of all will be the crowd that will be individualised and swayed by different motives. Reading the old histories I was surprised how interesting the life of the country was. Eureka and the goldfields are the most spectacular part, but other events are just as interesting in their own way.

I once thought when you tried to persuade Esmonde to do Australian history that your motive was biased and ultra-patriotic. I didn't think there could possibly be a rich field for research. I see now you were quite right, for there is a whole mass of fascinating and significant material. Please thank Nettie for her German sentences. They are intended for a German blacksmith manufacturing pikes in the opening of the first Eureka scene. (He was killed in the assault.) I would like another few German sentences (with translations at the side), for Vern, a flamboyant young man. He was a great ladies' man. How would 'Ah, the beautiful ladies!' go in the Germanic tongue. Or some expression of his romantic regard for the fair sex. Or a military sentence: 'I have studied the art of war'—or anything like that. I shall be very grateful for Nettie's assistance.

I don't know why I should bore you with all these details. We miss you both very much. I would explain things much better if you were here. It is a great help sometimes to tell somebody the plot. A few dark places are often illuminated in that way. I would like to write one or two plays next year; but it's not always easy to get a clear run. When I'm pulled up I find it hard to get into stride again.

P.S.—Bedford wrote a Eureka play, *The Flag of Stars*. Do you ever see him? I would like to know what his attack was. I'm told some novels deal with Eureka, but I haven't seen them, except Dyson's, which I've entirely forgotton. Do you remember any of them?

> # From Hilda Esson's Introduction to
> *The Southern Cross and Other Plays**

From his earliest years Louis Esson was familiar with the problem of giving artistic expression to this new and strange land. Though born in Edinburgh, in 1879, he lived all his life in Australia, and a close comradeship with his uncle, the artist John Ford Paterson, was one of the formative influences of his life. John Ford, like Louis himself, had an unfailing store of wit and eloquence, and never tired of talking on his favourite theme. He used to say, with a twinkle, that Cook only discovered the outline, it was for the artists to discover the real Australia. He delighted in pointing out the delicate and subtle tones of our landscape, comparing them with the heavy richness of European colouring, and explaining how the painter had to find a new palette to convey his impressions.

They looked at the country together, and with something of the same vision, freshly, without preconceived ideas or prejudices. Once, when they returned from a holiday in a remote part of Gippsland, Ford Paterson brought back a sketch of ghostly silver trees shining in a misty morning light, and Louis his short play, *Dead Timber*.

This quest remained for Louis always the chief motive of his existence.

---

* Melbourne: Robertson & Mullens, 1946.

Alan Seymour

Brian James (Wacka) and Bunny Brooke (Dot) in a scene from the 1970 Independent Theatre production of *The One Day of the Year*. Photograph by courtesy of the Independent Theatre, Sydney.

The One Day of the Year

The One Day of the Year was first performed by the Adelaide Theatre Group in Willard Hall, Adelaide, during July 1960, with the following cast:

ALF COOK	Terry Stapleton
WACKA DAWSON	Francis Flannagan
DOT COOK	Patsy Flannagan
HUGHIE COOK	Tony Ogier
JAN CASTLE	Georgina Mackie

Directed by Jean Marshall.

The One Day of the Year was later performed professionally at the Palace Theatre, Sydney, on 26 April 1961, with the following cast:

ALF COOK	Ron Haddrick
WACKA DAWSON	Reg Lye
DOT COOK	Nita Pannell
HUGHIE COOK	Lew Luton
JAN CASTLE	Judith Arty

Directed by Robin Lovejoy.

The Scene–The interior of a small suburban house in Sydney.
Time–The present.

ACT ONE

SCENE I

The Cook family's house in one of Sydney's inner suburbs on the western side of the city.

A multiple set, main areas being the kitchen; the "lounge"; and HUGHIE'S study, which is a glassed-in sleepout at the side of the house. Each of these may be presented as fully or as sketchily as is thought fit. Furniture throughout is cheap, dowdy, bought long ago on T-P.

The kitchen is the old enclosed-back-veranda type, with a table, chairs, gas stove, sink and primitive home-made kitchenette.

The lounge-room which should occupy central part of set contains an old lounge suite upholstered in brown Genoa velvet with flower patterns. Some of its springs have gone and in places it sags. An occasional table near lounge and an ashtray on a stand.

HUGHIE'S veranda room has bright contemporary curtains along its "louvres". In the corner a small bed, next to it a little table with portable radio, piles of books, exercise books, notebooks. On clothes closet nearby stands a modern camera of superior quality and a few packets of films for it.

DARKNESS. Noise is heard, men's voices, talking. Even before the lights are up we can tell one of them is drunk or at least on the way to it. Lights come up on kitchen. ALF and WACKA are seated at table. ALF is in truculent mood, WACKA negatively acquiescent.

ALF: I'm a bloody Australian and I'll always stand up for bloody Australia. That's what I felt like sayin' to him, bloody Pommy, you can't say anything to 'em, they still think they own the bloody earth, well, they don't own the bloody earth. The place is full of 'em. Isn't it? Wacka! Isn't it?

WACKA: Yes, Alf.

ALF: The place is full of 'em. Poms and I-ties. Bloody I-ties. Wherever y'look, New Au-bloody-stralians. Jabber, jabber, jabber. The country ain't what it used to be, is it? Is it?

WACKA: No, Alf.

ALF: 'E gets in the lift, 'e says "Seven". Like that. Not please, thank you, or kiss my foot. Just "Seven". I get'm all day, jumped-up little clerks, think they're God Almighty, well, they're not God Almighty, I know'm, I take'm up and down all day, you think I'm not sick of that lift. Well, it won't be for that long, I'll show 'em, won't be that long now. You see when I get my new job. Did I tell you about my new job? I'll be right when I get my new job. None of this up and down, up and down all day. (*He drinks*) 'E says "Seven". I says: "Wotcher say?" 'E looks me up and down as if I'm a lumpa dirt, his nose wrinkles up, he dunno he's doin' it but I seen it, I seen it so I says, more polite like, layin' it on only he don't see I'm havin' a go at him, I says Beg yr pardon, sir did you say

Act One

Seven or Second? I wish I had a quid for every time I've had to ask that in the last thirteen years. And he says, "I said Seven, old man." Gawd, when they start old man-n' me ... Bloody Poms. I thought of a few things I could've said but there was a dame in the lift, she was eight months gone if she was a day. I thought what I'd say'd make you drop that colt right 'ere and it'd be me who'd have to deliver it, wouldn't be the first time neither. You dunno what it's like, shut up in that thing, it's a bloody cage, being polite to every no-hoper every day, all day, holdin' yr horses when they tread on yr foot or ask silly bloody questions or bloody near insult you in front of the mob, they give me the dries, they do, they give me the screamin'—(*by now almost beside himself*) I'm as good a man as them, who says I'm not? Who says I'm not?

(*The front door bangs.*)

ALF (*continued*): Who's that?
MUM (*from hall leading from lounge room*): Me.
ALF: Frighten hell out of a man. (*To* WACKA) She bangs that door every time she goes through it, you wonder why I'm grey.

(MUM *has come through lounge unbuttoning overcoat.*)

MUM (*coming into kitchen*): Are you on it again? (*To* WACKA, *neither with nor without enthusiasm*) 'Ullo, Wacka.
ALF: You want one?
MUM: No, just had a cuppa tea at Mabel's.
ALF: Have one. Go on. (*He is pouring it.*)
MUM: I'm not havin' beer on toppa tea. It's too cold for beer anyway.
ALF: Never too cold for the old amber, love.
MUM (*glares at him*): How much've you had?
ALF: Oh, get orf me back. (*He pushes glass towards her.*)
MUM: I don't want it.
WACKA: I'll 'ave it.
MUM: You've got one in front of you already.
WACKA: I know. (*He takes glass, drinks.*)
MUM: Hughie not home?
ALF: Had a late lecture.
MUM (*getting electric jug*): I'm cold. Think I'll make meself a cuppa cocoa.
ALF: Cocoa! (*A long disgusted look at her, then*) I feel sick.
MUM: Gimme a look at you.
ALF: You put your jug on.
MUM: Gimme a look at your tongue.
ALF: I will NOT give you a look at my bloody tongue.
MUM: Don't you swear at me. Anyway, I don't need to look at your bloody tongue. I can see your bloodshot eyes.
ALF: Very funny. (*Turning his back on her*) Wacka, have another drink.
WACKA (*suddenly waking up*): 'E's awright, Dot. 'E's bin good as gold.
MUM (*at sink*): Oh yes, I believe you.
WACKA: He has. We just bin sittin' here waiting for you to get home.

MUM: Don't crawl to me. You'd stick up for him if he was paralytic. (*She fills jug, her back to them. A pause.* ALF *and* WACKA *exchange a "try-it-on" glance.*)
WACKA (*tentatively*): You look real nice tonight, Dot. You look nice in that getup.
MUM: You shut up, you old cow. (*But a moment later.*) Want a cuppa cocoa?
WACKA: Nup.
MUM (*indifferently*): All right. Well, if nobody else'll have any I can't be bothered makin' if for myself. (*At sink.*) Thought you was gunna do all them dishes for me after tea.
ALF: Oh, leave 'em. Leave 'em.
MUM: Yeah, leave 'em. I know who'll end up doin' 'em and it won't be you.
ALF: Don't take no notice of her. I know when she comes home a bit shirty, I know. Lose at the Housie-Housie, love?
MUM: I wasn't at the Housie-Housie. I was at the Euchre. And I won.
ALF: Bloody gambling. Still puttin' the kid through Uni, 'aven't got two bob to rub together and she's bloody gambling. The whole bloody country's living beyond its income. Look at Hughie's clothes. Clothes! What'd I know about clothes when I was his age?
MUM: He's got one suit and one sports outfit and he bought 'em out of his own money he earned drivin' the taxi for 'is mate in the weekend.
(*A pause.*)
ALF (*a long, satirical stare at her*): Well! Well! That's a turnup for the books, that is.
MUM: What is?
ALF: You stickin' up for him all of a sudden.
MUM: Drink yr beer.
ALF: Clothes and cameras, all Hughie thinks of.
MUM: He's got one camera.
ALF: Yeah, and all his money goes on it. The whole bloody country's living beyond its income. Like that bloody little jumped-up Pom in the lift today. Thinks 'e's Christmas in 'is suede shoes and 'is little 'at with the feather in it and his yeller vest, he's only a little clerk prob'ly; but do they turn it on? *Do* they? And why? That's what I want to know. Why? Why does he look at me as if I'm a bad smell and he's the bloody ant's pants, 'e's not worth tuppence. He's not. He's not worth tuppence. I wouldn't wipe me—
MUM (*from sink*): Alf—
ALF: Boots on 'im. 'Ow much did you win?
MUM: Two bob.
ALF: Two bob. And 'ow much did you lose last time?
MUM (*coming to stand over him*): How much did you waste on beer tonight?
ALF: You can see the bottles. Two bottles. If a man can't spend a few bloody bob on a coupla bottles of beer—
MUM: And how long was you on it before the pubs shut?

Act One

ALF: Now listen, Dot—
MUM: Alf. It's bloody this and bloody that every two seconds. I know how much you've had when you get to this bloody stage.
ALF: Listen, love. (*Puts his arm up around her waist.*) It's only a bit of a warmup.
MUM: I'll give you warmup.
ALF: Now, Dot—
MUM: All right, I know. I don't have to look at the calendar. You can go the whole year without hardly touchin' a drop and up comes April—
WACKA (*suddenly, into his beer*): Oh to be in England now that April's here.
ALF: England? Buggar England. I'm a bloody Australian, mate, and it's because I'm a bloody Australian that I'm gettin' on the grog. It's Anzac Day this week, that's my day, that's the old digger's day—
MUM: You can old digger y'self to bed.
ALF (*a sudden sting*): You bloodiwell leave me alone. (*They glare at each other.*) You leave me alone. Yr always pretty quick off the mark when it's me.
MUM: Well?
ALF: Well, y'mind yr ps and qs in front of the boy lately.
 (*She moves to the sink without speaking. He follows her.*)
 Ah! Got her on the soft spot. Come on. Tell a man. Let a man into the secret. What's the matter with Hughie? What's the matter with him all of a sudden? He's the same kid he always was. Well?
MUM: Shut up, Alf.
ALF: I won't shut up. (*They have suddenly quietened.*) I want to know.
 (*They face each other with the special deep hostility of people who have been a long time married.*)
MUM: Want to know what?
WACKA (*quietly*): She's right, Alf. Everythink's right.
ALF: She watches him. I've seen her. When he's in the room she just watches him all the time. Hardly says a word.
MUM (*biting*): I might if he said somethink to me—
ALF: Why's she got a snout on Hughie? What's he done?
MUM: Oh don't ask me. Wacka knows. He's noticed it.
ALF: Have you two been talkin' about my boy behind his back? Criticize, criticize.
MUM: Oh, of course you weren't, a minute ago, his clothes, his camera—
ALF: That's different. Hughie and me understand each other. I know you two buggers sittin' 'ere swillin' afternoon tea every day, mag, mag, mag—
WACKA (*meekly*): I haven't said a word, Alf. Haven't said a word.
ALF: She's got some bee in her bonnet. (*He turns on her again.*) Well?
 (*She shrugs, moves away. Impatiently ALF turns to WACKA.*)
 Well?

34   The One Day of the Year

WACKA (*hesitates, then*): Kids change.
MUM: They don't have to change that much. Get home, Wacka, yr landlady'll be worryin'.
  (WACKA *stands*.)
ALF: 'Is landlady can mind her own bizness for once. Siddown, Wack.
  (WACKA *sits*.)
  This is our last bottle. We're gunna finish this bottle.
  (ALF *begins to pour beer, looking up at* MUM.)
  And don't you worry about my young Hughie. He's all right.
  (MUM *turns back to sink*. ALF *and* WACKA *lift glasses and drink. Lights on kitchen scene fade. Voices are heard outside sleepout section. From the darkness comes* JAN'S *voice*.)
JAN: I hate them, hate them, hate them: How dare they?
  (*Light in bedroom flicks on*. JAN *has hurried into the room*. HUGHIE *stands at door, hand on switch*.)
HUGHIE (*laughing*): Sit down and stop talking!
JAN: I'm furious. I hate them. How dare they dictate to me?
HUGHIE (*coming into room*): You can't hate your parents.
  (*Grins*.) Hey—we're here.
  (*They stand and look at each other, suddenly nervous. He moves towards her; she deftly avoids him, looks around the room*.)
JAN: This your room? Isn't it gorgeous? So tiny.
HUGHIE (*slight chip on shoulder*): Oh? It's all right.
JAN (*at window*): Marvellous! You could almost touch the house next door.
HUGHIE: Haven't you got any neighbours?
JAN: We've the most gorgeous trees all around, one doesn't even notice them.
HUGHIE: Sit down.
JAN: On the bed? What if your mother comes in?
HUGHIE: Wouldn't matter. (*She sits as he throws cushions together for her. A moment of silence. He stands nearby, edgy, trying to drum up some social grace*.) Um—sorry I can't offer you a drink. Cigarette?
JAN: Thanks.
HUGHIE (*as he lights it*): It is cramped, isn't it? I've been at the family to buy a new home, but they're that conservative. It's pretty terrible when you want to bring anyone.
JAN: Hughie, you don't have to apologize.
HUGHIE: I'm not apologizing. How were they dictating to you?
JAN: Oh, being late every night, all that jazz. My mother has a special telephone accent, it's so damned AFFECTED! God, she's a snob. Daddy's not so bad, but oh brother, my mother! Hughie—you are, you know. The very best thing that ever happened to me.
HUGHIE: Here we go. Society renegade finds peace in arms of proletariat.
JAN: Don't send me up, Hughie, please.
HUGHIE: Well, don't you patronize me.
JAN: Me—? When did I ever—?

Act One

HUGHIE: My dear, you could almost TOUCH the house next door, where I live we have trees all around, nothing so vulgar as a human being in sight.
JAN (*gently*): It was being here—alone with you. I was just making conversation.
HUGHIE: Pretty bloody funny conversation. (*They both smoke furiously, annoyed. He quietens. A pause. Gently he kisses her.*) Why'd you want to come so much?
JAN: Now don't start.
HUGHIE: Don't start what?
JAN: That tired old sex stuff. I've had enough of that with the grade-one morons in my own set. I thought you'd be different.
HUGHIE: What, the virile, uncouth proletariat?
JAN: I thought your *values* would be different. I'm sick of elegant young men talking of tapered shoes and Jags and MGs, in fact I'm sick of everybody in our mob, everybody.
HUGHIE: She did upset you.
JAN (*quickly*): I'm glad I made you bring me, Hughie. It's lovely to see what they're like inside, these gorgeous quaint little houses—
HUGHIE: Your mother didn't want you to come here, did she?
JAN: My mother is a snob. (*At bedside table*) This the camera you're going to use? Isn't it ... (*tails away*) gorgeous?
HUGHIE: What does she know about me?
JAN: Nothing. (*Quietly; dropping all pretence.*) Hughie, I get so miserable. I told her weeks ago you were the most exciting thing ever, how we'd met through the Uni paper, how we were going to cook up the Anzac Day jazz, my words, your pictures—(*She hesitates.*)
HUGHIE: And—?
JAN: She just happened to ask if she knew your family ... You see, she took it absolutely for granted it would be one of our crowd. When I mentioned where you lived—
HUGHIE: She hit the roof, I suppose.
JAN: Hasn't come down *yet*. We've been fighting ever since.
HUGHIE: What does she think I am, some kind of village idiot?
JAN: Hughie, I want you to do something brave for me. Come up to our house for a weekend.
HUGHIE: Are you serious?
JAN: They'll only have to meet you, I know they'll fall, they couldn't resist that honest, wonderful face—and your nice manners. Hughie, it's true, you're as well-mannered as any of the social crowd I've ever gone round with.
HUGHIE: I couldn't come up to your place.
JAN: Why not? We've often had—(*checks herself*) well, we have had boys up for weekends before.
HUGHIE (*unhappily*): Oh.
JAN: Last year. (*Laughing.*) That was my Yacht Club phase. (*Looks at him.*) Hughie, you're not the very first boy I ever met.
HUGHIE: All right for them. I'd use the wrong knife or wrong fork or do something wrong. I'd disgrace you.
JAN: Those things don't worry me.

HUGHIE: They don't here. Now. In theory.
JAN: You've got to make an effort.
HUGHIE (*hesitates, then*): No. No, I couldn't. I'm just not sure of myself.
JAN: But you can't stay here burrowed down in your own class all your life. If you get a profession, go out in the world, you'll have to learn to mix with all kinds of people.
HUGHIE: That's what I'm afraid of.
JAN: Afraid? I'll help you! Promise. (*He shakes his head. A pause.*) It does worry you, doesn't it?
HUGHIE: You're dead right, it does. Mahleesh.
JAN: Huh?
HUGHIE: Mahleesh. Expression Dad brought back from the Middle East. "Never mind." "Forget it." (*Suddenly serious.*) Hey—did I hear you say—CLASS?
JAN: Yes, you did. (*Turning on him*) And you're not going to tell me there's no such thing here. That's one of our myths.
HUGHIE (*uneasily*): I've never thought about it.
JAN: That's not true, Hughie, it worries you every minute of the day. And you're right. (*Very dogmatic.*) I don't know any girl, any friend of mine who's ever married or gone out with or even MET a boy from—well, round here.
HUGHIE: Well, no. (*Then realizes implication.*)
JAN (*triumphantly*): We marry the people we mix with and we mix with our own class. Australia, the great democracy. Wow!
HUGHIE (*quietly*): We met. Because I'm at Uni. A—well, a— (*manages to say it*) a working-class kid. At Uni.
JAN: O.K., they dole out bursaries. It only covers your fees. Your parents still have to battle, now don't they, to get you through, buy your books, clothe you, feed you—Oh, they must have been wonderful.
HUGHIE: Ah, the proud peasant classes! Jan, my parents would bore you to tears.
JAN: I don't believe it.
HUGHIE (*quietly*): I was lying about us getting a new house. We couldn't afford a new house. They don't want one. They *like* it here!
JAN: But that's why I came. To see what produced Hughie Cook.
HUGHIE: But, Jan, you couldn't bear it! The conversations in this house! (*Does his parents*) Avea cuppa tea, luv, avea cuppa tea, I don't wanta cuppa tea, all right, don't avea bloody cuppa tea! (*They fall back on the bed, laughing.*)
JAN: I'd love to meet them.
HUGHIE: No, you wouldn't. (*He turns abruptly away from her. She watches him a moment.*)
JAN: Hughie ... You never talk about them. That's the first time. Don't you like them?
HUGHIE (*shrugging*): That's a funny question, isn't it?
JAN: You disapprove of me attacking my parents. Yes, you do. And yet ... What is it?

Act One 37

HUGHIE: Nothing. They drive me mad sometimes. They're so—so—
(*He stops, seems to be feeling for words.*)
JAN: Well? They're so what?
HUGHIE: Do you know I never can find the word? Somewhere in the back of my mind there's one word, one word that sums up all they represent, all I can't stand. But I can never find it.
JAN (*gently*): This Anzac Day story—wouldn't have anything to do with them, would it.
HUGHIE: I don't dig.
JAN: You get so burned-up about it. I don't know anybody who takes it so seriously. (*Pause.*) Why do you?
HUGHIE: Why do I? I wonder. (*A pause.*) I can't stand waste. Waste of lives, waste of men. That whole thing—Anzac—Gallipoli—was a waste. Certainly nothing to glorify. (*Impatiently*) God, there's been another war since then! Dozens of wars everywhere, thousands of lousy little victories and defeats to forget. But they go on and on about this one year after year, as though it really was something.
JAN: And so young Hughie's going to ride in on his white horse—
HUGHIE: Don't laugh at me. This time last year, all the week before, I watched him getting worse and worse. I thought, I won't go. I won't observe it any more. But I did. When it came to the point I did. Well, that was the last time. This time I'm going to celebrate Anzac Day my way, with my feelings, my photos from my camera, on paper, in print. Even if it rubbishes absolutely and completely all I've been brought up on, that's what I'm going to do.
JAN: Save it—I've already joined. I'll write you the best story you've ever seen, Hughie. But those photos will have to be magnificent.
HUGHIE: Oh, think I can't do it? (*He grabs up camera.*) This is how I get my kicks.
JAN: And this is how I get mine. (*Leans over and kisses him gently.*)
HUGHIE: Do you like me a bit? (*She nods.*) Gee, I wish—
JAN: What do you wish, Hughie Cook—?
HUGHIE: *Can* we like each other? Would it ever work?
JAN: Why shouldn't it? (*He shrugs.*) Oh, my mother.
HUGHIE: Not just her. My people too. The whole set-up.
JAN: *I* want it to work. I do, Hughie.
HUGHIE: Then we'll make it work.
(*They are suddenly embracing hungrily and fall across the bed. She pushes him away.*)
JAN: Hughie! (*They struggle.*) Hughie! (*They struggle.*) Hughie!!!
HUGHIE: Now don't go all moral on me.
JAN: I just want to be sensible.
HUGHIE: Sensible? CRIKEY!
(*He reaches up, flicks off bedlamp. Lights on bedroom scene fade. Lights up in kitchen.* MUM *has been groping in dresser drawer and cardigan pockets.*)
MUM: Got a shilling for the meter? I'm right out.

ALF: I'm broke.
WACKA (*feeling in pockets*): Got two sixpences.
MUM: That's a great help. (*She moves away.*) Hughie might have some in his drawer.
ALF: Don't go rattin' the kid's drawer. He's a growing lad, y'never know what y' might find.
MUM: I'd better not find anything.

(*She goes across lounge room, switching on light. Stops halfway across room, spots magazines and papers thrown on floor, starts tidying up and knocks ashtray over. The light in the bedroom snaps on, HUGHIE'S hand on it. One arm is still around JAN. They both listen.*)

HUGHIE: Dad.

(*In an instant they are apart, JAN adjusting her sweater, patting back her hair, HUGHIE putting pillow and cushions back in right place. MUM throws papers on couch, crosses, opens door to HUGHIE'S room. JAN is sitting primly on edge of bed. HUGHIE stands at cupboard at other end of room.*)

HUGHIE: This is the camera... (*Turns innocently to face door.*) Oh...
(*At sight of his mother, closes up.*) Oh. Hullo.
(MUM *is a little taken aback.* JAN *rises, realizes she has kicked her shoes off.*)
MUM: I'm sorry. Didn't hear y' come in. (*She eyes* JAN *over.*)
HUGHIE: We just got here. (JAN *is trying to slip foot into shoe.*)
This is Jan. Jan Castle, she's at Uni. Jan, this is my mother.
JAN: I'm very glad to meet you, Mrs. Cook.
MUM: Yes. Well, you'd better come into the lounge.
HUGHIE: Oh—Jan wasn't staying.
JAN: But I'd love to stay. I've been so wanting to meet Hughie's parents.
HUGHIE: But—(*embarrassed*) Dad'll be going to bed, won't he?
MUM: Dunno about that, he looks right for the night to me.
HUGHIE (*to* JAN): It's a bit late, isn't it?
MUM: What's the matter with you? (*To* JAN) You'll have a cuppa tea, won't you?
JAN: Please don't go to any trouble.
MUM: It's no trouble. Come on.
HUGHIE (*grudgingly*): Well, all right.
MUM: Oh, got a shilling for the meter? (*To* JAN) Gas meter. Drive you mad.
HUGHIE (*feeling in pocket*): Sorry, I'm flat.
JAN: Here (*Pulls some loose notes and silver from her pocket.*) There's sure to be ... Yes, there.
MUM: Oh, I wouldn't dream—
JAN: Go on.
MUM: Well ... Hughie can give it to you tomorrow. (*Takes money.*) Thanks.
ALF (*yelling from kitchen*): Where the bloody hell are you?
MUM (*yelling back*): Awright, don't get orf yr bike!

Act One

(*She goes.* JAN *stares after her.* HUGHIE *grabs* JAN'S *arm.* HUGHIE *switches bedroom light off at second switch near lounge door. They go through to lounge,* MUM *ahead.*)

HUGHIE: Don't take too much notice of Dad. I mean, if he's a bit ...
(*He is nervous, on edge.*)

MUM (*shaking cushions on chair*): Siddown and take the weight off yr feet.
(JAN *sits,* HUGHIE *perches on arm of chair next to her.*)

ALF: For Christ's sake, Mother, come on—!

MUM: We're in here.
(ALF *and* WACKA *come towards lounge, armed with glasses and bottle.*)

ALF: Where've y'been? Takes y'long enough to get a bob, don't it? Thought you'd gone to the dunny and fell in.
(*He stands in doorway and sees* JAN. HUGHIE *is mortified.* MUM *looks daggers at* ALF.)

MUM: Hughie's brought a young lady—from the University—
(ALF *has whipped bottle behind and is passing it back to* WACKA. WACKA *is on tiptoe, peering over* ALF'S *shoulder.*)

ALF: Yes. Well, that's real nice. (*His elbow connects with* WACKA'S *stomach,* WACKA *withdraws to kitchen, puts bottle and glasses down.* ALF *hitches up his trousers, comes into lounge with an attempt at dignity and sobriety.*) Any friend of Hughie's is a friend of ours.

HUGHIE: This is Jan Castle.

ALF: Pleased t'meetcher. (*He has approached her, is not sure whether to shake hands or not, finally doesn't, turns to* MUM.) Well, Mother, aren't you gunna give the young lady a cuppa tea?

JAN: I won't have one, thanks. (*Realizes this may sound rude.*) Really. I hardly ever drink tea.

MUM: Don't drink tea. What do you drink?

JAN: Coffee mostly.

ALF: Bad as Hughie. Hughie's startin' on that. See them black rings under 'is eyes? That's coffee.

HUGHIE: Sit down, Dad.

ALF (*sitting*): Well, don't have anything to drink if you don't want to.
(WACKA'S *head has come tentatively through door. Spotting* JAN *he hastily withdraws.* MUM *sits.*)

JAN (*offering cigarettes around*): Cigarette?

ALF: I've got the makin's.

JAN (*to* HUGHIE): Darling, light me.
(HUGHIE *whips out matches, lights her cigarette.* ALF *and* MUM *exchange a glance at the "darling". A silence.*)

ALF: Well ... (*Looks around with a large, uncomfortable smile. A silence.* JAN *smokes.* HUGHIE *is miserable.*)

HUGHIE: Jan drove me home.

ALF: You got a car?

JAN: It's the family's. I'm allowed to have it if Daddy's not using it.
(*A pause.*)

ALF: You English?

JAN: Who me? (*Laughs, then in speech perilously close to their own*) No, I'm a dinky-di Aussie.

ALF: Aussie? You kids aren't bloody Aussies.

MUM: Alf ...

ALF: Look at Hughie. Look at his clothes. He's done up like a Yank. I dunno ... what's happenin' to the country? When I was your age we was Australian and proud of it.

HUGHIE: Oh, don't start.

ALF: You kids, you aren't happy unless you're copyin' the Yanks, wearin' Yank clothes, singin' Yank songs, rock an' ruddy roll. (*To* MUM) I tell you ... me and Wack, we're the last of the Australians. When we're gone, when blokes our age are gone, what'll you have? A stinkin' lot of imitation Yanks, the whole damn country's goin' down the drain ...

MUM: Why don't you say a few words?

JAN: Don't you think, Mr. Cook, I mean all this change, don't you think it's good for us? We're not half so insular.

ALF (*to* HUGHIE): What does that mean?

HUGHIE (*biting*): It means we're beginning to grow up—

ALF: Chris', look who's talkin'.

HUGHIE: As a nation. We're not so isolated any more. The Europeans here—dozens of different nationalities—they're giving us something new—cutting right across the old Australian stiff-neck. (*His mother watches alarmed as his speech seems to turn into an attack.*)

ALF: What's 'e talkin' about?

HUGHIE: All that old eyewash about national character's a thing of the past. Australians are this, Australians are that, Australians make the greatest soldiers, the best fighters, it's all rubbish. (*His father is about to cut in.* HUGHIE *finishes in a rush.*) The Europeans here force us to see that all people are pretty much the same, and that's the best thing that ever happened to this country, maybe the next generation won't be so one-eyed.

(ALF *looks up quickly.*)

MUM (*embarrassed, tries to cover up*): Gets it from his father. Talk.

JAN: I think Hughie's quite right, you know. (*They turn to her warily. She smiles, hauls the conversation on.*) Take the migrants, as Hughie says. Look at the difference they've made to our eating habits.

ALF: I still eat three meals a day. Breakfast, dinner, and tea.

JAN: I meant their restaurants.

MUM: Restaurants? You can't get a good cuppa tea any more. Everything's espresso coffee. Gives me heartburn.

ALF: That's it! Poms, Yanks and bloody I-ties.

HUGHIE (*turning to him*): If you can't discuss it intelligently—

ALF: Oh! (*Pukka accent, to* MUM) Oh, I say, Mother, sit up, old girl, we're going to have an intelligent discussion. An intelligent discussion. (*To* HUGHIE) Well, go ahead. Go ahead, *old man*, go ahead.

Act One   41

HUGHIE (*tightly*): Let's skip it, shall we?
(*An uncomfortable pause.* ALF *relaxes a little, feeling he has scored a point, and turns to* JAN.)
ALF: Where you from?
JAN: Here.
ALF: Here?
JAN: Sydney.
ALF: What part?
JAN: Roseville Chase.
ALF: Oh. North Shore.
JAN: What work do you do, Mr. Cook?
ALF: I'm a lift driver. War wound.
JAN: Oh?
HUGHIE: Alamein.
ALF: Don't ask me to show you it. (*Laughs, suddenly belches.*) 'Scuse me.
JAN (*quickly, to cover* HUGHIE'S *embarrassment*): What a charming little place you have here. I was just saying to Hughie—
MUM: Dad's prob'ly not feeling too good.
ALF: Ay?
MUM: He's just been having a talk with an old friend.
ALF: Now look—now look, I'm not ashamed to admit I've been having a few drinks—
JAN (*to the rescue*): That's just what I'd like. I really honestly don't feel like a cup of tea but I'd love something stronger.
ALF: Good on yer. What'll y'have?
JAN: I don't mind. Can I have a Scotch?
ALF: Ay?
JAN (*immediately apologizes*): Oh—if you don't have any—
HUGHIE: We've probably only got beer.
JAN: Well, I don't care for it usually, but (*big smile at* DAD) I'd love one.
ALF: Wacka! (*To* JAN) Youse'll be sweet.
(WACKA *puts his head in.*)
Well, what's the matter with you? Come on.
(WACKA *starts to enter, empty-handed.*)
No, no! Where's the stuff? Go and get it—and a couple of extra glasses. You'll find another bottle in the back of the cupboard—
MUM: I thought that was the last one.
ALF (*yells*): Behind the Corn Flakes packet. (*To* JAN) Y'always want to get the big size, they'd hide anything.
JAN (*to* MUM): You must be very proud of Hughie.
MUM (*embarrassed*): Oh ... you know.
ALF: The Uni's made a lot of difference to Hughie. Smartened up 'is ideas.
HUGHIE: My public.
ALF: Oh? You still 'ere? Thought you'd gone to bed. (*To* JAN) Thinks he's real sophisticated now, Hughie. (*Grunts.*) Prob'ly is too.
JAN: I like him because he isn't. Well, not too.

ALF: Get out, he's bright, Hughie—
HUGHIE: Oh—Come off it.
ALF: He's good at his studies, isn't he?
JAN: I didn't say he wasn't.
ALF: Hughie's all right. He's all right. Gets a bit carried away but he's a good kid. (*He turns to* JAN.) I wisht I'd had half his chances. I do. I didn't ever get to any Universities. The University of hard knocks, that's all I ever had.
HUGHIE: I don't know what you're complaining about. You've done all right, haven't you?
ALF: Of course I done all right. (*To* JAN) I'm in a very good job, you know. This lift-driving, it's only temporary, see—(*his family is surprised*) and I've got a very good chance of getting into something better soon.
JAN: That's nice.
ALF: Better job, much better pay, and that won't be hard to take, putting him through. (*Jerking his head at* HUGHIE) Our staff superintendent, see Mr. Wilson, he's a very nice chap, nothing stuckup. Well, they're buildin' a new plant out of town, and they need a kind of supervisor out there, see.
JAN: Oh, that sounds quite important. That'd be an executive position, wouldn't it?
ALF: That's it, that's what it'll be. Kind of an executive position. (MUM *and* HUGHIE *are half-embarrassed, half-astonished.*) You'd have to look after the plant and prob'ly do a bit of maintenance. Well, I've always been good on that. Machines, like. Always had a bit of a kink about that sort of thing. Well, that's the kind of bloke they want. So when I see it advertised, I got hold of Mr. Wilson and I said to him, What do you want to go advertising for? You've got a good man right here and you don't know it, so we had a bit of a mag and I look pretty right.
HUGHIE: Dad ...
ALF: He said he'd put in a good word for me, see.
MUM (*flatly*): There's nothing definite, is there?
ALF: Ay?
MUM: The way you talk—
ALF: Of course it's definite. I told you about it a month ago when I spoke to him.
MUM: Yeah. You told me.
ALF: Well?
(MUM *and* HUGHIE *exchange a glance.*)
MUM: Aren't you a bit old?
ALF: Arr, go on. They want someone with a bit of sense.
MUM (*dubiously*): Hmmm!
ALF: Well, I keep reminding him, every time he gets in the lift I have a bit of a go at him, see. Well, he would've told me if they were gettin' someone else, wouldn't he? He says they're lookin' into it. They're lookin' into it. These things take time. Of course it's definite. (*To* JAN, *indicating* MUM) Gawd, talk about a wet blanket.

Act One   43

JAN: Well, I hope it comes off for you, Mr. Cook. It sounds very nice.
ALF: It'll come off, all right, it'll come off.
(WACKA *comes back, loaded with bottles and glasses.*)
(*Springing up*) That's it, Wack.
(WACKA *has put things on table, stands looking sheepish.*)
Wacka, this is a young lady friend of Hughie's. Miss—er—Miss—this is Wacka Dawson. Wack—Miss—
HUGHIE: Castle.
JAN: Jan.
ALF: Miss Jane Castle.
WACKA (*shyly*): 'Ow y' goin'? (*He opens bottle, starts pouring.*)
ALF: Wack and me are old mates. At the war together.
JAN: Which one?
ALF: Fair go. Second.
HUGHIE (*laughing*): Think I was a late baby or something?
ALF: A man ain't that old. Wacka was in the first though. Wack's a real old friend of the family. Wack goes back a long way, don't you, Wack?
WACKA (*laughs*): Yeah. Yeah. (*Then, embarrassed at his own presumption, mumbles*) The Dawsons and the Cooks was always mates. They was always mates.
ALF: Wacka's been in both shows, you was in the Fourteen-Eighteen and the Second one, wasn't you, Wack? He was at World War One with my Dad and World War Two with me. That's a record, isn't it, eh? That's a good record.
JAN: My word.
(*A pause. They seem to have come to a dead stop.*)
HUGHIE (*making conversation*): Wacka—I've been trying to work it out for years. Come clean now. How old are you?
(WACKA *proffers glass to* HUGHIE.)
WACKA: 'Ave a beer.
HUGHIE (*taking glasses from tray and giving one to* JAN): You're not going to wriggle out of it that way. How old is he, Dad?
ALF: Search me.
HUGHIE: Wack—?
WACKA: I dunno. (*Grins, shrugs.*)
MUM: He's lost count.
HUGHIE: You must have some idea.
WACKA: I dunno. (*Pause. They all look at him.*) What I did I put me age up to get into the First World War and down to get into the Second.
ALF: Gawd, you must be old.
MUM: He wouldn't know. True. He's got no one to keep count for him, have you, Wack? Now, go on, have you? (*To* JAN) 'E's never got married. 'E's never 'ad no one.
WACKA: I've had youse.
ALF: You said it, Wack. What d'y'mean 'e never had no one? We bin mates for years. I've looked after him, haven't I, Wack? I seen 'im through. (*To* JAN) What I c'n work out, my old man seen 'im through the first show, I looked after him all through the last lot.

And did he take some lookin' after? Two left feet. No fingers, all thumbs.

HUGHIE: He's a good barman anyway. Mind if we get this down.

ALF: Jeez. Sorry.

MUM (*indicating* ALF): He can talk the leg off an iron pot.

JAN (*smiles at* MUM): Hughie is like his father.

ALF: Hughie? Talk? You seen that turn he put on just now? He useter talk like that all the time once. Of course, nobody ever listened. But he's bin quietenin' down lately. (*To* HUGHIE) Why don't you rave on sometimes like you useter?

HUGHIE (*abruptly*): Can't get a word in edgewise. Well ... (*Lifts his glass.*)

(ALF, WACKA *and* JAN *follow suit.* MUM *is not drinking.*)

ALF: Good 'ealth.

JAN: Skoal. (ALF, WACKA, HUGHIE *drink.* JAN *has glass to her lips when—*)

MUM: You say you was drivin'?

JAN: Pardon?

MUM: You've got to drive home, haven't you?

JAN: Why, yes.

HUGHIE (*irritably*): Drink up. Go on.

ALF (*When* JAN *hesitates*) Go on, miss. Get it down. (*To* MUM) What's the matter with you? She's only having one. You're only having one, aren't you?

MUM: Y'know what it says on the wiless.

(*A slight pause.*)

JAN (*battling to keep even-tempered*): No. What does it say on the wireless?

MUM (*heavily*): When yr drivin' don't drink. When yr drink'n' don't drive.

HUGHIE: Mum, for God's sake.

ALF: Arr, get orf 'er back, the girl's only walked into the place and you start.

JAN: Mrs. Cook's right, really.

HUGHIE: Drink your beer and—

JAN: No really. But do you think just one little sip—?

MUM: I didn't mean to make a song and dance about it.

JAN (*takes a mouthful, puts glass down, beams at* MUM. HUGHIE *is annoyed with both of them.* ALF *and* WACKA *look uncomfortable,* MUM *disapproves*): There—Now, what were we talking about? I know, Mr. Dawson's age.

ALF: Bugger 'is age. 'Scuse me, miss.

JAN: But it is very interesting. He went through the Second World War with you—

ALF: I've known Wacka all my life. I grew up knowin' 'im. That man—(*pointing to* WACKA *rhetorically*) that man practically brung me up. 'E looked after me when me old mother was battlin' in the twenties, on her own. Me old man never came back, see, from the first one. (*An almost professional air of grief has automatically appeared in him.*)

Act One   45

JAN: Oh, I'm sorry.
ALF: 'E was done in by a Turk (*a pause*)—Gallipoli.
   (JAN *sits very still, tense, on the edge of her chair. Slowly she puts down her glass.*)
JAN (*softly*): Gallipoli? You mean ... (*to* WACKA) you were there? (WACKA *nods.* JAN *turns to* HUGHIE.) We've found one! Why didn't you tell me?
HUGHIE (*uneasily*): Didn't even think of it—
   (JAN *is almost bursting with excitement.*)
JAN (*to* WACKA): But this is wonderful. You must tell me all about it.
WACKA: All about what?
JAN: Hasn't Hughie told you—?
ALF: Told us what?
HUGHIE: Jan—
JAN: We're both on the Uni paper now. I write for it, Hughie takes the pictures. We're doing a feature on Anzac Day, for the next issue—
ALF: Well! That's nice. That's real nice. We're pretty strong on Anzac Day in this house—because of the old Dad, see. We always keep it up, don't we, Hughie? Hughie's been to the dawn service and the march with me every year since he was that high.
JAN: Yes, well—
ALF: And yr writin' a story about it? Gawd, that Hughie, he wouldn't tell y'nothin'. Well ... you've come to the right place. If you want to know something about the old diggers, you've come to the right place. (*Expansively*) What do you want to know?
JAN (*impatiently*): You weren't there.
   (*She gets up quickly, goes to* WACKA. ALF *is offended.*)
   Mr. Dawson, you've no idea how keen I am to get the real, the authentic feel of the thing, to contrast it with what's come after. I wonder if you would help me. This is what I have in mind.
   (WACKA *has been edging away, embarrassed.*)
ALF: He can't tell y'anythin'. He never opens 'is mouth about it.
WACKA: I dunno nothin'.
JAN: I'm sure you're just being modest, Mr. Dawson, and that's exactly what I want. (*She has him in corner chair, hemmed in.*) Now I have a theory about this. As you know there's been more rubbish written about Anzac Day than about any other subject in Australia. Now my feeling is that all the hot air comes from those who were never there and who just go on mouthing all the platitudes until they come to believe them themselves and—
   (HUGHIE *has glanced quickly at his father who has tried to follow* JAN *but has lost her.* HUGHIE *hurries across to* JAN.)
HUGHIE: Jan, it's a bit late, isn't it?
JAN (*turning to him*): What?
   (HUGHIE *takes her arm and gets her, in spite of herself, to her feet.*)
HUGHIE: I've got some work to do before I go to bed—this can keep.

JAN: But, Hughie, it's so wonderful. (*To* WACKA *who sits bolt upright, scared, staring at her*) I've never met one, you see, there can't be a lot of them left now, can there? I've been wanting—ever since Hughie got me interested—I've been wanting to talk, to question—
HUGHIE: Jan! (*She stops, turns to him.*) Knock it off, eh?
(*She looks past him to* MUM *and* DAD *sitting stiffly looking at her and begins to get the message.*)
JAN: Oh. Well, if you really think—
HUGHIE: Yes I do.
JAN: Well, when may I?
HUGHIE: Talk about it tomorrow. Everyone's tired. (*Appeals to others*) It is late, isn't it? This girl keeps such crazy hours.
MUM: Well, I don't. I've got to get up and get them two off tomorrow.
JAN: May I come again? (*She looks eagerly from* MUM *to* ALF, *is both sincere and patronizing at the same time and* HUGHIE *could kill her.*) May I, please?
MUM (*uncomfortably*): It's all right with me.
JAN: Oh, thank you.
MUM (*getting up*): I think Hughie'd better get y'off home. I bin out and I'm tired anyway.
JAN (*piqued*): Oh, I'm sorry. I didn't realize you'd been out. I thought you'd been home all evening (*too sweetly*) in the kitchen.
MUM: If I'd been home all evening these two wouldn't be the cotcases they are. I bin at the Euchre.
JAN: The what?
MUM: With the girls. Playin' Euchre.
ALF: She won two bob. Turnup for the books, she usually comes 'ome half a quid behind.
JAN: But how interesting. You don't like drink but gambling's O.K. Gorgeous!
HUGHIE (*tugging* JAN *away*): Well, we'll be getting along now—I'll see Jan out. Say Good night.
JAN: Good night ...
(HUGHIE *charges out of room pushing* JAN *ahead of him and carefully closing door behind him. For a second or two nobody in the lounge moves. Then* WACKA *pipes up.*)
WACKA: She's orf 'er nut.
ALF (*nods slowly*): What was it she was sayin' to you?
WACKA: I dunno.
ALF: Neither do I. Never understood a word of it. (*Turns to* MUM) What do you reckon?
MUM: She wears too much lipstick.
(*Lights in lounge out. Lights up in* HUGHIE'S *room.* JAN *is sitting on bed, combing her hair.* HUGHIE *turns to her.*)
HUGHIE: That wasn't funny.
JAN: What wasn't?
HUGHIE: Getting at them.
(*He turns away from her furiously. She rises, comes to him.*)

JAN: Hughie? Are you cross with me?
HUGHIE: Yes. No. Not just you.
JAN (*gently*): With them?
HUGHIE: With myself, for being—(*Shrugs.*)
JAN: They're very nice, Hughie. Terribly nice.
HUGHIE: They're not. They're—
JAN: They're what?
HUGHIE: They're so—so—oh, I don't know.
JAN: They're themselves. They're honest.
HUGHIE: And so quaint?
JAN: I didn't mean to sound rude.
HUGHIE: Oh forget it. It's just—sometimes I feel myself getting farther and farther away from them.
JAN: Isn't that natural? You've left them miles behind and so you should, it's right that you should. That's what I admire in you.
HUGHIE: True?
JAN: True.
(*His arms are around her. He kisses her, a long, slow kiss. She moves away.*)
I thought you said you had some study to do.
HUGHIE (*snapping mood*): Half an hour before I go to bed. Every night!
JAN: You're made of iron. (*Kisses him again, lightly.*) I'm going home.
HUGHIE: I'll see you to the car. (*They start to go.*) Hey, why for God's sake did you mention that damned Anzac Day story?
JAN: Well, why not?
HUGHIE: I haven't said a word.
JAN: Hughie, really. You can be too soft.
HUGHIE: You kidding? If Dad sees it—
JAN (*a pause*): Maybe you shouldn't have agreed to do it.
HUGHIE: I want to do it. It's what I believe.
JAN: Well, then ...
(*He shakes his head, worried.*)
Well?
HUGHIE: Come on.
(*They go out through outside door of his room. Lights up in kitchen. WACKA has gone. MUM is at sink drying glasses. ALF sits polishing his shoes. An electric jug is heating.*)
ALF (*quietly*): She was havin' a go at you, Mother.
MUM: If y'ask me she was havin' a go at all of us.
ALF: No. No. Wouldn't say that.
MUM: She sobered you up, I'll say that for her.
ALF: Poor old Wack. See poor old Wack when she had 'im in that chair?
MUM: What'd he shoot off for? I was gunna make 'im a cuppa tea.
ALF (*yawning*): Gawd, Mum, you're a buggar for that tea.
MUM: You want one?
ALF: No, I don't. I'd've asked if I'd wanted a cuppa tea.
MUM: Don't start again.

ALF: Well, I'm tired. I don't wanta keep bein' asked if I wanta cuppa tea when I'm tired.
MUM: Well, go to bed, why don't you?
ALF: I don't *wanta* go to bed.
MUM: Oh. (*She stands dead still.*)
ALF: What's wrong?
MUM: I just remembered. (*Fishing it out of cardigan pocket*) She give me a bob for the meter and I didn't use it.
ALF (*grunts*): She won't miss it.

(*The electric jug begins to boil.* MUM *attends to it, begins to make tea. Her back is to* ALF. *He sits a moment, looks at her thoughtfully.*)

(*Tentatively*) Didn't know young Hughie had a girl.
MUM (*without turning around*): Ay?
ALF: She his girl?
MUM: Who, her? She's not his girl.
ALF: How d'y'know?
MUM: 'E would've said.
ALF: Would 'e?
MUM (*turning to look at him over her shoulder*): Well, he would've said somethink.
ALF: 'E hasn't bin saying too much lately.
MUM: Oh. Wakin' up, are you?
ALF: Wakin' up—what to?

(MUM *has finished putting tea and hot water in pot, which she now covers with cosy and stands on mat. She turns to face him.*)

MUM: I told you. Hughie's changin'. In fact, he's changed.
ALF: Oh, he's just growing up. A boy gets restless.
MUM: It's more than that. You saw him in there. You heard him, making his speech.
ALF: Oh, he's always talked like that.
MUM: No he hasn't. (*Struggling to express it*) Well, he has, but now it's different. Before it was just—letting off steam. Now it's personal. Directed at us.
ALF (*after staring up at her to digest this*): Come 'ere, Dot. Siddown. (*She does so. He is quiet.*) That what you were gettin' at before? When Wacka was here? (*She nods.*) What is it, Dot?
MUM: Don't ask me 'cause you won't like what I say.
ALF: I am asking you, aren't I? What is it with Hughie?
MUM (*reluctantly*): Oh, I dunno.
ALF: Go on. Get if off yr chest. (*She shakes her head impatiently, lips set hard.*) Well?
MUM (*suddenly*): It's all this education, that's what it is.
ALF: Oh, go on with you.
MUM: All right.
ALF: We spent our whole life practically ever since he was born, makin' sure he'd have an education. What are you talkin' about, his education? It's his education that's making Hughie what he is.
MUM: That's just what I mean.
ALF (*in profound disgust*): Arrr. ...

Act One   49

MUM: All right. You know everything.
ALF: I know my own son.
MUM: Alf ... (*Her tone fixes his attention.*)
ALF: Well, go on. Don't just sit there lookin' niggly. What?
MUM: He's my son too. I don't get round singing his praises, but he's my kid. (*Slight nod.*) It's all right for you. You and him always got on all right. When he was a kid and you'd roar at him about something, I'd watch him nearly howling because it was you tearin' him to shreds. (*Quietly.*) I'd want to speak to him. But I could never speak to him. Hughie and me could never talk. (*She looks at him directly.*) That doesn't mean I don't—(*She stops.*) He's my kid. And all I know is he looks at me sometimes as though I'm nothing, as though I'm just nothing. He's not the same.
ALF: He's the same to me. I never seen no difference in my son and I never will. He'll always be the same to me.
MUM: Have it your own way.
ALF: Right. Hughie's O.K. Hughie's O.K. Where's my cuppa tea?
MUM: Your—? (*She gets up, goes to pot, pours furiously, banging every thing she touches, brings cup down and slams it in front of him.*) There, and you know what you can do with it.
ALF (*stirring sugar and mumbling*): You make me sick, criticizin' the kid. Y'ought to be proud of him, like she said.
MUM: Don't drag her in.
ALF: Pick, pick, pick, why don't you leave the kid alone?
MUM: I never said nothin' to the kid.
ALF: No y're not game to out with it and give 'im a piece of yr mind, y'drive me barmy instead.
MUM: Oh, shut up, Alf.
ALF (*standing now and beginning to roar even more irritably than when he was drunk*): I—WILL—NOT—SHUT UP. You get orf my back. You think I'm not sick of havin' people on my back all day goin' up and down, up and down, up and down, pick, pick, pick, think they're God Almighty and treat you like a bitta furniture, I'm a bloody Australian and I'm as good as anybody gets in that lift—
MUM: How did *that* get into it?
ALF: Don't you go me. (*He has worked himself into a fury again and is standing over her.*) You can try my patience just so far, Dot, but you overstep the mark and I'll—I'll—
MUM (*looking up at him unperturbed*): Y'll what?
ALF (*flinging away from her*): Arr, why don't you leave a man alone? (*He sits. She takes a mouthful of tea, looks down into cup as though suddenly wondering how and why she is drinking it, then gets up, takes cup to sink.*)
MUM: I'm getting ready for bed.
ALF (*mumbling*): Get ready—and bugger you.
(*He sits, sulking.* MUM *makes sure gas is off, goes to their bedroom door, turns to him.*)
MUM: You let Hughie get his work done. Don't you start on him. (*He doesn't answer.*) You leave him alone.

ALF (*turns slowly, eyes her coldly*): When did I ever stand in Hughie's light?

MUM: There's a cuppa tea there if he wants one. You better get to bed too.

(*She goes. ALF still sits, staring at nothing. Then, shrugging it off, he gets up, takes cup and saucer to sink, refills cup, tries pot, and slips a cosy over it to keep tea warm. Returning to table, he begins putting boot polish and brushes back into kit. HUGHIE comes back to his bedroom, collects his books, and with a certain restlessness gets notepaper, etc., together. The moment before he switches the light out in his bedroom he looks about the room, a hard, critical look. He moves into the main room and stands there alone a moment, looking up and about the whole room with a sudden excess of displeasure. Then with a shrug he moves into the kitchen.*)

HUGHIE: Where is everybody?

ALF: Yr mother's going to bed. Wacka went home. (*Carefully*) She scared him.

HUGHIE: Who, Jan? (*He laughs a little unconvincingly, starts putting books on table, thumbing through exercise books, looking through pockets for Biro.*)

ALF: There's a cuppa tea there.

HUGHIE: No thanks. (*He sits, finds place in book and is ready to begin work.*)

ALF: Where'd you pick her up?

HUGHIE: Mmm? (*Transfers his attention from book to ALF.*) Oh, she's in my year.

(*ALF nods. HUGHIE goes back to work.*)

ALF: Sure you won't 'ave a cuppa tea?

HUGHIE: No.

(*A break.*)

ALF: I'll get it for you.

HUGHIE: Don't worry.

ALF: It's no trouble, son. Won't take half a sec.

HUGHIE: Don't feel like it, thanks.

(*A break.*)

ALF: It's nice 'n' hot.

HUGHIE: Mmm?—Oh, no thanks.

ALF: Wouldn't take a minute. (*Impatiently, HUGHIE shakes his head.*) All right, I won't press you.

(*ALF sits down, watches HUGHIE. Gradually all the resentment in him fades. His head a little on one side, he begins to smile, eyes fixed on his son at work.*)

What are y' studyin' at tonight?

HUGHIE: Statistics.

(*HUGHIE continues to work. ALF sits watching him with a smile that is part-envy, part-awe.*)

ALF (*after a little while*): You must be clever, Hughie.

(*HUGHIE looks up, a little embarrassed. His father is sitting back*

Act One   51

contentedly, smiling at him. HUGHIE *manages a smile, returns to his work. Another pause.)*
  What are y'gunna be, Hughie? I mean, what are y' studyin' for?
HUGHIE *(as patiently as he can)*: I've told you.
ALF: Yeah, but I mean—well, tell me.
HUGHIE: Well, there's different things I could qualify for, I'll get my Economics degree—*(grins)* I hope—and then—see what's going.
ALF: Oh. *(Thinks about this.)* Don't you wanta be anything special, you know, when you leave?
HUGHIE: You know me, I'd like to spend my life taking pictures—but what you want to do and what you've got to do, to earn a living, are two different things, aren't they?
ALF: Huh! You're tellin' *me* that. But—you'll have to make up yr mind sooner or later, won't you?
HUGHIE: I wish I could. I think I've always wanted to be educated for the sake of—*(Breaks.)* Well, you always wanted me to—*(He hesitates.)* So I did. Oh, I'm glad I did.
ALF: You still like goin' to University?
HUGHIE: I like it all right. Why shouldn't I?
ALF: It'll make a difference, you know, son. You kids today, you get everything. I wisht I'd had your chances. *(A pause.* HUGHIE *goes on working.* ALF *is looking dreamily into space now.)* I always wanted to be an engineer, did I ever tell you that? (HUGHIE *is about to signify that he has but refrains when he sees his father's mood.)* I useter muck around with cars and engines and that all the time when I was a kid. But in those days ... well, the old Dad goin' off at the war and things bein' a bit hard—me Mum couldn't afford to do much for me, see. I had to get out and work. What work you could get. But I tell you someth'n', son. Tell y' someth'n'. All through the depression I tried to study, orf me own bat. I used to go to the Muni-cipal Library to get the books 'cause it was free, like, technical books and that, I spent hours over 'em, years. *(Grunts.)* Fat lot of good they did me. *(He turns to* HUGHIE *quietly.)* I hope you do someth'n' good with yr study, son. We can't do much for you, we've got no money, but we always do what we can, you know that, don't you?
  (HUGHIE *looks away, conscience stung.*)
HUGHIE: Yes, Dad. I know. *(A pause. He tries to work.)*
ALF: What was her name?
HUGHIE: Jan. Jan Castle.
ALF: She's a funny girl, isn't she?
HUGHIE: Is she?
ALF: Yeah, she's a funny girl. I thought poor old Wacka'd wet himself. Do you really think she's the type for you to be goin' around with?
HUGHIE *(getting angry, holding on)*: What do you see as my type, Dad?
ALF: Well, she bungs it on a bit, don't she?
HUGHIE: Now listen—

ALF: Now you don't have to take offence, I haven't said nothin' but it just strikes me—
HUGHIE: What just strikes you?
ALF (*growing a little heated*): You're only a kid, when you grow up a bit you'll see all her kind are the same. Got their money by keepin' the working man down and that's how they're gunna hang onto it.
HUGHIE: Oh, come off it.
ALF: Now, listen, my boy. I oughta know something. I know something about what goes on in the world. And I'm telling you, take it or leave it, I'm telling you, that young lady's too lah-dee-dah for us.
HUGHIE: Oh? What do you mean when you say US?
ALF: Our family. Us (*A pause.*) Or don't you see eye to eye with us any more?
HUGHIE: I'm trying to work.
ALF: Yr mother spotted it first. You're gettin' big ideas—tryin' to move up in the world.
HUGHIE: Of course I am. Why shouldn't I?
ALF: Because we're working people, we've always been working people, and working people we're gunna stay.
HUGHIE: I am doing what you want. Haven't you rammed it down my throat all my life, get an education, get out of the rut. Well, you can't do that without changing some way. If I'm changing it's through you, it's all through you.
ALF: That's not what I meant. A bit of study's all to get you through exams, get you a good job, but all this standin' around spoutin' big ideas, going round with smart-arsed little sheilas from the North Shore—(*He breaks, softens.*) It's all wrong, son. Can't you see?
HUGHIE: Look, I—
ALF: Yeah, I know something, I oughta know something. You'll see, son, you'll come round in time. Now you get on with your work.
HUGHIE: But—
ALF (*magnanimously*): I don't want to argue with you. You know I can't stand fightin'. You just get into your study. You're right there, son. The study's the thing. (HUGHIE *still furious, goes head down into his work again.*) Like me to clean yr shoes for tomorrow?
HUGHIE: Leave them, I'll do them.
ALF: I don't mind doin' 'em. Which ones are y'wearin'?
HUGHIE (*trying not to be irritable*): Haven't thought. These probably.
ALF: Well, give us 'em. (*He is on his knees, dragging shoes off.*)
HUGHIE: I said leave them.
ALF: No. No, let me. I c'n do yr shoes for you, can't I? Gawd. (HUGHIE *shrugs, gives up the shoes.* ALF *takes them up to do them near sink bench.*) Hah! If anybody else asked me to clean their shoes for 'em ...
HUGHIE: I don't like you doing that, Dad.
ALF: It's all right, it's all right, you get on with yr work.

(HUGHIE *does so but after a few seconds looks up and watches his father at work. Gradually he smiles.*)
HUGHIE: Ay, Dad. Thanks for doing them.
ALF (*looks up, hesitates, grins.*): She's right.

CURTAIN

ACT TWO

SCENE I

Anzac Day. Behind the house the sky is dark. It is before dawn. A light is on in the kitchen. MUM, in her dressing-gown, is getting a cup of tea. ALF, dressed in an old but neat blue suit, comes out of bedroom at rear, crosses lounge switching on light, and goes to door of HUGHIE'S bedroom. He knocks gently on door. His manner when he calls to HUGHIE is unsure.

ALF: Err—er—wakey, wakey. Rise and shine. (*Louder*) Hughie! Er—Hughie! (*Listens.*) Come on, matey. 'Urry up.
(ALF *hurries back across lounge, switches off light, switches it on again immediately and glares at a television set sitting in downstage corner facing up into room. Grunts, snaps light off again, goes into kitchen.*)
(*Grins at* DOT.) Got that cuppa tea ready, Mother?
MUM: No. I bin bakin' a cake. (*Hands him cup.*)
ALF (*taking it*): Wouldn't be surprised what you did. Gawd, that kid can sleep. (*He sits, starts putting new lace into shoe.*) Why do your laces always snap when y'r runnin' late? They never go when y'got all day to fix it, only when y'r runnin' late. (*Laughs.*) That's life, ay, Dot? (*He looks towards* HUGHIE'S *room, listens, the smile momentarily vanishing and a certain tension returning. Calls*) Ay, Hughie!
MUM: You make a fool of y'self over that boy.
ALF: Oh get out.
MUM: Y'give in to him. One minute you can't say enough about him, next thing you're all over him like a rash.
ALF (*smiles*): Don't pick me, Mother. (*Sits, sugars tea.*) Not today. (*Grins happily.*) It's the old digger's day today.
(ALF *suddenly looks around restlessly.*)
Knew there was someth'n wrong. No Wacka.
MUM (*nods*): Mmm. Funny without Wack.
ALF (*a bit piqued*): Never thought I'd see that you know. Wack not gettin' up to go to the Dawn Service. Not marchin' either.
MUM: Y'know 'is leg nearly went on 'im last year. It was me made him promise he wouldn't do no marchin' again. Standin' on his feet all that time with that leg.
ALF: You c'n be 'ard, Dot. Where's yr sentiment?

MUM: I face up to things. Not like you.
ALF: It's not the same without old Wack.
MUM: Lots of old blokes are droppin' out of it. Y'can't expect 'em to go on forever.
ALF: He's not that old. Lot of 'em older than him still march.
MUM: On a gammy leg? He'll be with y'in spirit, if that cheers you up. We'll be watchin'—in comfort.
ALF: Comfort. I dunno what this country's coming to. If I ever thought I'd see the day when people'd think of their own comfort on Anzac Day—
MUM: Well, I'm not sorry. It was Wacka's idea and it was a very nice thought hiring the television.
ALF: *Television.*
MUM: Don't you go 'im. If he gets 'ere before you go, don't you go 'im.
ALF: Television.
MUM: I noticed you looked at it last night.
ALF: Bloody cowboys and Indians. Bang, bang, bang—had a headache all night. I'll give 'im television.
MUM: You leave him alone. It was his idea and he's gunna enjoy it. (*Laughs.*) Best idea Wacka's had since we knew him.
ALF: Only one.
MUM: His landlady'll be wild he didn't put it in there.
ALF: I wouldn't care where he put it, he could shove it up his jumper for mine. (*Jumps up, drinks down last of tea.*) Well, while you two sit back like Lord and Lady Muck the two patriotic members of the family'll be there—in person. (*Yells.*) Hughie!
(*The slightest pause.*)
MUM (*softly*): Hughie won't be goin' to no march.
ALF: Hughie's never missed a Dawn Service yet and he always come and watched me march after. What are y'talkin' about? Where's my medals? Hughie!
(*He marches across darkened lounge and raps on* HUGHIE'S *door.*)
C'm'on, matey. Nearly dinnertime. We'll never get there. (*A pause.*) Hughie!
HUGHIE (*voice muffled, drowsy, from dark bedroom*): What do you want?
ALF: Y'know the mob they get in Martin Place—if we don't get goin' we'll be stuck up the back. Come on, hurry it up.
HUGHIE: Come on, I'm not going.
ALF: Come on, son, we haven't got that much—(*Then he registers.*) What did you say? (HUGHIE *doesn't answer.* ALF *suddenly rages*) What did you say?
(ALF *throws the door open, switches on the light.* HUGHIE, *in pyjamas, rolls over, props himself up on one elbow. They look at each other in silence.*)
HUGHIE: I'm not going.
ALF: You get up out of that bed or I'll—
HUGHIE: I'm tired.

Act Two 55

(*He reaches up, switches off light switch near bed. Out of the dark comes* ALF'S *roar of rage. He flings out of the room, slamming the door. And charges across the lounge into the bedroom at rear.* MUM *has heard it all from kitchen, now goes into lounge. She is about to switch on light when* ALF *comes charging out of bedroom. He is viciously jabbing his long-service medals into his coat and almost collides with her in centre of room. She grabs him by shoulders, steadies him. They stand still facing each other. Light spills across the room from open door of kitchen and their bedroom.*)

MUM: Alf—

ALF: Who does 'e think he is?

MUM: Gimme those. (*She takes medals from him and pins them carefully.*) You want them to look right, don't you?

ALF: What's the matter with the lot of yz? What's come-overyer?

MUM: Now ...

ALF: Well ... Gawd ...

MUM: Don't get y'self worked up, love.

ALF: Well, you know what day this is. This day used to mean someth'n' once, (*She opens her mouth to speak.*) Don't shut me up, I'm not ashamed of it. I'm proud to be a bloody Australian. If it wasn't for men like my old man this country'd never bin heard of. They put Australia on the map they did, the Anzacs did. An' bloody died doin' it. Well, even a snotty-nosed little kid oughta be proud of that. What's happened to him? Why isn't he?

MUM: Don't you go using this as an excuse for one of your—

ALF (*quietly*): One of my what?

MUM: You know what.

ALF: I don't need no excuse today. It's my day, see.

MUM (*as he moves towards door*): What time'll y'be home?

ALF: When I get here.

MUM: Alf—

ALF: You know I never know what time I'll get home on Anzac Day.

MUM: And what d'you think you're gunna get up to?

ALF: I'm gunna celebrate this day the way I always celebrated this day. That's all. (*He shoots one glance towards* HUGHIE'S *room.*) Little runt. (*He goes out quickly. A pause.* MUM *walks back to kitchen, switches off light. Stands thoughtfully in lounge. Crosses, stands outside* HUGHIE'S *room.*)

MUM (*quietly*): Hughie. (*A pause.*) You're not asleep.

HUGHIE (*quietly*): What do you want?

MUM (*after a pause*): Do you want me to get you a cup of tea?

HUGHIE (*softening a little*): No thanks, Mum.

MUM: All right. (*She is about to move away.*)

HUGHIE: I thought you were going to go off at me.

MUM: Hughie, what's the good in goin' off at you? (*Slight break before she manages to say it.*) Y'don't see things the same as us any more and that's that. I knew you wouldn't go with him. Y'might've give 'im a bit of warning, that's all.

HUGHIE: I'm sorry. How did you know?

MUM: I didn't come down in the last shower.
HUGHIE: Why didn't you tell him then, Mum? You could have softened the blow.
MUM: You fight your own battles. I'm not buyin' into any arguments. I get enough of 'em around here.
HUGHIE: Mum ... (*He stops.*)
MUM: What?
HUGHIE: Nothing.
MUM: Go to sleep. I'm going back to bed. (*She goes towards bedroom.*) Wacka can let himself in.

(*She goes into bedroom, shuts door. Its light goes out. General lighting fades momentarily to suggest a passing of time. Light fades in again, held down very softly. The sky behind the house has traces of pink through it. Very gradually it begins to lighten. In* HUGHIE'S *bedroom some slight movement. He lights a cigarette, lies back, hand behind head. Then he flicks radio on. Its small light glows softly in dark. Steps are heard approaching. The front door opens,* WACKA *is silhouetted against light from sky spilling through door. He comes in, leaving door open to give himself some light. Crosses to lounge windows, quietly pulls up blinds. Dawn light comes in. He looks around, moves quietly back to door. He is about to close it but a sudden quickening of light all through the sky stops him. He takes a step outside, looks up at the sky. It is dawn. He stands very still as though listening for something.* WACKA *turns, comes back to door. Stands another second or two then shrugs, laughs quietly to himself. But still he stands, looking out and up. There is absolute silence.*)

WACKA (*to himself, so quietly it can hardly be heard*): It was now. (*He stands still, remembering.*)

(*And out of the silence comes, soft and distant, the sound of a trumpet playing "The Last Post".* WACKA *stands as though paralysed. As it plays through, the bedroom door opens and* MUM *stands there without putting on the light. She is fussily wrapping gown about her but the sound stops her. She sees* WACKA'S *face, the dawn gradually lighting it, and she does not move. They both stand listening. The last notes die away. For a moment neither one moves.*)

(*Shakes his head, comes back to earth.*) Where'd that come from?
MUM: Hughie's room, I think. (HUGHIE *switches the radio off.*) He must've put the wiless on to hear the service.
WACKA: Didn't 'e go?

(MUM *shakes her head, stares across towards his room, her usually set expression about to break into a grudging smile.*)

MUM: Funny kid. (*Snaps out of it.*) Waste of time tryin' to sleep. May as well stay up now. I'll get you a cuppa tea.

(*They go towards kitchen. Lights fade.*)

Act Two 57

SCENE 2

A few hours later. Daylight.

WACKA sits in lounge room, his chair pulled out near centre of room watching TV. Noise is heard from the set ... marching feet, a band playing in the distance, a commentator's voice. Light from the television set plays up into the room and over WACKA'S face. The front door is shut and some of the window blinds down. One blind is up and lets some daylight into the room. WACKA watches in a kind of stupefied delight, wriggling in his chair, grinning, a look of half-disbelief on his face.

WACKA (*yelling*): Ay, Dot. Come'n 'ave a look. Ay, Hughie.
  (HUGHIE *comes out of his room. He wears sports slacks and thong sandals, is in T-shirt and carries coloured sports shirt and shoes.*)
  Look at it. Look at it.
  (*Over his shoulder WACKA sees that HUGHIE is occupied with his shoes and socks.*)
  Come on, Hughie.
HUGHIE (*irritably*): I don't WANT to look at it.
  (*Then is immediately sorry.*)
  March still going?
  (WACKA *nods without taking his eyes from it.*)
HUGHIE (*unable to resist a glance or two at it*): See anybody you know?
WACKA: Oh, don't be mad. Y'wouldn't see anyone.
HUGHIE: Why not? They get in very close.
WACKA: Y'see it better than bein' there. I reckon you do. Y'see it better than bein' there.
  (MUM *comes out of bedroom, in old floppy frock, loose cardigan, and slippers.*)
  Come'n look at this, Dot.
MUM: I've got to get into these dishes.
HUGHIE: Leave 'em.
MUM (*she joins him as he says above*): Leave 'em. I know. You and yr father.
HUGHIE: It's a holiday, isn't it? Why don't you sit down?
MUM: Where?
HUGHIE (*making room for her on the lounge*): Sorry.
MUM: I want to sit closer than that, I'll never see it.
HUGHIE: If we *must* look at it, this is the right distance. (*But despite himself he still keeps glancing at it.*) You're supposed to sit back from it.
WACKA: You was sittin' too close last night. Ruins yr eyes.
MUM: Ay? Oh well, all right. (*She goes to lounge, collapses in it. Sinking back into its deepest hollow and spreading herself.*) I didn't put me stays on. Not going out.
WACKA: Y'dont wanna get all dolled up. Relax'n' look at this.
  (MUM *watches it awhile.*)

MUM: It's different to what I thought.
HUGHIE (*still playing truculent*): Why?
MUM: I thought it'd be all blurred. Where's that from? They're up high there—
HUGHIE: Bebarfalds' corner. Camera must be on the awning. Catches each lot as they come round the corner.
MUM: It's real clear, look at their medals.
WACKA: It's good, isn't it?
MUM: Look, it's rainin'. You c'n see it comin' down. Ttt! Ever know an Anzac Day it didn't rain?
WACKA: Dozens of 'em.
MUM: Always seems to be rainin' to me. (*To* HUGHIE) You goin' out?
HUGHIE: I told you at breakfast time—
WACKA (*suddenly almost screaming, recoiling in his chair*): Look! *Look!*
MUM: What the hell's the—?
WACKA: Fred! Freddie Watson! 'E's comin' right into it ... look! ... 'E's gone. (*He sits again, mouth open, turns to* MUM, *who is laughing at him.*) I never thought ... (*Shakes his head.*) Well. (*Can't stop shaking it.*) Well.
MUM: Keep lookin'. Y'might see Alf.
WACKA (*after staring at her open-mouthed as he registers this new thought*): No. No, our mob ain't come down.
(*A car's brakes squeal outside. Horn starts honking.*)
MUM (*looking over her shoulder*): Make a noise, why dontcher?
(HUGHIE *jumps up, looks out of window.*)
HUGHIE: It's Jan.
MUM (*startled*): Ay?
HUGHIE (*tucking shirt in*): Jan. I told you I was going out with her.
MUM: You didn't say nothin' about her comin' here.
WACKA (*eyes on set*): Ssh, ssh.
(HUGHIE *has hurried to door, opens it, waves.*)
HUGHIE: Hi.
MUM (*sitting up*): She's not comin' in? (*In panic, struggling to get up from lounge.*) You little *bugger*. Why didn't y'tell me, I could've put on something decent. (*Grabs her spare tyre.*) Oh! Oh! Hughie!
HUGHIE: She won't look at you. (*Yells out of door.*) Come on!
WACKA (*registering for first time*): What's the matter?
MUM: It's her.
HUGHIE (*turning quickly to her*): You said she could come again.
(JAN *hurries in.*)
JAN: Couldn't find my cigarettes. (*Coming down to* MUM) Mrs. Cook—no, stay there, don't get up. Oh, Mr.—Mr.—
HUGHIE: Dawson.
JAN: Dawson. This must be a thrill for you.
(WACKA *is hit with shyness again, nods, grins, looks wildly at* MUM *then back at set.*)
HUGHIE: Where do you want to sit?

Act Two 59

JAN: Anywhere. (*She and HUGHIE perch up on arms of chair behind and higher than the others, looking down on the proceedings. They are close to each other.*) Good picture.
HUGHIE: No outside aerial either.
JAN (*takes one long look at picture on screen*): My God. Will you look at them? What *do* they look like?
(*A pause. WACKA and HUGHIE look at screen, commentator's voice drones on. MUM'S head slowly turns around and she looks up at JAN.*)
MUM: Well? What *do* they look like?
JAN: Oh, I wish Australian men would learn how to dress—
MUM (*she thinks about this, then*): What's dress got to do with it?
HUGHIE: You've got to admit, Mum, they are conservative. Look at all those double-breasted suits—
MUM: Your Dad's got 'is double-breaster on same as all of them. What d'you think 'e'd wear? Overalls?
JAN: 'Ray! Single-breasted suit. Nice stripe too.
HUGHIE: Off the hook.
JAN: Oh, of course, but quite smart. There's another. Younger chaps, of course.
MUM: You seem to know a lot about men's fashions.
JAN: Mmm? Don't know anything about them but, naturally, we're all interested in clothes—
(MUM *nods, lips pursed, looks back at set.*)
HUGHIE (*half-smiling*): They don't look real bad, you know.
(JAN *looks up at him, surprised.*)
JAN: Hughie!
HUGHIE: Look at them. Serious as anything. They're sort of proud but not—
JAN: Not what?
HUGHIE: I don't know. Not military. Not aggressive. You know?
JAN: Hughie, really.
WACKA (*suddenly*): Ssh!! (*He is pointing, almost paralysed with excitement.*) Ssh!
MUM: What? What is it? (*Looks at set. Flatly*) There's Alf.
WACKA: Look at him, look at him—he's up the back, he's comin' close now. (*On his feet.*) Look at him! Look! He's comin' straight towards us.
JAN: Who is it?
HUGHIE: Dad. (*He stands up, oddly excited.*)
(WACKA *is crouched in front of set.*)
MUM: What's he got his chest stuck out like that for, silly old cow?
WACKA: Gee, he looks good. He looks real good.
MUM: His suit looks awful. I don't know, I pressed it.
WACKA: Get the walk, will ya? Get the walk on it!
MUM: Cocky? Look at him!
(*And suddenly they all burst into laughter. Just as suddenly* HUGHIE'S *laughter stops. He looks at picture, a battle of feelings inside him, and chokes up.* MUM *and* WACKA *don't see.* JAN, *still laughing, looks up at* HUGHIE *as he turns away quickly.*)

MUM: He's gone. (*She sits back.*)
JAN: What is the matter, Hughie?
HUGHIE: Right as rain. (*Covers up quickly.*) Gee, he looked an old idiot, didn't he?
MUM (*who has been laughing to herself, stops*): No, he didn't.
HUGHIE (*recovering*): Well, you were laughing.
MUM: It was just the shock, seeing him, plain as day. I wasn't laughing *at* 'im.
HUGHIE: Well, I was! (*But the feelings are still mixed.*) He looked such a big aleck, marching along as though he'd won both wars single-handed. It was—pathetic.
JAN: Oh, they all are.
MUM (*huffily*): Turn it off, Wack.
WACKA: Ay?
MUM: Haven't y'seen enough?
WACKA (*looks from her to* JAN, *gets up reluctantly, goes to set*): Oh. Yeah, yes, Dot. It's all the same. (*He switches it off.*) Good seein' yr mates, but.
MUM: It was very nice. Pity more people don't appreciate it.
WACKA: Oh, they still get a good rollup. Well ... (*He stands about uncomfortably.*)
JAN: Are we going?
HUGHIE: Suppose so. Do we still want to do this?
JAN: I want to do it very much. Don't you?
HUGHIE (*slight hesitation. Nods*): It's just not as easy for me as I'd thought. I'll get the camera. (*Moves away, turns suddenly to face her. She has turned to watch* MUM *and* WACKA. *He turns and goes to his room. A silence.* MUM *sits drumming her fingers on arm of couch.* WACKA *goes up to windows, pulls up blinds. He begins to whistle softly "Take me back to dear old Blighty".* JAN *watches him, smiles, relaxes.*)
JAN: Mr. Dawson seems bright today.
MUM (*indignantly*): He is not. He 'asn't 'ad a drink.
JAN: That's what I mean. The other night he had had a drink and he seemed very quiet.
MUM: No one gets a look-in when Hughie's Dad's around.
JAN: Mrs. Cook ... Hughie thought I was rude the other night. I was too. I'm sorry.
MUM (*embarrassed*): Hughie's dopey. It was all right. (WACKA *comes down.*) Hughie's friend reckons she likes you better sober.
JAN (*laughs*): I didn't say that, really. But this is your day, isn't it?
MUM: Oh, don't start him on that, get enougha that from Alf.
JAN: But isn't it? You *were* there. Do you still remember it, Mr. Dawson?
WACKA (*nods shyly*): Yeah.
JAN (*prompting him*): What do you remember?
WACKA: Not much. It was a long while ago. (*Silence again.*)
JAN: Were you at the actual first landing? On this very day?
WACKA (*nods*): Yeah. Thought about it this morn'n'. Before sunup. Just about the time we started up them rocks.

Act Two 61

MUM: What was y'thinkin' then, love?
WACKA: 'Ow do I know, it was years ago.
MUM: No, I mean th's morn'n'.
WACKA: Oh. (*To* JAN) I was standin' in that door lookin' at the sky, I was miles away, dreamin' about it. And I 'eard the Last Post. Dinkum, I thought they was comin' for me.
MUM: Hughie had the service on on 'is wiless.
JAN: Hughie did? I thought he hated Anzac Day.
MUM: Hughie? Hughie hate—? Why should he?
JAN: Well, all it stands for. (*She looks at them as though they will understand. They don't.*)
MUM: Such as what?
JAN: The same old clichés in the newspapers year after year. All the public hoo-ha—it's so damned—
(MUM *and* WACKA *exchange a look. She sees they are not with her, struggles to explain.*)
I mean—I'm sorry—but—to us, to the people coming on, there's something quite—offensive in the way you all cling to it. Not Mr. Dawson, it really happened to him, he knows what he feels today and why, it's not just because it's expected. But with so many people it's—
MUM: It's what?
JAN (*shrugging*): Well, isn't it all rather phoney?
(HUGHIE *is back.*)
HUGHIE: Right? (*No one speaks. He looks around.*) What's up?
MUM: It's on again. (*She looks at* JAN *with the old disapproval.*
HUGHIE *crosses quickly, gets* JAN *to her feet.*)
HUGHIE: Best we get going.
WACKA (*looking at the camera*): Going for a picnic?
HUGHIE: What? No. (*Grimly*) A little job. A job I've been promising myself I'd do for years. (*To* JAN) But I'd feel happier if you weren't so—(*He stops.*) Come on.
(*They start to go.*)
MUM (*calling after them*): What time'll you be home?
HUGHIE: Expect me when you see me. Don't save tea.
JAN: 'Bye.
MUM: I wish someone in this house'd tell me occasionally where they're goin' and when they'll be back.
WACKA: What's the job? What was he talkin' about?
MUM: I don't know. What was *she* talkin' about?
WACKA (*shakes his head*): Didn't foller it. Didn't get a word. Never do when she starts.
MUM: Hughie's the same when he gets goin'.
WACKA: Gawd, we must be gettin' old, Dot.
MUM (*grimly*): Either we're old—or they're terrible young.
(*Lights fade.*)

SCENE 3

Anzac Day. Evening. MUM is in kitchen, washing dishes at the sink, from a meal she and WACKA evidently shared. The rest of the house is in darkness. WACKA comes in through back door of kitchen. He has had a couple of drinks, is not, however, even remotely drunk, just a little loosened up. He carries a bottle wrapped in newspaper.

WACKA: There, wasn't long.

MUM: Y'ave a drink?

WACKA: Coupla short snorts. (*He has put bottle down on table. Starts to get glasses to pour them a drink.*) Y'oughta see the mob in the wine bar. Real old blokes—and all the old girls.

MUM: I wouldn't be seen dead in those places. What did you get?

WACKA: Bottla muscat. All right?

MUM: It's too sweet, that stuff. I won't have any.

WACKA: Go on, be in it.

MUM: May as well. Right. (*The latter as she finishes drying dishes and puts tea towel up. Comes to table, sits.*) What's the time, Wack?

WACKA: Seven o'clock nearly. (*Looks at her quickly.*) He oughta be home soon now the pubs are shut.

MUM: I'm not worried about Alf. I'd like to know what that young Hughie's up to.

WACKA: Now. Give 'im a go with 'is girl. (*Drinks.*) Beats me, that girl. She's got Gallipoli on the brain.

MUM: Same as Alf. (*Then with a laugh.*) Wouldn't he be wild if he heard that? Him and her the same. (*Drinks.*) It's not Gallipoli with him, it's Anzac Day. This time o'year I get sick of the sound of it.

WACKA: He'll be right tonight when he gets home.

MUM: I hope he's had too much to drink.

WACKA: Ay?

MUM: I hope he's had too much. If he's had too much he's just sick, he falls straight into bed. If he hasn't had enough to make him sick he just gets steamed up and we'll cop the lot. Australia for the Australians.

WACKA (*smiles*): Poor old Alf.

(*She looks at him suddenly and is serious.*)

MUM: Well, that's a turnup. Him, he's always Poor old Wack and how y'need lookin' after.

WACKA: Oh, I let him say it.

MUM: Yeah, y'gotta nurse 'im a bit. (*Quietly.*) I don't begrudge him his few drinks with his old mates. Let him enjoy it, he doesn't play up much. (WACKA *laughs quietly, thinking about* ALF. *She looks at him.*) You've had a quiet old Anzac Day, haven't you?

WACKA (*shrugs*): Oh ...

MUM: Tell y'someth'n'. That upset Alf a bit before he even got goin' th's morn'n'. No Wacka.

WACKA: I didn't get on it with him last year, year before either, come to that.

Act Two

MUM: No, but it was the Service, not goin' to the Service.

WACKA: Oh I'm gettin' too old to care about all that, Dot. (*A bit sheepishly.*) That's terrible, accordin' to Alf, but—

MUM: You do as you please, don't let him bluff you. I d'know why he still sticks to it.

WACKA (*thinks about it; quietly*): Alf still hankers after things. I'm older, Dot. I don't hanker any more.

MUM: I wonder what he thinks about. Lotta nights he can't sleep, y'know. Lies there thinkin'. (*They have become very quiet, speak in a desultory fashion almost to themselves.*) He always wanted to be an engineer, y'know.

WACKA: I know. He told me often enough.

MUM: 'E should've gone into the Engineers during the war, that worried him all the war. He told me after.

WACKA: I know, I was there. (*Chuckles.*) The bloody Poms was runnin' the whole show and stoppin' 'im goin' where he wanted, accordin' to Alf.

MUM: They wouldn't take him without any qualifications, couldn't expect 'em to. He expected 'em to. Well, what qualifications would he have had? Done no trainin', went through the Depression pickin' up someth'n' here, someth'n' there, workin' on the roads, anyth'n'. He never even got started in engineering.

WACKA (*bottle over her glass*): Want another one?

MUM: Just a little one, may as well be silly as the way we are.

WACKA: All the best.

MUM: All the best. (*They drink.*) Poor old Alf. I s'pose he hasn't had much of a go. (*She flashes glance at* WACKA *who is smiling sympathetically into his plonk.*) Neither've you for that matter.

WACKA: Me? (*He is a little surprised.*) I been right, Dot, I always been right.

MUM: Go on. You was hurt worse than him, bin on the pension.

WACKA: I'm right.

(MUM *looks at him for some moments. He is rolling a cigarette and doesn't notice in her gaze there is a long-held rarely-expressed affection.*)

MUM: Y'know someth'n'? All the talk Alf does about the Anzacs, I don't reckon I've heard you say more than five words about it all these years.

WACKA (*laughs*): When Alf's around I leave the talkin' to Alf.

MUM: Now today when she was here—that's the first time I've heard you mention Gallipoli in years. Not that you said that much.

WACKA: I wouldn't tell her.

MUM: I think she was dinkum. She just wanted to know about what it was like bein' there. (*A pause.*) What was it like, Wack?

WACKA (*he doesn't answer right away, thinks about it, immediately becomes self-conscious*): Oh, I d'know.

MUM: Go on. Tell us.

WACKA: Nothin' to tell. It was just—Oh, I d'know. (*But he is dreaming away about it as he speaks.*)

MUM: Y'can't say y'dunno. You was at it, you seen the whole thing.

WACKA: No, I didn't. Nobody did. Want another one?
MUM: Haven't finished this. You can taste the grape in it all right.
WACKA (*pours his slowly. Sits thinking, continues quietly, almost to himself*): Nobody seen the whole thing that day. All you seen was what y'was doin' y'self. And then y'couldn't hardly see more than a few feet ahead of yer.
MUM: Why, love?
WACKA (*reluctantly*): Well ... (*feels for the words*) it was the terrain. (*He thinks about it, continues, gradually warming up*) Y'never seen such hills in yr life. They musta thought we was bloody mountain goats to send us up'm. (*Pause. She waits. He continues quietly*) When we landed on the beach it was still dark. The current'd carried us down a bit far, everything was disorganized. Well—we had to get up them hills just the same. Y'didn't know where the old Turk was or how many of'm was up top, but y'knew they was sittin' up there like Jackie waitin' to pick y'all off as y'climbed.
MUM: Was you scared?
WACKA (*nods*): Yeah.
MUM (*with rather automatic sympathy*): Must've bin terrible.
WACKA: It was the feelin' of not gettin' anywhere, that was the worst. (*He is hardly conscious of her now: stares straight ahead: goes over it all virtually to himself. Jerks his attention back to her again.*) It was all declivities, see. Declivities. 'Oles and slopes and dirty big boulders. And bare. Bare. I never seen country like it before or since, even out here.
MUM: But where was the fightin', the battle, like?
WACKA: All round yer. Noise, crikey. Y'd never know who'd come over the next rise at yer, burst of gunfire or bloody Turk. (*He slows: then gravely*) Then when the sun come up y'could see yr mates ... bodies ... corpses everywhere ... blood and everything ... (*A pause.*) Sometimes y'd be runnin' and y'd hear a noise and it'd be y'self sorta screamin'. Y'd have yr bayonet out and when they came at y' ... (*He stops.*) Y'couldn't stop 'n' help yr mates, that was the worst ... Y'had to keep pushin' on.
MUM: What happened in the end?
WACKA: We got together again, some'ow. Some of us. Soon we was all dug in, up and down them hills. We stayed there in the stinkin' heat with the stinkin' flies 'n' the bully beef 'n' dysentery and sometimes the Turk trenches not ten yards away—we stayed there nine months. Then we pulled out, whole bang lot of us. (*He pauses. Laughs softly.*) When we went in there we was nobody. When we come out we was famous. (*Smiles.*) Anzacs. (*Shakes his head.*) Ballyhoo. Photos in the papers. Famous. Not worth a crumpet. (*Drinks.*) Sorry, Dot. Didn't mean t'bash yr ear. Gett'n' like Alf.
MUM: Except you've got someth'n' to talk about. 'E's all wind. (*Studies him a moment.*) Well, I d'know. Y'bin through a lot. Two wars 'n' a depression. Y'got no family, a room in a boardin' 'ouse—and us. And that's the issue. Now, if Alf was you he'd have a

reason to be crooked on the world. But—y'never say a word.
WACKA (*reflects: smiles*): Well, I'm all right. I've settled for what I've got.
(*The front door opens, light goes on in the lounge. It is HUGHIE, home again and full of excitement.*)
MUM: That you, Alf?
HUGHIE: Me. (*Goes to his room, puts on light, is singing "77 Sunset Strip" or "Surfside Six" or some such. Holds camera tight and up to his face.*) Oh, you beauty. You little beauty. (*He kisses camera, puts it tenderly on top of cabinet.*)
MUM: Have you had any tea?
HUGHIE (*calls*): We had a hamburger at the Cross.
MUM: What was y'doin' up there?
(*HUGHIE is whipping shoes off, getting into his thongs. At her question he looks up impatiently.*)
HUGHIE: I just told you. Having a hamburger.
MUM (*to WACKA*): I d'know what we're sittin' in here for. Come inside.
(*WACKA and MUM rise, WACKA taking his glass and bottle. They go into lounge.*)
WACKA: Don't y'want another drink?
MUM: No, I've had enough of that stuff.
WACKA: Will we put the television on?
MUM (*impatiently*): In a minute. Hughie!
(*HUGHIE is lying flat on his back on the bed.*)
HUGHIE: What do you want?
MUM: You gettin' changed?
HUGHIE: No.
MUM: What are y'doin' in there?
HUGHIE: Smoking a reefer.
MUM: What?
HUGHIE: Having a drag. Marijuana. Feelthy pictures on the ceiling.
MUM (*to WACKA*): What'd he say? (*To HUGHIE*) You wouldn't say Hullo when you come in, would you?
HUGHIE: Hullo.
MUM (*sharply*): Hughie ...
HUGHIE: Oh, all right. (*He rises, gets pullover, comes out putting it on.*)
MUM (*before he gets there*): I'm gunna have a go at that boy before he's finished. Haven't said a word to 'im for weeks, he's gone his own way but I'm gunna have a go at 'im.
WACKA (*looks at his muscat bottle, grins*): It's a good brand all right.
(*HUGHIE has joined them. He stands looking a little defiantly at his mother, then relents.*)
HUGHIE: Hullo.
MUM: What y'bin doing all day?
HUGHIE: Had a ball! (*Going to lounge, flops into it.*) Oh, the pictures I got! You oughta see the pictures I got.
MUM: What pictures?
HUGHIE: For our story. I told you—for the Uni paper, story on

Anzac Day. Jan's writing it.

MUM: You started late enough, it was all over practically before you even left.

HUGHIE: WHAT was all over?

MUM: The march and everything.

HUGHIE: I wasn't after the march. You'll see half a page of all that crap in the Tele tomorrow. Oh, golly, and to think I nearly didn't want to go. Came to my senses all right once I saw it again. (*Slight pause.* MUM *and* WACKA *exchange a glance.*)

WACKA (*tentatively*): What sort of pictures did you take, son?

HUGHIE (*sitting up; faces them seriously*): Anzac Day. As it is. I got some beauties.

MUM: How do you know if they're any good?

HUGHIE: When we finished this arvo we shot in to a mate of mine, runs a photography place in town, and we could see right away.

MUM (*irritably*): But what was they pictures of?

HUGHIE: Everything. (*Sarcastically*) The celebration. There's one, one terrific one—pure fluke how I got it—of an old man lying flat on his back in a lane near a pub. Boy, had he had it?
(WACKA *starts to laugh, picturing it.* MUM *silences him with a look.*)

MUM: What'd y'want to take a picture of that for?

HUGHIE: That's the point of it. They're all like that. Outside a pub near Central there was a character sitting on the footpath leaning up against a post. He had the most terrific face, hadn't shaved, few teeth missing, very photogenic. I snuck up near him and squatted down and .. oh, just as I got it framed up, it was wonderful. He vomited. Just quietly. All down his chin, all down the front of his coat. I took it.
(WACKA *has been about to drink from his glass of wine, lowers it and pushes it away from him.*)

MUM (*evenly*): You're goin' to put that in a paper?

HUGHIE: Are we ever?

MUM (*after a blank pause*): Why?

HUGHIE: Because we're sick of all the muck that's talked about this day ... the great national day of honour, day of memory, day of salute to the fallen, day of grief ... It's just one long grog-up.

MUM: But—

HUGHIE: No buts. I know what you lot think about it, everyone your age is the same. Well, I've seen enough Anzac Days to know what *I* think of them. And that's what I got today in my little camera. What I think of it.

MUM: You can't put that sort of thing in a paper.

HUGHIE: Just watch us.

MUM: It's more than that. Anzac Day's more than that.

HUGHIE: Yeah, it's a lot of old hasbeens getting up in the local RSL and saying, Well, boys, you all know what we're here for, we're here to honour our mates who didn't come back. And they all feel sad and have another six or seven beers.

MUM: Hughie—

Act Two

HUGHIE: Look, no argument. You think what you like, I've had to put up with that all my life, well now you can just put up with my views. If they don't agree, bad luck.

MUM: Y'd better not let yr father hear y'talkin' like this. 'E'd better not know nothin' about this thing goin' in the paper.

HUGHIE: He's got to know sooner or later.

MUM: Yr gettin' carried away. Just because a coupla blokes get a few in—

HUGHIE: Couple? Everywhere you look—every suburb you go through—and we went through them today—every pub, every street—all over this damned country today men got rotten. This is THE day. (*In a dinkum-Aussie speech-maker's voice*) "When Awstrylia first reached maturity as a nation". (*His own voice*) Maturity! God!

WACKA (*shyly*): 'Scuse me, lad.

HUGHIE: What?

WACKA: That's not all it is.

HUGHIE: Oh, Wacka.

WACKA (*gently*): Can't you let 'em enjoy it? You don't have to agree. But they've got a right to their feelings.

HUGHIE: Wacka—you've been brought up on the speeches. They say what it's officially supposed to be. I've been looking at what it is. As far as I'm concerned, that's all it is. A great big meaningless booze-up. Nothing more.

MUM (*snapping*): Well, y'r wrong.

(*From outside a crash. Then* ALF'S *voice in a burst of drunken profanity.*)

HUGHIE (*gently*): Am I?

(*Another crash. A burst of bawdy song.*)

MUM: Alf.

WACKA (*listening*): 'E'ad too much?

(ALF *roars again.*)

MUM: No. Not enough (*To* HUGHIE) Now you be careful what you say.

(*The door flies open.* ALF *totters in. He is dishevelled. Hair flies wild, face is heavy with grog, trousers hang below his waist, shirt hangs half out. Clothes are sodden with spilled grog. He carries bottles, wrapped and unwrapped, and lurches to table, starting his dissertation as soon as he gets in.*)

ALF: 'Ullo!! You buggars on the plonk? (*Wags finger at* MUM.) Y'know what it says on the wileless, when yr drinkin' don't drive when yr drivin' don't drink, Christ, 've I 'ad a day? I've had a bloody lovely day. I seen everybody, Dot—Wack—Wack—I seen everybody, what y'doin', 'Ughie, siddown yr makin' me giddy, I seen everybody. Old Bert Charles, y'oughter see old Bert Charles, he s eighteen stone an'pisspot, c'n 'e drink? Oh, Jeez, we started at a pub in King Street straight after the march, I was with Bluey Norton an' Ginger Simms, did we get on it? We bin there 'bout an hour in comes ole Fred Harvey, I sung out You old bastard and 'e come up t'me y'know wot 'e did, 'e put on a voice like a bloody panz and 'e sez up high like, "Darl, 'OW ARE yer?" An' 'e kisses me, right in the bloody public bar, front of everyone, laugh, thought we'd bloody die, I hit him one and then we all 'ad a couple of grogs and then Ginge and I gotta meet me old mate down the Quay, come'n meet me old mate down the Quay, so we goes, whole lot of us goes and all the way down Fred does this act makin' up to the other blokes, laugh, I never laughed so much, on the way we picks up Johnny 'Opkins with 'is gammy leg—(*A foggy glare towards* WACKA.) *He* marched, he was in the march—and 'e was sittin' in the gutter lookin' for the lav so we got 'im to 'is feet and shot 'im into a public lav and in the lav there was a brawl, broken bottles flyin' everywhere and blood, Gawd, blood, and off we all went to Plasto's and there's Ginge's mates, we was there hours, then we says let's get out'f 'ere and we're off up Pitt Street, we went into every pub, every pub we come to, we went in every pub, there was ten of us by then, ten of us so someone says Come on let's get some other bastards 'n' make it a round dozen, so we grabs two ole blokes and turned out they was real old diggers, real Anzacs, 'ear that Wack, Anzacs, they was sittin' 'avin' a quiet yarn to themselves, we soon fixed that—we got 'em and shouted 'em and Ginge 'e made a speech, 'e said these are the blokes wot started the Anzac legend, these done the trick, soldiers and bloody gentlemen and we poured bloody beer into the poor old cows till they couldn't stand up, they was rotten, then silly bloody Johnny 'Opkins 'as to go 'n' muck things, 'e turns around too quick and gets all dizzy and spews, did 'e spew, brought it all up all over the bloody bar, all over the mob, in their beer, all over the floor, all over 'mself, laugh ... Jeez, I never laughed so much in all me ...

(*Very early on* HUGHIE *has turned to face his mother and* WACKA. *As* ALF *drives remorselessly on* HUGHIE *watches their faces gradually change.* MUM, *who has been laughing at first, looks at* HUGHIE *long and steadily then slowly sits.* WACKA *looks completely embarrassed, not at first but very gradually, finally drops his glance, can't face* HUGHIE, *makes feeble attempt to quieten* ALF, *then stands looking down uncomfortably.* ALF *has at last realized something is wrong. His voice dies away. He turns, looks groggily at them all.*)

ALF: What's the matter? What's up?

(*Nobody speaks.*)

HUGHIE: You've just proved something.

ALF: What? (*Sways, tries to focus.*) What'd I prove?

MUM: Y'didn't prove nothin'. (*To* HUGHIE) You leave him alone, Hughie.

HUGHIE: Nothing to say. It's all been said. (*He starts to go.*)

ALF (*blearily*): What'd 'e say? What'd 'e say?

HUGHIE: Forget it. You had a great day, that's all that matters.

ALF (*suddenly swinging* HUGHIE *around*): You bein' funny? You playin' up again, Mr. Bloody Brains Trust?

HUGHIE (*quietly*): Why couldn't you leave them alone? Those two

Act Two

poor old boys having their quiet talk? Does everyone have to be as rotten as you are before you can enjoy Anzac Day?

ALF (*very quietly*): Watch y'self. Watch y'self, mister. (*To* MUM) Is that what he's on now? 'E's pickin' on the old diggers now?

HUGHIE (*breaking away in sudden burst of complete exasperation*): Oh, frig the old diggers.

ALF (*weaving after him unsteadily*): Why—you ... you ...

HUGHIE (*swinging on him*): Do you know what you're celebrating today? (*To* MUM) Do *you*? Do you even know what it all meant? Have you ever bothered to dig a bit, find out what really happened back there, what this day meant?

MUM: I bin talkin' to Wacka about it just tonight—

HUGHIE: Oh, Wacka—what would he know about it?

ALF: Don't you insult my mate, don't you insult him. He was there, wasn't he?

HUGHIE: What does the man who was there ever know about anything? All he knows is what he saw, one man's view from a trench. It's the people who come after, who can study it all, see the whole thing for what it was—

ALF (*with deepest contempt*): Book-learnin'. (*Points to* WACKA.) He bloody suffered, that man. You tell me book-learnin' after the event's gunna tell y'more about it than he knows?

HUGHIE: Wacka was an ordinary soldier who did what he was told. He and his mates became a legend, all right, they've had to live up to it. Every year on the great day they've had to do the right thing, make the right speeches, talk of the dead they left there. But did any of them ever sit down and look back at that damn stupid climb up those rocks to see what it meant?

ALF: How do you know so much?

HUGHIE: How do I *know*? Didn't you shove it down my throat? (*He has plunged over to the bookcase against wall, drags out large book.*) It's here. Encyclopedia for Australian kids. You gave it to me yourself. Used to make me read the Anzac chapter every year. Well, I read it. The official history, all very glowing and patriotic. I read it ... enough times to start seeing through it. (*He has been leafing through book, find the place.*) Do you know what that Gallipoli campaign meant? Bugger all.

ALF (*lunging at him unsteadily*): You—

HUGHIE: A face-saving device. An expensive shambles. (*Evading his father*) It was the biggest fiasco of the war. (*Starts to read rapidly.*) "The British were in desperate straits. Russia was demanding that the Dardanelles be forced by the British Navy and Constantinople taken. The Navy could not do it alone and wanted Army support." (*His father by now has stopped weaving groggily and stands watching him, trying to take it in.*) "Kitchener said the British Army had no men available." (*He looks up.*) So what did they do? The Admiralty *insisted* it be done no matter what the risk. Britain's Russian ally was expecting it. There was one solution. Australian and New Zealand troops had just got to Cairo for their initial training. Untrained men, untried. (*He looks quickly*

back at book.) "Perhaps they could be used."
(*He snaps the book shut.*)
Perhaps. Perhaps they could be pushed in there, into a place everybody knew was impossible to take from the sea, to make the big gesture necessary ... to save the face of the British. (*He turns on his father.*) ... the British, Dad, the bloody Poms. THEY pushed those men up those cliffs, that April morning, knowing, KNOWING it was suicide.

WACKA (*roused*): You don't know that. 'Ow could anyone know that?

HUGHIE: You know what it was like. (*Grabs the book open.*) Show them the maps. Show them the photos. A child of six could tell you men with guns on top of those cliffs could wipe out anyone trying to come up from below. And there were guns on top, weren't there, Wacka, weren' there?

ALF (*almost shocked sober*): More credit to 'em, that's what I say, more credit to 'em they got up there and dug in.

HUGHIE: Oh yes, great credit to them—if you happen to see any credit in men wasting their lives.

ALF: Well, that's war, that's any war—

HUGHIE (*turning on him*): Yes, and as long as men like you are fools enough to accept that, to say that, there'll always be wars.

ALF: You're tryin' to drag it down.

HUGHIE: It was doomed from the start, it was a waste! Every year you still march down that street with that stupid proud expression on your face you glorify the—bloody wastefulness of that day. (*He turns away quickly, sits panting and trembling.*)

ALF (*speechless for a moment, then, furious, he turns to the others*): They don't care, do they? They don't believe in anything. What'd I tell you? What'd I tell you? The whole country's goin' down the drain. (*Then, turning on* HUGHIE) You telling him (*pointing to* WACKA) everything he's believed for forty years is wrong? You telling me what I've believed in is nothin'?

(*He makes a sudden dive at* HUGHIE, *drags him to his feet, but* HUGHIE *grabs him tightly and looks into his face.*)

HUGHIE (*quiet and firm, less hysterical now*): Believe in the men if you want to, they had guts. But the day ... it's a mug's day.

ALF: Get away.

HUGHIE: Why remember it? Why go on and on remembering it? Oh yeah, "that's war, that's war" ... Well, war's such a dirty thing I'd have thought as soon as it's over you'd want to forget it, be ashamed, as human beings, ashamed you ever had to take part in it.

ALF: Ashamed? Ashamed? To fight for your country?

HUGHIE: What did your country do for you after you'd fought? Arr ... don't feed me all that.

MUM: Alf! (HUGHIE *breaks away from his father. To* HUGHIE) Was you thinkin' all that today when we watched him on the television? Was you thinkin' that and never said a word?

HUGHIE: I've been thinking it for years.

ALF (*turns to her*): Did you see it? Did you see me in the march on that thing?

MUM: We did.

ALF (*to* HUGHIE): There! You seen em. Decent blokes, decent lot of blokes marchin' with their mates. Two wars that represents, two wars you don't know nothin' about, you jumped-up little twerp. You can stand there and knock those men?

HUGHIE: Yes, I can. (*But he is faltering.*) They looked ridiculous.

ALF (*threateningly: a step closer to him*): Yeah. Did they? How'd I look?

HUGHIE (*with sudden energy*): I don't care how you looked then. It's how you look now. When you came in that door—when you came in that door—(*words, feelings tumble out of him*)—Oh, God, if you only knew how you looked. (*Pointing furiously at his mother and* WACKA) THEY laughed at you. (*To them*) How could you laugh? Why is a drunk man so funny? (*Then turning on his father again*) Funny? Drunk or sober, you're not funny. You disgust me. You—*disgust*—me.

ALF: My kid! (*He flings himself at* HUGHIE. WACKA *gets hold of* ALF *and holds him back.* ALF *shouts and struggles.* HUGHIE *turns his back on them and strides to his bedroom, slamming the door.*)

MUM (*to* WACKA): Get him out. I want to talk to Hughie.

WACKA: C'm'on, Alf. C'm'on. (*Struggling, swearing, shouting,* ALF *is dragged into kitchen where he collapses in chair, buries his head on table. When they have gone* MUM *goes slowly, deliberately, to* HUGHIE'S *door, knocks on it.*)

MUM (*sharply*): Hughie! (*Silence.*) Hughie, listen to me. (*Silence.*) Hughie!

HUGHIE (*pressed against closet, shoulders heaving*): What?

MUM: I want to know one thing. You going to publish that article?

HUGHIE: Leave me alone.

MUM: Because if you are and your father sees it, it's the finish, Hughie. You can pack your bags and leave. I mean it. (*He doesn't answer.*) Right?

HUGHIE (*defiantly*): Right!

CURTAIN

ACT THREE

Early evening, some days later. ALF *is in the kitchen cleaning his suit with white spirit.* MUM *is putting away last of dishes from evening meal, hangs up tea towel. Looks at him as though she wishes to say something. He avoids her eye.*

She goes into lounge, switches on light. The TV set has gone. She does some half-hearted tidying up, stops near middle of room, stands aimlessly, thinking, restless. Then she goes to bookcase, takes out the encyclopedia HUGHIE read from and sits in near-by chair. She is reading when ALF crosses through lounge on his way to their bedroom to hang up his suit. He glances at her without stopping, goes into bedroom. She turns a page. ALF comes back from bedroom. He seems about to return to kitchen but stands, hesitates, is unable to contain himself.

ALF: What d'yer lookin' at that thing for?
MUM (*not looking up*): Ay?
ALF: What d'yer wanta read that thing for. Never looked at in yr life before last week.
MUM: Free country.
(*ALF seems about to burst into argument, restrains himself with a grunt and goes towards kitchen. Steps are heard outside. He turns. Looks toward front door. HUGHIE comes in. He has been hurrying, looks disturbed, unhappy. He and his father look at each other, look away. HUGHIE closes front door. ALF goes into kitchen. HUGHIE starts to go towards his bedroom, unzipping briefcase he carries. MUM has registered all this. As he moves she speaks. Quietly.*)
MUM: Thought you was comin' home for tea.
HUGHIE: I had it up there.
MUM: What's the matter?
HUGHIE (*after hesitation*): Nothing's the matter. (*But he doesn't move off.*)
MUM: All right. (*She returns to book.*)
HUGHIE: I had a row with Jan.
MUM: What about?
(*He hesitates then whips a newspaper out of his briefcase and holds it up for her to see.*)
HUGHIE: Ah, nothing. This. (*Throws it on table.*)
(*She gets up, gapes at newspaper.*)
MUM: You didn't ...
HUGHIE: It's more than the story, we disagreed over the whole thing.
MUM (*still eyeing paper*): Well? Go on.
HUGHIE (*about to speak, then*): It's private.
MUM: Please y'self.
HUGHIE (*suddenly miserable*): Mum—we agreed on everything, Jan and I, I thought we did.
MUM (*comes towards him, with a shade more sympathy than usual*): Is she worth worryin' about?
HUGHIE: Yes, she is. She's the first girl I ever met I really feel—(*He stops.*)
MUM: Don't see it meself. (*He starts to go.*) Hughie ... talk to your father.
HUGHIE: He won't talk to me.
MUM: I've had about enough, Hughie. Even when yr not here he gets round the house, won't hardly open his mouth. It's been days—

Act Three 73

HUGHIE: I can't help it.
MUM: Yes, y'can. I'm sick of it, son.
  (ALF *comes in quickly, heading for bedroom.* HUGHIE *turns his back to him. With barely a glance towards* HUGHIE, ALF *speaks on the move.*)
ALF: I'm goin' up the pub, Mother.
MUM (*as he reaches bedroom door*): Alf. (*He doesn't stop, goes into bedroom.*) (*She turns to* HUGHIE.) Hughie, please ...
  (ALF *comes back, getting into old raincoat.*)
  Alf ... (*He strides towards door, she speaks more urgently.*) Alf! (*He stops.*) Hughie. (*She is suddenly beginning to break, tries to toughen up*) Now, both of you, listen to me ...
  (*They are both embarrassed.*)
  I can't take much more. If you think it's any fun you two comin' and goin' never sayin' a word to each other ... I can't stand much more.
ALF (*softly*): Now, Dot.
MUM: Make it up. Both of you. Please. Make it up. For my sake.
  (*She sits down abruptly, takes out handkerchief, blows her nose.*
  ALF *and* HUGHIE *look at each other, neither giving an inch.*)
ALF: It's not my place. It's not my place to—
MUM: I don't care whose place it is. Someone has to go first.
ALF: It's not goin' t'be me.
  (HUGHIE *hasn't moved.*)
MUM: I s'pose it's not goin' to be you neither. (*She looks from one to the other as they stare angrily across the room at each other.*) You couple of stiffnecked—
ALF: You get orf me back. (*He turns away, sits, his back ostentatiously to* HUGHIE. *A pause.* HUGHIE *walks down, stands beside his father.*)
HUGHIE (*a pause*): I'm sorry. (*Quickly*) I'm sorry, Mum. (ALF *sits, head up, defiantly.*)
MUM (*to* ALF): Go on. 'E's said 'e's sorry.
ALF (*without turning to* HUGHIE): All right.
MUM: Alf.
ALF: 'Pology accepted.
HUGHIE: Thanks, Dad.
  (HUGHIE *goes towards his room.*)
MUM (*to* ALF, *sharply*): That all?
ALF: Well, what d'y'want me to do? I accepted his apology.
MUM: Don't strain y'self.
HUGHIE: It's all right.
ALF: Hughie! (*Turns to address him directly, with attempt at dignity.*) Just one thing, my lad. I'll never agree with what you had to say—you know what I'm referring to—and I reckon you 'ad no right to say it in the same room as me and Wacka after what we went through for you. For you. Just don't mention it any more. That's my feelings. Understand?
HUGHIE: I wish I'd never said it either.
ALF (*expansively*): Well! That's more like it. There y'are, Mother,

nothin' that a bit of friendly talkin' can't straighten out.
(He has moved up towards table. HUGHIE *has spotted university paper lying where he dropped it and as his father nears it attempts to pick it up quickly.)*
What's this? (ALF *picks it up, looks at front page. Excited)* Mother! Look at this! Look at this! *(Beaming)* "See Inside. Our story on ... Anzac Day." *(He fumbles through pages to find it.)* He done it. Fancy not tellin' us. There y'are, I knew the silly little cow had his heart in the right place all the time. After all that row he still put a wrap-up of the old diggers in, after all. *(The paper is open.* MUM *watches apprehensively.)* Listen to this. "Anzac Day, we are told every year, is the day which comm—which commemorates Australia's coming-of-age as a nation. One would never know from the way it is ... " *(He is suddenly doubtful)* "observed." *(Looks up quickly at* MUM *and then down at page again.)* "Look at these frank pictures below. This is the way Australia celebrates her national day ... "
(He stares pop-eyed at the pictures. Then roars.)
Hughie!
(HUGHIE *appears in the doorway.)*
You—! You—! *(He is almost speechless.)* You take these pictures?
MUM: Alf, don't start again.
ALF *(almost shrieking):* Look at 'em! Look at 'em! Men drunk—men fighting—look, a bloke vomitin'. YOU put that in there?
HUGHIE: You're not going to tell me it didn't happen.
ALF: Of course it happened, it always happens, you don't put that sorta thing in the paper—
HUGHIE: Why not?
ALF: You little hypocrite. A minute ago you was crawlin' to me, you was sorry y'd ever said—
HUGHIE: I didn't say I took it back. I don't take any of it back. I'm sorry because of the way I did it, to you and Wacka.
ALF *(looking at paper):* Who wrote this? You write this? No, it was that girl.
HUGHIE: It was both of us.
ALF *(holds the paper out to* MUM): Look at it, read it. Read it. *(Grabs it back from her.)* "It is a strange thing that men who for three hundred and sixty-four days have never given the nation a thought will on this day proclaim its greatness. How can it be great when—" *(His eyes bulge)* "—the winge-ers, whiners, and no-hopers shoot their big mouths off on Anzac Day and do nothing the rest of the year round?" That little bitch! That—
MUM: Alf—
ALF: Shut up! Listen to it! LISTEN to it! "This is the day we are supposed to be proud. But ... " *(He is suddenly very quiet.)* "I never feel more ashamed of being an Australian than I do on Anzac Day." *(A pause. He can't do anything but look at the paper and then stare at* HUGHIE.) Ashamed. Ashamed.
HUGHIE *(walking away from him):* I'm not fighting with you over it, Dad.

ALF: You can't see past a few drunks. You can't. Is that all you saw the other day? Is it? (HUGHIE *won't answer.*) Is that all that day means to you? (HUGHIE *won't answer.*) Then I'm sorry for yer. I am. I'm sorry for yer. Well what y'got to say to that? (HUGHIE *shakes his head. In disgust* ALF *turns to* MUM.) Are they all like that? All the kids today? They think like that?

HUGHIE: I don't care how the others think, that's how I think.

ALF: You'd take away everything. You'd take away the ordinary bloke's right to feel a bit proud of 'imself for once. You know what that march means? You saw it, on your television, you saw it. You know what that is? (HUGHIE *doesn't answer.*) March without uniforms, that's what that is. Y'don't get out there t'show what a great soldier y'was, y'r there as mates. Y'r there to say it was a job. Y'had to do it and y'done it. Together. Argue with that. Go on. Argue with that.

(HUGHIE *shakes his head.*)

No, 'cause you can't. Every city, every little town in this country puts on its service and its march on that day. Every year for forty years they done it and they always will do it. Y'think this (*he shakes newspaper*) c'n make any difference to it, a few pitchers and a few big words from a little squirt like you? Do yer?

(HUGHIE *doesn't answer.*)

(*To* MUM) He can't say anythin'. 'E can't say a word. (HUGHIE *has turned away, sits down. His father stands close, leans over him.*) Y'know why y'can't hurt it? Y'know why it's as strong as a rock? You ought to, cause you showed me. You said it yourself a week ago. And in that week I've seen it clearer that I ever did before. All them blokes like Wack'n' me and the lot of 'em get out there for someth'n' there's not too many men in not too many countries in this world'd want to do. That's not a victory we're celebratin', son. It's a defeat. All right, you said it couldn't never be a victory. Well, it wasn't. They lost. But they tried. They tried, and they was beaten. A man's not too bad who'll stand up in the street and remember when 'e was licked. Ay?

HUGHIE (*quietly*): Why not? Maybe it helps the great Australian laziness. Why worry about doing a good job? Fair enough's good enough. The only time we won our name was the time we lost.

ALF (*is momentarily taken aback at this jesuitical reasoning; covers quickly*): That's real cunning, Hughie. Real cunning. (*Turns to* MUM) Y'know what I think? Y'c'n get too smart for y'r own good. That's what that boy's doin'. (*He hits his finger against his own forehead.*) Everyth'n' comes from there. Nowhere else. Here. (*He turns to* HUGHIE.) Where's yr heart, Hughie? Hearts outa style with your new mob?

HUGHIE (*gets up quickly*): I think I'd better go out.

MUM: Leave 'im alone, Alf, he's just had a row with his girl-friend.

ALF: Her? That little North Shore tart. That's where all 'is ideas are comin' from. She started it.

HUGHIE: No, Dad. You started it. You started it years ago when I was a kid. When you dragged me by the hand through mobs of them like this—(*gesturing towards newspaper*) just exactly like this. That's all I ever saw on Anzac Day every year, year after year, a screaming tribe of great, stupid, drunken no-hopers.

ALF (*approaching him; very quietly*): Hughie. I didn't hear that, did I? You didn't say that?

HUGHIE: I said it all right.

ALF (*evenly*): Would you say it again?

HUGHIE: You've got to know, you'd better know once and for all how I feel. That's your famous old diggers to me. Great, stupid, drunken—

MUM: Alf!

(*For he has back-handed his son viciously across the face. HUGHIE staggers and is almost knocked off his feet. He collapses in chair, where he looks up at his father, astonished, but strangely without anger.*)

MUM: You get away from that boy.

ALF: That's men like my father he's talkin' about. Men who give their all.

MUM: Oh, give their all, where'd you read that? Don't talk rot.

ALF (*stunned*): ROT?

MUM: Didn't cost yr old man much to go out in a blaze of glory. It's the ones like Wacka who come back knocked up and get nothin', just about nothin' and go on without a word the resta their lives, they're the ones who give their all.

ALF (*furiously, almost choking*): Don't you turn on me now. I've had enough, Dot, don't you—

(*The front doorbell rings.*)

MUM: Who the hell's that.

ALF: I don't want any visitors. Don't want any visitors tonight.

(MUM *has gone and opened door. It is* JAN.)

JAN: Oh, Mrs. Cook, I'm sorry. I had to see Hughie.

(HUGHIE, *still nursing his face, gets up, startled.*)

MUM: Come in. (JAN *comes in.* MUM *shuts door.* JAN *smiles nervously at* HUGHIE. MUM *comes back into room.*)

JAN: Mr. Cook, I had to see Hughie. You don't mind?

ALF: Mind? No, this is the new branch, the Uni's just opened a new wing 'ere. Make y'self at home. (*Then firmly.*) But I'd be obliged if y'd say what y've gotta say and get goin'. You've started enough trouble round here—

HUGHIE: Will you get it through your head Jan didn't start anything? The newspaper stunt was all my idea.

JAN: Oh, it's that.

ALF: I don't believe yer. Yr standin' up for 'er. Well, I stand up for what I believe too. And if that little jumped-up snob can put a story like that in a newspaper there's someth'n' the matter with this country.

JAN: Why? We all have to agree with you before we can get into print?

ALF: Don't you cheek me, young lady. I dunno what y'do in yr own home but yr not comin' here upsettin' things.

Act Three

JAN: I'll upset who I like.
ALF: Don't you talk to me. I'm a bloody Australian—
JAN: You're so right, Mr. Cook. (*To* HUGHIE) Excuse me. I'm sorry I came. (*Starts to move away.*)
ALF: You hear 'er? You hear what she said to me? Nobody talks to me like that. I stood up and fought for this country ...
JAN (*turning quickly to face him*): Mr. Cook—
HUGHIE: That'll do.
JAN: Mr. Cook. My father went to the war too—but he doesn't go on and on about it.
HUGHIE: O.K., let it go—
JAN: You're nothing special, Mr. Cook. You're not the only hero on earth. You're just an ordinary little man.
ALF: Get her out! Get her out before I—
MUM: Leave her alone.
ALF (*beside himself with exasperation as they all gang up*): I won't leave anyone alone, comes insultin' me and buggerin' up my son, who does she think she is, bringing her bloody upper-crust ways here. She talks about me, what did they ever do for Australia? Ay? What did they ever do?

(JAN *faces back into room. Hesitates, then coolly.*)

JAN: I just told you, Mr. Cook, but you never listen. They fought for it, as you did. They haven't done any more than you—but they haven't done any less either.

(*It pulls him up short. He looks at each of them.*)

ALF (*to* HUGHIE): Get goin' with her. Go on. She wants t'talk t'yer. Get out in 'er car, talk about the great country it's gunna be when the whole mob's bright and clever like you. Go on. Get. Y'know where y'stand.
HUGHIE: Don't you push me around. Jan just tried to make you understand, you threw it back in her face. I'm sorry I stuck up for you now.

(*They are both startled by this slip.* ALF *is thrown a bit.*)

ALF: When did you ever stick up for me?
HUGHIE: A while ago. Up there. We had a row about the whole thing. I took your part. Don't worry, it won't happen again.
(ALF *suddenly caves in, almost breaks down, he sits.* HUGHIE *looks closely at his father and drops his aggressiveness, clumsily.*) The paper just came out today. All the week I've been asking myself, why did I do it? After that night here—I didn't know what I was doing. One part of me said go ahead, print it, publish it. I wanted to all the more out of—sheer spite. But another part of me was fighting all the time. Saying to me: That isn't all the story, there is something more in Anzac still, even now, even if I can't see it. Then the deadline came up, I had to make up my mind. You weren't talking to me, home was pretty rotten to be in, I wanted to hit out. So ... I did it. I went ahead with the story. I still don't know whether I should have or not.
(*A silence. It costs* ALF *a big effort to do so but at last he manages.*)

ALF (*roughly*): It's a free country. You got your opinion, you stick to it.

HUGHIE: But—(*Hopelessly*) Oh, I don't know. Up there—at Uni—it seems terrific to be—outspoken and—critical and everything. But ... (*He manages to face his father.*) I'm sorry. I didn't mean to hurt you.

ALF: Yes you did. Don't try to back out now. Go on. You go with her. She's right. (*Slowly he turns to face* JAN; *then quietly*) D'y' remember that job I was tellin' you about? (*With a half-smile*) The executive position?

JAN (*very quietly*): Yes, Mr. Cook?

ALF: I didn't get it. Missed out. (*Quietly*) Too old. No qualifications. (*He turns to* HUGHIE *and* MUM) I would've told you before—if we'd bin talkin'. You see? She's right.

(*He sits very stiffly, head up a bit, stiff-necked, and manages to say it without self-pity.*)

I'm nothin'. I never bin anythin'. I know it. I was gunna be somethn' when I was your age. I was. Well ... now I drive a lift. (*A pause.*) It meant a lot to me, that new job. (*Looks up at* HUGHIE.) You don't think I haven't known for ages what you think of me? That job it would've been—my last chance to show my son I could—be somethn' ...

HUGHIE: Dad ...

ALF: I'm not the only one. Some of me old mates ... when I think back to how we talked durin' the war ... when I think back to what they wanted outa life. Some of 'em done all right. But even those in decent jobs—(*Hesitantly, feeling it through*) It's more than jobs. It's ... (*He stops. The others all watch him, reluctant to break in.*) Boys I've known all my life. Went through the Depression with me, then the War. They're nothin' much either. Nothin' much ... (*Beneath his control he is trembling.*) But for one day they're somethn'. (*Quietly*) Anzac Day. They make a fuss of y' for once. The speeches and the march ... and y're all mates. Y're mates an' everyth'n' seems all right. The whole year round I look forward to it. Me mates, some grogs, and—and the feelin' y're not just ... not just ... (*He shakes his head.*) Y'know. (*He gets up, seems about to go, but turns to them.*) It's the one day ... the one day ... (*He almost unable to speak.*) I ever feel ...

(*They all look at him in profound embarrassment. He turns and goes quietly to kitchen.*)

MUM (*uncomfortably*): Poor old bugger. (*To* JAN) He knows 'e ain't up to much, why'd y'ave to rub it in?

JAN: Mrs. Cook. (*Goes to her.*) I'm sorry, honestly I am—

MUM (*patting her hand without thinking*): Never mind, love, it's not your fault. That Hughie started it.

HUGHIE (*with a kind of wonder*): I was sorry before. But I'm not now. I don't know why but I'm not. (*Very close to his mother*) Gee, I love him, Mum.

MUM (*not cracking*): Yeah. All right.

(*She goes to kitchen.* HUGHIE *and* JAN *face each other uncom-*

Act Three

fortably. He goes to table, gets cigarettes.)
HUGHIE: Cigarette?
(*She nods. He gives her one and lights up for her.*)
JAN: Do you want me to go?
HUGHIE: What's the use? The whole thing was so easy for you.
JAN: Hughie, I know that. You *had* to make your statement—as a man. Force them to accept it. I'm glad you did, still glad.
HUGHIE: A man? (*Quietly*) I feel as though I've been a priggish, hysterical kid, shooting his mouth off at something he's never understood. I *thought* I understood, I'd read all the books. The books don't tell you enough. (*He is struggling to make it clear to himself.*) It's funny ... I still dislike it as much as I ever did. But I know what they *feel* about it now.
JAN: Oh, don't be so damned sentimental. Nothing's changed just because one old man got upset. Anzac Day's still the same ghastly thing it always was.
HUGHIE (*exploding*): Who CARES about Anzac Day? I've got all that off my chest. (*Excited at his self-discovery.*) You see, it wasn't just that, it never was.
JAN: I know. It was him.
HUGHIE: It was him. I was hitting out at him. Everything about him. He's yesterday, he's the past. They both are. So they are. So I've got to put up with it. (*Suddenly almost breaking*) Avea cuppa tea, luv, go on, avea cuppa tea. I don't want, I don't want, I don't WANT a cuppa tea. (*He collapses into a chair.*) Jan, I hate it here. Hate it.
JAN (*rushing to him*): Then don't stay. Leave. Break free. You'll have to sooner or later. They're wonderful people, Hughie, I should never have spoken as I did, but—you'll never grow up properly until you can stand on your own feet without them.
HUGHIE: Maybe. Maybe I'll never grow up and I can learn to accept them as they are. And not be ashamed of them.
JAN: Ashamed? Hughie.
HUGHIE: My father thought you were a snob. *I'm* the snob. I can't help it. Jan, I can't BREATHE in this house. Everything they say and do just jars and jars on me. They're so—they're—I don't know—they're so—oh, I can never find the word. It's just that they're so ... (*a long moment as the word comes to him at last*) they're so—Australian.
JAN: Are they? They're what it was. We're what it's going to be. (*Smiles.*) You're going to stay, aren't you?
HUGHIE (*nods*): I'll walk out that door one day, Jan, I know I will. But not now. When I saw him sitting there, I made a pact with myself. I won't walk out on him now. You saw what losing that job's done to him. I don't care how rugged it gets here. For the time being I'll stay.
JAN: And I'm no use any more? (*He doesn't answer.*) But I'll help you. Help you.
HUGHIE: All right, you'll help me. And patronize my family without meaning to. And fight with your mother all the time—until you

get sick of the whole thing and drift back to the Yacht Club.

JAN (*hurt*): Hughie.

HUGHIE: You'll be able to laugh and tell them about your proletariat phase ...

JAN (*quietly, stubbing out cigarette*): As nice and polite a—brushoff as I ever heard. Well ... so long, Hughie Cook. (*She moves towards door.*) See you around.

HUGHIE: I don't know that you will. I think I might ditch my course. Leave Uni.

JAN (*coming back*): You can't do that. Hughie, you mustn't.

HUGHIE: That damned University's taking me farther away from them every minute.

JAN: I see. You do all the giving-in. To your father. Why shouldn't he give a bit too?

HUGHIE: He'll meet me halfway. After tonight it'll be better. He'll meet me halfway. And even if he can't ... (*He smiles.*) I made a pact with myself. Goodbye, Jan.

JAN: Hughie. You've got to believe one thing. Please. About you and me. I wasn't just—

HUGHIE: Slumming?

JAN: Hughie, don't. Can't you—? Can't you see I—?

(*She can't manage to say it and hurries blindly to door, opens it, takes one last look back at him, them composes herself and walks out slowly with an attempt at self-possession and pride. He stands staring after her, then moves quickly after her. But as he reaches door he restrains himself, comes slowly back, sees cigarette in ashtray, slowly stubs it out. Then, bracing himself, he goes steadily towards the kitchen. ALF sits at table, beer in front of him, head down. MUM is at sink making tea. HUGHIE goes to her, with forced brightness.*)

HUGHIE: Going out tonight, Mum?

MUM: Haven't thought about it. Don't think so.

HUGHIE: Why don't we all go to the local flicks? There's a musical on—a good one, I mean, not just rock-'n'-roll. It got good writeups. ... You like a good musical, don't you? Why don't we all go and have a look at it?

MUM (*a doubtful glance at* ALF): See how we all feel later on. (*Very gently*) Wanta cuppa tea?

(*He shakes his head.* WACKA *appears at back door of kitchen.*)

WACKA: G'day all. How y' goin'?

ALF (*roughly*): Come in and siddown.

(WACKA *sits.* ALF *pours beer for him.*)

WACKA: 'Ow are y', 'Ughie?

ALF (*quietly*): We had a fight. (WACKA *looks from father to son.*) I hit him. That's what it's come to. I hit my son.

WACKA (*a pause*): I bin waitin' for that.

ALF: All right. You know everything. (*To the room at large*) He knows everything. He'd stand there and be insulted. You stood there and let him insult you. Well, not me. Not me.

MUM: Where'd it get you?

Act Three

ALF: Well, now I know. I know what my son and his mob think of me. Well, all right, if he prefers to get around with that lot—(*He has still not looked at* HUGHIE.)

HUGHIE: I'm here, aren't I?

ALF (*turns to him; quietly*): Yeah? For how long?
(*A break.* HUGHIE *is having one of his small battles with himself. Finally he turns to them.*)

HUGHIE: Dad. Mum ... I want to talk to you about something. Dad ... (*He moves towards table.*) I think I might leave Uni.

MUM: What for?

ALF (*gaping at him*): Leave—? Leave University? What the hell do you want to do that for?

HUGHIE: I thought you knew what for. I'm sick of feeling—mixed up. You know it's changed me, I can tell how you both feel. Well—I want to do the right thing.

ALF: And what sort of work d'y'think y'd do?

HUGHIE: Drive a truck, take photos, anything.

ALF (*on his feet*): Oh no you don't. Oh no you don't!! You think I spent my whole life trying to get you somewhere to have you throw it away now? What's the matter with you? Don't you want to better y'self? Yr gettin' chances blokes like me and Wacka in our young days we'd've given anything to have. And you're not satisfied.

HUGHIE: I'm never SURE of myself. Wherever I am, whoever I'm with, I feel—I just feel—I'm forever uncomfortable.

ALF: Well, who said life was s'posed to be comfortable? Where'd y'ever get the idea it was anythin' but a bloody battle all the way? Battle! That's what it is. Just like fightin' in a war. You dunno whether you're gunna win or lose and in the long run it don't much matter, it's the fightin' that's important. Some people fight all their lives for someth'n' and never win, never win, end up with bugger-all. But at least they had a go. You'd give it away as easy as that. Gawd. What's the country coming to?

HUGHIE (*exasperated*): I was thinking of you. God, I don't know, whatever you do round here's wrong.
(ALF *has suddenly grabbed him by the shirtfront and in a final complete fury is shaking the boy.*)

ALF: I felt like knocking your block off in there and I still might, I still might. You're gunna stay at that University till y've done the lot. And if it's a battle for you, right, it's a battle.
(*He releases him, sits abruptly, pours a beer.* HUGHIE *turns to his mother.*)

MUM: He's right.
(*A moment as* HUGHIE *thinks of his future.*)

HUGHIE (*firmly*): But you won't like it. Because I can't—just to make you happy—I can't change how I think and feel. About— the most important things. (*He turns to* WACKA) Wacka, I haven't apologised to you for last week. I'm sorry if I offended you or hurt you. But—(*to his father*) I'm not sorry I said or did those things. I still believe them. I'd do them again.

MUM (*looks from* ALF *to* HUGHIE): I dunno who's worst.

HUGHIE (*to* ALF): I want us both to know how we stand. (ALF *nods, but won't look at him*) I *don't* respect what you all do on that day. I never will. And I don't respect what it stands for. But now I respect the way you feel about it, and if I'm going to stay here ... (ALF *looks up at him quickly*) that'll have to be enough. Now—do you still want me?

ALF (*battling*): I want you to have an education. I do. I do. But— (*Suddenly unable to cope with it any more bursts out to* WACKA) He goes too far, he gets above himself. They're all the same now, they think they run the country. Kids! Kids! You scrimp and save and give'm everything. For what? For what?

WACKA: Alf. (*It is quiet enough but they all turn to him. He hesitates, self-conscious as ever, then gently*) Your boy's growing up. You've got to face that. He's got the right to think and say what he likes. Any fightin' we ever did, you'n' me, in any wars, it was to give him that right. And if we don't agree with what he thinks—(*stops, then*)—Well, it's his world. We've had it. He's got it all ahead of him.

(*He turns to* HUGHIE. *A little shy smile.*)

Only—give the old blokes a bit of a go sometimes, son.

(*He looks down at table.* ALF *pushes a glass towards* WACKA, *ignores* HUGHIE. MUM *looks to her son to see what he will do.* HUGHIE *has listened intently and with sudden respect to* WACKA, *and now, managing a smile, he comes slowly towards his father. But as his father begins to speak, the smile vanishes.*)

ALF: That's all right about him. That's all right. I'm a bloody Australian and I'll always stand up for bloody Australia. I seen these jumped-up cows come and go, come and go, they don't mean a bloody thing, what did they ever do for the country, they never did nothing. It's the little man, he's the one goes out and gets slaughtered, we're the ones they get when the time comes, we're the ones, mugs, the lot of us, mugs. He said that. He said it. Did my son say that? Did he say that about me and my mates? That's good men he's talking about, men who give their all, that's decent men. I'll show the little cow. Someone's gotta show these kids. I'll show him, I know what he thinks, I'm nothin', but I'll show him, I'll show the lot of 'em. I'm a bloody Australian and I'll always ...

(*Through this* MUM *has stood very still, watching* ALF. *Then her gaze has gone to* HUGHIE *as he backs away slowly, hurt and disappointed. When he reaches the kitchen door he turns and hurries blindly into the main room.* ALF *has continued non-stop but as he reaches his last words he falters and stops as though really hearing his own voice for the first time. Slowly he pushes the beer away, looks off after* HUGHIE, *head raised a little, almost waiting to hear a door slam. Alone in the other room* HUGHIE *stands, angry and bewildered, and then charges towards the front door. He flings it open, but as he is about to dash out something holds him. He stands trembling, battling, and then slams the door. Head back,* ALF *listens, listens. Slowly* HUGHIE *comes back into lounge and sits down.*)

CURTAIN

Seymour on
*The One Day of the Year**

If I'd known *The One Day of the Year* was going to have such staying power, be performed in various parts of the world, be set for study in the schools, and so on, I might have taken a bit more care with it in the first place. That, of course, sounds such a square-off. Odd how a play means different things to different people at different times. About half a dozen times a film version has been planned, always to fall through, and it won't happen now because I won't let it—I am sure the play would show its age. But each person approaching me with ideas for a film has had his own angles on it. At first, within the first year of its premiere, British producers were interested because it showed a "unique side of Australian life". Then an American producer saw it—years later—as a symbol of the youth revolt of the '60s and wanted to update it to portray student attitudes to Vietnam. More recently Michael Thornhill, whose *Between Wars* is so good, actually wrote a complete screenplay based on *The One Day* (it was too reverent and loyal to the original stage play and should have been cut up and made more filmic) but was refused financial aid from the Australian Film Development Corporation on grounds which have never been clarified. I think he wanted to do it—and I'd have wanted him to—as a comment on the times in which it was written, just as the revival at the Independent Theatre in Sydney in the mid-sixties dressed the actors in the style of the late fifties. That revival brought forth the critical comment in a Sydney newspaper that the Anzac side of the play now seemed less important and what dominated the interest was the generation clash between father and son. The author was credited with having tapped the famous "generation gap" years before it became a popular cliché. I'd always thought it a staple of Western drama anyway for the last two and a half thousand years.

The most pleasing comment ever made by a critic on it came from a youngish Melbourne writer who saw the Actors Forum production in '74 and said that when he had seen the play in the sixties, at the height of the Vietnam era, he identified solely with Hughie, the son, and hardly registered the views of the older people. This time, half a dozen years older, he found himself very sympathetic to the father's views and able to see both sides. Which is what the play has always been about.

* These comments were written for this anthology, 1975.

Seymour as A.B.C. "Guest of Honour"*

On my first night back in Australia, in Sydney, I attended a performance of David Williamson's play, *Don's Party*. What was exciting was the sense of *necessity* in the occasion. How many plays have I seen in British and European theatres which gave no more than a pale, pretty evening. This, however, was vibrating with urgency as the audience, alive, alert, laughing, tingling with pleasure, responded to every nuance, recognizing the play's sharp and cutting relevance to their own lives and their own malaise. This is what theatre has always been for, to show us ourselves, then to go beyond that, to search out our private anxieties, to make us re-examine our own myths. In a modest but pungent way *Don's Party* does exactly these things.

But it is only one play. There have been many plays in this current resurgence of Australian drama, and there will, we hope, be many more to come. I have the impression of a society which, having recently taken a great step out of a long somnolence, is in a state of pleasurable turbulence, with much being thrown aside, not before time, and much that is new and provocative being tried. Such a society must keep re-evaluating itself, re-examining the unspoken assumptions on which it is based. The theatre—plays written by local people for local people—is already playing a vigorous part in this and will surely continue to do so. Are Australian audiences ready to follow along the paths Australian playwrights, if they're worth their salt, will want to lead them? Because it is also true that we must stop telling each other good yarns, we must get beyond the picturesque use of the vernacular to give audiences no more than the pleasant shock of self-recognition.

I am just beginning at last to have glimpses of this inner life of Australians, and I'm sure I'm not the only one wanting to see it probed, fingered delicately but mercilessly open to the public gaze. Surely Australians are not hollow men, surely when we open the vizor and look inside the tin-can helmet we won't find an empty space? Surely we do have an inner life?

---

* From a talk given in the Australian Broadcasting Commission's "Guest of Honour" series, 8 April 1973.

Autobiographical Article
"Encounters with the Great: The Prime Minister"*

Looking back, it seems to me now that most of my family were apolitical. The exception was my brother-in-law—let's call him George—who had a hand in looking after me with my eldest sister after my parents had died. George had a tough time. What jobs he had held before I went to live with them when I was ten, I don't know. They belong to that shadowy period, in childhood, before one was on the scene. For a while he was out of work and finally found a job as a clerk booking loads in and out of a Fremantle warehouse. Sometimes I visited him there after school. The high dark shed smelt of sawdust. George sat at a little desk at the top of wooden steps on the loading platform. He used to bring home small bags of boiled lollies twice a week. (I'm still having my teeth fixed.) George didn't know much about the world but what he did know was expressed with confidence. The royal family? Ought to be stood up against a wall and shot—which seemed a harsh fate for poor, mild, stammering George VI. The government? What are they doing for the working man? Nothing. He tried to help me get through the modest little East Fremantle state school I went to, poring with me over homework, shaking his head at my scrawny scribble and showing me the ornate old-fashioned copperplate of which he was proud.

My mother and others in our family had been explosive, given to the sharp slap and then tears of forgiveness. George went in for long moralizing lectures. I preferred the sharp slap. He also tended to torment my sister, sure she was unfaithful to him, as later she was. For months a small newspaper clipping was pasted to a light-switch mount in the kitchen. "What a tangled web we weave when we set out to deceive." I didn't understand the implication but its nagging presence seemed sinister. Even when George wasn't there I felt him breathing down my neck. That clipping possibly helped me become the proficient and colourful liar I was for a time during my early adolescence. I used to like getting home early from school and, finding the place empty, my sister still at work, would raid the huge old dresser to make up a mixture of cocoa, sugar and condensed milk

---

* Reprinted from *Meanjin Quarterly* 27 (1968): 351–57. Seymour's was one of a series of such "encounters" published by *Meanjin*.

in the bottom of a cup, which I would then eat off a spoon. Nobody had ever said in so many words I shouldn't do this but I knew it wouldn't be approved and enjoyed the delicious bowel-fluttering pleasure of washing the cup and spoon and returning everything to its place without leaving a sign.

George viewed most of the world with a mixture of contempt and anxiety. He had intelligence but little chance to develop or to use it. Suspicious and jealous of anyone different, he nevertheless urged me to better myself as much as I could, evidently unaware of the dichotomy. He hated and envied people with pretensions to a better life. His sister married a smooth, good looking charmer, Stan, who was trying everything, from photography to door-to-door salesmanship. "How's Stanley Harold?" George would ask, voice whip-lashing scorn at his baffled sister, and whenever Stanley Harold was mentioned George would snarl, "That poof."

One night doing my homework at the kitchen table I remembered a riddle I'd heard that day and tried it on George. His capacity for spoiling things came into full play. "If," said I, "England is the mother country and Germany is the father country, what's Greece?" It was an audio pun, the answer being "Two and six a tin". But instead of saying, fairly, that he didn't know, George roared an impromptu history lesson. "Greece is a bastard little country full of dirty sneaking thieving little runts. It's never been anything and it never will be anything." Many years later, standing on the edge of the Parthenon's cliff and looking across to the Philosopher's Hill and down on the two great open theatres, I suddenly remembered that night and George, whom I'd hardly thought about for years. Not that I could feel too smug: my own Australian education had told me little of any past culture but the British. Yet, xenophobia and all, George was good friends with the Yugoslav fishermen of our village-like community. They took us out to Rottnest Island one Easter weekend on their regular fishing trip, and big Guyo and little Rudi often called in at our flat and gave my sister fresh fish which she'd cook in sizzling oil.

George's greatest diatribes were directed against the conservative politicians of the day. And his favourite target was "Pig-Iron Bob". I remember very little coherent political argument from those monologues. All I gathered was that Pig-Iron Bob was on the wrong side, against Us, and embodied all of George's aversions. "Bob" fancied himself educated, even polished, a man of the world, which image no self-respecting Australian politician then projected or wanted to. He spoke "too Pommy", not like a real Australian. (Yet I'd been taught "alla-cution", no doubt as a helpful hoist out of the lower echelons and our wide but narrow Fremantle street.)

The next person to influence me politically was the youthful studio manager of the first radio station I worked at, in Perth. Another Stan, he seemed all that was mature, sophisticated and knowledgeable. He was twenty-three, promoted prematurely because of the war, to which he could not go because of a physical disability. Stan and his family, especially his brother, were more thoughtfully and consciously left-wing than anyone I had met. Politics, which had seemed remote and impersonal, suddenly became significant to me. Ploughing through a life of Lenin, trying to grasp something which I recognized later to be Shavian and Fabian rather than Marxist, I absorbed Stan's estimates of recent Australian history. The Depression, which had hardly been mentioned in my family, and the behaviour of Conservative politicians during the '30s—mumblings about an abortive "Iron Guard" on the Rumanian pattern—created a certain stereotype for me which shaped my political feelings for a long time ahead. "Pig-Iron Bob" (I am reluctant to leave that dated epithet alone, it has such a fine poetic resonance to it) was the least-liked rogue in their gallery. He had once, after a European tour in the '30s, come back praising Hitler (much later I was able to retort to them, "So did Walter Lippmann"—one of their idols) and would never be allowed to forget it. That he would ever be Prime Minister of Australia would have seemed to them beyond comprehension.

We all split up. My sister died of cancer, but years before had been divorced from George. George had a bad spell, I heard, had attacked his aging mother with a knife and was doing a stretch in Heathcote, a home for the mentally disturbed. I hadn't seen him since the night in my teens when I'd come home from late duty at the broadcasting station in Perth to find him, drunk, threatening my sister. They had been separated then for some months. He showed signs of wanting to have a go at me too, at which my sister interposed herself between us. George contented himself with sneering at my job ("gone up in the world, haven't we?"). I'd taken the job because I'd failed in my examinations and, miserable at my academic ineptitude, was surprised and excited to find I enjoyed the work in this new world. It was a humble enough job, I was the very junior of juniors, and in those pre-inflation days started out earning thirty shillings a week. But with an alarming tendency, even then, to agree with my critics and lacerate myself with guilt at my shortcomings, I found George's attitude just and understandable. He seemed to be saying I had betrayed all I had come from, including him, by moving into a more middle-class world. (A couple of years ago I heard that George, in his sixties now, going to a play of mine being performed in Perth, had said he wished we were still in touch, that he was proud of me, I'd really bettered myself.)

Through the 1950s, working in Sydney, I watched the growing embourgeoisement of Australian life with distaste. We could never go back to that lost and in any case unprepossessing world of the past. But wasn't there a better way to storm the future than from behind an electric motor-mower? As the hysterias of the Cold War lapped even our shores and a few hitherto outspoken persons began to hold their tongues I felt alarm at the illiberalism which, given a dogmatically conservative government in full spate, could easily spread. It seemed necessary to watch for any sign of repression or discrimination. The Petrov affair seemed a phony self-glorification, Australians delighted with the back-handed compliment that they were important enough, at last, to be spied on. Writer Ralph Peterson used to wax satirical about our orthodoxy's current obsessions. During the Korean war: "You can always tell a South Korean from a North Korean instantly. A South Korean is good, upright, democratic, like *Us*. A North Korean is a dirty crawling little communist toad. Moral, kill all North Koreans." Later, after a trans-continental flight: "They close all the curtains as you fly over Woomera. They're not silly, they know every plane is lousy with Soviet spies and communists craning to catch all the secrets of the installation."

But mostly life was placid, devoted to learning how to write for radio; then television and documentary films. As the hysteria somewhat ebbed people seemed to fall back into private preoccupations. I at last managed to get a play or two written and even performed. As Craig McGregor once pointed out in an article about political commitment, there is a period in life, late twenties to mid-thirties, when professional people seem to spend their energies on their professions. It's the younger and the older who make all the political noise.

Nevertheless, there was not much in the Australian scene to change my earlier sentiments. I was still solidly against the crawling orthodoxy of that great political party Australians inexplicably seemed unable to do without. So when I finally had my brief encounter with Sir Robert it was not the most comfortable moment of my life.

The Elizabethan Theatre Trust was doing a play I'd written. One Saturday night some friends were to be in the audience and I dropped in just before curtain-up, to see whether the dialogue in certain spots would sound as bad tonight as it had last time or whether the cast would perform more of their miracles of transmutation. At the stage-door entrance in the alley running between the Palace Theatre and the charming old Adams' Hotel, the Trust's business manager Elsie Beyer announced that the Prime Minister would be in the audience. Miss Beyer would be in attendance for a drink in the dress-circle office during the first interval. I was expected to be present.

As usual, I was unprepared. A dark business suit was obviously desirable. Writers in button-down collars were, I suspected, the only officially approved kind. Or it might be permissible to go to the other extreme and appear in a tweed jacket, rollneck sweater and brown corduroys. My apparel was strictly unsuitable. Grey sports slacks, which needed pressing. And a dark-blue black-checked jacket, vaguely Italian in spirit, purchased recently off the hook at DJ's menswear store in Market Street. It was way-out in the wrong way. Just unclassifiable. And, not for the first or last time, I'd been lax about polishing my shoes. My shirt and tie were passable but everything else that was visible was unimpressive. I probably needed a haircut too. I usually did.

The stage director, understudies, electrician, stood around making suggestions, Did I have time to go home and come back? Maybe, but what did I have at home much better than I had on? A suit that should have been at the cleaner's. Brown suede shoes. Oh Christ. So we battled, bourgeois conventions all-important it seemed, for my soul, or rather my unprepossessing body. The stage director offered to lend me his suit. It was two sizes too big for me, ice-blue, double-breasted which I disliked, and was anyway his older or working suit and looked it. I think he was joking. In the end I met the P.M. as I was.

From years of similar experiences (job interviews, meetings with editors, ABC department heads) I could tell, right off, I was not making a good impression. In the narrow office we stood along one wall, me wedged between the executive director on my left and Sir Robert on my right. I tried to stand kind of slopingly, with feet back against the wall, shoes in shadow I hoped, and my body and head leaning perilously, peculiarly out, pretending nonchalant interest, something like a slightly misplaced figurehead on an ancient galleon, except for the drink in my hand. How it looked I don't like to think. It succeeded only in making the P.M. look me up and down thoughtfully, run a scrutinizing eye over the Italian coat, and take in—I'll swear—my shabby shoes. His eye had a way of clicking open and shut as though a mysterious computer device inside were tapping out a metaphysical price-tag for each quality he noted. What, the cast of those eyebrows seemed to say, does this man do for a living when he's not writing plays? And a sag at the sides of the generous, carping mouth suggested his answer was: not much.

What did one say to a man who for decades has summed up all one dislikes in political life? What does one say in the interval anyway? I like to talk about the play but in this case I could hardly do that. Interval small-talk is always exasperating. The best theatre would be Greek-fashion, uninterrupted until the bitter end had been reached and the catharsis, if you still go for catharsis, achieved. And at official functions with official persons I can rarely drum up conversation, especially when it is expected, any more than I can write with someone standing by the typewriter looking over my shoulder. (In London, later, the backer of my play took me to the private opening of the London Film Festival and introduced me to Huw Wheldon of "Monitor", and several other influential newspaper and television persons. I know I was supposed to glitter and say witty or incisive things about the films we had seen, so that they would instantly succumb to my charm and want to interview me, plug the play, etc. I became tongue-tied and failed my producer.)

Whatever conversation passed between the Prime Minister and myself my memory has not retained. We filed out and back to our seats. I sat upstairs this time, not far from the official party. What Sir Robert thought of the play I don't know. I did note, and have always remembered, that his biggest reaction came when the leading character climaxed a long monologue with the words, "He turned round too quick and spewed. All over everything ... " Sir Robert's loudest laugh of the evening came on the word "spewed". One of those deep laughs, from the gut. When the word was repeated, he laughed again. Forced or genuine, product of slight trauma or his sense of humour, I've never known.

The fifteen-minute interlude in the interval was to be my only physical encounter with the Prime Minister. But some months later I wrote him a letter.

Overland had been refused financial help from the Commonwealth Literary Fund despite a good record of publishing Australian writers. The refusal was clearly, and frankly, political. The editor in his columns asked people to protest. I didn't think *Overland* the most sparkling jewel in Australia's literary crown but its presence, speaking for values other than the orthodox and established, seemed more important than ever. It was sometimes, I judged, too strident and over-simple. But I was hardly in a position to judge; these were two of my own worst faults anyway.

I joined the many sending protests and reminded the Prime Minister of our very brief meeting when he was good enough to come to the theatre, presuming upon that slight acquaintance to add my voice to the many disappointed by the recent *Overland* decision. I hoped, I said, he would be impressed by the fact that not only avowed left extremists but people of all political colours were alarmed at this tendency to discriminate against what was a good forceful journal doing a good job for Australian writers. I'd gathered, I added, that in some quarters the editor had been criticized for not being far *enough* to the left and was, so far as one could see, making an impressive effort to keep his magazine broader-based than it might have been and out of the hands of any lunatic fringe. Steve Murray-Smith when he saw a copy of this letter wrote that he liked it more than the routine paragraph I wrote to be published along with other protest notes in the magazine.

The answer came a fortnight later. A circular letter, roneoed, replied to the dissenters with some bumph about the government having more information on this matter than had its critics and acting, or choosing not to act, accordingly. Our views had been noted and the situation would be reviewed at a later date. In the margin the P.M. had written "kind regards" which, in the context, seemed fair enough.

David Williamson

Shane Porteous (Andrew) and Ron Haddrick (Ken) in a scene from the 1973 Old Tote Theatre Company production of *What If You Died Tomorrow*. Photograph by courtesy of the Old Tote Theatre Company, Sydney.

What If You Died Tomorrow

What If You Died Tomorrow was first performed by the Old Tote Theatre Company in the Drama Theatre of the Sydney Opera House on 9 October 1973 with the following cast:

ANDREW COLLINS, in his early thirties	Shane Porteous
KIRSTY, in her early thirties	Kirrily Nolan
HARRY BUSTLE, in his forties	Max Phipps
MICHAEL O'HEARN, in his early forties	Ron Falk
CARMEL SCOTT, in her early forties	Dinah Shearing
GUNTER, a twenty-one year old Norwegian	John Walton
IRENE COLLINS, about sixty	Ruth Cracknell
KEN COLLINS, in his sixties	Ron Haddrick

The voices of KIRSTY'S children are heard: SEAN, aged six; SEBASTIAN, aged four; and EMMA, aged three.

Setting designed by Yoshi Tosa.

Directed by Robin Lovejoy.

Setting:

The action takes place in the main room of KIRSTY'S home on the outskirts of Melbourne, 1973. The design is utterly naturalistic down to the smallest detail. The house is made entirely of natural materials: the walls are mudbrick and are broken by vertical lengths of telegraph poles or railway sleepers. The room is large and on several levels. On the right a door leads off to the kitchen; on the left is the front entrance to the house; at the back of the stage, one door leads to the bedroom and another to the bathroom and toilet. A steep staircase, almost rudimentary enough to be called a ladder, leads to a loft area above centre stage which is the children's bedroom. The room is in disorder. The slate floor is covered with magazines and newspapers. Bookshelves sprawl. The furniture is of adzed wood, rough and chunky. There is a centrally positioned brick fireplace with a large brick column as chimney. Reproductions of twelfth century Florentine paintings hang around the walls. A stereo set lies towards the back of the stage, with speakers on cleared spaces on the bookshelves.

Note: The characters in this play are fictional and any similarity to persons living or dead is purely coincidental.

ACT ONE

KIRSTY *enters, puts on some records and sits rocking gently in an old carved wooden rocking chair. A Mozart quartet of flute and strings plays softly on the stereo. ANDREW's voice descends from the loft, singing to KIRSTY's children—part of their going to bed ritual. The song is* The Owl and the Pussycat, *which he sings rather badly. The three unseen children, Sean (6), Sebastian (4) and Emma (3), raucously demand an encore. ANDREW flatly refuses. Their pleas become more raucous and insistent. He bellows at them.*

ANDREW (*off*): Shut up or you'll all get a belting. I don't want to hear one more word out of any of you, and I mean it. (*After a pause*) What happens to you if I hear one more word?
CHILDREN (*in gleeful chorus*): A belting!
ANDREW: Right, And I mean it.
(KIRSTY *doesn't react at all to this performance. She picks up a newspaper and idly flicks through it. ANDREW descends the stairs. He stops half way down and listens, waiting for the first sound.* SEAN *starts chattering, and he stomps up the stairs, making more noise than would be natural, in order to strike fear into the children. He virtually shouts as he ascends.*)
Right. I warned you. Didn't I? You're going to get a bloody thrashing, the lot of you.
(*He stops just at the top of the ladder and listens again. Silence. Pleased in a grim sort of way that his threat has been effective, he descends the stairs.*)
It's about time you were firmer with them.
KIRSTY: I don't believe in ordering them around.
ANDREW (*irritated*): You can't reason with them at that age. I don't care what the textbooks say, they're little psychopaths. All of them.
KIRSTY: If you treat them like adults, they will respond like adults.
ANDREW: I've watched you spend a quarter of an hour trying to convince Sean that it would be a good idea to let you put his pyjama top on him. Bloody ridiculous.
KIRSTY (*reading the paper*): Yes.
ANDREW: Don't just say yes.
KIRSTY: Right.
ANDREW: You've got to start being firmer with them.
KIRSTY (*reading*): They're much better than they used to be. You've done a lot for them, Puss. Miss Evans says that Sean's stopped stealing things at school.
ANDREW: That's not surprising. He would've damn near cleaned the place out by now.
KIRSTY (*reading*): If you and I were in a plane crash in the Arctic Circle and I died and you were starving, would you eat me?
ANDREW (*half thrown, half amused*): Of course I wouldn't.
KIRSTY: Why not? I'd be dead.
ANDREW: I just wouldn't.

Act One 95

KIRSTY: You should. I'd expect you to. This man feels guilty about it.
ANDREW: What man?
KIRSTY: The man who ate his dead passenger. When the rescue party reached him he yelled: "Go back. I'm a cannibal. You have rescued a cannibal. Go back." Wow! How's that for guilt? Probably a Catholic. Did you get much writing done today?
ANDREW: No, I er—
KIRSTY: I'd like to travel again soon.
ANDREW: What about the children?
KIRSTY: We could take them with us.
ANDREW (*dubious*): Where do you want to go?
KIRSTY: I'd like to live in India for a while.
ANDREW: India? What about cholera and dysentery?
KIRSTY: We'd have injections.
ANDREW: They don't give full protection.
KIRSTY: I lived in Turkey for a year when Sean was a baby, and we didn't get sick.
ANDREW: The shots only give something like sixty per cent immunity.
KIRSTY: I'd still like to go.
ANDREW: Where would we live?
KIRSTY: In a village.
ANDREW: Not just for a little while, eh?
KIRSTY: Early next year?
ANDREW (*dubious*): All right.
KIRSTY: You can write, and I'll go and meet people.
ANDREW: Mmm.
KIRSTY: Did you get much work done today?
ANDREW: No. The phone kept ringing.
KIRSTY: Take it off the hook.
ANDREW: I might miss an important call.
KIRSTY (*deadpan*): Yes. Mama read an interview you gave in *Vogue*.
ANDREW: I've never been interviewed for *Vogue*.
KIRSTY: She sent it to me. "His fine silky hair all but covers his big eyes and fabulous smile." Is that why you got your hair cut?
ANDREW: I seem to remember you interviewing me once.
KIRSTY: Not for a woman's magazine. Why do you let them do it?
ANDREW: They manoeuvre you into it.
KIRSTY (*imitating a breathless lady journalist*): "Yes, I know how precious your time is and you're probably fed up to the back teeth with giving interviews, but I wonder if you could just manage to squeeze me into one of your spare moments?"
ANDREW: That's just how they are. They're also very persistent.
KIRSTY: Have you *ever* refused an appearance or an interview?
ANDREW (*defensively*): Yes.
KIRSTY: When?
ANDREW: That television show a few weeks ago.
KIRSTY: Didn't they want you to do something odd?
ANDREW: No.

KIRSTY: Didn't they want you to play a trombone or something?
ANDREW: I forget.
KIRSTY: Can you play the trombone?
ANDREW: Yes. I've told you that about five times now. I was playing professionally at the age of sixteen.
KIRSTY: Did you know that I played the flute?
ANDREW: Yes. For the Junior Symphony Orchestra at the age of thirteen.
KIRSTY: Mmm. Who did you play for?
ANDREW: A jazz band.
KIRSTY: What were they called?
ANDREW: Oh, er, some stupid name.
KIRSTY: What?
ANDREW: Dirty Dick and the Yarra Valley Stompers.
KIRSTY: Really? I knew Dirty Dick. Sue Nicholls and Kiffy Myers and I used to go there occasionally. In the Union Hall.
ANDREW: That's right.
KIRSTY: Isn't that strange? I don't remember meeting you.
ANDREW: You'd hardly have taken any notice of me then, would you?
KIRSTY: I probably would have liked you.
(Pause)
The trombonist was a little fat chap.
ANDREW: I was only a stand-in.
KIRSTY: Why did they want you to play it on television?
ANDREW: They thought it would've been funny.
KIRSTY: I'm sure it would've been. You are a bit hard to draw out in those interviews sometimes.
ANDREW *(with a trace of a grin)*: What do you mean?
KIRSTY *(imitating interviewer)*: "Some critics have said that your work has a crackling surface but on closer analysis veers towards the superficial." *(Imitating* ANDREW*)* "Yes, they have!" "Can you answer that charge?" "No." "You agree that your work does veer towards the superficial?" "No." "Yet you don't care to answer the charge that it does?" "No." *(Searching for another question)* "I believe you cook a fair Stroganoff?"
Come here and sit next to me.
(She pats a cushion next to her.)
ANDREW *(picking up a paper)*: I'm comfortable here.
KIRSTY: Are you annoyed with me?
ANDREW *(although he isn't and she knows it)*: Yes.
KIRSTY: If I wasn't around to keep your ego in check, you'd be a menace to the community. *(Looking at the billiard table)* Can't we put that billiard table in the shed?
ANDREW *(reading)*: We've been through this ten times before and the answer is no. No. You can win on everything else, but you're not winning this one.
KIRSTY *(after a pause)*: It's easy to bring it out when you want to play.
ANDREW: No.

Act One

KIRSTY: Please.
ANDREW: No.
KIRSTY: It sort of jars with Botticelli.
ANDREW: It stays here. Right?
KIRSTY: It wouldn't—
ANDREW: How did your interview go?
KIRSTY: Everything went wrong. I just made it to the crèche to collect Seb before it closed. Mrs. Harris always looks at me as if I am likely to have him there all night.
ANDREW: Who were you interviewing again?
KIRSTY: A young film maker.
ANDREW: Bright?
KIRSTY: Interesting. I would've liked to spend longer with him.
ANDREW: Did you get enough to write the article, or do you have to see him again?
KIRSTY: No. I got enough. Who were all those phone calls from?
ANDREW: Michael rang about three times.
KIRSTY: He's very fond of you.
ANDREW: Shit.
KIRSTY: We have long talks about you over the phone when you're not here.
ANDREW: Well don't.
KIRSTY: You're lucky to have an agent who takes a close personal interest in you.
ANDREW (*pointing at her, trying to stop grinning*): You'll go in a minute.
KIRSTY: What did he want?
ANDREW: He's bringing someone over tonight.
KIRSTY: Again?
ANDREW: It's business. He's got another offer for my manuscript.
KIRSTY: Ooh, I forgot ...
ANDREW: What?
KIRSTY: Harry Bustle rang while you were bathing the children.
ANDREW: Was that Harry?
KIRSTY: Mmm. He's coming over.
ANDREW: Tonight?
KIRSTY: Mmm.
ANDREW: Shit. Why didn't you tell me?
KIRSTY: I forgot.
ANDREW (*irritated*): Look, I'm damned if I'm going to go bathing your kids and putting them to bed if you can't even remember to give messages.
KIRSTY (*calmly*): Now come on. This is the first time you've put them to bed for weeks.
ANDREW: He can't come tonight. Michael is bringing Carmel Scott with him. What'd he want?
KIRSTY: I don't know. He just said it couldn't wait. Usual Harry line.
ANDREW: Would you ring him and tell him I'm sick or something?
KIRSTY: Who's Carmel Scott?

ANDREW: The publishing editor at Chisolms.
KIRSTY: Chisolms?
ANDREW: That's right. Chisolms. Would you ring Bustle please?
KIRSTY (*going towards the phone*): I thought you said it was definite that Bustle was publishing it?
ANDREW: No. I didn't.
KIRSTY: Well he thinks it's definite. He said he wanted to "really make an impact with this one."
ANDREW: When?
KIRSTY: Before. On the phone.
ANDREW: Yeah, well he's jumping the gun. I haven't signed anything yet.
(KIRSTY *dials.* ANDREW *pours himself a claret, draining the bottle. He holds the glass up to the light, sniffs it and glances nervously towards the phone. He looks at the claret again and drinks it.*)
KIRSTY: He's not answering.
ANDREW: Shit. He's probably on his way. I wouldn't mind betting he's heard about Chisolms on the grapevine. (*After a pause*) Shit.
KIRSTY: Why do you want to change publishers?
ANDREW: Why shouldn't I? Bustle's done nothing for me.
KIRSTY: He thinks he has.
ANDREW: Evidently he got up at dinner the other night and said—get this—that he not only published, marketed and distributed my books, but he practically had to write them as well.
KIRSTY: Who told you that?
ANDREW: I heard.
KIRSTY: Are you sure? You are inclined to be a bit paranoid.
ANDREW: He said it.
KIRSTY: He was probably referring to Freddie Hubbard.
ANDREW: Well let's face it. He really does have to knock Freddie's stuff into shape, but the only thing he's ever done for me is bloody near ruin two of my books.
KIRSTY: I thought you said that some of his suggestions were quite helpful.
ANDREW: Helpful? I'll be sitting there thinking and he'll suddenly burst in and yell: "Try this one for size: a desecration fuck of the whore goddess figure." At least Carmel's got some sensitivity.
KIRSTY: Have you met Carmel before?
ANDREW: Once. For lunch. With Michael.
(*He drinks his claret.*)
God, that's good.
KIRSTY: Is there any left?
ANDREW: Really good. No, I've just finished it. We take this sort of wine for granted these days. A bottle with every meal. Do you know how much this stuff retails for?
KIRSTY: I didn't think it was all that good.
ANDREW: That's a great wine. Full bodied and a firm tannin finish. Needs another year or two in the bottle. I'll put a couple of dozen down when I start the cellar. (*Becoming expansive*) You get used to having money. You really do.

Act One 99

KIRSTY: We could manage with less.
ANDREW: That's what you'd like to think, isn't it?
KIRSTY: We've managed with a lot less.
ANDREW: You hate to admit it, but the money's made everything a hell of a lot easier.
KIRSTY: Money seems to be your favourite topic of conversation these days. You work for years on a relative pittance for a trade union clinic, and suddenly Bustle talks royalties and film sales and you practically start salivating.
ANDREW (*defensively*): I know. I'm seducible, but by Christ you wouldn't have half the freedom you do if we didn't have it. Do you know how much we spent on baby-sitters for your kids last week?
KIRSTY: We needn't go out as much. When we do it's usually something to do with your career, in any case.
ANDREW (*tersely*): You don't have to come if you don't want to.
KIRSTY: I don't particularly enjoy a lot of it.
ANDREW: You were pretty eager to get to the opening of the Festival Theatre even if I did have a temperature of a hundred and three.
KIRSTY: I thought it was just a cold.
ANDREW: It was a virus, and a bloody strong virus at that.
KIRSTY: I'm sorry. I really wanted to hear the concert.
ANDREW: Bullshit. You wanted to meet Don Dunstan.
KIRSTY: I wanted to hear good music played under ideal conditions.
ANDREW: Ideal conditions. I would've been dying right next to you.
KIRSTY: You could've asked me if I wanted to go by myself.
ANDREW: The invitation was for me. Not you.
KIRSTY: I don't see that that matters.
ANDREW: You can't go sending a substitute on an occasion like that.
KIRSTY: Substitute?
ANDREW: Yes. Substitute. I was invited and not you. If you only admitted it, you get to a lot of interesting places and meet a lot of interesting people because you're living with me.
KIRSTY: I wouldn't've thought it was a question of who gets the invitation. We do things together.
ANDREW: Then why did you want to go to the Festival opening by yourself?
KIRSTY: You really think you're terrific, don't you?
ANDREW (*nodding*): Mmm.
KIRSTY: Look at you. A little kid who's just won a fight. Aren't you?
ANDREW (*smiling*): Mmm. Come here.
KIRSTY (*unable to restrain a grudging grin*): Now that you've won a little point, you're ready to have me.
ANDREW (*nodding*): Mmm.
KIRSTY: You are just like a little boy sometimes.
(*She goes over, grabs the back of his neck and mock chokes him. He grabs her and does the same.*)
ANDREW: You like the money. Admit it.
KIRSTY: I will admit that I've got expensive tastes. When I was living with John, he'd go crazy because I'd go out and buy a

beautiful piece of pottery or a painting instead of food. Sometimes I had to steal groceries from the supermarket. Don't say that about me using you to meet people, though. I knew a lot of interesting people before I met you. What's the matter?

ANDREW: You're heavy.

KIRSTY: I'm not heavy.

ANDREW: You're cutting off my circulation.

KIRSTY: I'm getting disillusioned with you. You didn't even make love to me last night.

ANDREW: I'm run down. That virus killed thousands in Europe.

KIRSTY: When we first started living together, we used to spend half the night making love.

ANDREW: I know. I've never fully recovered. Will you get off my knee?

KIRSTY: Do you remember our first little flat with the sun streaming in and the stereo playing?

ANDREW (*nodding*): My wife ringing up distraught and your husband driving around the block with a shotgun in his car. I remember it all right. I still panic every time I hear Mozart. Hey, have you seen that last letter from my parents lying around? Would you get off my knee?

(*KIRSTY gets off his knee and sits beside him.*)

KIRSTY: No, sorry.

ANDREW: I think they're getting back sometime this week. I'd better be there to meet them, or my mother will throw a fit.

KIRSTY: Do you want me to come?

ANDREW: Er, perhaps it might be better if I saw them first.

KIRSTY: Don't you want me there?

ANDREW: Oh, well, er, look, if you'd like to. Fine.

KIRSTY: Please yourself.

ANDREW (*after a pause*): It's just, er, that my mother will probably be a little, er, difficult until I've, er, had a chance to, er, calm her down. She's, er, very emotional at the best of times.

KIRSTY: I would have thought that the sooner we got it over with the better.

ANDREW: All right. If you want to, but I'm warning you that she can make people feel very uncomfortable when she wants to. She really can.

(*There is a loud thumping at the door. ANDREW jumps up, a little startled and runs to open it.*)

That's probably Michael and Carmel now. Have we got something to drink?

KIRSTY: I don't know.

ANDREW: Shit. Nothing is ever organized in this bloody place.

KIRSTY: I wasn't expecting any visitors.

(*ANDREW opens the door. It is HARRY BUSTLE. He utters the first part of his speech unseen from the doorstep.*)

HARRY: Locked doors out here? Christ!

ANDREW (*smiling*): How are you, you bastard?

HARRY (*stepping in*): When I lived out here at the colony, we didn't

Act One

lock our doors. Leave the bloody thing open.
(*He sees* KIRSTY, *moves across and kisses her passionately.* ANDREW *winces in the background.* KIRSTY *is less than overwhelmed.*)
Hello there, gorgeous. Has he been treating you well enough and often enough?

KIRSTY: He's not too bad.

HARRY: Well, if you've got any complaints, come and see me.

KIRSTY (*tongue-in-cheek*): I'll hang on for a little while longer.
(HARRY, *gloriously thick-skinned, doesn't pick up the irony.*)

HARRY: Have you both seen the old colony? (*Pointing*) It's just over there.

ANDREW (*nodding*): Mmm.

HARRY: Incredible place in it's day. No one much of note left up there now, of course. A handful of the old guard and thousands of pseudos. I'm renting out my old mudbrick to—get this—a Yank Professor and his family who're slumming it amongst the arties during his sabbatical. Wants his kids to grow up in a stimulus-rich environment. (*Laughing uproariously*) Get that.

KIRSTY: To develop their creative intelligence.

HARRY: Poor little bastards will suffer permanent retardation, his wife'll get screwed by some junk sculptor who's still learning to use a blowtorch; and he'll get sold some shoddy pottery goblets that'll give him lead poisoning if he's mad enough to drink out of 'em. I love Yanks. They're so fucking stupid. How about getting me a drink?

ANDREW: You've caught me on the hop. There's beer in the fridge, and I think there might be a bit of flagon red.

HARRY: Better stick to the rough red. I'm not allowed to put on weight. My doctor says I've got the blood pressure of a healthy eighty year old.
(ANDREW *goes.* HARRY *turns to* KIRSTY.)
You knew the Penfields, didn't you?

KIRSTY: Yes I did. I had a room in their house for two years when I was a student.

HARRY: The Penfields were forces for good up at the colony. They were the first of the old guard to leave. I'm not sure why.

KIRSTY: I think it all got a bit too much for Mary.

HARRY (*alert*): Did she say that, did she? Mmm. I suppose the bohemian thing got a bit much at times.
(ANDREW *returns carrying a flagon of claret, two-thirds full.*)

ANDREW: I think it's been open a fair while.

HARRY: Really. (*Turning up his nose*) I'll have the beer.

KIRSTY (*as* ANDREW *turns to go again*): I only opened it yesterday.

HARRY (*grabbing the flagon*): That should be drinkable. (*Indicating that he has no glass*) Let's not be too primitive.
(ANDREW *gets a glass from the cabinet.* HARRY *changes it for another one.*)

ANDREW: What brings you out here, Harry?

HARRY: I hate to bother you with business Andy, so I'll only stay a second, but that fuckwitted agent of yours is really driving me right off my brain. Look, I don't expect anyone to lick my arse, but an agent isn't doing his clients a service by shitting off his best customers now, is he? (*As* ANDREW *shakes his head*) I'm not up myself by any means, but I do expect to be treated with a little bit of civility and respect. If I leave a message to call back, people call me back, and they call me back quickly. If they're selling and I'm buying, they maybe pay me the odd compliment now and then. Quite frankly, I've come to the end of the road with that agent of yours, Andy, and unless he starts treating me with the sort of respect I get elsewhere, I'm just not going to do business with him. I have had the contract for that manuscript of yours with him for five weeks. Now you were happy with the terms, weren't you? That's what you told me.

ANDREW: Well, I was. Yes.

HARRY: Right. That's what I thought, so I expected the thing back in a matter of days. After three weeks I do get onto him and he's completely evasive. I ring him up three days ago and he says: "We're still considering the terms." And today I hear on the grapevine that he's considering another offer. Another offer? Is he kidding? I'm not going to beat around the bush. I'm the top of the pork barrel, boy. If I knock a manuscript back, that's the time to go chasing after something else. Do you know anything about this?

ANDREW: Not really.

HARRY: It's Shorthorn and Mulligans, isn't it?

ANDREW: I'm not sure.

HARRY: It's not bloody Chisolms, is it?

ANDREW: I'm not sure.

HARRY: Chisolms? He's got to be joking. Do you know who their publishing editor is? Carmel Scott. Fuck!

ANDREW: What's wrong with her?

HARRY: Look, I know your agent's got to consider all offers, but Chisolms'd have to be the last gasp. He can't seriously consider they'd put up a better deal than I have.

ANDREW: I don't know. I haven't heard the details.

HARRY: Well, you listen to the details by all means. You listen to them, but I'll tell you what, I've got no worries on that score. No worries at all. Distribution and promotion wise we piss on them, and as far as the artistic side of it, if you let Carmel Scott edit you, you'll come out something like Australia's answer to the Bronte sisters.

ANDREW: Chisolms have a good reputation for tactful editing ...

HARRY: Look, I know Carmel from way back. I've fucked her in fact—she used to hang around up at the colony, and in all fairness she used to have some sort of spark; but the word around the industry is that she's gone ratshit. All precious and Gothic. I'll tell you what. You'll never get a film sale if she edits your book. We've had our disagreements over editing but you've got to admit that we're a pretty formidable team when it comes to knocking a

Act One

manuscript into shape. Right? I don't do much more than stand back and yell encouragement but there's some chemistry there, isn't there? A few of my shafts strike the occasional odd spark in the old creative cauldron. (*Tapping* ANDREW's *skull*) Eh? Isn't that right? Eh? Our track record's up there on the board for everyone to see. Right?

(HARRY *has a habit of placing his face close to his target when making strong assertions. He is doing so now.* ANDREW *backs off.*)

ANDREW: I suppose it's just a case of Michael considering every offer.
HARRY: Well, you're the one who has the final say, and remember this also; I wouldn't be surprised if he advises you to take the Chisolms deal against his and your interests.
ANDREW: Why?
HARRY: He hates my guts. It's the homo-hetero thing. Did you know he was queer?
ANDREW: Of course.
HARRY: I shouldn't make sweeping generalizations, but I've never met a poofter who wasn't manipulative, predatory, devious and snaky, and your agent is no exception. Has he ever had a go at you?
ANDREW (*defensive*): No.
HARRY: Just wondering. I saw him clutching your arm very determinedly at that Freddie Hubbard launching last month.
ANDREW (*embarrassed*): He gets a bit inclined to grasp arms when he's been drinking.
HARRY: What do you think, Kirsty? Do you find him devious?
KIRSTY: I rather like him.
HARRY (*shrugging*): I may be wrong.
KIRSTY: He's taken it upon himself to fill in the gaps in Andrew's literary eduction.
HARRY (*laughing*): Yeah?
ANDREW (*indicating a shelf on the bookcase*): Yes, I've got a, er, whole shelf full of Greek translations that he's given me. I haven't had time to read them yet.
HARRY (*looking at them and frowning*): If you want my advice, stay right away from the classics. Your writing power stems from the fact that you're an illiterate.
ANDREW: Thanks.
HARRY: I mean it. You go fucking around with the Greeks, and before you know it you'll be reading Proust and writing like a turd. There's a little bit of limpness crept into this latest manuscript that I'm a little worried about.
ANDREW (*sharply*): Where?
HARRY: The centre section lags and the end needs an explosion or two.
KIRSTY: I think the end's fine.
HARRY: Oh, it's all there. It's all there. These are only minor points.
KIRSTY: I don't think the centre lags either.

HARRY: A bit too much time spent elaborating on the women.
KIRSTY: It's needed. Otherwise they become stereotypes.
HARRY: Look, let's face it, honey. We're writing a book and not a propaganda treatise. You want your man to write them how you'd like them. I'd like him to write them how they are.
KIRSTY: There's an awful lot of women who aren't stereotypes and it's about time he started writing about *them*.
HARRY: You might have a point. (*Nodding*) You might have a point, but in this case the main narrative drive is with the men, and that centre section tends to dissipate the line of development.
KIRSTY: But if you're talking about ...
HARRY: Look, we'll thrash these things out once we start working on it. (*To* ANDREW) Can I get you to tell O'Hearn that either the deal goes through in a couple of days or forget it? I've already spent one hell of a lot of money and time setting up the machinery and I can't afford to be fucked around any longer.

(HARRY *drains his glass and turns to go.* ANDREW *gets up to accompany him to the door.* HARRY *turns to him.*)

And just remember, Andy, O'Hearn's only your agent. Whatever he says you've got the final word.

(HARRY *stops on his way to the door to examine some of the reproductions.* ANDREW, *who wants him out as quickly as possible, continues toward the door. He looks wryly at* KIRSTY *behind* BUSTLE's *back.*)

I like this place. Who designed it?
KIRSTY: I did.
HARRY: Hmmm.

(*He turns to go. There is a knock at the door. Before* ANDREW *can open it,* MICHAEL *and* CARMEL *let themselves in.*)

CARMEL: Hello, Andrew. Sorry we are late.
ANDREW: Oh, er, Carmel, this is Kirsty.
CARMEL: Hello, Kirsty.
ANDREW: And, er, you've met Harry, I suppose.
HARRY: We have indeed. Hello Carmel.
CARMEL: Hello, Harry.
ANDREW: Well, er, go and warm yourselves by the fire.
HARRY: Hello, Michael.
MICHAEL: Hello, Harry.
ANDREW: Kirsty will get you both a drink.

(MICHAEL *gives* KIRSTY *a polite but affectionate kiss.*)

KIRSTY: I can only offer you claret or beer, I'm afraid.
ANDREW: Sorry about that. I must remember to stock up.
HARRY: You must remember to stock up.
MICHAEL: I might just have a small claret.
CARMEL: Same here.

(ANDREW *stays near the door hoping* HARRY *will leave.* HARRY, *however, starts up a conversation with* CARMEL *and crosses back to the fire with her as it continues.*)

HARRY (*to* CARMEL): It's a long time now since our paths have crossed. How's Sydney?

CARMEL: Fine. I like it a lot.
HARRY: Who are you mixing with up there these days? The Balmain laundromat push?
CARMEL: No, I'm really leading quite a quiet life.
(KIRSTY *pours two clarets.*)
How's your family, Harry? I've been hearing good reports of young Alan.
HARRY (*pricking up his ears*): Really?
CARMEL: He's evidently taking to the publishing game like a duck to water. Like father like son.
HARRY: Just so long as he doesn't get too smart. I've got enough competition already.
CARMEL (*ignoring the jibe*): Someone told me that he's been going steady with a girl in the ABC for over two years.
HARRY (*nodding and grimacing*): Yeah.
ANDREW: It's a reaction against his father.
HARRY: It is too. A couple of years ago we had a party at home, and I had a gorgeous young dancer lined up. Quite stupid—apologies to you feminists—but very rootable. Half way through the night she disappeared upstairs, so I went up to find her and, given the sound effects, I pretty quickly came to realize that I'd been beaten to the gun. I hung around out of curiosity and who should come out but Alan. Seventeen he was. Nowadays if I start to talk sex openly in front of him he gets hostile. Silly little prick says he's in love.
CARMEL: Maybe he is.
HARRY: Maybe he is. I don't know. I've been in love myself three times in my life, and do you know a curious thing? Each time it lasted exactly nine months. Oh, the actual relationship lasted longer, but the wham-wham-wham stuff only lasted nine months. Don't you think that's curious? Maybe nature only programmed the love thing to last as long as a pregnancy.
MICHAEL (*with an edge of derision*): Your personal experiences are hardly enough evidence to go building a theory on, Harry.
HARRY (*also with an edge in his voice*): Maybe not.
CARMEL: It all depends on your age, I think. I used to fall in and out of love with incredible speed when I was younger.
HARRY: Yes, I must admit you'd hardly be strong support for my theory in the old days. You had the hottest pair of pants in the colony. (*Laughing*) I've heard that you've slowed down a bit now.
CARMEL (*embarrassed*): The basic sex drive gets a little less insistent as you get older, I suppose.
HARRY: Hasn't been my experience, but still.
CARMEL: No, it wouldn't be.
HARRY: How about moving that flagon in this direction? (*After a pause*) Didn't I hear you were living with someone?
CARMEL (*embarrassed*): Yes, I am.
HARRY: A young journo or something.
CARMEL: That's right.
HARRY: For how long?

CARMEL: Two years.
HARRY: Really, Hmm?
CARMEL: Over two years.
HARRY: And it's all there?
MICHAEL: What is this? An inquisition?
HARRY (*to CARMEL, ignoring him*): Well that's good. That's fine. (GUNTER *struggles through the doorway carrying two huge suitcases. They notice him. He stops.*)
GUNTER (*nervously*): Andrew Collins?
CARMEL: House guest?
ANDREW: Not to my knowledge.
GUNTER (*louder*): I am looking for Andrew Collins.
ANDREW (*frowning and looking at KIRSTY*): That's right. (IRENE, ANDREW's *mother, enters, closely followed by his father,* KEN. IRENE *is overweight but still has attractive features. She is expensively but a trifle garishly dressed. She is irritable and tired.* KEN *is an upright, tall, dignified man with craggy features and greying hair. It is important to note that despite the surface malice of the dialogue between* KEN *and* IRENE, *there is an obvious affection and concern for each other under much of it.*)
IRENE (*to ANDREW, curtly*): Don't you read our letters?
ANDREW (*confused*): Oh, er, hello Mum. Did you just arrive?
IRENE (*tartly sarcastic*): No. We're still on the ship.
ANDREW: Hello Dad. I didn't expect you both till next week. (KEN *has been frowning at the architecture.*)
KEN: Hello son.
IRENE (*accusingly*): Well. Are you pleased to see us or aren't you?
ANDREW (*jolting out of his stupor and moving towards them*): It's great to see you both ... (*kissing his mother on the cheek*) looking so well.
IRENE: Well? I'm not well, and neither's your father. He had a turn just out of Bangkok.
KEN: Don't start that straight away, Irene.
ANDREW: Mum, this is Kirsty. The girl I wrote to you about. Do you remember?
IRENE: Yes, I do. (*With a frozen smile*) How are you Kirsty?
KIRSTY: I'm very pleased to meet you, Mrs. Collins. Andrew's told me a lot about you.
IRENE (*grimly*): I could tell you a lot about him, too.
KIRSTY (*to KEN*): Did you have a good voyage, Mr. Collins?
KEN: Quite good. Quite good. I don't think I'd travel on an Italian line again but, er, quite good.
ANDREW (*to IRENE*): A good voyage back was it?
IRENE: It was fine until we docked and found ourselves the only ones on board who weren't met. Edith Marshall was on the same ship and her son Ronald came down from Alice Springs to meet her. "You're lucky," I said. "Mine couldn't even get off his bum and come thirty miles."
KEN: Be fair, Irene. The ship was seven hours early.
IRENE (*angrily*): He could've rung. It's not too much trouble to pick

up a telephone. (*Turning to* GUNTER) This is Graeme. He had a little bit of trouble on the ship, so we're looking after him for a while.
ANDREW: Oh, er, hello Graeme. Er, Mum and Dad, I'd like you to meet Michael O'Hearn my agent, Harry Bustle the publisher who you've no doubt heard about, and Carmel Scott, who's also in publishing.
(KEN *shakes hands with them in turn. A short embarrassed pause.*)
GUNTER: I'll get the other cases, Mrs. Collins.
(*He leaves.*)
HARRY: Don't know about anybody else but I'm busting for a leak.
(*He exits.* KEN *is still looking at the house.*)
ANDREW: Like the house? (*after a pause*) Kirsty designed it.
KEN (*lying*): Looks very nice. Did you, er, do some of the carpentry yourself?
ANDREW (*puzzled*): No.
KEN: Oh. Are those sort of rough joints the fashion now?
KIRSTY (*laughing*): Yes. Everything's getting back to the raw and primitive.
KEN: Yes. Workmanship's a thing of the past these days. Working in wood was my hobby for many years.
KIRSTY: Yes, Andrew's told me.
KEN: It's all a matter of pride, I suppose. I'd spend up to three hours on a dovetail joint and if I wasn't satisf—
IRENE: Shut up about your damn joints. Everywhere we go it's your damn joints. You bore everyone silly.
KEN: I'm not boring anyone silly. All I'm doing is remarking that I can't understand how a professional carpenter can allow himself to do shoddy work.
IRENE: Because they've got to make a living. That's why.
(KEN, *as is his habit, refuses to be budged once he is in an argumentative frame of mind.*)
KEN: People should be prepared to pay a little extra for the satisfaction of a good joint.
IRENE (*losing patience with him and turning to* ANDREW): I want you to look after Graeme, Andrew. He's had a very bad time. He was bringing his fiancée out here to get married and she ran off with an Italian purser on the ship.
KEN: People pay for quality in other things. Why not in carpentry?
IRENE (*to* KEN, *sharply*): Shut up. (*To* ANDREW) I could see it coming a mile off, actually. Couldn't keep her eyes off those Italian officers from the moment she got on board the ship. A real little sexpot.
KEN (*to* IRENE): Don't tell me to shut up. Always telling me to shut up. I'll say what I think. Be damned to you, woman.
IRENE (*ignoring him, to* ANDREW): He's still very upset, so I'd like you to look after him.
KEN (*at the billiard table*): Nice table, son. Now that's a good piece of carpentry.

ANDREW: Yes. I made it. What do you mean, look after him?
IRENE: He's new in the country and he hasn't got anywhere to stay.
ANDREW: He can't stay here.
IRENE: He's got nowhere else to go. Besides, you're a doctor. You can give him sedatives and things.
ANDREW: It's not just my house. It's Kirsty's too.
KIRSTY: I suppose we could find room.
IRENE: You can give him tablets and things to calm him down.
ANDREW: Christ, I'm only a physician, not a bloody psychiatrist.
KEN: Have you given up practice for good, son?
IRENE: Yes, well we can't have him. We've decided to shift from Brooksbank into somewhere nearer the city, and we won't have any room.
KEN: Your mother's always the same. Picks up these lame dogs then tries to foist them on someone else.

(GUNTER *comes in through the door carrying another two large cases.*)

KIRSTY: Would you like something to drink? There's claret and plenty of beer in the fridge.
KEN: Actually I wouldn't mind a cup of tea.
KIRSTY: I suppose you're hungry. Would you like something to eat?
KEN: No. I'm right thanks.
IRENE: I certainly wouldn't mind something. We were four hours getting through customs.
KIRSTY: I'll make you a Capricciosa.

(GUNTER *leaves.*)

IRENE: You wouldn't have something plain, would you? We've had six weeks of Italian stuff.
KIRSTY: It'll be nothing very fancy. It just means everything I can get my hands on tossed into one pan.
IRENE: Thank you, but I think I'd rather have steak.
KIRSTY: I'm sorry. I'm afraid I haven't any. I haven't done the weekend shopping yet.
IRENE: I wouldn't mind normally, but it's just that we've been having so much Italian stuff we're fed up to the back teeth with it.
KIRSTY: I'm sorry, but I'm afraid we haven't got anything but a bit of pasta and bolognaise. Would you like a little of that, Mr. Collins?
KEN: Sounds fine.
KIRSTY: Would you like to try just a little bit, Mrs. Collins?
IRENE: I think I'll just settle for a cup of tea.
KIRSTY: Are you sure?
IRENE (*smiling falsely*): I should be watching my figure in any case.

(KIRSTY *goes to the kitchen.*)

KEN: Well it's not going to help your figure if you die of starvation. Have something to eat and don't be bloody silly.
IRENE (*tensely emotional*): I'm not all that hungry.
KEN: Well, you just said you were.
IRENE: I'm not all that hungry.
KEN: Don't be so bloody stubborn.

IRENE: Will you just shut up!
(GUNTER *comes in carrying two more suitcases, to fill an awkward silence.*)
IRENE (*to* ANDREW): Would you pour Graeme a beer.
ANDREW: Right. Just a second.
(*He goes to the kitchen.*)
GUNTER: No, please. I am not feeling thirsty.
IRENE (*to* ANDREW): He always refuses at first. He's too polite.
GUNTER: No, please. Really.
(ANDREW *emerges with a bottle of beer, which he opens.*)
No. Please, really. I am not yet thirsty.
IRENE (*to* ANDREW): He's just being polite.
(ANDREW *has a glass but hesitates to pour it.*)
KEN (*irritably*): If the lad doesn't want any, he doesn't want any.
IRENE: Rot! Every time I poured one for him on the ship he soon drank it.
ANDREW (*to* GUNTER): A claret, perhaps?
GUNTER (*embarrassed*): Later, perhaps. I will get those other cases.
(*He leaves. It is a hurried escape.*)
KEN (*irritably*): I wish you'd damn well let people make up their own minds for a change.
(*There is an awkward pause.* HARRY *enters.*)
HARRY (*to* KEN *and* IRENE): How long have you been away?
KEN (*brightening*): Oh, er, over fifteen months now, Mr. Bustle.
HARRY: Harry, for heaven's sake. Fifteen months. A lot's happened to your boy since you've been away.
IRENE (*blackly*): It certainly has.
HARRY: I suppose you realize that he's the sensation of the Australian publishing industry.
KEN: Yes. He certainly seems to have become, er, quite well known since we left. (*To* ANDREW) Have you given away your medicine completely, son?
ANDREW: Mmm.
KEN: I mean you had a secure income at the clinic. Is there a good living in writing in this country these days?
HARRY: Only if you're right at the top, Mr. Collins, and that's where your boy is!
ANDREW (*embarrassed*): Now come on, Harry—
HARRY (*to* KEN): I've just concluded a big international film sale on the rights to Andrew's last novel, Mr. Collins, and I won't mention the sum involved because it's positively indecent—
(KIRSTY *enters to get a pot from the shelf.*)
ANDREW (*embarrassed*): Most of it's going to go to the tax man in any case.
HARRY: Let's just put it this way. He'd have to hand out a lot of prescriptions to make as much as he's making this way. I'm not patting myself on the back, but I've made him a pretty hot property.
(KIRSTY *returns to the kitchen.*)
IRENE (*looking to the kitchen*): So it seems.

MICHAEL: Sometimes I think you really believe your own PR department, Bustle. You didn't show a glimmer of interest in the first manuscript until three other publishers were negotiating for an option.

HARRY: I don't stand up and do handsprings until the moment's right, O'Hearn. (*To* IRENE *and* KEN) A really hot property. In fact, if I can ever pin Michael down for long enough to get him to sign the contract, I'm about to clinch a deal which will get Andrew a simultaneous publication in London, New York and Sydney. First time ever in Australian publishing history.

KEN: That's—

HARRY (*nodding*): That's pretty incredible, don't you think? Mind you, it couldn't be done as late as two years ago, and when I first broached it in London, the Brits sneered in their cufflinks. Shitarses! If ever you want to cure the world of arrogance in one hit, drop a bloody bomb in London.

MICHAEL: Or your office.

KEN: We read a big article on you while we were in London. They describe you as the Aussie buccaneer of publishing.

HARRY (*alert*): I haven't seen that one. What was the tone of it?

KEN: Oh, it was very complimentary as I remember it.

HARRY: A bit flippant, pouring shit on me?

KEN: No. It said you had enormous energy and drive, if I remember correctly.

HARRY (*sourly*): Yeah, well that's a sly Pom way of pouring shit on you too. They think lassitude and indolence are the mark of a superior civilization. Can you remember what you read it in?

KEN: It was a magazine of some sort.

HARRY: You wouldn't've kept it by any chance?

KEN: We might've put it away in a case somewhere.

(GUNTER *comes in carrying another two cases. He leaves again immediately.*)

HARRY: Glossy cover job?

KEN: Yes it was.

IRENE: You read it in a doctor's surgery.

KEN: No I didn't. I think it might be in one of the cases.

HARRY: Well, if you do find it I'd like to have a look at it. You've got to keep up with what they're saying about you or you might be accidentally polite to some journalist you should have punched in the teeth.

CARMEL: Andrew—

IRENE (*to* ANDREW): Are we going to get a chance to have a few words with you tonight, or are we not?

ANDREW: Can it wait till the morning? I've got a bit of business to discuss tonight.

KEN: Of course. Your mother's tired and I am too. We'll be off to bed.

IRENE: For heaven's sake. We've just arrived. If he can't spend a bit of time with us on our first night home, then we may as well not be his parents.

HARRY: Look. I can save anything I want to say until tomorrow. You talk to your parents, Andrew. *(To* MICHAEL) If we could slip back to the city, Mike, perhaps we could finalize the deal tonight and Andrew could sign in the morning.

MICHAEL: We haven't decided whether we're accepting your offer, Harry.

(There is a long pause. HARRY *looks incredulous.)*

HARRY: Not accepting?

MICHAEL: Chisolms have submitted another offer.

(HARRY *looks at* CARMEL *in mock disbelief.)*

HARRY: Chisolms? An alternative offer? Are we talking about Andrew's new manuscript?

MICHAEL: That's right.

HARRY: Are we talking about Andrew's new manuscript which you have verbally assured me several times I am to handle?

MICHAEL: Don't carry on like a prize turd, Harry.

(HARRY *looks at* MICHAEL *for a second or two, still with an expression of disbelief.* KEN *moves off to toilet area.)*

HARRY *(with his face close to* MICHAEL's): You'd better have some sort of explanation for this, O'Hearn. I don't really expect you to exhibit integrity, but I draw the line at straight out treachery.

MICHAEL *(moving away with a look of distaste)*: If you don't mind.

HARRY: What?

MICHAEL: Don't breathe on me.

HARRY *(temporarily dropping belligerence for a tone of enquiry)*: Why? Have I got bad breath or something?

MICHAEL: I just object to you thrusting your head two inches from my face and shouting.

HARRY *(moving close again)*: For Christ's sake, man. I'm giving your boy a simultaneous release in London and New York. Chisolms'll be lucky to get you a release in Toowoomba. What kind of game are you playing?

CARMEL *(angrily)*: Don't be so bloody childish, Harry. We might not go in for gimmicky stunts, but we've got a very efficient distribution system.

HARRY *(wildly turning on her)*: It's all very well to use words like gimmicky. The media just loves writing me off with a few cutesy little adjectives now that I've done the very thing that three years ago their feature writers were saying was impossible. I'm just getting sick of the whole bloody deal. A man tries to build this country a cultural identity. Rips years off his life fostering the talent he damn well knows is here. Shoves it down the throats of the Brits and the Yanks and makes them acknowledge it and gets shit poured on him in his own country by paranoid little cretins who never made it themselves. I'm getting out of this deal and buying myself a farm. Fuck the lot of you. *(To* MICHAEL) A New York-London release means nothing to you obviously; because there's one thing I do know, and it's that Chisolms won't get you that.

MICHAEL: We can't be absolutely sure that you will either, Harry.

HARRY: Now come on! That's just plain bastardry. I've showed you every cable and all the correspondence.

MICHAEL: There's nothing signed. They could still get cold feet. It only needs a slight dip in the Dow Jones Index.

HARRY (*with his face close to* MICHAEL's): Listen, you little viper. Don't fuck around with me. If I tell you I'll do something, I do it. (*To* ANDREW) It's your decision ultimately, but just let me go on record right here and now as saying I will never again deal with this excuse for an agent in my life. And let me tell you another thing. I am not leaving here tonight until I get a definite decision one way or another. I've got too much at stake, so I'm going to walk outside the door, walk down that drive, and when you've listened to it all, and come to some decision, call me.

(*He goes to walk outside but returns to collect the wine flagon, which is still nearly half full.* GUNTER *returns with two more suitcases.*)

Does anyone want this?

ANDREW: No. Help yourself.

(HARRY *turns to go again, clutching his flagon, but turns back at the last moment.*)

HARRY (*to* ANDREW): I don't want to use a word like loyalty, Andrew. There's no such thing in this game, but shit! We've done a lot together. You think about it. We've done a lot together. I've made money from you. Sure. But I've contributed to your success and I've taken risks. (*Moving close to* MICHAEL) The only risk O'Hearn ever takes is that he might have a bad hangover one morning and forget to deduct his ten percent.

MICHAEL (*moving away from* HARRY's *close-thrust face*): You have got bad breath actually.

HARRY (*losing his cool, loud*): I don't often resort to physical violence, O'Hearn, but I don't take shit from anyone, and I don't intend taking it from you, so don't push me. Right?

MICHAEL: When's the last time you saw your dentist?

(HARRY *grabs him by the throat in a flurry and shoves him towards the door.* ANDREW *leaps in and separates them. The noise wakes the children upstairs.*)

ANDREW: That's enough, Harry. Now just piss off outside for a while.

HARRY (*to* ANDREW): I mean it, Andy. I'm never dealing with that smartarse little ... poofter, again.

MICHAEL: I wondered how long it would be before you brought that up.

HARRY (*as he goes*): Well, you're all so fucking proud of it these days I'm surprised you find the term offensive. (*As* ANDREW *ejects him*) The worst sin you can commit these days is to be white, male and hetero-fucking-sexual.

(*The children are making quite a deal of noise now. As* KEN *enters, the trapdoor opens from above and a tin clatters to the floor. It narrowly misses* KEN, *who jumps. The trapdoor closes. The noise from above continues.*)

Act One

KEN: My God. That only missed me by a whisker.
ANDREW (*yelling*): Sean! Sean!
  (*There is no answer.*)
  If you don't look before you drop that thing, we'll stop the whole business altogether. (*To* KEN) It's his message tin.
  (ANDREW *opens the tin and extracts a piece of paper on which the message is written. He reads it, puts the note down with a frown and starts climbing to the children's room, from which noise is still emanating.*)
KIRSTY (*off*): Would you attend to those children, Andrew.
ANDREW I am. (*Disappearing*) Now just what are you doing? I warned you, didn't I?
CARMEL: Don't worry, Mrs. Collins. All children carry on like that nowadays.
  (KIRSTY *enters.*)
KIRSTY: Do you both have milk in your tea?
IRENE: Mr. Collins has milk but no sugar and I have black tea with no sugar and a slice of lemon.
KIRSTY: No lemon, I'm afraid.
IRENE (*mock pleasantly*): Every household should have a lemon. Cook's first rule.
KEN: Take what you're given. Guest's first rule.
  (IRENE *glares at him.*)
KIRSTY (*going to kitchen*): One milk, no sugars.
GUNTER: All the cases are in now, Mrs. Collins.
IRENE: Thank you, Graeme.
KIRSTY (*off*): What nationality are you, Graeme?
GUNTER: Oh, er, I come from Norway.
KIRSTY: That's a strange name for a Norseman.
IRENE: It's his Australian name.
KIRSTY: Oh. What's your real name?
GUNTER (*looking at* IRENE, *embarrassed*): Oh, er, Gunter.
KIRSTY (*off*): Would you like some food and something to drink.
GUNTER: Have you got some coffee?
KIRSTY (*off*): Instant.
GUNTER: Fine.
KIRSTY (*off*): Would you like to come out here and pour it? I've got my hands full.
GUNTER (*looking nervously at* IRENE): Yes. Thank you. Of course.
  (*He goes out into the kitchen.* CARMEL *and* MICHAEL *have retreated to a couch at the back of the room and are discussing business. They have both produced documents.* IRENE *picks up the note that was in the message tin and reads it. She looks at* KEN.)
IRENE (*reading*): "If you ever hit me again my Dad'll come with an axe and split your head and jump on your brains." That's lovely, isn't it?
KEN: Bound to be a bit of friction.
  (ANDREW *descends the ladder carrying a huge box of children's plastic building blocks. At the same time,* HARRY *returns and*

makes a bee line for MICHAEL. *He is still carrying the flagon by its neck. The trap door opens and more bricks are hurled down.*)

HARRY (*to* MICHAEL): Just one thing, boy. Just one thing. I have a copy of a letter which I sent to you confirming your telephone offer, a letter to which you did not reply, which in any court of law represents a tacit acknowledgement of the truth of my letter. If you go ahead with this deal I'll sue for breach of contract.

MICHAEL: Look, don't try and bluff me, Bustle. (*To* ANDREW) Can Carmel and I go somewhere quiet so we can thrash out the proposal?

ANDREW: Sure. Go down to the end room.

(*They go.*)

HARRY (*to* ANDREW): It's all right for him to pass it off as bluff, but you're the one who gets it in the neck if I do go ahead and sue.

ANDREW: What letter are you talking about?

HARRY: When he first read the manuscript, O'Hearn rang me up and offered it to me. I wrote back straight away accepting and he didn't reply. A court could very well rule that there was the basis of an implied contract.

KEN: Make sure there are no legal complications, son. You can very easy get yourself into some awful tangles.

HARRY: I don't want to get Andy into any kind of hassle, Mr. Collins, believe me. It's that damn agent of his. Have you had some experience with the law?

KEN: Not directly. I was in Insurance, but I often had dealings with our legal department.

HARRY: Well, you'd know exactly what I'm talking about. Could you try and point out to him the sort of risks his agent is leaving him open to?

(*He leaves, still carrying the flagon.*)

KEN: The legal side is very important, son.

ANDREW: I know.

KEN: Do you think you've done the right thing, son?

ANDREW: I think so, Dad.

KEN: What about your house and car and furniture?

ANDREW: Meredith gets that.

KEN: All of it?

ANDREW: Yep.

KEN: That's ten years' work.

ANDREW: Yep.

IRENE: Stop saying yep.

KEN: What about Robin and Mark?

ANDREW: I'm paying maintenance.

KEN: That's all very well, but what if something happened to you, son? What if you died tomorrow? Where would they be then? You'd better let me fix up an insurance cover for you.

ANDREW: Right.

KEN: What about Kirsty's children, are they covered?

IRENE: Damn Kirsty's children. It's his own children he should be worrying about.

Act One

KEN: If he's taken on a new responsibility, then he'll have to cover that as well.
IRENE: They've got their own father.
KEN: Are they covered, son?
ANDREW (*irritated*): I don't know.
KEN: We'd better take out a short term fixed insurance till we find out, and back it with a big whole of life.
(KIRSTY *enters carrying the tea and* GUNTER *carries the coffee.*)
GUNTER (*looking at the paintings*): Botticelli da Firenze.
KIRSTY: Piace Firenze?
GUNTER: Non so perchè non ho vista. Ma credo è una città bellissima, è vero?
KIRSTY: Si, è vero. Sono stata in Firenze per due anni una volta. Non in Firenze esattamente, ma in Settignano nelle colle sopra.
GUNTER: Che cos'ha fatto per due anni in Firenze?
KIRSTY: Hanno una borsa di studio all'Università. Ho fatto l'architettura, l'arte, la politica e la musica. Tutte insieme.
(*She laughs.* ANDREW *tips the bricks out of the box and starts building with them.* KIRSTY *turns to* KEN.)
I hope you're very hungry. It's not exactly a gourmet dish.
KEN (*enthusiastically*): Looks pretty good to me.
(*He starts to eat it.* KIRSTY *puts down the cups of tea within reach of* IRENE *and* KEN. IRENE *looks enviously at* KEN *who is obviously enjoying the food.*)
KIRSTY: Have you travelled a lot?
GUNTER: No, I've never been out of my country before. Not even to Sweden.
KIRSTY: Where did you learn the languages?
GUNTER: At school. English was compulsory, and Italian was my choice. (*Looking at the paintings*) I admire always Italian art. It is so disappointing to find the real Italians are so vulgar.
KIRSTY: Australians can be pretty vulgar too.
GUNTER: So I am noticing.
KEN: If this is just thrown together, I wouldn't mind one of your carefully prepared meals.
KIRSTY: I lived on pasta for a year once.
KEN: Where?
KIRSTY: In Italy. I was a student at Florence University.
KEN: We visited Florence. Didn't we Irene?
IRENE: Yes.
KEN: Fine old buildings, but not very well kept. In fact the whole of Europe struck me as rather grubby. Didn't you think so Irene?
IRENE: Filthy. Absolutely filthy.
KEN: We had a good guide in Florence. Spoke quite good English. He was really quite funny, wasn't he Irene?
IRENE (*irritated*): I suppose so.
KEN: When we stopped in front of the statue of David he said that Michelangelo's grasp of anatomy was perfect except for the head which was too big, and another part of the anatomy which was too small.

(KEN *laughs heartily.* KIRSTY *smiles politely.* IRENE *glowers.* ANDREW *looks up from his building and winces.* KEN *is encouraged by* KIRSTY*'s reaction to try a joke of his own.*)
I must admit there wasn't much for him to be big-headed about. (*Chuckling*) Was there Irene?
(*She remains grim-faced.*)
I rather liked Italy.

IRENE: I don't really think Graeme wants to hear about Italy at the moment.

KEN: No, I don't suppose he does. I'm sorry Graeme.

KIRSTY (*to* GUNTER): You'll find the landscape here very different from Europe. Would you like to see some Australian bush? You can see for miles from the slope outside.

GUNTER (*glad of the escape*): Yes, I would.

KIRSTY: It's really quite a dry, hot country in summer. And the trees will probably seem rather tough and gnarled, but they've got a strength that you get fond of after a while.

ANDREW (*still building*): Isn't it a bit dark out there?

KIRSTY (*as she goes*): We won't go far down the hill. Besides, there's a full moon.

(*They exit.*)

IRENE (*to* ANDREW, *after a pause*): Your father wants a word with you.
(KEN *looks embarrassed.* ANDREW *keeps building his structure.*)
Stop fiddling with those damn blocks!
(ANDREW *keeps building.*)
Your father had a turn on the ship you know.
(ANDREW *stops building and looks up.*)

KEN: It wasn't really a turn, Irene.

IRENE: Your heart raced like a steam engine all night. I know it did. (*As* ANDREW *resumes building*) That letter was a great shock to us both. Stop fiddling with those damn blocks!
(ANDREW *stops. There is a pause.*)

KEN: Do you think you've done the right thing, son?

ANDREW: I think so.

IRENE: What's behind it all? Sex?

ANDREW: Partly.

IRENE: Well, I hope that you can explain that to your children when they're old enough to know why you walked out on them.

KEN: Cut it out, Irene.

IRENE (*emotionally*): Well, it's pretty weak, that's all I can say. Pretty weak when a man leaves his children simply because he isn't getting enough of what he wants in bed. You ought to be horsewhipped!

KEN: He didn't say it was the only reason.

IRENE: I know what Meredith had to go through. You don't, but I do. I've got her letters right here.

KEN: What letters?

IRENE: Never mind.

KEN: What letters are you talking about?

IRENE: Never mind. She wrote to me when it happened. (*Weeping*) I didn't show you. It would've killed you. Killed you.
KEN: What would've killed me?
IRENE: Two days before they were married he took some girl up to a house in the mountains and spent the weekend with her. It would've killed you.
KEN: That's a bit much, son.
IRENE (*emotionally*): I know a lot more besides that. A lot more.
KEN: I don't want to hear it.
IRENE: I wouldn't tell you. I wouldn't tell anyone. Meredith walked into his surgery and found him having relations with a seventeen year old patient. It would've killed you.
KEN: It probably would've.
IRENE: She could've had him struck off the register.
KEN: That's a bit much, son.
ANDREW: She was nineteen and she was my receptionist.
IRENE: Does that make it any better?
ANDREW: No. I would've preferred the seventeen year old.
IRENE: Listen to him. Listen to him. He just thinks it's all one big joke. You just get back to your family right away while Meredith will still have you. Your father and I had problems, but he didn't leave me.
KEN: That's got nothing to do with it.
IRENE: He wouldn't walk out and leave you without a father. He had some sense of responsibility.
KEN: That has got nothing to do with it.
IRENE: You just get back to Meredith straight away.
ANDREW (*still building*): Shut up!
(IRENE *moves across in a fury and tweaks his ear viciously. She grits her teeth and appears to obtain some gratification from the action.*)
IRENE: Don't you tell your mother to shut up. Don't you dare tell your mother to shut up.
(ANDREW *grimaces in pain and looks sourly resigned. He keeps building.*)
Get back to your children.
ANDREW: Get to hell!
IRENE (*letting go his ear*): Don't you tell me to get to hell. I know what's going on around here. (*Producing the note from the message tin*) Split your head with an axe. These children don't want you, that's obvious.
KEN: It's probably a bit hard for them to understand.
IRENE: Yes, well it's a bit hard for me to understand too. (*To* ANDREW) I've been on this earth longer than you have, my boy, and I'll tell you one thing. Sex isn't everything. Sex doesn't plan ahead and make sure there's always something in those kitchen cupboards. Sex doesn't take a pride in the place and make sure it isn't looking like a pigsty. Sex doesn't—
ANDREW (*loudly*): Are you obsessed with sex or something? It's all you bloody well ever talk about. I can remember when I first

started taking girls out I'd come home and you'd be sitting up waiting for me in a pink dressing gown with your teeth out and your hair in rollers, howling wild accusations at me through your gums.

KEN: It was your mother's troubled time, Andrew.

ANDREW: It was mine too. Christ. At least most mothers had the decency to divert their Oedipal hangups into something constructive like bottling fruit or baking scones. I got the bloody lot. What kind of sex life did you two have?

IRENE: Don't you dare ask your mother questions like that.

ANDREW: What kind of sex life did you have?

KEN (*embarrassed*): Your mother had a, er, medical problem, son. It made things very difficult.

IRENE (*emotionally*): Yes, and your father didn't walk out and leave us both. He didn't take the easy way out!

ANDREW: What in the hell was wrong?

KEN (*embarrassed*): Well the, er, doctor said it was, er, sort of mental thing.

IRENE: I wasn't mental. That was nothing to do with it. There was something wrong and it wasn't my fault.

KEN: I didn't say you were mental. I said it had mental origins.

IRENE: There was something wrong with my nerves.

ANDREW: For Christ's sake. What were the symptoms?

KEN: Your mother got, er, very tense. In, er, her middle regions.

ANDREW: Dyspareunia.

KEN: Dys ... what?

ANDREW: Dyspareunia. (*Quoting*) "A contraction of the vaginal musculature making penile penetration difficult if not impossible. Almost certainly due to psychological causes." Christ, how long did this go on?

IRENE: Ever since I was married. There was something wrong with my nerves.

ANDREW (*throwing blocks at random targets around room*): Christ. Why me? Piss off, you mad old crone, and stop bothering the shit out of me.

IRENE (*to* KEN): I told you he needed a break.

KEN (*his memory jolted*): Oh, er, how about us getting away from all this, son? Would you like to come fishing with me up the Murray for a week or two? Might get onto a big cod. Give your mind a chance to settle down.

ANDREW: Thanks, Dad.

KEN: We've got that caravan sitting around not being used. We could take that.

IRENE (*still emotional*): We bought presents for those children of yours in every country we visited. Where's the pleasure now?

KEN: We mightn't get onto a cod but there's sure to be no shortage of redfin.

ANDREW: Thanks very much, Dad, but I'm really pretty pushed for time right at the present.

KEN: Remember when we went right up to the red cliffs and caught

a sugarbag full in three hours? The red clay of the cliffs, the deep greens of the river and the swallows flying inches from the surface. Do you remember that?
ANDREW: Yes I do.
(*The children wake up and start making a noise.*)
KEN: We wouldn't catch them like that these days, son. That was a freak year in times of plenty.
ANDREW: We ate five of them and had to bury the rest. There's a moral there somewhere.
KEN: There is. There is. We've raped this country. Mainly in ignorance, admittedly, but we've raped it none the less.
IRENE (*still emotional*): We can't talk to anyone these days without him getting into an argument.
(*The noise from the children increases.*)
ANDREW: I'd better go and see to those kids.
IRENE (*half-tearful*): I'll go and attend to them. They sound like they could do with some discipline.
(IRENE *starts to climb the stairs to the loft. The noise stops.*)
KEN: Don't underestimate your mother, Andrew. She's got her faults but the household always ran like clockwork, and she made every sacrifice for you.
ANDREW: Mum said something about you both shifting from Brooksbank.
KEN: Yes. We, er, decided on the trip home.
ANDREW: Why, for Christ's sake? It's absolutely beautiful out there.
KEN (*embarrassed*): We feel we should be closer in.
ANDREW: Closer in?
KEN: We're both getting on, you know.
ANDREW: What's that got to do with it?
KEN: We need to be near all the amenities.
ANDREW: What amenities?
KEN: Shops and things.
ANDREW (*incredulous*): You're trying to tell me that you want to sell that beautiful bit of forest so that you can be near the shops?
KEN: And a hospital.
ANDREW: A hospital?
KEN: My heart's not the best, son. I'm a year older than my father was when he died.
ANDREW: You're on the phone.
KEN: I was sitting next to him when it happened. One minute he was sitting there laughing, and drinking a brandy. Next minute, he was dead. It's something that stays with you.
ANDREW: When are you moving out?
KEN: As soon as we can find a buyer.
ANDREW: What about all your plants and shrubs?
KEN: Somebody else will enjoy them. I've had a lot of pleasure from building a few pieces of furniture and watching a few hundred trees and shrubs grow. I gave most of the furniture away because your mother didn't like it. But somebody's got it, and the trees will

still be there when we leave. Oh, we got a note from our neighbour about those shrubs you planted.
ANDREW: Oh my God. I must get them out before you move.
KEN: He said they looked like weeds so he pulled them out and burned them.
ANDREW: Burned them?
KEN: Yes. He felt dizzy for two days after. I'd check your nursery man if I were you.

(*He walks off to the back room to sleep, shoulders bent and tired. ANDREW watches him go, then sits there building his structure. The shape is beginning to become clinically correct, but is as yet a long way from completion. He continues to build as the house lights come up to indicate interval. He continues to build through interval. ANDREW puts on a record. It should play until the start of* ACT TWO.)

INTERVAL

ACT TWO

Children's noises. The start of ACT TWO *is signalled by the appearance of* IRENE *descending the stairs from the loft.* ANDREW *is still building his structure.*

ANDREW: How're the kids?
IRENE (*still emotional, sadly resigned*): Your father lost over a stone. He worries about you all the time.
(*It is obvious to* ANDREW *that she is speaking her own feelings rather than his father's. He gets up, looks at his structure, goes across and puts his arms around* IRENE *in a genuine display of warmth.*)
ANDREW: It's good to see you back.
(IRENE *clutches him and cries. He gently disengages himself.*) How were the kids?
(CARMEL *comes out from the room where she and* MICHAEL *are discussing the manuscript.*)
CARMEL: Sorry to interrupt. I was just wondering if I could have a beer or something. I'm getting quite hoarse.
ANDREW (*indicating the bottle opened for* GUNTER *earlier*): Help yourself.
IRENE: What's the little girl's name?
ANDREW: Emma.
IRENE: She's an absolute little angel.
ANDREW: What did you think of Sean?
IRENE: He's a very good looking child, isn't he? Very well behaved when you approach him in the right manner.
ANDREW (*cynically, building again*): Yeah. With a riding whip in your hand.
CARMEL: My children took a long while to adjust to my new man.

Act Two

They focus their resentments at him in all sorts of subtle ways.
ANDREW: You should be so lucky. Sean hit me in the vitals with a cricket bat yesterday.
CARMEL: Yes. That's hardly subtle, is it?
ANDREW: No. He wasn't exactly penitent either. He said he'd hit me there again if I didn't stop poking his mother with it.
IRENE: Has he seen you doing it?
ANDREW: Yes. He seems to prefer it to television.
IRENE: That's a pretty sad comment on your personal standards.
ANDREW: I tend to think it's a pretty poor comment on the standard of television.
IRENE: Don't joke. I mean it.
ANDREW: We don't invite him, I assure you. He just comes.
CARMEL: All kids are intrigued by sex, Mrs. Collins. We'd just finished making love the other day only to find my youngest sitting on the end of the bed. "What are you doing?" she said, so I thought, "Here goes, let's be honest." "Brian and I were making love, dear." Silence. "What's that?" "It's something that two people who love each other like doing and it gives them a lot of pleasure." She sat there and thought a minute and said: "Do it again. I only saw the part where you both yell."
ANDREW (*to* CARMEL): I thought I was really getting somewhere with these three, doing all the right things: not forcing myself on 'em, warm and open when they made a positive approach towards me. In fact just the night before, I'd been boasting to Kirsty that I'd broken the back of the problem, when I walk into the kitchen next morning and there are the three of them eating their muesli. I nod and beam good morning at the three of them, without the slightest trace of condescension. Deathly silence, the three of them. Frozen in mid-spoon. Orange rind stuck between their teeth, muesli dribbling from the corners of their mouths. I become a bit suspicious of the depth of their positive feeling for me, so I walk on and wait where they can't see me. "Piss off, you fucking idiot," says Sean, and the other two nearly choke themselves laughing.
(HARRY *enters.* CARMEL *laughs and looks at* ANDREW *affectionately. She is attracted.*)
CARMEL: Must go back and battle it out with your agent.
(*She goes, carrying the beer bottle and glasses.*)
IRENE: Isn't there something around here I could eat?
ANDREW: Muesli?
(IRENE *goes out into the kitchen.*)
HARRY (*to* ANDREW): Sorry I flew off the handle a bit there earlier.
IRENE (*off*): There's a few eggs here. Are they for the children?
ANDREW: You have them.
HARRY: I'd never take you to court over this. You know that. If O'Hearn advises you to take Chisolms' offer and you take his advice, then that's it as far as I'm concerned. No hard feelings. (*After a pause*) And I'm sorry about pulling that loyalty bullshit.
(HARRY *is a little drunk and becoming a touch maudlin.*)

You don't owe me anything. I took on your work because it was good. No other reason. Because it was good, and if there's one damned thing I can do and do well it's spot quality. I am a talent sniffer. That's it. That's me. Pure and simple. A talent sniffer and I can sniff it out better than anyone else in this country, and consider this, consider this, boy. Talent is a commodity just like anything else, it's a commodity that's got to be found and mined and processed, and I found you and I mined you and I processed you for one reason and for one reason only—because I knew you were good and because I knew that if I treated you fairly and honestly you would make us both a fortune one day. That's the reason I've always been straight with you. Not any phoney honesty or principles or any of that crap. Because you were good, and I knew that if I did anything sharp or shady or tricksy with you, sooner or later you would find out and say, "Up you, Harry", and there would go my golden goose flying right out of the window. Get me?

(ANDREW *continues building methodically.*)

So forgive me for peddling that loyalty bullshit. All I've done for you I've done out of pure self-interest. My Christ. I've been dishonest in my time. I could tell you some things I've done that I'm still ashamed of, but never to you, boy. Never, never to you, and it's not that I'm patting myself on the back, as I've said a few times already, it's out of pure self-interest.

ANDREW: Yes, you have.

HARRY: What?

ANDREW: Said it a few times.

HARRY: And I'm not going to try and appeal to you on the grounds of what I've done for you as an editor, either. It's getting that work onto the paper that's the hard part. Shuffling it around a bit after that is easy. Relatively easy.

ANDREW (*embarrassed*): Look, for Christ's sake—

HARRY: Your agent may be right. Who knows? Perhaps I am crass. Perhaps Carmel might point you in more sensitive directions, but I would point out the warning that sensitive and precious are often synonymous.

ANDREW: Look, for Christ's sake shut up will you, Harry. I'm not going to sign with Chisolms.

(HARRY *pulls up with a jolt, surprised.*)

HARRY: You're not?

ANDREW: I'm not.

HARRY: You're not going to sign with Chisolms?

ANDREW: I'm not.

HARRY: You're going to sign with me?

(ANDREW *adds a block and nods.*)

I'll remember this. In amongst all the deceit, the character assassination, the back-stabbing, there is a remnant of loyalty in all of us. Let's face it, if there wasn't it wouldn't be worth being human, would it? What was it that decided you?

ANDREW (*tongue in cheek*): Loyalty.

Act Two

HARRY: Bullshit. I know what it was. I'm a bloody good editor and a bloody good promoter, and I'll get your book into the kind of shape that'll make people want to read it, and make film producers want to buy it. That's why! You shitarse! You really enjoyed pulling this kind of stunt, didn't you?

ANDREW: Yes, well you stop blowing off about how you bloody well near write my books for me. You have a certain facility for spotting structural weaknesses but you have no bloody facility for knowing how to go about remedying them. I know the last one had faults but if I had've taken your advice about how to rectify them the bloody book would've been a disaster!

HARRY: Now just you wait a minute. That's the line you peddled in that *Cleo* article and I resent it. I bloody well resent it.

ANDREW: Yes, well I started to feel that it was about time I retaliated.

HARRY: When have I made these alleged statements about writing your work for you?

ANDREW: That bloody *Four Corners* interview. The one you conveniently forgot to tell me was on.

HARRY (*embarrassed*): Did you watch that?

ANDREW: Yeah.

HARRY: I was goaded into it by the interviewer.

ANDREW: He goaded you into it?

HARRY: Yeah.

ANDREW: Well, he must have pretty provocative eyebrows, because he certainly didn't get a chance to open his mouth.

HARRY: You forget pretty easily.

ANDREW: Look. You're a good editor. You can spot the flaws, but your remedies are ratshit.

HARRY: What about cutting back on Helen?

ANDREW: I'll pay that one, but what about Morton Gould?

HARRY (*shrugging and shaking his head*): I still think he should've been bi. Hey! Did you know Jimmy Hogg is bi?

ANDREW (*interested*): Yeah?

HARRY: Interesting, isn't it? He got off with one of the male leads in the RSC.

ANDREW: Yeah?

HARRY: I should've suspected it, actually. He's the sort of guy who compartmentalizes everything but in such a way that he's bound to be caught. His wife found out.

ANDREW: Yeah?

HARRY: Interesting, isn't it? Did you see what he wrote about you last week?

ANDREW (*sharply*): No.

HARRY: Don't take any notice of it. It was just bitchy crap.

ANDREW: What did he say?

HARRY: Look, don't worry about it. He just drew a rather unfavourable comparison between you and Freddie Hubbard.

ANDREW (*paranoid*): Freddie Hubbard is a precious little wordmonger.

HARRY (*enjoying the revelation immensely*): Don't worry about it. All that critical stuff is shit.

ANDREW: When was it in?

HARRY (*with relish*): Last Sunday.

ANDREW (*yelling*): Kirsty! (*Receiving no answer*) She hides all the bad crits. I wish she'd bloody well show me. I find out sooner or later.

HARRY: Count yourself lucky. Arna shows me all the bad shit with great relish. (*After a pause*) How're things?

ANDREW (*still brooding*): With what?

HARRY: With your new woman.

ANDREW (*curtly*): She's not exactly new and her name's Kirsty.

HARRY (*musing*): She interviewed me once for *The National Times*. Said I had beady eyes.

(*He pauses, relishing a secret knowledge.*)

Lovely night out there.

(*Pause.*)

I suppose you've got a, er, fairly flexible sort of relationship?

ANDREW (*suspicious*): What d'you mean?

HARRY: I expect you permit each other a fair degree of freedom?

ANDREW: No. Not particularly.

HARRY: Oh.

ANDREW: Why?

HARRY: Just wondered.

ANDREW: We've had one or two little blow-ups on that subject actually.

HARRY: Really? Mmm?

ANDREW: I'm a bit of a compulsive groper when I've got a bit of alcohol in the bloodstream.

HARRY: Mmm.

ANDREW: I just have to look at some women's eyes and I'm gone.

HARRY: Yeah. It comes out a bit heavy in this manuscript, actually.

ANDREW: What d'you mean?

HARRY: Bit too much of the old "eyes meeting across the crowded room" stuff. But not to worry, it's only a small point. I've heard you've been caught out a few times?

ANDREW: Mmm. Bloody stupid of me. I really love that woman and it doesn't help things. I must be compulsive or have self-destructive impulses or something.

HARRY (*smugly*): Does Kirsty ever retaliate?

ANDREW: No, she doesn't. (*As HARRY raises his eyebrows*) Why?

HARRY (*savouring it but keeping a straight face*): I could be wrong, but she seems to be getting very involved with our Scandinavian friend. I could be wrong. The light's pretty bad ...

(ANDREW *looks at him.*)

Does that worry you?

ANDREW (*exploding*): Of course it fucking worries me!

HARRY (*clinically interested*): What're you going to do about it?

(ANDREW *moves towards the door, looking very angry.*)

ANDREW: What do you bloody well think I'm going to do about it?

Act Two 125

HARRY (*grinning*): Leave them be. Play it cool. (*As ANDREW exits*) It puts you in a hell of a good bargaining position.
(KEN *enters, looking worried, and starts to count the cases.* HARRY *addresses him jovially.*)
Making sure they're all still there?
(KEN *doesn't hear him. He looks worried and begins to count the cases again.*)
Making sure they're all there?
(KEN *turns around.*)
KEN: We've lost one of the cases. (*Genuinely worried*) Irene! We've lost one of the cases.
HARRY: You've got to watch them on the wharves. They'd pinch anything.
(HARRY *exits.*)
KEN (*agitated*): No. I counted them coming off the ship. Irene! Irene! We've lost one of the cases.
IRENE (*coming from the kitchen carrying a plate of eggs*): What?
KEN: We've lost one of the cases.
IRENE: How many were there?
KEN: Twelve. I counted them on the wharf. We'd better go back there straight away.
IRENE (*irritated*): There'll be no one there at this time of night.
KEN: Someone will be on duty.
IRENE: Ring them up.
KEN: Yes. Yes. That's a good idea.
(*He goes to the phone.* IRENE *counts the cases. There are eleven standing together and one apart from the others.*)
IRENE: There are twelve here.
KEN (*pointing to the one apart*): That one's Gunter's.
IRENE: Well, that was with us on the wharves too.
KEN (*thinking*): Was it?
IRENE: Of course it was. He brought it through customs and put it down next to ours. Don't you remember?
KEN (*genuinely relieved*): That's right. You're right. He brought it through customs and put it down next to us.
IRENE (*gentler*): That's right. Now go off to bed.
KEN: That's right. He said, "So now I'm in Australia". And I said, "Yes. Put your case down on Australian soil." Linoleum actually, but I was speaking figuratively.
IRENE (*ushering him off*): That's right. Now go to bed.
(*She is worried.* ANDREW *enters, looking distracted and angry.*)
Your father's getting impossible.
ANDREW: Yeah, he's getting old.
IRENE: He's a fine man, but he's getting impossible. Do you know that he stood up and shouted at a waiter in France. The most embarrassing moment of my life. He thought the man was cheating us, but there was only a little mistake in adding up. He thinks everyone's getting at him.
ANDREW (*glumly*): Yeah. He's getting old.
IRENE: What's the matter?

ANDREW: Gunter's broken down.
IRENE: Broken down? Where is he?
ANDREW: Down the hill. Kirsty's with him. He's crying his eyes out.
IRENE: He did that on the ship. He'll just have to learn to take a grip on himself. Your father's a fine man, but he's just getting impossible to live with. Everywhere he goes he takes over the conversation, and if anyone disagrees with him he just abuses them. Why did you ever fill his head with politics? You might be right about your damn Labor Party, but all I know is that he was a hell of a lot easier to live with when he was a Liberal.
ANDREW (*trying to concentrate*): Yes. He does seem to be a lot jumpier than when he went away.
IRENE: Yes, well it's no wonder, the trouble you've given him. It's hard for us to understand this sort of thing, son. I know Meredith wasn't perfect, but it's hard for us to understand. Why don't you talk to your father? He gets hurt very easily. He can't remember the last time you talked to him.
ANDREW (*guiltily*): You've been away for a year and a half.
IRENE: He said to me on the ship back: "Irene, I don't think I've ever really had a heart to heart talk with Andrew." He feels things like that. He's no fool. Why don't you go on this fishing trip with him? It'll make him very happy. (*As* ANDREW *looks towards the front door*) Surely your father's important enough to let you tear yourself away from this Kirsty woman? Who paid for this place?
ANDREW: I paid half and Kirsty paid half.
IRENE: Don't try to pull the wool over my eyes, son.
ANDREW (*irritated*): She did. She got a bank loan.
IRENE: He argued with an Italian taxi driver over the quickest route to the Colisseum. A man who'd lived there all his life, and he'd get so agitated about something going wrong that we arrived at every airport over an hour before the plane loaded. (*Noticing* ANDREW's *lack of concentration*) Can't you even pay attention for two minutes when I'm telling you these things?
(*She was close to tears. Again it is genuine emotion.*)
I was at death's door for four days having you. I sometimes wish I had've died. You didn't even phone us on our fortieth anniversary. Your father sat up by the phone all night.
ANDREW (*irritated, guilty*): Look, I've been absolutely flat out. I'm sorry but I haven't had time to think for the last few months!
IRENE: I reminded you three times in my letters.
ANDREW: I tried to get a booking but I left it too late.
IRENE (*still upset*): You'd rather I was still over there, wouldn't you? Your father's the only one I can rely on. The only one.
ANDREW (*irritated, guilty, genuinely concerned*): Don't be so stupid.
(*He puts his arms around her and she sobs. He looks despairingly over her head.*)
IRENE: They didn't want him to marry me, you know.
ANDREW: Who?
IRENE: May and Andrew. They wouldn't even visit our house.

Act Two

Bloody snobs. (*Bitterly*) May didn't even come to Dad's funeral. Over a hundred of his workmates came, but not May. Said she had a headache. She called me a slut one day when your father went out of the room. She'd never dare say it while he was there. I don't care what they say about your father. He wouldn't hear a word against me from his mother or anyone.

KIRSTY (*off*): Andrew!

(IRENE *notices that* ANDREW, *while trying to be as sympathetic as possible, is still distracted.* KIRSTY *enters, looking worried.*)

Will you talk to him, Andrew? I can't get him to move.

ANDREW: Is he still howling?

KIRSTY: No. He's just sitting there staring straight ahead and he won't move.

IRENE: Go and do something. You're a doctor.

ANDREW: You go and do something. You adopted him.

IRENE: Go down and help him. Go and do something.

KIRSTY: Please, Andrew. He's very upset.

ANDREW: I'll give him some sedatives and put him to bed. (*He goes.*)

IRENE: We're all upset. Mr. Collins has just gone off to bed again with his heart pounding.

KIRSTY: Andrew didn't tell me he had a bad heart.

IRENE: We've both got bad hearts. Not that Andrew would care.

KIRSTY: Sit down and rest.

IRENE: Rest? How can I rest? My nerves are completely on edge. Could you look in that red case over there? There's a bottle of brandy in there somewhere.

(KIRSTY *moves across and starts looking.*)

I had three turns myself on the ship.

KIRSTY (*still looking*): Heart turns?

IRENE: The ship's doctor said it was only nerves, but he was an Indian and I don't think they know all that much. I think it's somewhere near the front under the clothes. We were both hit very hard by that letter. I had my differences with Meredith, but we both felt they had a happy marriage.

(KIRSTY *finds the bottle and goes to get a glass.*)

KIRSTY: It's often hard to tell from the outside. Would you like anything with it?

IRENE (*with a false smile*): No, thank you. How exactly did you meet Andrew?

KIRSTY: I interviewed him.

IRENE: I see. Where?

KIRSTY (*puzzled*): Where?

IRENE: In his house?

KIRSTY (*puzzled*): Yes. I think I did.

IRENE: Did it happen right then?

KIRSTY: What?

IRENE: The monkey business.

KIRSTY (*incredulous*): The what?

IRENE: Don't you worry. He's done it before.

KIRSTY: What?
IRENE: Done things to women he's just met. Meredith sent me some letters. I know what she had to put up with. Did he do something right there and then?
KIRSTY: No he didn't.
IRENE: Was Meredith home?
KIRSTY: Yes she was.
IRENE (*nodding*): Mmm.
KIRSTY (*slight smile*): I'm sure he wouldn't've jumped on me even if she hadn't been.
IRENE (*dubious*): Mmm. Did you speak to her?
KIRSTY: Meredith?
IRENE: Mmm.
KIRSTY: That day?
IRENE: Mmm.
KIRSTY: No.
IRENE: Did you see her?
KIRSTY: No.
IRENE: Did you see his children?
KIRSTY (*puzzled*): Yes I did, actually.
IRENE: He's very fond of his children.
KIRSTY: Yes, he is.
IRENE: Very fond of them. Why didn't he introduce you to Meredith?
KIRSTY: She was in bed, recovering from a severe bout of depression.
IRENE: Yes. Well we all have our ups and downs.
KIRSTY: She seems a lot happier now.
IRENE (*outraged*): Happier? No father of her children? Happier?
KIRSTY: She hasn't been depressed again since he left.
IRENE: Depressed? She hasn't had time to be depressed. She's managing those children and working at the same time. She's been left with all of the responsibility. If you don't mind me saying so, that's a very callous attitude to take. I've got her letters. It's been very difficult for her.
KIRSTY: It's been very difficult for all of us.
IRENE (*tight-lipped*): I thought perhaps you'd at least be sorry for what you've done.
KIRSTY: Look. I don't know what you've been told in those letters, Mrs. Collins, but I didn't drag Andrew away from his family. He came very much of his own free will.
IRENE: Why didn't you send him back? I was prepared to give you a fair chance but you're making it very difficult for me.
KIRSTY (*tensely*): I'm sorry. But I've been made to feel guilty for quite a while now and I'm getting pretty sick of it.
(ANDREW *bursts through the door in a fury, frog-marching* GUNTER, *who is protesting listlessly. He hurls* GUNTER *violently onto the couch.* GUNTER *says nothing. He lies there limply.*)
ANDREW: Just stay there and don't move.
KIRSTY (*alarmed*): What happened?

(ANDREW *goes to the kitchen to get tablets.*)
What happened?
ANDREW (*returning*): Stupid bastard tried to kill himself.
GUNTER: I want to die. I just want to die.
ANDREW: Shut up that whining or I'll fucking well oblige you.
KIRSTY: Andrew!
ANDREW (*directing her away from* GUNTER): Just stand clear.
(*He makes* GUNTER *take some pills.*)
KIRSTY: Don't be so—
ANDREW (*tersely*): Just move off. It was your motherly solace that got him all geared up to do it. Now get lost. (*To* IRENE) You too.
KIRSTY: How did he try and kill himself?
ANDREW: By knotting his tie around his neck and launching himself from one of your tough sturdy Australian eucalypts.
KIRSTY: Is he all right?
ANDREW: Yeah. The branch broke. (*To* GUNTER) Swallow those bloody pills.
(GUNTER *shakes his head.* ANDREW *grabs him, forces his mouth open, forces the tablets into it, pours brandy down his neck, and holds his nose to make him swallow.* GUNTER *struggles and spits the tablets out.* ANDREW *slaps him hard across the mouth, shocking him so that on the next try the manoeuvre is successful.* KIRSTY *is horrified by the violence.*)
KIRSTY: Stop it! Stop it! What are you giving him?
ANDREW (*irritated*): For Christ's sake, will you get lost.
KIRSTY: What've you given him?
ANDREW: Sedatives. They'll knock him out. (*To* GUNTER) I'm going to take you back there and put you to bed, and if you try anything stupid I'll belt the Christ out of you. Right?
(HARRY *enters.* ANDREW *frog-marches* GUNTER *towards the bedroom.* MICHAEL *and* CARMEL *have come out from the back room to see what the noise is all about.* GUNTER *sees* CARMEL *and seizes the opportunity to expound to an audience.*)
GUNTER (*enraged*): What is it that women want? Tell me. What is it that women want? Foul-mouthed Italians?
CARMEL (*not understanding the situation*): I suppose they'd be a change from foul-mouthed Australians.
GUNTER (*to* CARMEL *and* KIRSTY): Every morning I would pass him on the deck, and every morning he would stop me to make some crude gesture relating to some by-standing woman, which I found highly sickening and quickly moved on.
(*The children wake up again.* KEN *enters.*)
ANDREW (*as he hauls* GUNTER *off*): You try anything stupid and I'll smash you. I mean it.
CARMEL: What happened?
KIRSTY: Gunter tried to kill himself.
(*She follows* GUNTER *and* ANDREW *anxiously.*)
HARRY (*interested*): Kill himself? How?
IRENE: He tried to hang himself.
HARRY (*raising his eyebrows*): Hang himself? Did he actually get to jump?

IRENE (*to* KEN): Go and talk to him. He respects you.
KEN (*irritated*): Is he injured?
IRENE: No, the branch broke. Go and talk to him.
KEN: Talk to him? What would I say to him? You talk to him. You're the one who picked him up.
IRENE (*glaring at him, then going*): You're a great one in a crisis. I'm the one who chased the thief out of the room in Paris.
KEN: Your face would scare anyone.
(IRENE *hesitates at the door, her tone is less peremptory, more conciliatory.*)
IRENE: Go and talk to him about getting him a job in Insurance or something.
KEN: He doesn't want a job in Insurance and I don't blame him.
(*The noise from the children increases.* IRENE *comes back and starts up the stairs.*)
IRENE (*irritably*): What *is* the matter with those children?
KEN (*retreating to a chair or couch at the back of the stage*): Pen-pushing for forty years. Who'd let anyone in for that? He's suicidal already.
(*He pours himself a brandy and sits on the couch. There is a distinct pause as everyone contemplates the implications of the suicide attempt.*)
HARRY (*drinking meditatively*): Suicide puzzles me. I have never, ever been suicidal.
MICHAEL: Certain temperaments aren't prone to it.
HARRY: Not once. (*Thinking*) No. Not once.
MICHAEL: I can't say I'm surprised.
HARRY (*sharply*): What d'you mean by that?
MICHAEL: Certain temperaments aren't prone to it.
HARRY: You said that. What are you getting at?
MICHAEL: I'd imagine that before you wished to commit suicide you'd need to have certain doubts about your personal adequacy, which you obviously never do.
HARRY (*looking at* MICHAEL *musingly*): You're a smart little prick, aren't you?
MICHAEL (*shrugging*): I was merely making an observation.
(HARRY *looks at him, musing, then turns to* CARMEL.)
HARRY: Do you ever get suicidal?
CARMEL: Yes.
HARRY (*nodding, his expectations confirmed*): What about you?
MICHAEL: I do, as a matter of fact.
HARRY: When was the last time?
MICHAEL: Two months ago, actually.
HARRY: Did you seriously consider it?
MICHAEL: Very seriously.
HARRY: Why did you want to commit suicide?
MICHAEL: That's rather private.
HARRY: Come on. Don't be a fucking prima donna. What does it take to get a sensitive man ready to knock himself off?
CARMEL: Cut it out, Harry.

Act Two

HARRY: It's not good enough to sit there and bask in an enigmatic aura. Why did you want to kill yourself?
CARMEL: Stop it Harry.
MICHAEL (*to* CARMEL): I think we've just about finished here. Would you like a lift?
CARMEL: Thanks, Michael, but I think I'll stay here and discuss a few things with Andrew, if that's all right.
MICHAEL: Perfectly.
HARRY (*to* MICHAEL): You've settled things then.
MICHAEL: I can't discuss anything further until I've spoken to Andrew, Harry, and I'm not speaking to Andrew until tomorrow.
HARRY (*nonchalantly, knowing he's got the book*): Suit yourself. What made Chisolms suddenly get interested in a Collins manuscript, Michael?
CARMEL: I persuaded them they should publish him.
HARRY: What made you interested?
CARMEL: I think he's a fine writer.
HARRY: He overwrites to buggery and makes monstrous structural errors.
CARMEL: In your opinion.
HARRY (*to* MICHAEL): You've engineered this whole deal, haven't you?
MICHAEL: I took the manuscript to Carmel. Yes. You fucked up the last one and I didn't want to see it happen again.
HARRY (*taut, hard*): Fucked it up? Fucked it up? It made you a bloody fortune, didn't it?
MICHAEL: Yes, it did. Maybe I'm a bad agent, but unfortunately quality still means something to me.
HARRY (*hard, venomous*): Fucked it up? The biggest success the local industry's ever had. Film sale within six months, English Book Society choice within two months of publication. I wish I had someone to fuck things up like that for me, and as far as quality is concerned, O'Hearn, remember this. You can sell the public shit and you can sell the public quality, but the one thing you can't sell the public is boring shit or boring quality, because, strange as it may seem, the public does not enjoy being bored shitless. The only difference between you two and I is that you think he's a genius and I know he isn't, so don't let him indulge himself.
MICHAEL: I certainly think he's more talented than you do.
HARRY: Well you're eminently more qualified to make that judgment than I am, aren't you? I am a first class Honours graduate in English Literature ...
CARMEL: Second class, and it was Economics if I remember correctly ...
HARRY: And I can paint, sculpt and play three musical instruments.
CARMEL: Have you ever seen his paintings?
MICHAEL: Does he play the instruments simultaneously or one at a time?
HARRY: I'm sure your years as a public service clerk gave you all

kinds of insights into the artistic process, O'Hearn.

MICHAEL (*to* CARMEL): Will you give my respects to Andrew and Kirsty?

HARRY: I'll tell you what art is, O'Hearn, and it's not about geniuses. It's about Shakespeare's scripts being knocked into shape by his actors. It's about T.S. Eliot being edited by Ezra Pound. I'm not exactly for democracy in art, but there's often more than one person involved.

MICHAEL: I'm not disputing that, Harry. I just wish the other person wasn't you.

HARRY: Why did you nearly kill yourself, O'Hearn? It's really pricking at me. I want to know.

MICHAEL: I fell in love, Bustle. The boy had all kinds of hang ups which I nursed him through. And when I had, he left me to live with a woman. I suppose you find that a pretty trivial reason for contemplating suicide?

HARRY: It did sound vaguely like the second verse of *The Poofter's Lament*.

MICHAEL: I thought you might react like that.

HARRY: You thrive on drama, O'Hearn.

MICHAEL: I certainly didn't realize I was enjoying myself at the time.

HARRY: You thrive on it.

MICHAEL: The trouble with you, Harry, is that right down at your core you have absolutely no feeling. Goodbye, Carmel. Tell Andrew I'll phone you both tomorrow.

HARRY: Why didn't you kill yourself?

CARMEL: He knew how happy it'd make you.

(MICHAEL *doesn't answer. He looks at* HARRY *venomously and goes.* HARRY *calls after him.*)

HARRY: Come on. Why didn't you kill yourself?

CARMEL: Just shup up, Harry. I've had enough of you tonight.

HARRY: Well. We have become a sour old stick, haven't we?

CARMEL (*explosively*): And stop telling people that you've fucked me!

HARRY: I don't.

CARMEL: I've heard it from about three people in the last year.

HARRY (*slightly guilty*): I can't remember having told anyone.

CARMEL: You'd probably be surprised to hear that I wouldn't count it as one of my more notable accomplishments, even if it were true. But seeing as it's not, it makes me very angry.

HARRY: Not true?

CARMEL: That's right.

HARRY: Now come on. I didn't make a conscious policy of it but it just so happens I fucked every woman in the colony at some time or another.

CARMEL: Everyone except me. In that whole period of my life it's the only thing I can look back on with pride.

HARRY (*musing*): I could've sworn I did. That night up at Marcus's place.

Act Two

CARMEL: We were always up at Marcus's place.
HARRY (*musing*): It might've been Di Calderstone.
CARMEL: Or Mary Penfield.
HARRY (*sharply*): Did she say that?
CARMEL: Yes. She left the colony straight after.
HARRY: That's a rather nasty inference to draw, Carmel. (*Becoming high-spirited suddenly as he recalls the colony*) Hey, were you there the night Marcus fucked the horse?
(KEN *nearly falls off his chair.*)
CARMEL (*irritated*): He didn't touch the horse.
HARRY: He did. As true as I'm standing here. Charlie Griffiths'd been trying to get a stallion to mount his mare for two days, so Marcus went out to show the stallion what to do.
CARMEL: I've heard it all before and I don't believe it.
(CARMEL *exits to toilet.*)
HARRY (*ignoring her*): Just as Marcus started on the mare, the stallion stopped watching and walked away, and Charlie yelled: "The stallion's just gone off." And Marcus just yelled back: "That makes two of us."
(CARMEL *slams the toilet door.* HARRY *laughs raucously.* KEN *pours himself a drink.* ANDREW *appears, followed by* IRENE. HARRY *turns to* ANDREW.)
Have I told you about Marcus and the horse?
ANDREW: Mmm.
HARRY (*laughing*): Marcus wanted to marry the mare but her father said neigh.
(*He laughs raucously at his pun.* KIRSTY *appears.*)
IRENE (*to* ANDREW): How's Graeme?
ANDREW: He's out to it.
KIRSTY (*to* ANDREW): You needn't've been so rough with him.
ANDREW: He'll be all right now. He's asleep.
IRENE: What a stupid thing for him to do. (*To* ANDREW) Those children are sleeping in filthy sheets. Don't you ever wash?
ANDREW (*irritated*): Yes I do. Every Monday.
IRENE (*incredulous*): You wash?
ANDREW: Yes I do. Every Monday, except that I got pissed at a lunch with my accountant and missed out this week.
IRENE: Why do you do the washing?
ANDREW: Because the sheets get dirty.
IRENE: Why do *you* do the washing?
ANDREW: Because it's my job. The washing and the washing up. Sometimes I put the children to bed but not all that often, thank Christ.
IRENE: That's ridiculous.
ANDREW: Why?
KEN: Stop that Irene. It's none of your business.
IRENE (*angrily*): It is my business. I'll make it my business. She can't expect to have her cake and eat it too.
KIRSTY (*coldly*): I'm sorry. I don't understand.
ANDREW (*to* IRENE, *very angry*): Will you please go to bed?

IRENE (*to* KEN): See how he talks to me?

KEN: Don't shout at your mother, son.

ANDREW (*to* IRENE): It's about time you started minding your own business.

IRENE: That's right. Turn on your mother. I'm the only one who'll stand by you in the end. Remember that.

KEN: Now come on, Irene.

IRENE: If she's determined to grab herself someone who's famous, then she can't expect him to do the bloody housework.

ANDREW (*exploding*): For Christ's sake!

IRENE: Well it's about time someone cleared the air.

KIRSTY (*with controlled anger*): I thought I made it clear that I did not grab Andrew.

ANDREW: You don't have to answer her.

KIRSTY: As for him being well known, I loathe it.

ANDREW (*more insistent*): There's no need to answer her.

KIRSTY: Do you think it's fun to come home from a day's work and find a fuckwitted television crew clambering over your living room and telling your kids to shut up, or to find that you aren't getting to see your old friends any more, and all that you're meeting in their place are monsters with elephantitis of the ego.

(*She looks at* HARRY. *He waves cheerfully to her.*)

It's a ball I can tell you. My work is deteriorating rapidly; but I nearly got to meet Don Dunstan once.

(*She storms towards the bedroom.* ANDREW *moves to go after her, but stops as she turns and delivers a last broadside.*)

And as far as Meredith not having a father for her children, she's luckier than I am. I've had to sit and watch mine get physically battered—

ANDREW: That's an exaggeration.

KIRSTY: You threw Sean against a wall once. So all right. I know you miss your own children, I know you feel guilty about what you've done and I know that my children are copping the consequences, and I know that it will all come together in time, but sometimes it's very hard for me to sit there and wait.

(*She exits.* ANDREW *returns to his structure, adds a block, then follows* KIRSTY.)

IRENE (*to* KEN): Are you coming to bed?

KEN: No.

IRENE: Why not?

KEN: I'm sitting up here and finishing my drink.

IRENE: You know how you'll be tomorrow if you don't get your rest. You'll get your pains and think you're dying and I'll have to chase around after you all the afternoon.

KEN (*stubbornly*): I'm finishing my drink.

IRENE: All right. Don't say I didn't warn you.

(*She storms off to bed.*)

KEN: A man's a fool to have ever got married. I'm going to put on the kettle.

(ANDREW *returns looking disgruntled.* HARRY *picks up the*

flagon and pours himself a drink.)

HARRY (*to* ANDREW): I want to start work on that manuscript as soon as possible.

ANDREW: Get stuffed.

HARRY: What? You've changed your mind again, have you? You're going to give it to them?

ANDREW: I'm not going to give it to any bloody one. I'm going to burn the bloody thing. Now piss off!

HARRY: Now you listen to me, son. When some jumped-up little clerk tries to double-cross me because he believes he knows what's best for you artistically, then he'd better know his stuff one hell of a lot better than O'Hearn does. I've been in this business long enough to know what creativity is all about. It's a sweaty, dirty, bitchy, tough little business of trial and error, suck it and see, and learn the tricks of your bloody trade. You *need* me, Collins.

ANDREW: Just piss off.

HARRY: Joking aside, Andrew, I want your signature by tomorrow or the deal's off. I mean it. I've got better things to do than be pushed around by your agent. Kirsty'll calm down in a day or two. When she does, give her a big kiss for me.

ANDREW: Piss off.

(HARRY *goes.* KEN *appears at the door.*)

KEN: Hello son. Kettle's boiled. Would you like a cup of tea?

ANDREW: Thanks, I would.

(KEN *brings in a teapot and two mugs. He puts them down and pours the tea.*)

KEN: Nothing like a cup of tea. They can't make the stuff properly on these Italian ships. (*Looking at* ANDREW) Did you know your agent is a homosexual?

ANDREW (*still building*): Yes, I did.

KEN (*after a pause*): Did you, er, travel much with him on, er, business?

ANDREW: No. Not much.

KEN (*nodding*): We had a homosexual working in our office once. He spoke with a lisp. We didn't find out for years. He was a very good worker. (*After a pause*) That Harry Bustle is a bit hard to take.

ANDREW: He, er, is a little flamboyant at times.

KEN: He, er, told you about his friend who mounts horses?

ANDREW: Yes. Several times.

KEN (*laughing*): He's got a very vivid imagination. I'll say that much for him. (*Laughing*) I mean how in the blazes would you do it? (*Laughing*) The damn things are about this high.

(ANDREW *grins and laughs.*)

ANDREW: Bustle always exaggerates. It was probably only a pony.

(KEN *laughs a little dubiously and looks at* ANDREW *to see whether he's serious.*)

Or maybe he used a box.

KEN (*laughing dubiously again*): Do you think this chap actually did carry on with the horse?

ANDREW: I wouldn't be surprised.

CARMEL (*returning*): Neither would I, on reflection.
KEN: Oh, hello there. Look, I'll be off to bed now. You two have probably got things to discuss.
CARMEL: Don't hurry off, Mr. Collins.
ANDREW: Finish your tea, Dad.
KEN: No. I only have a few sips before I go to bed. Otherwise I have to get up during the night. I'll see you in the morning, son.
CARMEL: Good night Mr. Collins. Nice to have met you.
(KEN *nods and goes, walking slowly, tired.* CARMEL *looks at* ANDREW. *She pours them both another brandy. Already one senses that the sexual attraction is there between them.*)
I suppose you've gathered how much I admire your work?
ANDREW: Thank you.
CARMEL: Look, I won't beat around the bush. You mightn't be a genius but I think you're a lot more talented than Bustle thinks you are, and I want to edit you. I read the first draft of your last book.
ANDREW (*looking at her sharply*): Michael was asked not to show it to anyone.
CARMEL: I know. I pressured him.
ANDREW: He shouldn't've done that.
CARMEL: I think that just about everything Bustle took out should've stayed in.
ANDREW: For instance?
CARMEL: That beautiful section where Helen begins to assert her independence.
ANDREW: How would that square up with her vulnerability in the last chapter?
CARMEL (*taken aback*): But that's often how it happens. (*Doubtful*) Isn't it?
ANDREW: Is it?
CARMEL: Why have Helen so vulnerable in any case?
ANDREW: Because Tony could've shot off and left her in the first chapter and I wouldn't've had a book.
CARMEL: I don't agree.
ANDREW: You might be right.
CARMEL: A person can be vulnerable and independent at the same time.
ANDREW (*without interest*): You might be right. How long did you live at the colony?
CARMEL: Too long. I was only nineteen when I first went up there. Completely naive. Straight out of suburbia into this land of godlike creators. All of them men. Christ, and was it sexist! It makes me so angry in retrospect that I howl in rage sometimes. They swapped us, shared us, fucked us in public, and if we felt that something was vaguely wrong, that in some way we were being exploited—they shamed us by attributing it to our sexual repression. You know, I really thought they were gods in those days. All it needed was the ability to slap some paint on a canvas or throw a crude pot and I thought they were gods. Now they're all

scattered around the country either dying of cirrhosis of the liver or exhibiting symptoms of paranoia. Bustle's the only one that's done anything at all, and he was the most repulsive of the lot. I got very drunk one night and let him fuck me. One of the things I still hate myself for. I've always been easily attracted to men. I suppose that's why they recruited me up there. Do you get strongly attracted to people?

ANDREW (*looking at her*): Mmm. It's got me into a lot of trouble.

CARMEL: It's something about the eyes that does it for me.

ANDREW: Faces and eyes.

CARMEL: Right. (*Jumpy*) Faces and eyes. Mainly eyes. (*Looking at him*) I'm still the same. I'm attracted to you. It's eyes. It's caused me trouble, too. I'm controlling it these days. It's worth controlling. Don't you think?

ANDREW: Mmm.

CARMEL: My new man tells me straight out that if he catches me out, that's it, forget it. He's really beautiful. You'd like him. He's a lot younger than I am, but I don't give a damn. He's an activist. He met Abbie Hoffman in the States. He writes counter-culture stuff. Can't spell but he's very good. I help him with his spelling. Do you feel attracted to me?

ANDREW: Yes, I do. You've got beautiful eyes.

CARMEL: It's really a problem, isn't it? Really a problem.

ANDREW: Mmm.

CARMEL: Do you want to fuck me?

ANDREW: I do actually. Mmm.

CARMEL: It's a real problem, isn't it? Are you pretty committed to Kirsty?

ANDREW: Mmm.

CARMEL: She's very beautiful.

ANDREW: Mmm.

CARMEL: And what else?

ANDREW: Sane.

CARMEL: That helps. That helps. And you're pretty committed?

ANDREW: Mmm.

CARMEL: Then why me?

ANDREW: I'm a moral imbecile.

CARMEL (*really jumpy*): Christ! Where can we do it?

ANDREW: Here.

CARMEL: Here?

ANDREW: The bedrooms are all the way down the back, and Gunter's doped up on sleeping tablets.

(*He starts taking off his clothes.*)

CARMEL (*taking off her clothes*): I don't like this sort of thing. A guy took me home once and fucked me on a billiard table while his wife was asleep upstairs. I found out later he was an undertaker. Chilled me in retrospect. You're not going to see anything spectacular, I can assure you.

ANDREW: Neither are you.

CARMEL: You're not impotent, are you?

ANDREW: No. I'm monotonously reliable.
(They are both down to their underwear. They embrace passionately. Their embrace slows.)
CARMEL: What's the matter?
ANDREW: I got small again.
CARMEL: Yeah. I noticed that.
ANDREW: Do you want me to keep trying?
CARMEL: Do you want to keep trying?
(ANDREW shakes his head glumly.)
I wish I had've been the one to freeze up. I could've gone back to my man brimming with virtue.
(They sit there, half-dressed. GUNTER, stumbling along like a somnambulist, staggers out on his way to the toilet.)
ANDREW *(pointing)*: It's through there.
GUNTER *(staring at them, slurring)*: You? You shouting at me? Copulating like dogs while your wife is asleep. I'm going to punch you in the morning. *(Staggering off to the toilet)* I am going to punch you very hard.
(He slams the bathroom door very loudly. ANDREW starts dressing hastily in case someone has heard. CARMEL is drunker and slower. IRENE comes to the door in an old pink dressing-gown.)
ANDREW: Christ! It's déjà vu. I'll swear it's the same gown she had twenty years ago.
IRENE: What do you think you're doing?
ANDREW *(softly, urgent)*: Look. Go to bed.
IRENE *(louder)*: Don't try and push me off. I'm your mother. I'm entitled to know what you're doing. You walked out on Meredith and your children, and now you're up to your same old tricks. *(Cuffing him)* What is wrong with you?
(She cuffs him again. KEN appears at the doorway looking embarrassed.)
You've nearly been the death of your old father, you know. He can't fathom you out. Neither can I. Speak to him, Ken.
KEN: This is not good enough, son.
IRENE *(pushing him in the side with short sharp thrusts)*: What *is* wrong with you? *(Loudly)* Answer me! *(Hitting him in the side as she speaks)* I thought you'd be a joy to your mother when you grew up. Take me to shows and on picnics. Show me a little bit of appreciation for the sacrifices I've made for you. I nearly died having you. For four days I hovered on the brink.
(KIRSTY appears and sizes up the situation. ANDREW and CARMEL are still only partly dressed. KIRSTY walks up to ANDREW and looks at him.)
ANDREW *(lamely)*: Caught with my pants down.
(KIRSTY hits him powerfully and cleanly with a punch to the jaw. CARMEL moves up to KIRSTY.)
CARMEL: I'm sorry, I had a lot to drink.
KIRSTY: I don't know what he's told you, but he'll publish with Bustle. One, they're both men. And two, they've got a lot in common.
(KIRSTY nods to her, not unkindly, and leaves for her bedroom again.)

Act Two

IRENE (*to* ANDREW): I should've done that to you years ago. Don't sit there looking sorry for yourself. Someone should've done that to you years ago.

(*She goes.*)

CARMEL: I'll call a taxi.

ANDREW: You'll never get one out here at this time of night. There's a spare bunk up in the kids' room.

(CARMEL *nods and climbs the stairs.* GUNTER *comes out of the bathroom, still drugged, and glares at* ANDREW *as he passes.*)

GUNTER: I'm going to punch you in the morning.

ANDREW (*to himself*): It's all right. It's been done.

(GUNTER *looks at him suspiciously and moves off.* ANDREW *resumes work on his structure. It is approaching completion, having moved away from the order to a more rambling chaotic shape.*)

KEN: You've got yourself into a bit of trouble again, son.

ANDREW: Mmm.

KEN: Do you think this girl's the right one for you?

ANDREW: Kirsty?

KEN: Mmm.

ANDREW: Mmm.

KEN: Mmm.

(*Pause.*)

She seems pretty volatile.

ANDREW: Mmm.

KEN: Mmm.

(*Pause.*)

What makes you sure she's the right one?

ANDREW: She's only eight stone. Meredith was twelve and she could knock me unconscious.

KEN: Yes, well you bring a lot of it on your own head.

(ANDREW *looks at him and rubs his jaw, but sees that his father's pun is unintentional.*)

We've had some terrible trouble with your girl friends. Do you remember the one who broke your mother's leg?

ANDREW: I think she meant to miss. She only had her licence a week.

KEN: Mind you, Meredith could be pretty ferocious. She used to remind me a lot of your mother. Very efficient, but very irritable. Is Kirsty irritable?

ANDREW: No, and she's not very efficient either.

(KEN *nods.*)

KEN: Mind you, your mother's a fine woman in lots of ways. I always had clean shirts.

ANDREW (*still building*): How did you manage for so many years without sex?

KEN (*very embarrassed*): Oh, er, we, er ... Your mother often helped me out.

ANDREW (*irritated by the sadness of it*): Why didn't you separate?

KEN: It wasn't so easy in those days, son.

ANDREW: No.

KEN: And it would have hurt your mother a lot. She's a fine woman in a lot of ways. She's got an awful lot of friends.

ANDREW: I'd have to agree.

KEN: Yes. Bore me stupid. I used to just go to sleep in the chair. She got over a hundred and fifty Christmas cards last year. Mind you she sent over three hundred. She says I won't have one friend at my funeral. (*Watching* ANDREW *building*) That reminds me of the way you used to play with your meccano set when you were young. You'd spend hours and hours at it.

ANDREW: Did I have many friends?

KEN: No. You were like me. Happy with your own company. I couldn't get to the toolshed quick enough.

(*A pause.* KEN *pots a billiard ball.*)

My brother and I had a table at Partridge Street. We used to play billiards every night for five years. Best five years of my life. (*After a pause*) Are you sure you've done the right thing? Leaving your family?

ANDREW: I think so.

KEN: Your mother's very upset about Robin and Mark. She brought clothes for them in every country we visited. You know how grandmothers are. You see them still?

ANDREW: Alternate weekends. I still get guilt dreams about them. I dreamt that Robin ran towards me and I stabbed her in the chest. Do you still have those nightmares about the office?

KEN: No. Not now.

ANDREW: The one where you were two minutes late and your feet kept slipping and you couldn't get to the office door?

KEN: No. Not now. If I have a nightmare these days it's about dying. Sometimes I dream I have an awful pain in my chest and I wake up shivering and wondering if it was a real pain or not.

ANDREW: Have you been exercising regularly?

KEN: Yes. I walked a mile around the ship every day when the weather was fine.

ANDREW: Keep it up.

KEN: Yes. I want to avoid that guestless funeral for a while.

ANDREW (*half smiling*): Kirsty and I will come, and I'm sure there'll be a few others.

KEN: I'll try and hold it off for a while. If you took any notice of the statistics, a man would give up. Did you read about the ex-footballer the other day?

ANDREW: Yes, I did.

KEN: Forty-four. Who could be fitter than an ex-footballer? Coronary at forty-four. Are you going to bed?

ANDREW: In a minute.

KEN: Things will be a lot more settled now. (*As he moves off to bed*) I'll see you in the morning.

(ANDREW *builds his structure. It is chaotic, but not randomly so. The light dims. He stands up, looks at it, moves off, stands on a chair to survey it from a new vantage point, comes back, adds a few blocks, then one more. He moves off towards the room he shares with* KIRSTY. *The structure remains in the dim light. It is quite aesthetically pleasing. Fade to blackout.*)

CURTAIN

Williamson on
*What If You Died Tomorrow**

What If You Died Tomorrow is not autobiographical. It contains elements extracted from my experience but the total structure of the play is built to its own internal laws and is not a segment of tape recorded reality. Andrew, a young writer, has left his wife and family to live with Kirsty, a journalist, and her three children. There are hints in the play that his previous wife, Meredith, was not responsive to him sexually and that her temperament was one of dominance and irritability, characteristics that Ken, his father, has endured in Irene, his mother. Both Andrew and Ken are self-absorbed and timid, preferring to construct things (Ken's furniture, Andrew's novels and, as the play proceeds, his building of the model) than to relate to people and confront complex human questions.

Ken has stayed with Irene and they have evolved a working relationship which is satisfactory on one level but which has severely limited the personal growth and perspectives of both of them. ("Fine old buildings," says Ken, "but not very well kept. In fact the whole of Europe struck me as rather grubby.")

Andrew, perhaps subconsciously fearing a similar constriction of his view of life, has taken up with a girl who refuses to allow him to be timid—she is already planning to take him to live in villages in India—and who refuses to be cowed and hindered in her own personal growth by Andrew's "success". Although Andrew feels a deep affection and sympathy for his father, and indeed his mother, he is ashamed and irritated by his father's narrowness and timidity, making direct communication between them difficult, if not impossible. The question Andrew desperately wants to ask and finally does is "Why didn't you two separate?" The only answer his father can give is "It wasn't so easy in those days, son."

It's true. It wasn't so easy in those days when pressures of social disapproval were greater, and even now, with guilt feelings about his own children and troubles in relating to Kirsty's, Andrew isn't finding it easy. He hopes that Kirsty's words, "It will all come together in time," will prove true.

---

* These comments were written for this anthology, 1975.

Commenting on the charge that in What If You Died Tomorrow *he betrays his characters for an easy laugh, David Williamson says*:

I certainly agree that my characters have substantial problems to face. I don't betray my characters for an easy laugh—the characters themselves attempt to make little of their considerable difficulties as an act of denial, or courage. It's just a mechanism of coping. In many instances in my plays, I've had characters trying to make light of a difficulty, only for it to be revealed later in the play as a more serious difficulty that their earlier behaviour tended to suggest. Witness Andrew joking with Carmel about how Kirsty's children have rejected him. We think he's coping quite well. Later we find that he's been so enraged at their rejection that he's thrown Sean bodily against a wall. A lot of my so-called refusal to face up to the characters' real problems is in fact a refusal to show them acting in any other way than they *would* act in that particular social situation. I don't want to "peel the layers of the onion" but to show accurate patterns of social interaction.

... Another example is Andrew's answer to Carmel when she asks, "Why are you doing it?" He answers, "Because I'm a moral imbecile!" It's not a glib joke line—it's an attempt to pinpoint a fundamental terror that grips him—namely that he has no fixed set of values or norms that he can believe in and hence use to order and control his behaviour. He may say it in a lighthearted way, but the fear is there all the same. He *is* a moral imbecile and is perhaps a little relieved to be caught and punished, as this demonstrates that other people have value systems *they* believe in.

From a *Cinema Papers* Interview*

Cinema Papers: We've discussed an instance of visual humour in your work. Now for an example of verbal humour. It occurs in *Jugglers Three* during a confrontation between Elizabeth and Neville, who are separated. They grow more and more angry, hurling insults and accusations at each other. Finally, Neville recounts what to him was the worst outrage of all, that he had received a phone call at 2 a.m. from a woman screaming at him for having run out on Elizabeth. Elizabeth replies, "That was me." Neville counters, "I might have known!" That's an extremely funny verbal exchange in the context, as the fact that Neville only *might* have known reveals the extent to which he is emotionally estranged from Elizabeth. It was both very funny and thematic.

Williamson: Yeah. Well, I think that humour is often aggression released, and I think that humour and aggression are often related in my work. There's an awful lot of aggression in the world, and one way of coping with higher levels of interpersonal aggression is rather black, sardonic, cynical humour.

Cinema Papers: In this instance it wasn't the character who was being cynical or sardonic as I read it, but it was the author.

Williamson: Yeah.

Cinema Papers: More often, though, your characters are that way. In much of your work there seems to be one character who is wry, sardonic, very cynical.

Williamson: Yeah, in some of the plays, yeah, there is this character who is like that, but I think that to some extent it may be the shared characteristics of Australians and Americans. I think there is an awful amount of cynicism in Australia. Anyone who starts to have higher motives or expound on the more spiritual aspects of life gets put down in an awful hurry in an Australian context and perhaps in an American one. I remember years ago being impressed by the wave of the American satirical novel, novelists like Heller and Purdy and Barth, who seem to have this black, cynical conception of life.

Cinema Papers: Cops figure in your stuff a lot. Are you preoccupied

---

* Published in January 1974.

with police, or is it mainly as a dramatic focus for aggression that you're interested in them?

Williamson: No, I'm really not preoccupied with them. *The Removalists* came about because the situation in part was related to me by a removalist. I thought it was a great dramatic situation. The cop in *Jugglers Three* was perhaps a bit gratuitous in retrospect. He added a slightly farcical effect to the proceedings. But the one in the new film, well, I think Tony Peterson brings it on his own head. He virtually wants the cops to bash him up. He's in such a dejected frame of mind that he provokes them, and I certainly don't see it as being a comment on police brutality. I think that if anything the cops just wanted to take him quietly to the police station.

Cinema Papers: Beer or alcohol seems to figure in your stuff a lot. You use it to allow characters to change their line or change their attitude to something. Is that because of its alleged prominence in Australian society?

Williamson: (laughter) Yes, it has got an alleged prominence in Australian society, yeah. It is a social lubricant to the extent that more telling things are revealed under its influence. That's perhaps why I've used it. People who get plastered tend to say things that they otherwise wouldn't. This certainly happened in *Don's Party*. Alcohol gave rise to events that wouldn't have otherwise occurred. In the latest play, *What If You Died Tomorrow*, there's quite sparse drinking in it, so maybe I'm conscious of the fact that perhaps I've used too much grog in my earlier days.

Cinema Papers: (laughter) I didn't necessarily mean it as a criticism.

Williamson: Other people certainly have. They say, "A lot more beer cans," but the fact is that the three plays were written in the space of a year, so there are bound to be common elements in them, and there was beer in each of them.

Cinema Papers: Aggression—verbal and physical—seems to pervade your work.

Williamson: Yeah. The plays are concerned with the sexual and the aggressive impulses that most of us do have, and I'm interested in the way that people cope with them. For example, *The Removalists* should be a worrying play, because the audience laughs right through it at often quite gratuitous and pleasurable violence. The sergeant enjoys beating Kenny, and Kenny in a strange way for most of the play is enjoying being beaten up, or at least he's egging the sergeant on to greater heights of violence. It's a society-wide problem, because violence and sex are the most expedient ways of coping with the great modern problem of sheer boredom. The surge of gratuitous violence in most Western countries is related to the boredom of most people's lives. Young guys just go out now and roam around in cars and find somebody to beat up. It alleviates their boredom. There should be other ways of doing it, but I'm terribly interested in this sort of problem.

Cinema Papers: In your work so far, you seem to have described this problem of gratuitous violence fairly thoroughly and consistently, but there doesn't so far in your work seem to be a vision of some possible alternative. Are you, in your future work, interested in exploring other possibilities, even if they might not be real ones?

Williamson: Well, I can't see any role for me as a writer in the social and political restructuring of society, which is the ultimate answer. It's a question of people's attitudes, and in the present materialist and capitalist type of society, there is a permanent disadvantaged group. All our western suburbs show the highest rate of bashings and gratuitous violence simply because the young guys are industrial prisoners. They work in boring, shit-house jobs. They are given no social esteem whatsoever. They very smartly realize they're the shit at the bottom of the barrel. The only way to gain any relief from the boredom and gain group identity is to elevate a negative characteristic like brutality to a positive mode of identifying.

Cinema Papers: Your plays suggest that the perhaps less disadvantaged groups like the middle class or the upper class are equally violent, equally bored, but that the higher one goes up the social ladder the more verbal the violence gets.

Williamson: Yeah, it's only a change in emphasis because it's a relative thing. ...

Cinema Papers: There seem to be no reasonably sound people in your work. I mean, most of them are equally guilty, except the really bad cop in *The Removalists*, perhaps.

Williamson: No. Actually, I felt rather sympathetic towards the two cops in *The Removalists* because I accepted the fact that the sergeant got a bit of gratuitous pleasure from the violence, as he usually kept this sort of thing within human bounds ... It was just that the sergeant let the situation go beyond the normal bounds that he could handle.

Cinema Papers: From what you've said, there seems to be a political context to most of your work. But there's never been any political content overtly in it. Do you think you prefer to keep it that way, or do you think that later you may explore some of these questions even if you don't know what the answers are?

Williamson: Oh, I'm intensely interested in exploring them personally, but not in my writing. I'd rather write about the situation as it is, because I really don't pretend to know the answers. I'm quite bewildered. Do we opt for a homogenous society with only one set of values as in China, or do we adopt a pluralist society in which there are an incredible number of attitudes and value systems to choose from? There are unpleasant side effects in both. Do we have some intermediate type of system which allows ... As I say, I'm completely bewildered.

Cinema Papers: I take it from that that your hesitance to be overtly political in your plays and films is not from any theoretical antagonism towards political writing, but from what you feel to be your particular talents and abilities.

Williamson: Well, it's more that I have no firm belief in any political line. I just observe and report ... But reporting and commenting on society without specifying the political solution can still be useful politically in that other people can cogitate on it. It may be a spur to other people to press for some solutions. I don't know. I do have certain beliefs. I think there's something wrong with excessive materialism. (And here I am. I own a quite spacious house here in the bush.) I can sort of see the disaster to which materialists are striving. They're bleeding the world at the moment. And if anything, there's that sort of vague feeling in the back of my head that humanity's got to be diverted from its basic pursuit of material acquisition to interpersonal harmony. But how one does it, Christ knows.

From a *Cleo* Interview*

From time to time, Williamson has been accused of creating stereotype characters. He is both slightly amused and slightly hurt by this criticism. "They are real to me, very real," he said. "Without giving anything away I can say they are as real as it is possible to make them."

Is there a typical Australian male, then? "No, not really ..." And now it is the psychology student speaking, rather than the playwright. "The Australian male has a huge range of temperamental differences, call them socio-economic differences if you like, cut across by certain common surface characteristics. He still tends to show a lot of chauvinism, mistrust and fear of women. The rugged individual thing is a myth. I think a large percentage of men tend to assume a veneer of boorishness to mask an otherwise unassuming interior.

"When the male adopts this rather brutish attitude—which may stem from the fact that in the early days of settlement here women were in such short supply they were regarded as objects for the bedroom or the kitchen (well, that's one theory, anyway)—Australian women, in turn, develop definite reactions.

"Shrewishness is about the most dominant. There are an inordinate number of shrewish, manipulative women in Australia—understandable perhaps, when they are left with only limited channels through which to express themselves. And I think that expression is sometimes not very healthy."

Williamson is interested in the phenomenon of the liberated woman. At this stage, however, he hasn't yet written one into a play—mainly because he is concerned with realism and he believes that most women, as yet, are not wholly liberated.

"A woman has to be pretty strong in her mind, pretty bloody tough, to play it out and not just adopt certain liberated attitudes, then fall back on the old familiar woman's role when it suits her," he said.

"Take the two girls in the segment I wrote in *Libido* (although their roles were a bit diminished in the final version). They're not really liberated women but they're playing at it. Liberated women

---

* Anne Yuille, "Will success spoil David Williamson?" *Cleo*, August 1973, pp. 24–25.

wouldn't have gone off with the two men. They woudn't have taken the outrages calmly; they would have blown up on the spot. But these two were playing the situation for its sensuality.

"I've been abused by real liberated women—and there are a few of them around Carlton—for most of my female characters. They feel I should be writing about liberated women, to combat possible stereotyping. But this would not be as dramatically viable. And I have to write reality rather than propaganda."

Douglas Stewart

Tawhai with her golden lover, Whana. A watercolour by Norman Lindsay illustrating *The Golden Lover*. Photograph by courtesy of Douglas Stewart.

The Golden Lover

A Comedy in Verse

The Golden Lover was first broadcast, in a slightly abridged version, on A.B.C. radio on 24 January 1943, with the following cast:

TAWHAI, a young Maori woman	Patricia Kennedy
RUARANGI, her husband	Robert Burnard
WERA, her mother	Hilda Dorrington
NUKUROA, her father	Howard Smith
KOURA, an old woman; friend of Wera	Ruby May
TIKI, a youth in love with Tawhai	Keith Hudson
Women and men	Maud Fyfield Margaret Reid John D'Arcy Austen Milroy
TE KAWAU, the tohunga or witch-doctor	Marshall Crosby
WHANA, the golden lover; a man of the faery "People of the Mist"	Keith Eden
RAURIKA } TEINA } women	(not included in first broadcast)

Produced by Frank D. Clewlow.

SCENE I

Sound of snoring.

TAWHAI: Wake, volcano!
RUARANGI: Eh? What is that you said?
TAWHAI: I asked if my noble husband would deign to wake.
  It is morning, if I may say so without offence
  To your dignity, Ruarangi.
RUARANGI: And the food is cooked?
TAWHAI: Not quite, Ruarangi.
RUARANGI: Ach, you are lazy, Tawhai.
TAWHAI: You are right, of course, Ruarangi; you are always right.
  And yet it is true that you are still in your bed
  On the soft warm fern, and I have been out an hour
  And down to the river to take an eel from the trap
  While you were snoring, and no one else in the village
  But myself and the wild duck were at the water.
  I think—it is just a whim, and probably wrong—
  You could go to the river yourself.
RUARANGI: Tawhai, my dear,
  The morning air tastes bitter on your tongue,
  And you will become a scold. Be bright at daybreak!
  It is true that the perils of fishing are a husband's burden
  And to-morrow morning, as long as I do not sleep,
  I shall certainly go to the river. But also by custom
  It is not your place to speak to me of such things.
  You are young, and have much to learn. I do not snore.
TAWHAI: You gurgled and whistled all night like a boiling spring.
RUARANGI: I have never snored in my life. I have known myself
  For longer than you have, remember.
TAWHAI: I have been your wife
  Two years, Ruarangi, and every night you have snored.
RUARANGI: By immemorial custom I may snore if I please.
  Go and see if the eel is cooked.
TAWHAI (*going*): Yes, Ruarangi.
  The day is bright. It is time you saw the sun.
RUARANGI: It is time I had my food. And time you were gone
  To your work in the fields. A sunny day of the spring;
  That is the fine time to fell a tree
  And hollow out a canoe, if one were younger;
  And a fine time to be setting snares for the birds,
  If the birds were not far in the forest, and one were not fat;
  And a fine time to be catching the little crayfish
  Where the creek runs into the Waipa, if the water were warmer;
  A fine time, indeed, to be doing everything,
  And also a fine time to sit in the sun
  And not be doing anything very much.
  I shall look at my fishing-lines and undo the knots.
  (*Calling.*)
  Tawhai!

TAWHAI: Coming, Ruarangi. It is ready now.
RUARANGI: The good eel with the silver belly from the river!
   The wind in the tea-tree does not smell so sweet
   And wind you cannot eat, without discomfort.
TAWHAI: It is a fine eel. You like it, my husband?
RUARANGI: Fresh from the clear stream and the oven of earth—
   Aye, Tawhai, it is good. Sometimes I think
   Of that lovely Waipa leaping down from Pirongia,
   From the wild bush all the way down to the sea,
   And an eel in every pool. Ten eels, Tawhai—
   All the river an eel! When I think of that
   My belly he sings like a bird.
TAWHAI: You are a poet.
RUARANGI: Give me a kumara with it, the sweet potato.
TAWHAI: Here; there is plenty of food. Tell me, Ruarangi,
   I am a good wife? You are pleased with Tawhai?
RUARANGI: It is true you could have brought another eel—
   One is not much for a warrior. But, yes, Tawhai,
   You are a good wife, when you do not scold.
TAWHAI: Then I will tell you now what is in my mind.
RUARANGI: Ha! What is that? Do not disturb my breakfast.
TAWHAI: I was frightened, Ruarangi, at the river this morning.
   Except for myself and the birds there was no one there
   And the white mist had not gone back to the bush.
   Who knows that the faery people, the people of the mist,
   Do not come down from the mountain, from dark Pirongia,
   When the mist comes down, and move about in our fields?
RUARANGI: The faery people, the patu paiarehe!
   It is better not to speak about such people.
TAWHAI: No, but they move in the mist.
RUARANGI: They move in the mist.
TAWHAI: And this morning a white mist on the water of the Waipa.
   Ruarangi, one bell-bird cried, and then no more.
   The white mist that turns the air to snow
   And kills the heat of the sun had come from Pirongia,
   Walking like spirits through the Hakarimata bush,
   And it was over our fields where the kumara grow
   And over the eel-traps. The mist, Ruarangi, at the river.
RUARANGI: You did not see a man of the faery people?
TAWHAI: The mist swirled, and I ran. I felt them around me.
RUARANGI: You did not hear a flute? If you heard a sound
   Like the crying of a flute, lost in the white mist
   Or the dark bush, or out upon the water,
   You should stop your ears and run; run, Tawhai!
   You did not hear the flutes of the demon people
   So close to the village?
TAWHAI: I heard no sound at all,
   Except the bell-bird once, and the crying of the water.
   When I frightened the wild duck and she flew away
   I thought there was no one alive in all the world

Except myself and the river; and the mist was round us.
I am frightened to go to the river, Ruarangi,
At sunrise again. Sunrise is the cold time
When the world comes from its dark mother called Night
And the light is new, and the mist moves in the bush,
And the birds worship their god, and something could happen
That has never happened before upon the earth.

RUARANGI: This is a fine talk to talk to a husband
At his peaceful breakfast, Tawhai. This talk of devils.
I am a warrior, and I do not like to be frightened.

TAWHAI: So you are frightened, are you? And what of your wife?
They are tall and beautiful men, and fierce with women.

RUARANGI: That is enough of all this unpleasant talk.
There is danger, Tawhai; enchantment! It is best to be silent
On all such matters as ghosts and monsters and demons
In case one is overheard, and one's words are offensive.

TAWHAI: It is true they are great enchanters. In all the old stories
They steal the Maori women by their wicked behaviour
And their magic flutes.

RUARANGI: Now you have made me think
That the eel in my belly may well have been bewitched.

TAWHAI: I do not think they would bother to bewitch an eel.

RUARANGI: It squirms and bites inside me.

TAWHAI: You eat too fast.

RUARANGI: That is no way for a wife to talk to a husband
Whose belly is alive wth enchanted potatoes and eels.
I shall go to old Te Kawau, our wise tohunga,
And ask him to work a magic. I think I am poisoned.

TAWHAI: You, a warrior, to be afraid of an eel!

RUARANGI: I am, it is true, a warrior. I was born ferocious.
But what can my stone axe or my whalebone mere
Or my wooden spear avail against enchantment?
No, I must go to Te Kawau.

TAWHAI: I hate that man!
He is old and yellow and evil and feeds on horror
Like fungus on a rotting log. That man should die!

RUARANGI: You are wicked, Tawhai! If you say such a thing again
I shall beat you hard. The tohunga knows our thoughts
Before we think them and can strike us dead in our whare
With a blast of his mind like lightning. You think politely!
It is time you went to the fields.

TAWHAI: To the fields again!

RUARANGI: Young wives should not be lazy.

TAWHAI: I am tired of working.
I do not see why a wife should do all the work.

RUARANGI: It is a law of nature, not to be questioned.

TAWHAI: Day after day to toil in the kumara patch.
What will the husband do while the wife is grubbing
With her pretty hands in the dirt?

The Golden Lover

RUARANGI: I, too, shall work.
 A warrior's work. I shall sit out here in the sun
 At the side of the whare, and look at my fishing-lines.
TAWHAI: You must not exhaust yourself. And this afternoon
 The sun will have moved, you will toil in the cold shadow.
 What then will you do, Ruarangi?
RUARANGI: This afternoon
 I shall walk with my lines to the other side of the hut
 And sit down there and work.
TAWHAI: Ah, you are lazy.
RUARANGI: How dare you say such a thing! I am a warrior.
TAWHAI: You have never been to battle in all your life.
 The men are all women now. My mother says
 When she was a girl the men were men indeed.
 She says one time——
RUARANGI: From all we know of what happened
 When she was a girl, Tawhai, it is best to forget it.
 You must not fill your head with loose imaginings.
 You are far too ready to do so.
TAWHAI: You are jealous still.
 Although I have been your wife for two long years,
 You think I would cast my eyes on younger men
 And not so fat, perhaps. Why, Ruarangi,
 I should never dream of doing such a thing!
 It is true that several youths, especially Tiki
 (Who, I think, is insane), watch me with eyes like dogs'
 And even invite me to go for a short walk,
 But I do not see them or hear them.
RUARANGI: I believe you, Tawhai.
 After all, you are married to me; which is an honour.
 Yet it is true, before you became my wife,
 You were somewhat gay with the impudent youths of the pa.
TAWHAI: There were only three or four.
RUARANGI: You told me two!
TAWHAI: Ah, well, I forget.
RUARANGI: Do not forget, Tawhai,
 My stone axe, my whalebone mere and my spear.
 Should you happen to go for a walk with that young Tiki,
 I think he will take a longer walk one day
 With a split skull, and he will not come back.
TAWHAI: I shall never walk with Tiki. He is just a boy.
RUARANGI: Then that is good. Hurry to the fields, Tawhai,
 Lest you be the last at work, and I am disgraced.
TAWHAI: Ach, I am tired of the fields. I am tired of work.
RUARANGI: Tired of growing food! Why, I, myself
 Have many a time walked almost as far as the field
 And sat on the hill and watched you women toiling.
 Nothing could be more refreshing. And healthy, too.
 It will make you strong.

TAWHAI: It will make me one great lump
Of fat and gristle like my mother.
RUARANGI: You are cross this morning.
Why, if you do not like it, do you stay so late,
Working on in the dusk when the others have gone
And the mists are beginning to move? Hear me, Tawhai,
Be early away from the kumara patch to-night.
Here we are few in number, and all around us
Is the dark bush, full of many unusual things
Which are pleasant no doubt, and certainly well-intentioned,
But best not met with.
TAWHAI: I am not afraid in the sunset.
For then the earth is old and glows with knowledge
And nothing will happen by field or forest or river
That has not happened before and is harmless enough.
RUARANGI: You will not say it is harmless if the people of the—
The people you spoke of before should come down in the mist
And steal behind you as you work and snatch you up
And smother your cries and carry you off to the bush
And you never come home again. And well you know
That that has been known to happen.
TAWHAI: The people of the mist,
The men, that is, of the patu paiarehe,
Are said to be very handsome. They are strong and fierce
And their skins are fairer than ours, the colour of honey,
And their eyes are blue, and their hair is the faery red,
The urukehu hair, like a fire in the night.
I should like to see one, I think, if it were safe.
RUARANGI: It would not be safe for you who alone in the village
Refuse to anoint yourself with that pleasant oil
We squeeze from the dead sharks, and the smell of which,
Like the smell of our cooking pots, for some strange reason
The faery people dislike. The shark-oil, Tawhai——
TAWHAI: Ruarangi, I do not wish to hear about shark-oil.
I am not a shoal of fish. I am a woman.
RUARANGI: But all the Maoris use it.
TAWHAI: So you said before.
How many times have you said it these last two years?
RUARANGI: But now, Tawhai, if the faery people are about——
TAWHAI: Not now or any time. I should be ashamed
If a man with the wild red hair who chanced to see me
Should have to run from my beauty, holding his nose.
RUARANGI: Better to hold his nose from the smell of shark-oil
Than to run off holding you. You are foolish, Tawhai.
You should not joke on such matters.
TAWHAI: It is not a joke.
I should like to see such a man—just once, for a minute,
From behind a bush—somewhere where I am safe.
RUARANGI: If you should see such a man, you foolish girl,
He would snatch you away to the bush, to the cold mists

The Golden Lover

    And the cold winds and the cold inhuman people
    High up and far away where wild Pirongia
    Is lost in the sky of the gods, and never again
    Would Tawhai see the dogs and children playing
    In the village where she was born; never again
    See mother or father or sister or brother or friend;
    Nevermore our twisting Waipa and our fields of food,
    Nevermore her husband's whare. Alas, poor Tawhai!
TAWHAI: I have not yet gone, Ruarangi.
RUARANGI: Eh, Tawhai,
    You had better not go at all to the fields to-day.
    You have made me afraid.
TAWHAI: Of course I shall go to the fields.
    You are always trying to stop me doing what I wish.
    I am not afraid. It is day, and the women are there.
RUARANGI: Go, then, if you wish. But do not linger in the dusk.
    A woman, although she is married, is a plump brown bird
    That tempts the hawk to strike.
TAWHAI: You are jealous of Tiki.
RUARANGI: We were talking, Tawhai, of the demon people you mentioned,
    Notorious snatchers of women and bewitchers of eels.
    Besides, when you are late, I have to wait
    Too long for my dinner, and my belly roars in pain.
TAWHAI: You could cook the meal yourself.
RUARANGI: I, a warrior!
    The son of a warrior
    And the grandson of a warrior
    And the great-grandson of a warrior
    And the great-great-grandson of a warrior
    And the great-great-great-grandson of a great great warrior indeed!
    To do the work of a woman. Take that!
    (*Slaps her.*)
TAWHAI: Oh!
RUARANGI: From a woman I will suffer much, expecting no more
    Than a man should expect from a bird or a female dog—
    A song, that is, or puppies; but I will not suffer
    Insult, Tawhai, to the dignity of a husband.
    No! take that!
    (*Slap.*)
TAWHAI: Oh!
RUARANGI: I will not allow you
    To speak to me of your multitudinous lovers
    Before you became my wife, you shameless creature!
    I will not allow you to roll around your tongue
    The name of Tiki like a savoury piece of eel.
    I will not allow you to speak of handsome faeries
    Except with proper repugnance. I will not allow you
    To suggest I could cook a meal.

TAWHAI: How much would it hurt?
RUARANGI: It will hurt you, Tawhai, if you do not show me respect.
If you make me beat you again I shall take a stick.
Not merely slap you gently where you are soft
In a way that gives us both a certain pleasure.
Go to the fields before I am really angry.
TAWHAI: I am angry myself. I do not like to be slapped.
You should slap yourself if you think there is pleasure in it.
RUARANGI: Go; and be home early.
TAWHAI: I shall go to the fields.
To talk to my mother of scandal and the people of the mist.
But as for work—I shall please myself, Ruarangi.
And as for coming home, I shall come when I choose.
RUARANGI: If you come home early, you take an eel from the trap;
Then neither of us would have to go to the river
In the mist to-morrow morning. Come home by the river
And bring an eel from the trap.
TAWHAI: I shall do what I please.

(*Music.*)

SCENE 2

WERA: Koura, my friend, you are the mother of lies.
KOURA: I am old, and so to be mocked. My truths are lies.
At least, Wera, I am not the mother of scandal,
As some fat persons are, nor yet the mother
Of a scandal waiting for its chance, by the name of Tawhai.
Let your daughter, who flirts with Tiki, see what I saw,
And then we shall see some truths.
WERA: I think you are lying
Did you truly see this man?
KOURA: With my eyes I saw him,
Before I hid them and howled.
WERA: Eh, you old crayfish
Koura, they named you well, for whenever you see
A thing worth seeing you run away from it backwards.
KOURA: Fat as you are, Wera, and fat you are,
You'd have run yourself from that man. His hair was flame,
He was tall as a totara-tree; and the mist all round him;
And round me, too, wet and silver on my skin
Like the very cloak of witchcraft. On my wrists and ankles
Cold, the bonds of enchantment. And I breathed it, Wera,
The mist he breathed and exhaled from his demon body
Like dank leaves burning in my nostrils, the air of enchantment.
WERA: And all day long, you sly old crayfish, Koura,
You have worked at my side in the field here, weeding the kumara,
And kept to yourself this news that the very potatoes
Would sprout from the earth with popping ears to hear.
You, my friend, whom all my life I have known,
Whose secrets I know, including some small scandals,

The Golden Lover 159

And you did not tell me. A man of the faery people!
KOURA: Old friend as you are, Wera, my oldest friend,
  Whose life I have lived as my own, sharing your secerts
  And some fine large scandals, too, I could not tell you,
  For the frost of fear that clenched on my heart at the sight
  Has taken all day to thaw. I am still afraid
  And think I should not have told you, lest now on you,
  As well as on me, bad luck shall fall for talking
  Of a thing that is not to be talked of. I have done you evil.
WERA: Bad luck and good luck both live in my whare, Koura,
  And stir the pot in turn.
KOURA: But this is witchcraft.
  Who knows what evil the people of the mist can do,
  The patu paiarehe with their hair like fire?
WERA: From all that I have heard they are not an evil people
  And though they are famous for carrying off our maidens—
  Young women, perhaps I should say—to the dark of the bush,
  I am much too large and far too middle-aged
  For a faery twice as strong as a totara-tree
  To carry off in comfort. And you are too thin
  And bent, and too sparsely favoured with hair and teeth
  For any faery in his senses to look at you twice.
  Even if he did, you would howl and spoil his fun.
KOURA: Wera, you should not laugh. See, it is dusk;
  The women are beginning to go. When it is dark
  The mist will be here, and the strange people of the mist—
  Here where we are, on our village kumara field
  Where I saw that one this morning. We two, perhaps,
  Being middle-aged and a shade too thoroughly married,
  Have little to fear from immoral faery persons,
  But the young umnarried girls are in danger, Wera!
  And the married, too, who by some miraculous chance
  Are plump and pretty still. You have a daughter.
  Aye, and where is she? Where is Tawhai your daughter?
WERA: Eh, crayfish, you have touched me with your cold claws.
  She is surely somewhere on the field.
KOURA: I cannot see her.
  All the women but Tawhai! She has vanished in the air.
WERA: Her dust's too sweet and warm to a man's hands
  And a faery's too for the winds to have it yet.
  But where has she gone? If she were still my daughter
  And not the wife of that mountain stuffed with nothing,
  Ruarangi, I'd teach her not to wander. I'd slap her.
  Is she down in the gully there, cutting the flax?
KOURA: There is no one down in the gully. The women have gone,
  And a thin mist, Wera, a mist is rising.
  See, see now, from the black earth at our feet
  A little steam of mist, the first white fingers
  Feeling for the throat of the light. Where is your daughter?
WERA: She cannot be far. She is always the wandering one.

    Is it Tawhai there, coming up the hill towards us
  With the others going home?
KOURA: Raurika is there;
  Teina is there. Tawhai—where is Tawhai?
WERA: Do not scuttle so quickly, Koura, Koura the crayfish,
  Under the dismal rocks.
  (*Calling*) Raurika! Raurika!
  Do you know where my daughter is?
RAURIKA: Look in the bushes.
  You will find her there with some fine bird or other.
  It runs in the family.
WERA: It is good to know, Raurika,
  My daughter is not such a damp and dismal hag
  As only a frog could love.
                  Tell me, Teina,
  When did you last see Tawhai?
TEINA: This afternoon
  She said she was tired of scratching in dirty ground
  Like a swamp-hen looking for worms; so she left the field
  And went alone to the forest.
KOURA: Alas, to the forest!
TEINA: Is Tawhai lost?
KOURA: Do not tell these women, Wera.
  Talk is unlucky. They will spread it all over the village.
WERA: I think, Teina, my daughter went home early
  To cook her good husband's dinner.
RAURIKA: She would do more good
  If she cooked her husband. I think you will find her, Wera,
  Discussing cooking and other domestic matters
  With someone young and hungry. Tiki, for instance.
WERA: There are some who live in virtue and disappointment
  Like a frog in a swamp. Go home to your tadpoles, woman.
TEINA: We shall see you to-morrow, Wera.
RAURIKA: We shall, Teina.
  One cannot miss a mountain.
WERA: Swim, frog!
KOURA: And now they are gone. And all the women are gone.
  And who knows who will meet in to-morrow's sun?
  See where they climb the rise to the pa on the hill
  Where the fires burn and the men wait for their food
  And the children go to the whares like birds to their nests,
  Darting and rustling and fretting before they sleep.
  And now we are two old women alone in the dusk
  As the sky fades and the mountain grows dark and vast
  And voices like women drowning, spirits perhaps,
  Cry in the running river, and Tawhai is lost.
WERA: Do not say such a terrible thing.
KOURA: Aye, she is lost,
  Your daughter of the proud breast and the mouth of love
  And the fierce high-curving nostrils. See, my friend,

Darker grows Pirongia, darker the bush
WERA: There is too much bush. The men should burn it down
As they did in the old days once when the faery people
Learned of the horror of fire. All night, all bush;
All mountain and sky and moaning water and bush.
KOURA: And something is burning there with a cold flame
To make that smoke of mist that creeps from the ranges
And glides along the river and fumes at our feet
From the earth we Maoris tilled. The fire of the dead,
So coldly burning; the fire of witchcraft, of evil,
Of the earth that does not love us.
WERA: Where has she gone?
And all that bush and the mist.
KOURA: Bad luck is upon us.
And look, Wera, look! Worse than bad luck.
There in the white mist! They are coming, Wera!
WERA: Aye, there is someone there.
KOURA: Quick, we must run!
We cannot wait for Tawhai. See, they are coming,
Three tall men—look! Three men as tall as trees,
The patu paiarehe! Do you see them, Wera?
WERA: I see one crayfish dithering in her second childhood,
And my daughter Tawhai approaching. Three faery people!
Look, you old fool, it is only my lazy daughter
Who has been asleep in the fern.
(*Calling*) Tawhai! Come here!
KOURA: She has no right to look like three tall demons,
But that is enchantment perhaps. Perhaps a prophecy.
Let us go, then, Wera. I do not like the dark
And this morning I saw what I saw.
WERA: Eh, old Koura,
I think you walk in a dream not proper to your age
Where you see these red-haired faeries. Three of them now!
KOURA: I saw that man this morning. And now it is late,
And hands reach for your daughter.
WERA: It is true she is foolish
To stay so late in the bush; and the mist so close.
Tawhai!
TAWHAI: What monster of the night bellows my name?
WERA: Come here, you cheeky!
TAWHAI: Ho, you old Maori women,
You are working late to-night. Koura the crayfish,
Your husband will drop you in the pot and boil you pink
If you stay so late in the field.
KOURA: You should beat her, Wera.
WERA: Hear me, my daughter, this is no time for laughter.
Koura has seen a thing in the fields this morning
That will make your tongue crouch down like a bird from a hawk,
You who are young and shudder from the Maori shark-oil.
TAWHAI: She has seen a man of the patu paiarehe!

WERA: She has indeed. But how did you know it, Tawhai?
KOURA: The bird foresees her doom. She knows it all.
TAWHAI: Koura, you did not truly? Not truly see one?
    A man of the faery people, and you so old?
KOURA: Old, and the sport of the young, but I saw that man.
TAWHAI: When? What was he like?
KOURA: Darker it grows,
    And the bush is heaving towards us. Let us go to the village.
WERA: Yes, let us go.
TAWHAI: Tell me about that man.
KOURA: I saw that man of the demon people this morning.
TAWHAI: How early this morning?
KOURA: Early indeed, Tawhai,
    While the mist from the bush was white on the field and the river.
TAWHAI: He was not at the river, Koura?
KOURA: Below us there,
    Where the bracken comes to the edge of the kuamara field.
TAWHAI: Eh, was his hair red and his skin like gold?
    Was he tall and strong and fierce?
KOURA: Aye, he was tall.
    Tall as a totara-tree was this man of the mist,
    With the mist around his shoulders like a cloak
    And his body strong and golden and his hair like flames.
    Taller and stronger than any man of the Maoris
    And fierce, and his eyes flashed, and his arms were long
    And he leaped towards me and made a sound like laughing
    (An evil spell, no doubt) and I covered my eyes
    And howled and ran. And again he made that sound
    Like the laughter of devils, and shouted enchantments at me.
TAWHAI: Ah, what did he say?
KOURA: "Go home!" he shouted.
    "Hag, reeking of shark-oil, go home to the pot!"
WERA: That does not sound like a spell.
KOURA: It was vile enchantment,
    Working by opposites. He wished me to stay and be seized.
    But I was too cunning.
TAWHAI: I wish I had seen that man.
WERA: Tawhai, my daughter, do not say foolish things.
    We do not wish you lost to us for ever.
TAWHAI: Why, Koura, were you out on the field so early?
KOURA: I came for food to the pit where we store the kumaras,
    And there I saw him.
WERA: And there you saw that man!
TAWHAI: I was out myself in the morning mist at the eel-trap.
    The faery man with his wicked and beautiful hair
    And his golden and dangerous body and very long arms
    Was not in the mist by the river, else I and not Koura
    Would be telling this terrible story.
WERA: You, my daughter,
    Would not be here to tell it. The man of the mist

Would seem to have spared Koura because she is old,
But only a fool of a faery would pass you by.
TAWHAI: How dangerous it is to be so lovely.
I wish I were fat as you or skinny as Koura;
Although, of course, it is lovely to be so lovely.
KOURA: You would not be lovely long in the mountain places
Where the wind tears a woman as it tears a tree
And the cold devours you with the shining flames of snow
And the mist is heavy in your breast.
TAWHAI: Ah, you are horrid.
It is not at all like that in the mountain places.
WERA: There where the faeries live, maybe as here,
The fire burns and the whare is warm in the night
And children, though pleasant, are very much of a nuisance,
And husbands, though also pleasant, are more of a nuisance,
And the best thing is a talk with another woman
On the old days, or the latest news if scandalous.
But when a woman is seized by the people of the mist
If she goes to no great harm, she goes for ever.
And the yearning for her own people is colder than the snow
And a heavier thought than mist to lie on her heart.
Tawhai, there is your whare. Go home to your husband
And try to forget how lovely it is to be lovely,
Or at least be careful, and do not go out at night
While this danger threatens the village.
TAWHAI: Eh, my mother,
I am tired of going home to that snoring stomach.
And this morning he beat me.
WERA: I thought Ruarangi too lazy
To slap a mosquito. You must have stung him hard.
TAWHAI: He is jealous of boys I knew before we were married,
And also jealous of Tiki.
KOURA: With reason, I think.
TAWHAI: If I have been slightly unfaithful from time to time,
It is most unjust to beat me on mere suspicion.
KOURA: When you are as old as I am, time will beat you
With a hard stick, and stone you with heavy stones
For no crime, except being born a woman.
My old bones have cracked, climbing this hill.
But better here, safe at the gates of the village
Than back in that horrible hollow of night and mist.
TAWHAI: The moon is rising, Koura.
KOURA: The moon is coming,
And I am going. Good night, Wera and Tawhai.
Go to your whares quickly, and all will be well.
WERA: Will you tell your husband, Koura, about this man
You think you have seen in the mist?
KOURA: I will tell him nothing.
It is not an affair for men. I tell him the thing,
And he will be off to Te Kawau, and I shall be questioned,

And spells will be made and the rites of terror performed,
And I do not like such things.
TAWHAI: There is nothing to tell,
You think you saw a man of the faery people,
But nothing happened, and it may have been all a dream.
That is no tale for a husband.
WERA: All men are fools,
Though I do not think a whare is a whare without one.
Let us not tell anyone then. There will only be talk.
KOURA: Talk is unlucky. It made me enough afraid
To see the man. I will not talk about him.
He might enchant me.
TAWHAI: Ah, you silly old Koura,
Who would want an enchanted crayfish?
KOURA: Once I was young!
WERA: She is just a cheeky girl; and her husband will tame her.
KOURA: An evil fate will befall her.
WERA: Tawhai, go home.
TAWHAI: I did not mean to offend her.
WERA: She has gone away
With her lean kneebones knocking each other in rage.
I shall see her safe to her whare and soothe her down.
Go home, my daughter; and see that no evil befalls you.
TAWHAI: Good night, then, Wera.
WERA (*going*): Good night, Tawhai. Go home.
Your husband will want his dinner.
TAWHAI (*alone*): What a fool I am.
It is all their fault for talking of the faery people.
Now he'll be angry again.
TIKI: Tawhai!
TAWHAI: Who's that?
TIKI: It is I, Tiki.
TAWHAI: You, you fool of a boy,
You gave me a fright. Why do you spring at my feet
When I think of an eel for my husband? What do you want?
TIKI: I watched for you to come home. I wanted to see you.
TAWHAI: You have seen me, then. Now go and drown yourself.
TIKI: Why should you be so angry with me, Tawhai?
I am burning for you, and you tell me to jump in the water.
TAWHAI: Eh, Tiki, I am angry. I forgot the eel
From the trap for my husband's dinner. And I do not wish
To go all the way back to the river.
TIKI: Let me go, Tawhai.
TAWHAI: You are only a stupid boy. A proper lover
Would hit my husband with an axe, not run to the river
To bring him eels.
TIKI: I will do whatever you like.
TAWHAI: You would be afraid to go to the river, Tiki,
If you knew what Koura saw. In the mist of the morning,
The patu paiarehe.

The Golden Lover

TIKI: The people of the mist!
TAWHAI: A tall and golden man; and fierce and wicked.
    You would be afraid to meet a man like that.
TIKI: I do not believe it. I am not afraid to go.
    Koura is old and mad. Come to the river.
    And I will protect you, Tawhai.
TAWHAI: If you think, Tiki,
    You might catch at the river a better fish than an eel,
    You have made a mistake. I am not to be taken with a worm.
    But still, we will go to the river, and you shall protect me
    If by any mischance that savage and beautiful man
    Should leap from the bushes.
TIKI: I will protect you, Tawhai.
    He is only a man of the mist. Give me a kiss.
TAWHAI: No, I must hurry. Run.
TIKI: I'll race you there.
    Look at the mist on the water.
TAWHAI: It is like a dream.
    The silver water shining in the silver mist
    And the moon bright in the sky.
TIKI: It is not like a dream
    To be running behind you and never catching up.
TAWHAI: You never shall.
TIKI: But why not, Tawhai? Why not?
TAWHAI: I am not for puppies to worry.
TIKI: My love is Pirongia,
    Sombre and huge on the skyline, but you do not see it.
TAWHAI: Pirongia is where the faery people live.
TIKI: Oh, curse the faery people!
WHANA (*shouting*): Ha!
TAWHAI: Tiki!
    There! It is he!
TIKI: The patu paiarehe!
    He is tall as a tree. Golden! His burning hair!
    Flame from the darkness—run, Tawhai, run!
TAWHAI: Tiki, I am falling!
TIKI (*in the distance*): Hurry, Tawhai!
TAWHAI (*calling despairingly*): Tiki!

(*Music.*)

SCENE 3

WERA: And how was the hunting of the duck to-day, my husband?
NUKUROA: Good was the hunting. We shall not go hungry, Wera.
    What was the chatter in the fields?
WERA: Just women's nonsense.
NUKUROA: You spoke with Tawhai? How was our daughter to-day?
WERA: The thought of Ruarangi sits on her spirit
    And flattens her, Nukuroa. But she burns deep down
    And will make him jump some day.

NUKUROA: All Maori women
Are crazy, Wera. When a drake sits on the water
The duck does not come up behind and set him on fire
To make him jump. Let a husband sit down if he pleases.
I am tired to-night. We travelled far in the swamp,
The dog and I.
WERA: I am tired myself, Nukuroa.
NUKUROA: From a day in the kumara field? That is no great hardship.
WERA: I hurried back to the pa, and the hill is steep.
The gods should have made the world all sloping downhill,
Then women who are not so slim as they were could roll.
I am short of breath, Nukuroa.
NUKUROA: Then why do you hurry?
WERA: Some gallant young man might offer me love in the dark.
NUKUROA: Some brave young man who is not afraid of monsters.
RUARANGI (*calling*): Wera!
NUKUROA: Ah, the voice of the lover.
RUARANGI: Nukuroa!
WERA: That is the voice from the belly of Ruarangi.
Tell him to go away.
RUARANGI: Nukuroa! Wera!
NUKUROA (*calling*): Is it you, Ruarangi?
RUARANGI: It is I indeed, Nukuroa.
May I talk to you in your whare?
NUKUROA: Come in, Ruarangi.
Be careful you do not treat on my good dog
As you step inside, for you are a heavy man
And he has a very short temper.
RUARANGI: Ah, yes, indeed.
(*Noise of* RUARANGI *entering. Dog yelps and then snarls.* RUARANGI *shouts.*)
NUKUROA: Outside, you over-fed mongrel!
WERA: Not you, Ruarangi.
RUARANGI: For two years now—and before I married Tawhai—
Every time I come to your hut that dog bites me.
Why do you keep such a monster?
NUKUROA: He is good for hunting.
I am sorry he hunts you, though. I will beat him for it,
When I can catch him.
RUARANGI: And I will beat your daughter
If I do not catch her soon.
NUKUROA: Why? What has happened?
WERA: Has she not come home?
RUARANGI: No, she has not come home.
I thought perhaps she had come to your whare to gossip,
Forgetting that all there is in her husband's belly
Is a roaring hollow.
NUKUROA: Tawhai has not been here.
Where did you leave her, Wera?

WERA: I have not seen her.
NUKUROA: But you said you were talking together.
WERA: Well, then, we talked.
But I have not seen her to-night. She is working late,
Or perhaps she is visiting someone.
RUARANGI: But how late it is!
WERA: Perhaps she did not notice that night had fallen.
NUKUROA: Perhaps she is up to no good and you are protecting her.
RUARANGI: Except to her father I would not say such a thing,
But Tawhai lately has needed much correction.
WERA: She is not the sort to be deeply in love with correction;
She could do without it, I think.
RUARANGI: Am I, Wera,
To do without my dinner and my wife to cook it?
My stomach gapes like a crater and my anger rises.
WERA: I see you are like a volcano about to erupt.
I will give you some food, Ruarangi.
RUARANGI: I am too upset.
What have you got?
NUKUROA: There is some of that dried shark
We got on that journey to Kawhia, six months ago.
WERA: The stink is beautiful now. Ah, you are lucky.
That is a special treat for my daughter's husband.
Here, Ruarangi. And here is a dish of kumara.
RUARANGI: Ah it is good indeed. Shark is delightful,
If it is not too fresh. When it reeks like this
I can never understand why Tawhai refuses
To anoint herself with the oil. Eh, I am worried!
NUKUROA: I remember when Wera disliked the scent of shark-oil.
She is wiser now she is fat.
RUARANGI: Tawhai is slender.
WERA: She will not be far away. It is early yet.
You eat the shark of Kawhia and do not worry.
RUARANGI: Ah, there are wonderful foods that swim in the sea.
I like your shark, Nukuroa.
NUKUROA: The shark of Kawhia!
Eh, Ruarangi, you should have come on that journey.
RUARANGI: Indeed I should have liked to go on that journey
Through the dark-green bush where our people's enemies live,
And also devils—through the long, hard, hostile forest
Till you saw the shining water and all the fish,
But my toe was sore at the time.
WERA: Yes, we remember.
RUARANGI: On a journey where battle and being cooked and eaten
By ferocious tribes of the bush were distinctly possible,
I should have loved to be present. But then as a warrior
I felt it my duty to stay and protect the women.
It was much more dangerous. And somebody had to stay
And attend to the business of the village.
WERA: Oh yes, Ruarangi.

NUKUROA: Aye, Ruarangi; but that was a great journey.
   The bush like a long life, sunlight and shadow,
   Mountain and gorge, and never any rest in either,
   Only struggle and journeying on, and danger in the night,
   Danger in the daytime, waiting; and then that moment
   On the last spur, with all that bush behind you,
   When you looked down a mile of light to the water of Kawhia
   Like youth again or the shining land of the spirit,
   And the mullet leaped like a spear shaken in the sun.
   The good times, Ruarangi, the times of fishing!
   Cockles in the mud when the tide goes out to the ocean,
   Flounder in the shallow water when the tide comes back,
   Snapper feeding on the shellbanks or the mussels at the heads,
   And sometimes the black fin, the swirl in the channel
   As the shark comes in from the wild blue water to the green.
   Eh, I will tell you what I have seen, Ruarangi,
   In the green water of Kawhia, I have seen the kahawai!
   I have seen the kahawai shoaling, the silver murderer.
   Up from the white cliffs of Pukearuhe
   Or in from lonely Karewa, the gannet's island,
   The herring rolled to Kawhia, a tide of fish,
   The little millions banking to the crests of the waves,
   Ruffling the harbour surface, jangling the water
   Like a wind from the sky, and behind and below the herrings
   And among them, bringing them death, the kahawai rushed,
   The silver killers shoaling after the herrings.
   I stood at the heads where the ridge is broken down
   To a crooked back of stone, old rock and old man,
   And together we watched that slaughter, death in the sea;
   And over our heads, Ruarangi, in the blue of the sky,
   The seagulls screamed and dropped for their share of the kill.
   War in the sea, Ruarangi, war in the sky!
   That is the thing I saw when I came from the bush
   And all its dangers to the quiet waters of Kawhia.
   And around the coast a little on a big grey rock
   Naked to the spray but out of reach of the sea,
   Two seagulls had their young in its nest of sticks,
   The helpless little fellow, bald and ugly.
   Those seabirds watched me; soared in the air and watched me,
   And screamed and were helpless. I saw that, too, Ruarangi,
   Around from the heads at Kawhia. You should go on a journey.
RUARANGI: I shall have to go on a journey to find your daughter.
NUKUROA: If you had been to Kawhia and seen the seabirds,
   You would know it is not worth troubling. You can do nothing!
   Let Tawhai come when she pleases.
RUARANGI: Eh, Nukuroa,
   We cannot all be as old and as wise as you
   To soar above our troubles and watch and not scream.
   I cannot sit here and digest my shark in peace
   While my wife is walking the night.

WERA: The shark was no good?
RUARANGI: It was sweet as a dead dog. But my heart is troubled.
  A wife should come home to her husband.
NUKUROA: Aye, that is true.
  Hear me, Wera, our daughter must obey Ruarangi.
WERA: How, Nukuroa, will you hold the mountain stream
  In her busband's cooking-pot? You are silly men.
  You know about war and fishing, old man; Ruarangi,
  You know about sitting and eating; but neither of you knows
  The mind of a girl like Tawhai.
NUKUROA: I know your mind
  And the fish that cooks in that pot, and that is enough
  To make quite certain the girl should come home to her husband.
  Where did you leave her, Wera?
WERA: I have not seen her.
NUKUROA: I think you are lying, woman.
WERA: Why should I lie?
NUKUROA: Habit.
RUARANGI: Tawhai is lost!
NUKUROA: Found, more likely.
  By a thing called Tiki.
RUARANGI: No! I do not believe it.
WERA: She would never waste herself on that naked fledgling.
NUKUROA: I think he can hop.
WERA: For a harmless crumb or a worm.
RUARANGI: I have heard myself a story about this Tiki,
  But here I sit, fearing a far worse thing.
  Nukuroa, if your daughter had such little sense
  Of her husband's rights and importance as to play him false
  With some crumb or worm of a Tiki, why should she linger
  So late with her lover and so let her shame be known
  And my terrible wrath be aroused? She is not a fool.
NUKUROA: Aye, that is true. Even Wera always deceived me
  With circumspection.
WERA: I never deceived you; or seldom.
  You are right, Ruarangi. Tawhai is not with Tiki.
RUARANGI: She cannot be with a man. But she spoke this morning
  Of a man not a man at all, but a being of the mist.
  I am much afraid. Women have strange forebodings.
NUKUROA: The patu paiarehe! It is long, Ruarangi,
  Since they troubled the Maori women. You have made me uneasy.
RUARANGI: We are a little people and the bush surrounds us.
  A handful of warriors, a handful of women and children
  And detestable dogs, a few little huts of raupo
  And the meeting-house and the fires where the women cook,
  And all around us the great dark lonely bush
  Where our enemies live, and half-mad wandering outcasts,
  And the hooting birds that hunt for their prey in the night.
  At the gates of the pa the enormous cave of darkness!
  And the creatures and spirits of the dark, older than the Maori,

170   The Golden Lover

Old as the forest, hide in that cave by day,
And at night come out to hear us sing in the whares
Or watch us cook at the fires. They move in the night,
They move in the mist. And Tawhai said this morning
She had sensed at the river the patu paiarehe.

WERA: You have frightened me, Ruarangi.
RUARANGI: I have frightened myself.
    (*The dog snarls and then barks outside the whare.*)
WERA: Eh! who is that? Listen!
    (*Dog snarls.*)
RUARANGI: Is it Tawhai, Wera?
NUKUROA: The dog would not bark at Tawhai.
RUARANGI: See who it is.
WERA: I do not like it.
RUARANGI: Someone is standing at the door!
NUKUROA: They would never come to the village where the shark-
    oil reeks
And the steam rises from the pots.
    (*Dog barks.*) Go, Wera.
RUARANGI: Tawhai is gone. They have come to tell me she is gone.
WERA: Koura, come into the whare. Lie down, you dog.
What has brought your old bones creaking through the village
In the dark of the night, Koura?
NUKUROA: Welcome, old Koura.
KOURA: Welcome you say, Nukuroa. But a harsher word
Your dog speaks at your door.
RUARANGI: That dog is a devil.
KOURA: You here, Ruarangi? Well, I am not surprised.
Your pretty wife is not in your whare to-night.
RUARANGI: How! What do you know?
KOURA: I know a little.
Oh, yes, I know a little of what goes on.
A woman, perhaps, is a silly old knock-kneed crayfish,
No use to a man and fit to be mocked by a girl,
And yet she need not be blind. Old and skinny,
But not yet blind, Ruarangi. Old crayfish eyes
That still can see what the little fishes do
Behind the weeds when they are two together
And the big fat eel is asleep.
RUARANGI: It is hardly courteous.
To speak of anyone here as an eel, and fat,
But we shall let it pass. Speak, Koura,
Your terrible news of Tawhai and the people of the mist.
KOURA: I do not think it was a man of the faery people
The useless and laughed-at crayfish saw to-night
Leading the laughing Tawhai down to the river.
Not a faery lover. Go and find your wife in the tea-tree
With a water-rat called Tiki.
RUARANGI: Ha! I will kill him!
NUKUROA: No, Ruarangi, no. He is only a boy.

The Golden Lover 171

RUARANGI: But a boy is easy to kill. I will dash his brains out.
And Tawhai, too. What thing shall I do to Tawhai?
WERA: What will Tawhai do to you if you kill her friend?
Koura, why do you come to my whare with lies?
You have dreamed this thing because you are angry with Tawhai.
KOURA: I did not mean to tell her husband, Wera.
Husbands should go away and get bitten by dogs.
But I came to tell you to save your daughter from folly,
For I saw her go with that boy.
NUKUROA: Women! Women!
I knew that spark of a Tiki danced in her eyes.
Where did you see them, Koura?
RUARANGI: I will kill them both!
KOURA: From my whare door I saw those shameless ones.
She must have met him as soon as we left her, Wera.
WERA: Now you have said it!
NUKUROA: My wife is the queen of liars.
You will put me to shame, Wera, before all the tribe;
And your daughter, too, and this good man, Ruarangi.
You came from the fields with Tawhai. You gave her to Tiki.
RUARANGI: Do not say that person's name. It is like a beetle.
I will crush that thing with my foot.
KOURA: Sit on him, fat one.
WERA: Believe me, Nukuroa, it is none of my doing.
NUKUROA: Then why did you lie?
WERA: Well, it is Tawhai's affair.
I thought she had gone for a walk. It does no good
To ask where a woman has gone when a woman has gone
Wherever a woman goes when she goes for a walk.
It is not an affair for men. It is women's business.
Koura goes out of her mind and tells you the truth
And now we have all this nonsense. This talk, this fuss!
This talk of killing poor Tiki.
NUKUROA: I wish all women
Were fish at the bottom of the sea, to be caught when wanted,
Thrown back if useless—which is nine times out of ten—
And never able to talk.
KOURA: You are quite right, Wera,
I should not have spoken to men of sacred matters.
RUARANGI: Women are a babble of birds. There is all this chatter
And my wife is still in the tea-tree down by the river,
Not behaving herself at all. It is not to be borne!
And I will not bear such a thing. I the descendant
Of generations of warriors, I who am I,
Ruarangi!
WERA: Eh, what a noise!
RUARANGI: To be shamed by a beetle of a boy!
My body is an earthquake of anger. It will start me wheezing.
WERA: Sit down, Ruarangi.
RUARANGI: No, I will not sit down!

Let me go and kill that person.
NUKUROA: No, be patient.
WERA: The dog is outside, Ruarangi.
RUARANGI: I will kill the dog!
NUKUROA: Ah, you are brave with rage. But listen, my friend,
You cannot kill that boy or the village will laugh.
RUARANGI: Even so, I will kill him.
WERA: Tiki is only a boy.
RUARANGI: Even so, I will kill him.
KOURA: I have seen that boy with the spear
And also the axe and club. He is very strong.
WERA: A terrible boy.
NUKUROA: To kill him would start a feud.
RUARANGI: Sorrow is upon my head like night on the forest.
My wife is unfaithful and now my life is in danger.
NUKUROA: The talk! The talk! Every fish can be caught
With time, Ruarangi, and patience.
RUARANGI: Confusion is on me.
And whatever thing I do the village will laugh.
NUKUROA: Truly, Ruarangi, this thing must be kept a secret.
You women, you are not to talk.
WERA: We shall be like stones.
NUKUROA: Then do not get up and jump with a splash in the pond.
RUARANGI: Secret, yes; but how shall the secret be kept
If in spite of the skill with weapons of that mighty boy
My warrior's blood overcomes me? I do not think
I could see that person who has stolen my devil of a wife
And let him live.
NUKUROA: No. You are not to kill him.
    (*The dog barks.*)
WERA: More trouble, more trouble. Who is it coming now?
NUKUROA: We do not want any strangers here to-night.
Tell them to go away.
RUARANGI: Let them see me kill him.
WERA: Tiki!
TIKI: Nukuroa!
KOURA: Shameless!
NUKUROA: You, you puppy!
RUARANGI: Ha! Tiki! Now you will die a death.
TIKI: You here, Ruarangi! I have jumped in the boiling mud.
RUARANGI: Now I will kill him. Watch me!
    (*Sound of scuffle.*)
TIKI: Help! Nukuroa!
WERA: Quick, he is choking him.
RUARANGI: Ha, you rat, you devil!
KOURA: We are seeing murder done before our eyes
And the feud of blood will last for generations.
NUKUROA: A little choking will do that boy much good.
RUARANGI: Tiki, beetle, what have you done with my wife?
Answer!

The Golden Lover

WERA: The boy could answer you better, Ruarangi,
  If you let his tongue slip back inside his mouth.
  You will squeeze him to death.
RUARANGI: What have you done with Tawhai?
  Tiki, answer!
TIKI: A terrible thing has happened.
RUARANGI: Ah, I will choke you some more.
NUKUROA: No, let him go.
  Boy, what have you done?
TIKI: It was all a mistake.
  I meant no harm. We only went for a walk.
  Then suddenly it happened.
WERA: Ah, yes; we know.
  It always seems to happen by the purest accident.
RUARANGI: I will take this boy in my hands and break him in half.
TIKI: You do not know, Wera and you, Ruarangi,
  If you dare to touch me again I shall run to my whare
  And get my spear and stab you. Leave me alone.
  Your wife is lost for ever.
RUARANGI: You are a thief!
NUKUROA: How is she lost? Speak, you shrimp of a Tiki.
TIKI: Indeed she is gone for ever, Nukuroa.
  Gone, gone, gone.
WERA: Alas, she is gone.
TIKI: It was none of my doing. I am not to be blamed for this thing.
  I did not know it would happen. I could not help her.
  The patu paiarehe took her away.
NUKUROA: The patu paiarehe!
RUARANGI: Alas, it is true.
WERA: Eh, Tawhai! Alas it is true indeed.
  Did you not see the man of the mist, old Koura?
KOURA: I saw the man. I saw the demon who took her.
NUKUROA: Is it so then, Tiki?
TIKI: He sprang at us out of the mist.
  His skin was gold and his hair the faery red.
  And Tawhai sank to the ground before him and screamed.
  I shall never see her again.
WERA: Tawhai! Tawhai!
  Never to see you again, my beautiful daughter,
  Lovelier than the wild birds, and flown for ever.
  Empty is the nest, silent is the tree at morning,
  Broken, broken is my heart.
NUKUROA: Aye, it is bad.
KOURA: She will never come back to the village; never again
  Will the hand of Tawhai be dipped in the water of the river,
  Never again her hand in the earth of the fields
  With the hands of the other women; never her head
  Bowed at the cooking fire; never will her body
  Lie down again on the bed of fern by her husband.
RUARANGI: In my folly I forgot that her hands that grubbed in the field

Were a dance of light like sunlight moving through water.
In my blindness I did not see that her curling hair
That took the steam of the pot was a dark river
All down the rapid of her back; in my sleep and deafness
I did not know that her voice was a well of water
Sweeter than the singing river in the gloom of my whare.
In the death or the madness of stone on the bed of fern
While Tawhai lay beside me I did not stir.
Eh, she said that I snored; and I woke in the morning
Bad-tempered, and spoke harsh words; and now she is gone,
Aye, and I struck her. O Tawhai, Tawhai, Tawhai!

(*Music.*)

SCENE 4

TAWHAI: You wild beast of the forest, you beast of the mist,
  Let go! Oh, let me go!
WHANA: Eh, the soft bird,
  How it cries and flutters in my hand.
TAWHAI: A bird, am I?
  Can a bird bite you like this? Has a bird these nails
  To tear your face to shreds? There, you beast!
  I will bite and scratch, I will beat your face with my fist
  If you do not let me go.
WHANA: You are not a bird, then,
  Nor a woman, Tawhai, not even a woman of the Maori
  But a little wild beast yourself, struggling and biting
  And tearing with your claws in the dark.
TAWHAI: Now you insult me.
WHANA: Never did I say you were not the loveliest beast
  That ever bit the blood from the back of my hand.
TAWHAI: You laugh! Ah, you are horrid. You swoop from the dark,
  Pounce like a hawk from the mist on an innocent girl,
  Carry me miles through the forest, not caring the slightest
  That the branches scratch me and your grip bruises my flesh,
  Then set me down in the lonely bush—and laugh.
WHANA: Tawhai; I laugh because you pretend to be angry
  And I do not think a woman of such beauty as yours
  Could dislike the love of the patu paiarehe.
  Here, I will kiss your bruises.
TAWHAI: No! No!
WHANA: How shy it is! You must not tremble like that.
TAWHAI: There is no one to help me. No one to come if I call.
  And the bush all dark and lonely. What shall I do?
WHANA: It is not so dark as you say. Look at the moonlight.
  Nor is it lonely, Tawhai. Not far from here
  Are many more of my tribe, asleep in their shelters.
TAWHAI: More of your tribe! The strange wild faery people,
  The patu paiarehe, people of the mist!
  You who live in the dark and walk in the night

The Golden Lover

And work your enchantments—woe to the Maori people!—
In the mountain gorges where the air is heavy with mist
And the earth is black and the water of the creeks is black
And out of that black earth and that black water
Are born the creatures of evil, and the dark-stemmed tree-ferns
Spreading their still green wings, and you and your tribe.
Do not come near me! No, I will scream if you touch me.
I lived in the sunlight. And you, you will take me away
To the deep forest, where the growing trees are like logs
Sunk in some lake of nightmare, heavy with moss,
Wet with the mist, silent in a dream of evil.

WHANA: What staring old mopoke of a woman, or perhaps a husband,
Has hooted such dismal nonsense into your ear?

TAWHAI: You, the invisible ones who walk in the mist!
You who are shadows, watching us out of the forest,
You who shake the bracken when the air is still,
You to have caught me! I am lost in the web of the mist.

WHANA: It is dark when you shut your eyes. Open them, Tawhai!
There is no mist here, no dark, no strangeness, no evil.
There is only the bush where by day you have often walked
And the trees in their calm grace accepting the moonlight
As a woman should accept the love of a man in the night.
I who am with you, what more am I than a man?

TAWHAI: A man of the faery people!

WHANA: But still a man,
And no stranger to you, Tawhai.

TAWHAI: No stranger to me?

WHANA: You have dreamed about me. All your life you have dreamed.
I know you, Tawhai. You have had lovers, a husband,
And lovers and a husband they were not to be despised;
But always beyond them, Tawhai, there was a dream.
You lay, I know you have lain, with your lover in the bracken,
You have lain with your husband in the bed of fern in the whare,
But who did you lie with in dreams? With your golden lover!
With a tall man like a shadow on the fringe of the morning
Who turned and was gone before you could ask his name.
With a golden man who vanished in the green of the bush
Before you could see his face. Look in my eyes!
The golden lover haunting the fringe of your dreams
Laughed and was gone and left you forlorn and angry
In the depths of your heart, and hungry—hungry, Tawhai.
Look in my eyes and be glad. You cannot be frightened.

TAWHAI: I am still afraid. Let me go home to my husband.

WHANA: To that fat potato!

TAWHAI: Home to my own people.

WHANA: If you, who know that you lay in my arms in your dreams
When you turned in your sleep and sighed for the golden stranger,
Can deny me now—go! If you who have kept

Your body fragrant for love, you I have carried
To the clean bush that smells of fern and moonlight
Can go now to the whare reeking of cooking
And the heavy fool you married—go, then, Tawhai.
Go! You are free. Go!

TAWHAI: How unfair you are!
How can you say I am free and tell me to go
When you know you have fastened me here with your wicked spells?
Your hair is a dark fire, and you lean above me
Like a column of golden moonlight, and your hands are strong.
You have muttered some charm and bewitched me.

WHANA: You are free to go.

TAWHAI: I am not at all free to go and you should not say so.
I am quite bewitched. My will is as water before you.

WHANA: Ah, let me look at you, Tawhai. "As the graceful kotuku
Was she, the bird seen once in a lifetime."

TAWHAI: Is it so?
To you who have your choice of the faery women
And could have leaped on any woman of the Maori
As we toiled in the field, I am the white heron?

WHANA: On the cold sands of my life, between the forest
Where all is sombre, and the water where all is death,
You, the white heron, sacred and solitary,
And all that the world holds of grace and beauty
Shining where the light strikes on your folded wings.
Ah, keep them folded, Tawhai. Do not fly away.

TAWHAI: I do not think I would go now if I could.
What do they call you?

WHANA: Whana. My name is Whana.

TAWHAI: Whana. The wild name, the wild name,
Like a stone in a mountain stream.

WHANA: Ah, you are perfect!

TAWHAI: No, do not touch me yet. How do I know
That all your beautiful words are not a snare
Of the faery people? Is it truly me you love,
Or were you not waiting there on the edge of the forest
For any woman of my people not as ugly as Koura?

WHANA: Eh, that old kiwi, how she scuttled for her life in the morning!
But I waited for you, Tawhai, you with the wings.
How many weeks have I watched you at work in the fields,
Ventured at night to the pa reeking of your people,
Yearning to see you, burning for a chance like this.

TAWHAI: You watched and waited for me! But why for me?
There are many beautiful women among the Maoris,
Or nearly beautiful.

WHANA: But only one white heron.
Tawhai, I love you.

The Golden Lover

TAWHAI: But why?
WHANA: When the tui sings,
  The bell through the green of the forest, clear and deep,
  Some form arises trembling among the music
  Like a silver ghost, my darling. You are that ghost.
  When the kowhai breaks into flower and the honied blossoms
  Flow down to the earth in a waterfall still and silent,
  Some form that is not a tree laughs there and sings
  And bathes her hair and her hands in the golden pool:
  Your hair and your hands, you heart of the spring and its flowers.
  A green spirit in the forest, a dark in the earth,
  A fire of silver burning now with the stars—
  Tawhai, Tawhai, you are all the earth and the heavens.
TAWHAI: To me in my life no one has said such things.
  It is sweet to be here with you in the bush and moonlight
  And to hear you speak. Eh, my wild Whana
  With your strange name and your mountain torrent of words
  And your auburn hair, fierce face and body of gold,
  You might indeed be a lover out of a dream.
WHANA: You are not a woman beside me but the earth burning.
  Your dark hair smoulders, and your body under my hand
  Is all one flame. And yet how the blaze takes form!
  It is not the long loose wandering flame of aurora
  Rose and green when the sky catches fire in winter,
  That stretches far out of reach and shrinks as you watch it;
  That is the flame of your spirit. But the fire of your body,
  It is here, it is close, I can touch it, ember and flame.
  See how it branches, the lovely leap and the flash
  In your arm, your hand, the wavering light of your fingers,
  And there, where your mouth is, the glowing heart of the embers;
  And the long, adorable, curving streamers of flame
  Flowing to your breast and down the lines of your body,
  Then branching again. Fire of the sky in your spirit,
  Fire of the earth in your body! Tawhai, Tawhai,
  Our spirits met in the burning sky together
  How long ago! And now you are mine on earth.
  And I, I am fire like yourself; these hands of mine
  Can hold you and not be afraid, not wither to ash.
  See, I can lift you, fire in a cradle of fire,
  And take you away to be my own for ever.
TAWHAI: Ah, Whana, Whana my lover! And yet I am frightened.
WHANA: Frightened? You cannot be frightened. Are you not Tawhai?
TAWHAI: I am Tawhai indeed. Tawhai of the Maori people,
  And you are Whana of the patu paiarehe.
WHANA: No, you are not of the Maori, you who have kept
  From that sweet brown skin the degradation of shark-oil.
  Why did you do that, Tawhai, if you did not know
  That somewhere a lover waited and would come to claim you
  For the life of the bush with the patu paiarehe?

TAWHAI: You make me afraid with your knowledge. It is true indeed
  I could not smear my body with that dirty oil
  And I felt in my heart I did not belong to the village.
WHANA: Out of that Maori village, the stench and corruption
  Of life without passion, standing in its own squalor,
  You have grown as the rata grows on the rotting tree,
  The tall vine climbing, lifting its scarlet flowers
  High over death into the air of delight.
TAWHAI: Ah, it is true! The red flower in the sky,
  And I grew for you, Whana.
WHANA: You are mine for ever.
TAWHAI: Hold me close. I am cold. Whana, my dear one,
  I cannot leave my people.
WHANA: But you must, Tawhai.
TAWHAI: No, but I cannot. I cannot leave them for ever.
  Never again to see the little whares
  And the smoke of the fires and the fields where I worked with the women,
  Never again to see all the people I know—
  I could not bear it, Whana.
WHANA: Poor little Tawhai!
  But I will be your whare and the warmth of the fires,
  The earth for your tilling and all the people who love you.
TAWHAI: You are all the world, but you cannot be my home.
  I would hunger for ever for the place and the people I know,
  The thoughts and the songs and the laughter of my own Maoris
  That are part of my being but could never be part of yours—
  My own village, Whana, and my own people.
  Eh, what are they doing? What are they saying?
  They are mourning for Tawhai.
WHANA: Then let them mourn.
  What have you, my flower of the forest, my bird of the air,
  To do with the Maori village? There where the women
  Grow shapeless with childbirth and gross with middle-age
  And bowed and bent and broken with toil in the fields;
  Where the smoke of the cooking-fire stains and begrimes their faces
  And the stench of the cooking-fire fouls their skin and their hair;
  Where their fingers grow blunt and dirty with grubbing in the earth
  And their fingernails are broken. You, my heron,
  To grovel in the dust and ashes!
TAWHAI: And yet there is Wera,
  My mother who makes me laugh. And crooked old Koura
  Whom I tease but love. And sometimes in the fields, Whana,
  It is pleasant to talk with the women.
WHANA: You are still a child.
  Well, there are women, Tawhai, among my people.
TAWHAI: But not the women I know. There is also Tiki.

The Golden Lover 179

Eh, poor Tiki, how he ran from you to-night!
WHANA: I will catch him and keep him for you. There are things
    like Tiki
To be found on the dogs in my village. Ho, how he ran!
TAWHAI: I wonder if Tiki dared to tell them what happened?
I think there will be much talk about Tawhai to-night
In my people's village. Whana—my poor fat husband!
He will howl for me and his dinner like a dog for the moon.
Eh, I would love to see it!
WHANA: And so would I.
Tawhai, what made you marry that decaying shark?
TAWHAI: My father made me. But I do not mind Ruarangi.
He is pleasant for a husband, a kind of walking joke
Except in the mornings or when he happens to remember
His warrior's blood and makes ferocious faces.
Whana, how shall I face my father?
WHANA: Tawhai,
You will never have to face that old Maori again.
TAWHAI: Nukuroa is silent and thinks of nothing but fishing,
But if anything happens to take his mind off fish
He is dangerous, Whana. Of course, I could run away,
But then he would go to that evil old wizard Te Kawau
And I do not like that man. The tohunga, Whana,
He can read a woman's thoughts, and he rarely approves
Of what he reads. He mutters and works his spells.
He would work no good to our love.
WHANA: Te Kawau the tohunga,
Father, husband—all this is nothing to me.
They do not exist. They are nothing. There is only you,
And you I shall carry away from them all for ever.
I, I am Whana! Among my people I am chief.
I choose to take you. I do not care for your fears,
Nor all your tribe, nor even your will against me.
No! I take you. Now!
TAWHAI: You are my master,
My will is as water before you. You are fierce and beautiful.
Eh, Whana, you would not want me in the forest
Without my love.
WHANA: Love me, then.
TAWHAI: I do.
But never could I leave for ever the people of my tribe
Who make me laugh and whom I have known so long.
No, it is not to be thought of. We must find a way——
WHANA: I could find a way to turn you over and smack you.
TAWHAI: Although, Whana, you are certainly my golden lover
And of faery blood, and handsome as the sun to look at,
You behave at times surprisingly like a husband.
WHANA: Although, Tawhai, I could not doubt for one moment
That you are my crimson blossom and the song of a tui,
You argue at times disconcertingly like a woman.

TAWHAI: Ah, no, Whana. Ah, no. We begin to quarrel.
And I love you truly for ever, beyond all the world.
WHANA: And I love you.
TAWHAI: And you want your Tawhai happy?
You would not take me by force to be cold and sullen,
Cold as Pirongia?
WHANA: Aye, I would like you happy.
TAWHAI: Then you must let me love you but keep my people.
WHANA: Oh, you are woman indeed. You cannot have both.
You ask the impossible.
TAWHAI: Do be reasonable, Whana!
WHANA: I see why your father prefers to think about fish.
Hear me, you greedy child, you cannot have both.
TAWHAI: In myself, of course, it is only you I want,
But my wretched Maori blood keeps interfering.
Think, my dear one, it is only at night you want me.
At night we shall lie with your face between mine and the stars
In the sweet and lonely bush.
WHANA: How lovely you are!
TAWHAI: So really you do not care where I spend the day
That was only made for sleeping. Let me go home
Each day when the sun comes up, and return to you
Each night when the sun goes down.
WHANA: It is madness, Tawhai.
TAWHAI: And yet we could do it.
WHANA: Eh, come away with me now,
And never come back.
TAWHAI: Some day, perhaps, I will.
Soon I will do it. Yes, I promise it, Whana.
Now it is all so strange. I cannot think.
Wait just a little while and then I shall come.
Am I not worth waiting for?
WHANA: Well, I could wait.
TAWHAI: Then let me go home at daybreak and come to your arms
When the mist comes to the fields and the women are gone.
Every night I will come. I promise.
WHANA: They will stop you from coming.
TAWHAI: Let them try to stop me! I say I will come to my lover.
WHANA: I do not like it. Death in the reeking village!
The death of love. They will put their mark upon you.
TAWHAI: Do you not know the mark of your hands is upon me
And the mark of your mouth?
WHANA: They will smear you with shark-oil.
TAWHAI: Let them dare to touch me! And besides, I can wash.
WHANA: It will bring us no good. I should never have let you talk.
TAWHAI: You love me because I am strong as you are strong.
WHWNA: You are a devil!
TAWHAI: Whana, we talk and talk,
And the sky in the east grows light. Let it be as I say

The Golden Lover

For a little while, and then I will come for ever.
WHANA: Each night you will come to me, each morning go home
To the Maori village and your people. Ho, you devil,
You will have that fat husband in a fit! For that alone
I love you and will do what you wish. But not for long.
Eh, you can try it! He will roll on the ground
And bite himself like a dog chasing its tail
When you say farewell each evening. You will drive him mad.
You are wicked, Tawhai, and I love you.
TAWHAI: It will do him good.
Never was he tender with me as you are tender.
He is full of his own importance and too many eels.
WHANA: There must be no nonsense, mind you. He need not think
Because he's your husband he can take any liberties, Tawhai.
TAWHAI: I can manage Ruarangi.
WHANA: I am not surprised.
You have managed me to-night.
TAWHAI: Oh, no, Whana.
WHANA: I told you, Tawhai, you were patu paiarehe.
You have bewitched me.
TAWHAI: Oh, you are laughing at me!
WHANA: Ah, no, not laughing. Only asking for music
From the loveliest bird that ever sang in the forest.
Tawhai, come here. The night is slipping away.
TAWHAI: Eh, my Whana! My will is as water before you.

(*Music.*)

SCENE 5

Sound of RUARANGI *snoring.*
TAWHAI: Aha, the song of the husband! Sleep on then, fat one.
The day is bright but I do not think you will like it.
   (RUARANGI *snores.*)
When you wake, Ruarangi, you will have some reason to roar.
Eh, the same old husband and the same little whare,
The posts of tree-fern, the thatch of raupo from the swamp,
The flax mats on the floor and the bed of fern.
How long since I left you? Only a night? And yet
How dear you are since that one wild night in the bush,
That night with Whana. Eh, my dear little whare,
I might have lost you for ever!
   (RUARANGI *snores.*)
And you, little whale,
I might have lost you for ever. Hey, Ruarangi!
RUARANGI: What! And the food not cooked?
TAWHAI: You have forgotten.
RUARANGI: Ha! Tawhai!
TAWHAI: My husband!
RUARANGI: You are a ghost.
TAWHAI: My poor dear husband.

RUARANGI: Quick, go away, Tawhai.
You are a ghost!
TAWHAI: Alas, my poor Ruarangi.
RUARANGI: I am afraid of ghosts. Do you not remember?
You must go away.
TAWHAI: This is a pretty welcome.
You send me away!
RUARANGI: Alas, if they killed you, Tawhai,
If they ate those pretty limbs, and the rounded portions,
It is not my fault. Eh, do not come to haunt me!
TAWHAI: My unhappy husband.
RUARANGI: Never did I mean to hurt you.
My father also snored, and my grandfather too.
Why should you come in death to stare at me so
And stand in the door of our whare with your arms outstretched
And the blue of the morning behind you?
TAWHAI: Let me come to your arms.
RUARANGI: No, I am not accustomed. I do not know
What to do with a ghost in my arms.
TAWHAI: I am not a ghost.
I am your wife Tawhai, come home in sorrow
And shame to the husband who nonetheless will forgive her,
Knowing how awkward it is when a girl is bewitched.
RUARANGI: You are your ghost.
TAWHAI: Let us be clear about this.
I had planned to come to your arms and weep a little
As is only proper, and you make it very difficult,
Shrinking there in the corner with your hair on end
And your stomach rippling with emotion. I am not my ghost!
RUARANGI: Where have you been, you daughter of a female dog?
TAWHAI: Ah, you brute! Now I shall weep indeed.
I shall vanish again, Ruarangi. It will serve you right.
That I, who all night long in the dark of the forest
Endured such terrors and fought, and all for you,
Should have such a welcome home! Is there no justice?
RUARANGI: Alas, what have I said! I am sorry, Tawhai.
TAWHAI: I had thought, Ruarangi, "Here is the wounded bird
Dragging her broken wing home to the nest.
There, at least, will be one who will understand,
One who will heal her poor bruised broken body
And her bleeding heart. He, the generous husband,
Who, cold and forlorn, sits on the egg of his sorrow.
How glad he will be to see me!" So I had thought.
RUARANGI: Forgive me, Tawhai.
TAWHAI: No, I shall never forgive you.
RUARANGI: I am all confused. I do not know what I say.
They said you had gone for ever with the faery people.
Late, late we talked. And all night long
I did not sleep a wink. And when I woke up

You were there: standing: looking. You are looking now;
Like a ghost; you are strange. Your eyes are looking beyond me.
What terrible thing that you saw in the dark of the night
Is stamped on your eyes?
TAWHAI: He is the golden hawk
Who hangs in the sky of my dreams. When I was young
I shrieked. How silly I was! But that was in dreams.
The golden hawk struck from the sunset sky
When I was a woman awake, and if I shrieked
I shrieked with joy.
RUARANGI: Am I to understand
You have been insulted by a bird?
TAWHAI: You little man!
You slug that creeps on one little leaf of life,
What do you know of birds? High up there are branches
Where the tree holds up the coloured cups of the flowers
For the birds and the winds and the gods of the sky to drink,
And such a flower am I, for he told me so.
You, Ruarangi, who snore on your bed of fern
When morning stands at the door, you are a slug!
RUARANGI: How wild you are. I do not understand you.
TAWHAI: Perhaps I should have explained. I am bewitched.
RUARANGI: Do not say such words. I do not like these things.
And even if you are, you need not insult me, Tawhai.
TAWHAI: How can I help what I say? I am bewitched.
You must not object, or I might say terrible things,
Being a woman under a spell and not responsible.
RUARANGI: At daybreak you come, before I have eaten food,
When the light is cold and so is my liver inside me,
And you speak strangely and harshly. It is not to be borne.
Last night they said that the patu paiarehe
Had taken you away to the lonely bush of Pirongia
Never in life to return. And I mourned for you.
Fool that I was to mourn! For here you are
To scold and not cook as usual; aye, and pretending
You are under a spell and therefore free to be rude.
Young Tiki said you had gone—what mischief, woman,
What sly and scandalous game by the light of the moon
Were you and that Tiki playing?
TAWHAI: Alas, Ruarangi!
RUARANGI: Alas indeed! Have you made a thing of me
That the village will laugh at?
TAWHAI: Alas, Ruarangi.
RUARANGI: Stop saying "Alas", Tawhai! You will drive me mad.
TAWHAI: Alas, Ruarangi.
RUARANGI: Why do you say it so strangely?
TAWHAI: How shall you bear the news I have to tell?
Come to my arms, Ruarangi.
RUARANGI: Speak! What has happened?
TAWHAI: Hold me, my husband.

RUARANGI: My poor little frightened bird.
TAWHAI: Ach, let me go, Ruarangi!
RUARANGI: What is it now?
TAWHAI: Alas, I have just remembered that I am bewitched
And therefore tapu, taboo for you to touch.
It is sweet to lie in your arms and breathe the incense
Of you and shark, hardly knowing which is which;
But it is not safe, Ruarangi. Your life is in danger!
You will be bewitched yourself if I let you touch me.
I am taboo!
RUARANGI: I touched you, Tawhai, just now.
Do you think I have caught it?
TAWHAI: I think you are safe, Ruarangi.
But be very careful never to touch me again.
RUARANGI: What a horror to come upon me before my breakfast!
Is it true then, Tawhai?
TAWHAI: Aye, it is true, Ruarangi.
I have been bewitched by a man of the faery people.
RUARANGI: Horrible! Horrible!
TAWHAI: Yes, it was very horrible.
I, too, have not had a wink of sleep all night.
RUARANGI: Yet he did not take you away to the forest for ever.
Did you not please him, Tawhai?
TAWHAI: Of course I pleased him.
RUARANGI: He has sent you home bewitched to torment your husband?
TAWHAI: Not to torment you. My heart is throbbing with pity.
RUARANGI: But I cannot touch you.
TAWHAI: Ah, well you can always go fishing.
RUARANGI: Perhaps the spell will wear off.
TAWHAI: I fear it will not.
RUARANGI: Ho, I must go to Te Kawau. The wise tohunga
Is skilled in enchantments and all these terrible matters.
He will set you free.
TAWHAI: Never do that, Ruarangi.
Then you would lose me for ever. My fearsome lover
Would never let me come home to you each morning
If he thought you could be so mean as to plot against him.
RUARANGI: Let you come home each morning! What thing have you said?
TAWHAI: Eh, I forgot. It was such a little thing.
Oh, yes, I must tell you that.
RUARANGI: What must you tell me?
Is there never an end of trouble in my whare this morning?
TAWHAI: You are not to take that complaining tone with me.
I will not have it. Ah, how ungrateful you are!
Are you not pleased to see me back in your whare?
RUARANGI: Indeed, I may be. Yes, of course I am pleased.
Are you not my wife whom I thought I had lost for ever?
My heart is brimming with joy.

TAWHAI: Well, then, in your gladness
When you might have lost me for ever, you will never object
If my wretched lover of the patu paiarehe
Compels me to leave your whare at dusk each evening
And return to his loathsome embrace?
RUARANGI: What is this I hear?
TAWHAI: If it causes you pain, do not think about the nights.
Think only how glad you will be to see me each morning
When I come back from the forest.
RUARANGI: I shall be glad?
TAWHAI: You will rejoice, Ruarangi. "Here," you will say,
"Here is my pretty bird come back to the nest
Where her husband sings forlorn."
RUARANGI: You think I will sing?
TAWHAI: "Here," you will say, "here is my pretty wife
Returned once more to her loving husband's whare
From the molestations of that wicked, bewitching man
Who held her all night in the forest. How tired she looks,"
You will say; "I am sorry for her." And then you will comfort me.
Our life together is going to be so beautiful.
RUARANGI: Is it, indeed?
TAWHAI: Am I not a clever wife?
RUARANGI: Indeed you are clever.
TAWHAI: I thought of it all myself.
Of course he wanted to take me away for ever
But for ever is much too long. It is for ever!
So I thought of my plan. I talked till I made him agree.
He did not like it at all, but I told him plainly
That, bewitched as I was, only on my own terms
Could I overcome my repugnance to the faery people.
I said I would hate him for ever, and then he agreed.
It was all for you. "Poor Ruarangi," I thought,
"He will pine and die and never get proper meals
If he loses his Tawhai for ever." So I thought of this plan
By which we can all be happy. All day I am yours
To admire and talk to, and then at night I am his
To endure as best I can his insulting behaviour.
I shall suffer it all for you. At first, Ruarangi,
You will find it a little strange; I do myself.
But soon you will grow resigned; I am resigned.
Let us look on the happy side. And you know, Ruarangi,
Even to have to look on a man of the mist,
In spite of his beautiful hair, would make me sick,
Were it not for his wicked spells. I am quite bewitched.
My will is as water before him.
RUARANGI: Ha, you are water!
You are all one wicked river of nasty behaviour.
How many lovers before I took you to wife—
Fool that I was—six, seven, thirteen,
Nobody knows how many lolloping puppies

Who should have been drowned at birth you led to the bush
And found that your will was water! Eh, you Tawhai,
You swamp of a thousand surrenders——
TAWHĀI: Listen, Ruarangi——
RUARANGI: No, no, I am deaf!
TAWHAI: I wish you were dumb.
RUARANGI: I will not stand and listen to a woman's impudence.
And I will not have you sneaking to the river with Tiki
And running away for the night with some faery person
Who pokes his nose through the bushes. And now I will tell you
That I will not have you going to this person each night
And returning to me each morning. Bringing your shame
Home to the whare like a dog with some bone it has found.
Am I, the son of a warrior and a warrior's grandson
And a warrior myself to sit all night in the whare
With the dark and the fleas while my wife is at large with her lover?
TAWHAI: I shall think of you all the time.
RUARANGI: Think of dead dogs!
Shall I who am great in the village, important, respected,
Be known as the man whose wife comes home each morning,
Comes home for breakfast? No! No! No!
I, Ruarangi, to be laughed at by boys and warriors,
Tittered at by women, mocked by hoots from the forest!
TAWHAI: You say these words, but what can we do about it?
I am too much bewitched even to try to think
Of a way to help you.
RUARANGI: Ha, that devil who bewitched you.
Something is there to be done; and I, Ruarangi—
Give me my whalebone battle-axe; give me my spear!
TAWHAI: No, Ruarangi, no!
RUARANGI: Out of my way!
TAWHAI: I will not let you. No, you will go to your death.
RUARANGI: It is death for him this morning. Ah, the white whalebone
That drank of the red blood in my father's time.
TAWHAI: You cannot fight the patu paiarehe.
Whana will kill you or make you mad with enchantments
Before you have even seen him.
RUARANGI: I will kill this Whana.
TAWHAI: He is strong and fierce and skilled with weapons as with spells,
And a chief among his people. Ruarangi, beware.
RUARANGI: I think Ruarangi is as good a man as he is.
TAWHAI: I think you are not.
RUARANGI: Well then, perhaps you are right.
A faery, no doubt, is beneath a warrior's notice.
But you Tawhai, you who betray and insult me,
I do not think that you are as good a man as I am.
No, I will kill you! I think I can kill you, devil!

The Golden Lover

TAWHAI: Oh, no you cannot! Ho, be careful, Ruarangi!
   Would you touch a woman bewitched? You dare not do it!
   You would fall down dead to the ground and foam at the mouth.
RUARANGI: Who shall I kill!
TAWHAI: Enough of this talk about killing.
   Stop waving that axe, Ruarangi; you will knock your head off.
   Put it there in the corner. This talk of killing is nonsense.
   You cannot do it; and besides, you do not mean to.
   You know I am not to blame for any of this.
   I told you my will was as water.
RUARANGI: All this comes
   From a woman refusing to anoint herself with shark-oil
   And so be decently disgusting to handsome strangers.
   There is shark-oil here. You take it and rub yourself
   And then we will see how this red-haired person receives you.
TAWHAI: That is no use. He said he would wash it off.
RUARANGI: Then I must go to Te Kawau and ask for a spell
   To unbewitch you.
TAWHAI: You cannot do that, Ruarangi.
   I have told you already. If that old wizard Te Kawau
   Should try to break this powerful spell that is on me
   Whana will know; he will take me away for ever.
   Or else I shall die.
RUARANGI: Then I shall go to your father.
   Nukuroa can help me in this.
TAWHAI: You cannot do that.
   How, Ruarangi, could a woman respect a husband
   Who ran to her parents to help in these trifling affairs?
   To see my father now, much as I love him,
   Would have grave effects, I am sure, upon my bewitchment.
   I should take a fit. Or else I might run away.
   I am just as distressed as you are; but truly, my husband,
   There is not a thing you can do. No, not a thing.
RUARANGI: Ha, I can stamp my foot and bounce on the floor!
   Do not tell me I cannot do that. I stamp my foot.
   I bounce. You will drive me mad!
TAWHAI: You will start an earthquake.
   (Dog barks furiously.)
RUARANGI: Ha, you devil! Bark!
TAWHAI: Nukuroa's dog!
RUARANGI: Eh, you devil of a dog! Keep away, you brute.
   Tawhai, watch. He will bite me.
TAWHAI: You could always brain him
   With your father's whalebone battle-axe. Outside, you cur!
RUARANGI: I would hang that mongrel. Is it Nukuroa and your mother?
   Can you see from the door, Tawhai?
TAWHAI: Yes, they are coming.
RUARANGI: They are looking for you. They said they would come this morning.

Now we shall find some plan.
TAWHAI: They are all coming.
　Wera and Nukuroa and funny old Koura
　And Tiki trailing behind.
RUARANGI: Good, good!
　Now we shall soon put a stop to all this nonsense.
TAWHAI: Oh, no; I must go. Ruarangi, I cannot stay.
　The spell of that wicked Whana is upon my feet
　And they run away like water. I shall see you to-morrow.
RUARANGI: Tawhai! Come here!
TAWHAI: Alas, how bewitched I am.
　Good-bye, Ruarangi.
RUARANGI: Come here! Tawhai! Alas.
　Eh, I will chop his head off. I will kill them both.
　She is gone again, Nukuroa.
WERA: It was Tawhai we saw.
KOURA: I say it was the ghost of Tawhai.
TIKI: She is running to the bush!
NUKUROA: What is all this fuss, Ruarangi?
　(*Dog barks.*)
RUARANGI: I will eat that dog!

　(*Music.*)

SCENE 6

WHANA: How she steps towards me, pushing the bracken aside!
　And the way she holds herself, black hair in the sun
　Held high, a torch sweeter than the light; brown breast
　And shoulders leaning back from the chill of the fern,
　My little queen of the forest.
TAWHAI (*calling*): Whana, where are you?
WHANA: Sing, birds, my lady is coming to meet me!
　(*Calling*) Higher, Tawhai! You will find a track in the fern.
　Why were you running?
TAWHAI: I was frightened of Nukuroa.
WHANA: Here, this way, my darling. So you came to your wild man?
TAWHAI: Oh, Whana, my dear one. Of course I came to you, Whana.
WHANA: Ah, you are lovely. When I hold you so in my arms
　I cannot believe I agreed to let you go.
　How did the fat man like it?
TAWHAI: I left him moaning.
WHANA: The lamentation of the oyster for the seagull.
TAWHAI: You see, I came as I promised. Early, to-day.
　Was it cold, waiting in the fern?
WHANA: I was warm within me,
　And when I saw you coming, climbing through the fern
　To the edge of the forest where you knew I was waiting, Tawhai,
　I thought I stood like a beacon, one blaze of delight.
TAWHAI: You stood like a tree of fire. I burn in your shade.

The Golden Lover

WHANA: Ah, but you do not know, how could you know
   What it means to a man when his lover is walking to his arms!
   You girls thirsting for love, you are living fire,
   Not women at all. A woman is earth walking,
   Two legs of earth for walking, two arms for working,
   A body to cover with a rag and fill with food
   And put to sleep in the night, no more alive
   Than the clay it is made of that sleeps all time away.
   But a woman awake with love is a burning spirit
   Carrying in pride and joy her burden of fire,
   The gift of her body to lay at the feet of her lover.
   I could have forgiven you, Tawhai, when you came just now
   With your proud head high and your body gleaming in the fern
   If you had brought it all to some other lover
   And all I could do was watch, and worship in the distance:
   It was sweet enough for that! But you came to me.
   It is mine, all this. You, you are mine to take.
   well, I will take you; and worship while I am taking.
TAWHAI: You make me ashamed, Whana. I am only Tawhai.
   It is I who have come to worship my golden lover.
WHANA: Lovely beyond all that is lovely in the earth or the sky
   And coming so to my feet! Beautiful, Tawhai,
   Is the silver Waipa, but the water runs from our fingers;
   Beautiful is the rimu-tree, the green-haired dreamer,
   But her eyes are blind and her feet are fastened in the earth;
   Beautiful is the blue sky and the sky of stars,
   Beautiful the white clematis and the wild white heron,
   But sky and flowers and water and tree and bird,
   They will not come to the hand. And you, you are here!
TAWHAI: I saw you standing here at the edge of the forest
   Like a tower of sunlight. Oh, Whana, take me away.
   Quick, far in the bush, wherever you like.
WHANA: You are my Tawhai indeed.
TAWHAI: You are my Whana.
WHANA: You have been with your Maori people; and yet you came back.
TAWHAI: And earlier even than I promised for this first day.
WHANA: I could not believe my eyes when I saw you coming.
TAWHAI: Did you think I would not come? I was afraid
   You would not wait.
WHANA: I would wait for you for ever.
   And I thought you would come. And yet I was afraid, Tawhai.
   It is cold in the fern, the bush will be lonely to-night,
   And your whare is warm and safe.
TAWHAI: Wherever you are
   It is warm and safe for me.
WHANA: Tawhai! my darling!
   And yet the track is wild through the bush to Pirongia,
   And love is no easy journey.
TAWHAI: I am not afraid.

WHANA: Ah, my flower, you do not know what it is,
　　Love with a man like me. The cold and the dark,
　　Where our hearts will live in fear, the journey of pain
　　Our spirits must go before they can rest in peace;
　　And deep in the bush, Tawhai, and high on the mountain,
　　The fire crouching and leaping. Always the fire!
　　Love is a fire in the fern, a fire in the bush,
　　A fire on the mountain, Tawhai. Will you burn with me?
　　Ashes, charred relics of bone, that is what we shall be
　　Before this love is finished.
TAWHAI:　　　　　　　　　When a Maori speaks
　　Of a fire in the fern, Whana, he means there is war.
WHANA: Aye, there is war! War between you and me,
　　War between you and your people, you and yourself.
　　You have seen the village; you have entered the door of your whare;
　　You have seen what the village calls love in the pulpy rubbish
　　They call your husband. Choose between that and my war.
　　You have seen what the village calls women in the fat grotesques
　　Or the lean and angry hags. Between their lives
　　That reek in peace and the war you will fight with me,
　　Choose, Tawhai. In the odour of Maori shark-oil,
　　In the fume of the cooking-pot, stench of dogs and children,
　　You have smelled the Maori earth. You who are fire;
　　And that defilement! Choose between earth and fire.
　　Tawhai, now you must choose.
TAWHAI:　　　　　　　　　　　I cannot choose.
　　I am fire for you; but when I was born I was earth.
WHANA: You have already chosen. Did I not see you
　　Running away in horror from all the old life,
　　Running to the new with me?
TAWHAI:　　　　　　　　　I saw them coming,
　　Wera, Koura, Tiki and Nukuroa,
　　And I wanted to meet them, but I ran. They would talk and talk,
　　And nothing they could say would help. They would try to stop me.
　　I cannot lose you. Whana, take me away.

(*Short interval of silence. Then sound of* RUARANGI *snoring.*)

TAWHAI: Wide awake as usual. I am here, Ruarangi.
　　Ruarangi, Ruarangi, I am back!
RUARANGI:　　　　　　　　Oh, you are back.
　　Well that is nothing to make such a song about.
TAWHAI: You do not know how lucky you are, my husband.
　　Last night, Ruarangi, you nearly lost me for ever.
　　I promised Whana, or at least he thought I promised,
　　Never to come back to the whare. He wants me so much,
　　And of course my will is simply as water before him.
RUARANGI: Then why did you come? We get on well enough

The Golden Lover 191

    Without you scuttling in and out of the village
    Like a crab in the seaweed.
TAWHAI: You are grumpy this morning.
    I have learned, of course, not to expect thanks
    From a man for all that one does; but I hoped, Ruarangi,
    That at least you would be resigned. Give me a smile.
    I came because I am fond of you after all,
    But I will not come if you cannot behave properly.
RUARANGI: Behave! Behave! Who has been out all night
    With a monstrous thing in the bush? Do not come to the whare
    And speak to me of behaving.
TAWHAI: How grumpy you are.
RUARANGI: Well, I am upside-down.
TAWHAI: That is awkward for you.
RUARANGI: Eh, do not laugh, do not laugh. My world is in pieces.
TAWHAI: Ruarangi, I am truly sorry. But what can I do?
    If only my will were not as water before him——
RUARANGI: If you say that again I will hit you hard on the head.
TAWHAI: But I am as water. I have never been bewitched like this
    In all my life. I simply cannot resist him.
    All that is happening is against my will as you know,
    But I cannot help consenting to its happening.
RUARANGI: Ach, that disgusting beast, that monster of the mist,
    How dare he lay his hands on my wife's person!
    It is an outrage, Tawhai.
TAWHAI: It is shocking indeed.
    Although, Ruarangi, it is not completely revolting.
    Whana is strangely handsome.
RUARANGI: He is a devil.
TAWHAI: I think it is hardly fair to call him a devil.
    He is, of course, of the patu paiarehe,
    But they, after all, though shameless in bewitching women,
    Are human enough in their way.
RUARANGI: He is a dog.
TAWHAI: Oh, no! You must not say such a thing, Ruarangi.
    It is true he is not polite to bewitch me like this,
    But that is just his nature. We must not blame him.
RUARANGI: I am going to Te Kawau to have you unbewitched.
TAWHAI: It is best to leave well alone.
RUARANGI: It is not well!
    I will not have my wife coming home in the morning
    From nights in the vile clutches of that beast of the mountains.
TAWHAI: Ah, he is not so vile. I wish you could meet him
    And see how nice he can be. I am sure you would like him.
    You would get on well together.
RUARANGI: Tawhai, hear me!
    I will not meet him and I would not get on well
    With a red-haired devil of the forest who has stolen my wife.
    You are shameless even to suggest it.
TAWHAI: How cruel you are.

I am only trying to do what is best for you both.
You are jealous, that is the trouble.
RUARANGI: I?—Jealous!
I am not jealous of a red dog of the wilderness,
Not even of Maori blood. I am a warrior.
He is beneath my contempt. I do not even
Spit upon such a person. I ignore him completely.
TAWHAI: That is the thing! Ignore him.
RUARANGI: I do ignore him.
But I will not have this scandal. I, Ruarangi—
My name is upon the wagging tongues of this village
Like a snapper on a line. Yesterday all day long
As I tried to sit in the sun outside the whare
And think my gloomy thoughts, the women came
And the warriors came and the children—the dogs came!—
To lick my shame with their tongues. Ach, how they talked!
I am not a person for impudent Maoris to stare at—
Some huge and improper god carved on a pole—
Indeed I am not!
TAWHAI: So all the village is talking.
What a stir I must have caused. But we cannot blame them.
It is strange and exciting that such a thing should have happened,
And only human nature to want to see me.
RUARANGI: It is I they come to stare at.
TAWHAI: They are jealous of you
For having a wife that even the faeries desire.
Not every man has a wife as pretty as you have,
And loyal to you, too. They envy your cleverness
In making this arrangement with the man of the mist
By which you are able to share me, not lose me for ever.
You are much too wise to notice these jealous Maoris.
RUARANGI: It is true they have always been jealous of my importance.
And this affair, as you say, reflects much credit
On me as your husband. I greatly admire myself
For my patience in such an awkward situation.
But, Tawhai, they came and laughed.
TAWHAI: Ignore their laughter.
Between ourselves, Ruarangi, we might admit
It is not without its humour, my being your wife
But spending my nights in the bush, and you not able
To touch me for fear of bewitchment; or even to complain.
Oh, yes, it is funny.
RUARANGI: Oh, no, it is not funny!
I will not have you coming to my whare and laughing.
I will not be pelted by the shrill laughter of children,
As I sit at peace in the sun; I will not be clubbed
By the laughter of warriors; I will not be stoned to death
By the howling and sneezing of the lewd old women of this pa.
(Dog barks.)

I will not be barked at by dogs!
TAWHAI: Wera, my mother!
WERA: Aha, you owl of the night! Have we caught you at last?
TAWHAI: And Koura and Nukuroa. I am glad to see you.
KOURA: You have been consorting with devils.
WERA: Is it true, my daughter?
TAWHAI: Nukuroa, how is the fishing?
NUKUROA: Eh, it is good!
There was an eel I almost caught last night——
TAWHAI: Tell me about it.
RUARANGI: No!
NUKUROA: Eh, my daughter,
My cunning daughter, I think we shall talk about you.
What have you caught, you shameless, on the fishing-line
Of a woman? Trouble as usual!
RUARANGI: Enormous trouble.
KOURA: To go for a walk and come home to her husband bewitched!
WERA: Aye, my daughter. Tell us about this bewitching.
This time you shall not run away.
TAWHAI: I do not wish to.
Ah, my mother, how glad I am to see you.
And you, too, Koura. And you, of course, my father.
I have missed you all.
NUKUROA: You missed us yesterday morning!
TAWHAI: I was bewitched, my father. But how I have missed you all
In the bush with my golden lover.
WERA: It is true then, Tawhai?
You are loved by a man of the patu paiarehe?
RUARANGI: As I told you before, Wera, she has had the misfortune
To become enchanted. It is much against her will.
KOURA: Eh, she will come to no good.
WERA: What is he like?
RUARANGI: She finds him revolting.
TAWHAI: Mother, he is tall and golden
Like a tree in the sky of morning, and his hair is auburn
Like embers glowing in the dusk. And his hands are fire.
WERA: And you love him truly?
TAWHAI: Wera, my will is as water.
WERA: So I believe you said.
RUARANGI: She is always saying it.
Soon she will drive me mad.
NUKUROA: In my youth, Ruarangi,
In a moment of folly I begot a scandalous daughter.
I owe the world an apology.
RUARANGI: Not at all, Nukuroa.
TAWHAI: That is right, Ruarangi. I have just been telling him, mother,
That since there is nothing to be done about this affair
It is best to treat it as a joke.

RUARANGI: And I have been saying
  It is not at all a joke to be the joke.
NUKUROA: Indeed it is not. This affair is an open scandal.
  It is going to stop.
TAWHAI: It cannot be stopped.
KOURA: Hear her!
  She is bold and bewitched. I am glad she is not my daughter.
WERA: Tell me about him, Tawhai. What is his name?
TAWHAI: His name is Whana. A pleasant name, do you think?
WERA: A tall and golden man by the name of Whana.
  Yes, you would be bewitched. What does he say?
TAWHAI: He says the village stinks.
WERA: That is true enough.
TAWHAI: He says that women here grow bent with work
  And shapeless with childbirth and grey and ugly with age.
KOURA: That is a lie. Old age is often beautiful.
TAWHAI: Is it a lie, Koura? He says that I
  Am a flower too fine to seed and wither in the pa.
  I am his own kind, of the faery blood.
NUKUROA: That, I think, is not true. I do not recall
  That your mother ever deceived me with a faery.
WERA: Tawhai, you do not believe your lover's nonsense?
  You have too much sense. It is pretty nonsense, I know—
  I should like to see this Whana, or once I should have—
  But you, as you know, are my daughter; a Maori woman;
  And you in your time will be just as fat as I am.
TAWHAI: Not quite so fat. He says these things, Wera,
  And though I do not believe them, not quite believe them,
  It is pretty to hear him talk.
NUKUROA: Women! Women!
KOURA: And how many others, Tawhai, women of the Maori,
  And women of his own tribe, too, has he lured to their doom
  With his pretty words?
TAWHAI: I am not a fool, Koura.
  I have also thought of that. But I do not intend
  To go away for ever as he begs and commands me.
  So I see no harm whatever in what I am doing.
RUARANGI: No harm, she says!
NUKUROA: You are doing harm to me.
  With all this talk I cannot fish for thinking.
  I forbid you, Tawhai, ever to see him again.
TAWHAI: But my will is as water before him. I am bewitched.
NUKUROA: I will smear you with shark-oil, then.
TAWHAI: He would wash it off.
NUKUROA: Well, we shall go to Te Kawau. The tohunga's magic
  Will break the spell of the other's. I mean it, my daughter;
  Never again must you see this golden lover.
TAWHAI: I cannot do it. I cannot give him up.
  Wera, I cannot do it.

The Golden Lover

WERA: I think, Tawhai,
  You had better submit. There have always been two moments
  When a man is deaf to argument; one is the time
  When he asks you to smile on him; and the other time
  Is when he forbids you to smile on someone else.
  There is too much talk in the village. You had better submit.
TAWHAI: You, Wera? I thought you would understand.
WERA: Aye, Tawhai, I know. But what is your life
  To be with such a lover? Will you sleep in the bush
  And live on roots and berries? Here is your home,
  Your warm whare and the place and people you know.
  Will you lose them all? Love is a fine thing,
  But so is a whare; and so are your own people.
TAWHAI: You make it hard for me, mother.
KOURA: It is life, Tawhai.
TAWHAI: It is death if I lose Whana. You do not know.
NUKUROA: Has he land, this Whana?
TAWHAI: He is chief among his tribe.
NUKUROA: A landless people! A wandering life in the forest.
KOURA: That dark bush, the mist, and the darker enchantment.
WERA: And here you have food and fire; and a good husband
  With nothing enchanting about him whatsoever.
  You had better keep him, Tawhai.
RUARANGI: Indeed she had better.
TAWHAI: Food, fire, whare and my own people—
  Aye, they are good. But what is all that to me
  Without that wild man's love?
NUKUROA: You are shameless, daughter.
WERA: Tawhai, this wild man's love—what is it like?
TAWHAI: Fierce.
WERA: You are frightened of him.
TAWHAI: He said it is dark
  Like the dark of the forest, cold like the wind on Pirongia,
  And always the fire waits and leaps from the darkness.
  It is more than the love I know.
WERA: You are frightened, Tawhai.
TAWHAI: Eh, my mother, his love is so fierce and strange,
  But I love him so much.
WERA: You must never see him again.
TAWHAI: Oh, let me hide my face! I am torn by the winds.
KOURA: And there outside the whare, there is someone walking.
  I, old Koura, have heard him.
NUKUROA: It is only the dog.
KOURA: Who comes, bringing enchantment?
TAWHAI: Ah, you Tiki!
  You little brown worm, how you wriggled away that night.
  This is all your fault.
TIKI: Put all the blame on me.
  Go on. I have learned to expect it.

TAWHAI: Well then, wee worm,
I am glad to see you.
NUKUROA: Enough then, Tawhai. Enough.
Will you stay in your whare to-night, or am I to go
To Te Kawau and traffic in magic?
WERA: Tawhai, my daughter,
Stay home to-night.
KOURA: Stay and be safe.
RUARANGI: Tawhai!
Is it nothing to you that your husband is a valiant warrior?
Stay and be safe in my whare.
NUKUROA: Aye, you must stay.
TIKI: It is madness to go, Tawhai.
RUARANGI: Tiki is right.
TAWHAI: Eh, my people! You call with so many voices.
   (*Short interval of silence.*)
WHANA: You are cold, Tawhai. You shivered.
TAWHAI: Oh, Whana, my darling.
WHANA: I will hold you close and warm you.
TAWHAI: Oh, Whana, Whana,
Why did you awake me, beloved? It is day too soon.
WHANA: It is not yet day.
TAWHAI: See in the east. It is light.
WHANA: That is only the moon, my darling.
TAWHAI: The moon has gone.
And that star in the east—see it above the ridge
Where the dark trees stand, shaggy, like giants with clubs—
Is fading now as we watch it.
WHANA: There are tears in your eyes,
That is why the star seems pale. You must not be sad.
TAWHAI: I am sad because a bird sang, and I heard it.
WHANA: My heart sang for love. The birds are asleep.
TAWHAI: A tui cried in the valley. Down near the village.
WHANA: No, it was the river, Tawhai. You heard the Waipa.
TAWHAI: Look now in the east. It is glowing. Oh, Whana, my heart,
  They are burning the night we have loved. They are burning the world.
WHANA: If you will close your eyes and lie in my arms
I will bring you a darkness, Tawhai, blacker than midnight
But flashing with all its stars; the dark of the ocean,
Cool and black and immense, wave after wave,
Where the weed sways and the fishes burn like comets.
I will bring you the blazing darkness, and then you will sleep.
Let me hold you, Tawhai.
TAWHAI: No, it is daybreak, Whana.
And I am awake. It is cold. I must go to the village.
WHANA: Stay just a little longer.
TAWHAI: No, I must go.

The Golden Lover

WHANA: But a little longer, Tawhai. The day is so long
And the night has been so short.
TAWHAI: I have loved the night.
But now it is daybreak. I must go to my own people.
WHANA: I am your people.
TAWHAI: Ah, that is true, Whana;
But still I must go. I will come again at sunset.
WHANA: Black is the day when you go. I will keep you here.
TAWHAI: I must go to my people, Whana.
WHANA: Your people! Your people!
It is all the fault of your fat dog of a husband.
TAWHAI: Eh, he is not so bad.
WHANA: I believe you love him.
TAWHAI: It is only you I love. And yet it is true
That if I lost him I should lose the fat round stone
That holds the canoe at the moorings.
WHANA: May he lie for ever
At the muddiest bottom of the river.
TAWHAI: Do not speak so harshly.
Ruarangi is pleasant when you know him. Some day, perhaps,
I should like you to meet him. You would get on well together.
WHANA: Do not play those tricks on me, you woman, you!
I am jealous enough already.
TAWHAI: How cruel you are.
I am only trying to do what is best for you both.
WHANA: Hear me, Tawhai. I am old in the ways of women.
Do not say such things to me. You are trying to do
What is best for little Tawhai; and I do not mind it
So long as you do not insult me with foolish pretences.
TAWHAI: Eh, you are harsh! If you only knew it, Whana,
You are lucky I came last night. I promised my husband,
Or he thought I promised, never to see you again.
WHANA: Did you intrigue against me with that fat dog?
TAWHAI: Eh, do not shout at me. I never intrigue.
It is not Ruarangi alone. They are all against me,
And you are not there to help me. They were at me and at me,
And I promised, or nearly promised, not to come;
But I had to see you, Whana. I slipped away.
WHANA: Why do you listen to the howling of Maori dogs?
TAWHAI: They are my people, Whana.
WHANA: Aye, it is true.
But hear me, Tawhai. Among my people I am chief.
Slaves and dogs and women do not plot against me
And a woman I choose does not dispute my will.
From you, because you are Tawhai, much have I borne.
Because you are Tawhai and hunger for you own tribe
As a Maori would, I have borne your rebellion with patience,
Knowing you would come to heel. Because you are Tawhai,
And it made me laugh to know that you were a woman

As well as a fire and a flower, I have watched in patience
While you played your woman's games. Because you are Tawhai
And proud, I do not take you away—now,
As I could; now!—to be my slave for ever.
Because you are Tawhai I love you. But now it is finished.
Go; yes, go to the village. But do not come back
Unless you are coming for ever.
TAWHAI: Ah, let us, Whana,
Go on as we are for just a little longer.
WHANA: Each time you go to the village, you come to me
With the taint of it on you, Tawhai. More of the taint.
More lies, more women's tricks, more need of your people,
More fear of love. Eh, I am hard, Tawhai.
But if I am soft, as my love would like to make me,
I lose you for ever to the cooking-fire and the whare,
The husband and the gabble of hags. No, it is finished.
Go this once. I want you to be quite sure.
Look at your people; decide; bid them farewell,
And come to me for ever.
TAWHAI: When I go to the village
They will shut me away perhaps. They will guard me with spears.
WHANA: I am not afraid of their spears. And they cannot hide you
Where I will not find you, Tawhai.
TAWHAI: You would come to the village?
WHANA: Wherever you are I would go. I am not afraid.
TAWHAI: They will call out old Te Kawau who is strong in magic
And an evil man.
WHANA: I am not afraid of spells.
TAWHAI: And what if they smeared me with shark-oil?
WHANA: If they smeared you by force,
Why should I blame you, Tawhai? Hear me, my dear one,
I am not afraid of anything they may do,
I am only afraid of what you may do to yourself.
Do not listen to the words they say. They will snare you with words
And make you even as they are, dogs and hags.
You, my flower of midnight! Do not hear them, Tawhai.
TAWHAI: They speak with so many voices.
WHANA: And I with one.
Yet that voice—Tawhai, is it not true?—
Is stronger than all the village. Ah, my white heron,
When I talk to you like this, do you know the voice
That speaks to a woman's heart?
TAWHAI: It is true, Whana.
Never has a man so spoken to me before
In a voice that melts my body until I am nothing
But water flowing towards him. Ah, light on the water!
And Whana, it is true that I played you a woman's tricks
And listened to the voice of my people. I am ashamed.
You are my golden lover, my heart for ever.

WHANA: You flower of the kowhai that the winds and the bellbirds love,
  You are mine, now, for ever. Eh, my Tawhai,
  I will lay my mountain at your feet. Come with me now.
TAWHAI: I am so sure now, so surely yours,
  That more than ever I must go to my Maori village
  Once more, to look at it all, to see them all,
  Once more to say farewell, then never again.
  Already in my mind I have said that long good-bye,
  And a little grief is buried in a corner of my heart
  And all the rest is yours. You need have no fear.
  I will go, I must say farewell or their hearts will break.
  But at sunset, Whana, I will meet you here again
  To go on that journey you spoke of, that lasts for ever.
  If I do not come, you will know I am held by force,
  And come for me, Whana, come. You are sure you can free me?
WHANA: I am sure that nothing in the world can hold me from you
  Unless you should wish it so. They can do nothing
  To end our love if you do not consent to end it.
  Do not consent. Can you be firm against them?
TAWHAI: You know my will.
WHANA: The fire has gone out of the east.
  It is morning now. When it burns again in the west,
  The sign of my love, you will come to the edge of the forest
  And vanish in the mist with the patu paiarehe.
  You are not afraid?
TAWHAI: No, I am not afraid.

(*Short interval of silence.*)

A MAORI: Hey, Ruarangi! You are early abroad this morning.
A WOMAN: I thought he liked to sleep.
SECOND MAN: Did you dream, Ruarangi?
FIRST WOMAN: Perhaps he has indigestion.
SECOND WOMAN: That is not likely
  When his wife is so devoted and such a good cook.
SECOND MAN: Why should a fat man rise so early in the morning
  And stand at the gates of the village like the god of thunder?
FIRST WOMAN: It is silent thunder.
SECOND WOMAN: Tawhai is cooking his breakfast.
  Am I right, Ruarangi, or wrong?
FIRST MAN: He has lost his tongue.
FIRST WOMAN: No, it is stolen. Tawhai took it to her faery.

FIRST MAN: Hey, Ruarangi, have the patu pairehe
  Run away with your tongue?
SECOND MAN: And your wife as well, Ruarangi!
RUARANGI: Go away, you chattering birds. Go away, go away!
FIRST WOMAN: He wishes to brood alone.
SECOND WOMAN: We must help him brood.
  We mourn for our wife who has not come home to breakfast.

FIRST WOMAN: We rise at daybreak from the lonely bed of fern
   And come to the gates of the pa and wail for our wife
   Who is out in the bush with a stranger with wild red hair.
FIRST MAN: But I cannot hear him wailing. No, we are angry.
   We want our wife and our breakfast.
SECOND MAN: Hey, Ruarangi,
   Do you miss your wife at nights? You should tie her up
   By the leg to a post in the whare.
RUARANGI: Go away, you rabble!
FIRST WOMAN: Perhaps he is waiting to meet his red-haired rival.
   We intrude at a sacred moment.
SECOND WOMAN: I am sure you will like him.
   Ruarangi, you will get on well. For after all
   You have much in common.
FIRST MAN: Tawhai, for instance.
RUARANGI: Will you go away and leave me to wait in peace!
SECOND MAN: You must not lie, Ruarangi. That is not nice.
   I do not think we can say we are waiting in peace
   When our face is frowning and our belly rumbles with thunder.
   We are out of humour this morning.
FIRST WOMAN: Perhaps he has seen
   What I can see, and that is someone like Tawhai
   Who is climbing the hill towards us out of the fern.
SECOND WOMAN: Ha, she is coming! How glad you must be,
   To be able to borrow your wife for another day.
FIRST MAN: This is one of those tender moments between husband
      and wife
   That reveal all the beauty of marriage. We are lucky to see it.
SECOND MAN: Perhaps although she is tapu, dangerous to touch,
   She will let him hold her hand.
RUARANGI: Ha, I am mad!
   Wera, Koura, here! Tawhai is coming.
   Send these women away. I will kill them soon.
WERA: Go away, you silly women. Let a husband and wife
   Conduct their affairs in private. Have some respect
   For me, if not for yourselves.
   (*Calling*) Tawhai, come here!
KOURA: Eh, she will come to no good.
FIRST MAN: She has been to no good.
FIRST WOMAN: The poor girl looks so tired.
SECOND WOMAN: With struggling,
      doubtless.
RUARANGI: Ha, will you go away!
FIRST WOMAN: No, we will not.
SECOND WOMAN: We want to see you kill her.
SECOND MAN: Her red-haired
      Whana
   Will not be pleased with that.
RUARANGI: That devil of the mist.

FIRST MAN: Ruarangi; now is your chance. The red-haired man
   Must be somewhere close, since Tawhai is coming from his arms.
   Run down in the fern and kill him.
KOURA: He will be bewitched.
SECOND MAN: The faery people hate the smell of our shark-oil.
   It makes them sick. Roll on him, Ruarangi.
FIRST WOMAN: They cannot bear the smell of our cooking-pots.
   Go and breathe on him, Ruarangi.
RUARANGI: Dogs and thunder!
   Am I who have stood among you like a totara-tree
   Vast in importance, extending my leaves and branches
   For you to roost in like birds, to stand and be mocked
   Because of a woman? Shall I who have worked like a slave,
   Sitting and fishing and in other arduous ways,
   To feed this woman, allow her to approach like this
   Not in shame and tears, walking on her hands and knees,
   But calm and smiling from her red-haired demon of a lover?
   No, I say. No! By the blood of my father, no!
   And I will not permit you sniggering women to snigger
   Nor you men of the tribe to laugh. I have borne enough!
   I, Ruarangi! By my father's whalebone battle-axe
   I am not a thing to be laughed at!
FIRST MAN: Well, we will go.
FIRST WOMAN: Yes, let us go.
RUARANGI: I will not permit you to go.
   No, you shall stay and watch the shaming of this woman
   And hear what a warrior says to a faithless wife.
   Stay! Come close! Hear what I say to this woman
   Who has shamed me before you all but will do it no more.
   You, Wera, and you, too, Koura, stand beside me.
   You others stand aside and let her approach.
KOURA: Aye, do not crowd about her. She is a witch.
   And true they are, the words her husband says.
   He is betrayed. He is mocked. He is shamed by a wanton.
WERA: My daughter is hardly a wanton. She is careless, perhaps.
KOURA: Who knows what far worse shame is to follow these days?
   What will the village say when a child is born
   With hair not Ruarangi's—aye, red hair!
TAWHAI: What are you saying, Koura? You were talking scandal.
RUARANGI: Ha, you thing called Tawhai that walks the earth
   And has not died of its shame, answer me this:
   Are you come home for ever, or still will you roam
   The bush at night with a red-haired father of devils?
TAWHAI: I do not know, Ruarangi. What is all this fuss?
RUARANGI: Answer me now and for ever.
TAWHAI: I cannot answer:
   Send all these people away. I am not to be stared at.
RUARANGI: You witch and mother of devils I will kill you here!
   Answer or die!

TAWHAI: Kill me if you must, Ruarangi.
But I cannot give you an answer.
RUARANGI: I am insane!
The dogs howl in my head. Speak, you Tawhai!
TAWHAI: I cannot speak.
RUARANGI: Am I to be the father
Of seventeen red-haired devils?
  (*Laughter from the Maoris.*)
TAWHAI: What a fuss you make.
  (*More laughing.*)
RUARANGI: Yes, you laugh. And yes I make a great fuss.
And before this day is finished I will make more fuss,
A greater fuss than this village has ever imagined,
And no one will laugh. I, Ruarangi, tell you.
Turn; look! Now who will wish to laugh?
You will not laugh at Te Kawau.
FIRST WOMAN: Oh, the tohunga!
FIRST MAN: It is Nukuroa coming, and hobbling beside him
Te Kawau!
SECOND MAN: I will go, I think. It does no good
To be present when magic is done.
SECOND WOMAN: I am going to my whare.
KOURA: No, you will stay. You will see it, all of you women.
Great and terrible times are upon our village.
FIRST WOMAN: Eh, I am frightened. What will Te Kawau do?
KOURA: The dark work of witchcraft.
RUARANGI: Make way for Te Kawau!
SECOND WOMAN: This is all that Tawhai's doing. We shall all be
  bewitched.
RUARANGI (*calling*): Here is my wife, Te Kawau.
TAWHAI: You, Ruarangi,
To do such a thing to me! Why have you brought
That old and evil man to do magic against me?
Wera, why did you let him?
WERA: Eh, I am sorry.
Now all your love is over. But what could I do?
Your husband and Nukuroa arranged this thing
And would not hear my voice. They were stern and angry.
It is man's work this, and no good luck for a woman.
I do not like Te Kawau with his old black eyes
And his shaking, crooked hands. And that evil smile!
TAWHAI: Mother, where can I run?
NUKUROA: Stay where you are.
This is my daughter, Te Kawau.
TE KAWAU: You, Tawhai,
With the spell of your lover upon you, who think of running,
Run if you like. And my thought will run at your side.
I do not think you will care to come back to this village
If you run, little flower of love.

WERA: Do not run, my daughter.
TE KAWAU: Aye, good Wera, you speak with the voice of a mother
  And her father speaks as a father, her husband as a husband,
  But to what voice of all the voices of her people
  Does Tawhai listen when her lover speaks as a lover?
  To none! She is deaf. Her blood drums in her ears
  The song of passion and she will not listen to your voices.
  But I think there is one she can hear; one voice of the village,
  Old and deep and dark like a hidden water.
  You, little flower, whom the wild man wears for a garland,
  Can you hear one voice?
TAWHAI: Aye, I can hear you, Te Kawau.
TE KAWAU: And why can you hear my voice? I am old, I am ugly,
  I am hated and feared and avoided. Yet they send for me
  When things have come to their worst, and you hear my voice.
  I am skilled at enchantment and dark and evil matters
  And men are afraid of my shadow; and you are afraid;
  And yet they send for me, and you stay and listen.
  I, Te Kawau, the witch-doctor, I am not one
  For a girl to hold in the arms of love in the night;
  I am one to make you shudder; and yet if you shudder,
  You do not run; and run you may if you wish.
  I am not one whose tongue is the honey of love,
  Sweetness and fire to taste, the burning blossom
  That a young girl sips at midnight—no, I am gall!
  Bitter the tongue of an old man sour with wisdom,
  Bitter are my words, Tawhai, cutting and withering
  The dreaming flower of a girl. And yet you listen.
TAWHAI: Aye, Te Kawau, I listen. You will break my heart.
TE KAWAU: Break then, break! For you know that I speak the truth.
  I speak your own thoughts to you, the truth of your heart.
  That is why you stay, that is why you listen, Tawhai.
  I am Te Kawau; my name is the name of the cormorant.
  The black shag of my mind, the swift one, the deadly,
  Flies high and far over the troubled waters
  And all on the shining surface and all that is hidden—
  The shadows that hide in shadows, the fish in the reeds—
  Is clear to my evil eyes. I am the cormorant.
  And what does the shag see, Tawhai, the fierce black eyes
  In a trembling water called Tawhai?
TAWHAI: Ah, you are loathsome!
TE KAWAU: I am only the truth of your heart. Only the knowledge
  That never again must you go to your golden lover.
TAWHAI: It is false, Te Kawau! You are old and evil and jealous.
  Whana is my man of the mist, and I love him for ever.
FIRST WOMAN: Hear her talk to Te Kawau!
SECOND WOMAN: She to defy him!
KOURA: A doom will come upon her. He will strike her dead.
TE KAWAU: Take her away, Nukuroa. Take her away.
TAWHAI: You cannot take me away from my golden lover.

TE KAWAU: Shut her away in her whare. And guard the door.
TAWHAI: Whana will come. He has said he will come to-night
  If you shut me away. He will set me free and take me.
NUKUROA: I think, my daughter, we are enough for your lover.
TAWHAI: He is not afraid of your warriors.
NUKUROA: Nor we of him.
TAWHAI: He is skilled in magic. He is not of the Maori people
  But the patu paiarehe.
NUKUROA: Te Kawau also
  Has no small skill in magic.
TAWHAI: No thing you can do,
  Unless by my own consent, can harm our love.
  And never will I consent.
TE KAWAU: Take her away.
  I think, little Tawhai, that all these things will be answered
  When your lover comes to-night. Take her away!
TAWHAI: Alas, what evil are you plotting for my lover to-night?

(*Music.*)

SCENE 7

FIRST WOMAN: How the fires flare now the light has gone from the sky.
SECOND WOMAN: They will light a flare of fear in her lover's heart.
  He will never come. She has lost him now for ever.
  Sunset and dusk and the night—he is late already.
FIRST WOMAN: Te Kawau believes he will come. See how he stares
  At the darkening bracken, there where the mist is creeping.
SECOND WOMAN: Maybe her lover of the patu paiarehe
  Is crouching there in the fern, watching, afraid.
  Te Kawau's thought, the flying shag of his mind,
  Will seek him out wherever he is in the fern
  Or the bush beneath the stars and compel him here
  To face the tribe and the fires.
FIRST WOMAN: See Tawhai there
  With her head down and her hands at her sides twisting.
SECOND WOMAN: The wings of the bird are broken.
FIRST WOMAN: No, she is angry.
  When her lover comes we shall see her fly to his arms.
SECOND WOMAN: Te Kawau will never allow her.
FIRST WOMAN: He will not hold her.
  He has said she may go if she pleases.
SECOND WOMAN: Then she will go.
  She has sworn she will. And Te Kawau has lit the fires
  And kept us all standing here outside the gates
  In the dangerous dark for nothing.
FIRST WOMAN: Te Kawau is strange.

The Golden Lover

SECOND WOMAN: Aye, he is strange; and evil. I am frightened of magic.
He should work his spells by himself, and let us go home.
I do not know what it means. I am frightened of it.
The seven great fires, flaring against the stars,
And the steam rising from the pots; and behind the steam
Wera and Koura kneeling, and the other old women;
And behind the women, Nukuroa and Ruarangi
And Tiki too, standing there straight and silent;
And behind those three, the warriors, row on row,
With their spears and clubs and axes—eh, the fine men!—
Row after row from the firelight back to the shadows
Where we who are not important may stand and watch.
The warriors, the men of Tawhai and Tawhai's women,
The steaming food and the seven great leaping fires,
And beyond the fires, alone in a pool of light,
Te Kawau stands with Tawhai! What does it mean?
FIRST WOMAN: Te Kawau's magic. We stand in a great enchantment
At the gates of our village, waiting for Tawhai's lover.
SECOND WOMAN: From the darkness beyond the two, where the firelight ends
He could leap and snatch her away.
FIRST WOMAN: The men will kill him.
SECOND WOMAN: He is fierce and sudden, so Tawhai said this morning;
A flame that leaps from the dark. He will come like that!
FIRST WOMAN: And yet his tribe, they say, are afraid of fire.
One time our people, perhaps in revenge for a woman,
Set the fern and the forest on fire over all the country
And many perished of the patu paiarehe.
SECOND WOMAN: They fear the fire; and they hate the steam of our cooking.
FIRST WOMAN: They hate old women like Koura; or fat ones like Wera.
SECOND WOMAN: When Whana comes for Tawhai, if he dares to come,
He will see all the things that he hates. Cunning is Te Kawau!
FIRST WOMAN: What is that gourd he holds in both his hands?
SECOND WOMAN: It is one of his sacred vessels. There is magic in it.
FIRST WOMAN: I think it is powerful magic. I think it is shark-oil!
SECOND WOMAN: Aye, it is shark-oil for certain. The people of the mist
Hate it or fear it, because it is the sign of the Maori
And our bodies reek a little. That Tawhai there
Would never anoint herself, that is why he took her.
She was too fine, she thought, to be smeared with oil.
FIRST WOMAN: When her lover comes, Te Kawau will lift the gourd

And drench her body in the oil. So Whana will hate her
And go, and Ruarangi will have her.
SECOND WOMAN: No!
She will go to her lover. Nothing the Maoris can do
Will end their love, unless by her own consent.
She said it this morning.
FIRST WOMAN: Watch!
TAWHAI: People of the Maori!
SECOND WOMAN: Tawhai is speaking.
TAWHAI (*loudly and clearly*): Am I to stand before you
Shamed, with my head bowed, like a captive woman,
Like a slave? Women and men of my tribe, hear me!
I am not ashamed, I stand here in pride before you
And wait for my lover to claim me, my golden Whana
Of the patu paiarehe. Oh Whana my lover,
If you hear me now, there in the dark and the mist,
If you are crouching there in the fern or the bush,
Uncertain, waiting—no, not afraid of the Maori,
But doubtful of me, not trusting a woman's love—
Come to me now!
FIRST WOMAN: Hear! She is calling her lover.
TAWHAI: O women and men of my tribe, farewell for ever!
You, my husband; you, Nukuroa the fisherman;
You, Wera my dearest mother; you, Koura and Tiki,
Farewell forever and remember I love you always.
You, whare that I love, village that I love,
Lost in the shadows, farewell.
SECOND WOMAN: She is going to her lover.
TAWHAI: O women of my tribe, you will know. And you, you men,
You will try to understand. Do not judge me harshly.
Remember me when I am gone for my days of laughter
And the way I could make your smiles dance in the sun.
Remember me always as one who loved my people.
I loved you all, how much have I loved my life
Of which you are part, and so to be cherished for ever.
I have tried to be true to my love; against all persuasion
To cling to you all for ever. You do not know,
You cannot know, how in the dark of the night
And the blaze of day I have fought against myself
And against my heart to keep the faith of a Maori.
But also do you not know—how could you know—
The spell of my lover of the patu paiarehe,
The golden storm that has washed away my will.
What can I say that will help you to understand,
To forgive, if that is needed? I stand before you
In the light of the wise man's fires, and you think you see
A woman of the Maori here; I am the sky
Blazing with stars, that is washed away in the morning;
I am the river that rushes on the stones to the sea;

I am the sea herself, the moving ocean
That floods to the light of the moon. O Whana, my light——
WHANA: Tawhai! My love! My love!
FIRST WOMAN: Whana has come!
(*The Maoris shout.*)
SECOND WOMAN: Did you see him leap from the shadows? His body is gold.
FIRST WOMAN: He strides towards her. He is going to take her now.
TAWHAI: Whana! Whana!
RUARANGI: Ho, men of the Maori!
Kill this beast of the night!
NUKUROA: Kill! Kill!
(*Warriors shout.*)
SECOND WOMAN: Alas, they will kill him.
FIRST WOMAN: Watch Te Kawau. Listen!
TE KAWAU: Peace! There will be no killing. Stand, you warriors.
It is I, Te Kawau, who say it. There will be no killing.
This wild man of the patu paiarehe
Has come to claim his woman, and no one shall stay him
But Tawhai herself if she pleases. You of the mist,
Speak! Do you take this woman?
TAWHAI: O Whana, my darling.
WHANA: Look well on your people, Tawhai.
TAWHAI: Long have I looked.
WHANA: Look in the furthest shadows to the whare where you lived
And the little village you loved.
TAWHAI: I have seen them, Whana.
WHANA: In the shadows where the firelight ends, the slaves and the dogs
And the women of no importance.
TAWHAI: I have seen them also.
WHANA: Rank upon rank, with mere and spear and war-club,
The mighty warriors of your race, they who protect you
From the fire in the night, the raid, the leap and the screaming.
TAWHAI: I have said farewell to the brave, strong fighting men.
WHANA: At whom I laugh. Of whom I will meet the strongest,
Spear against spear.
(*Warriors shout.*)
TE KAWAU: Peace. Let him speak to his woman.
WHANA: In front of the warriors, close before us, Tawhai,
Look on your father. Look on the man you married,
With whom you have lived in peace. Look on the youth
Who follows with a dog's eyes your lightest movement.
TAWHAI: Whana, take me away.
WHANA: No, not yet.
Look there, kneeling at the fires, on Wera your mother
And Koura your mother's friend, and the women of your tribe.

TAWHAI: Take me away. I have looked and said farewell.
WHANA: Now, for the last time, look on this wise old man
　Who knows the secrets of your heart and stands beside you
　With a gourd of the oil of the Maori. Tawhai, my heart,
　Take the bowl. Cover yourself with the oil.
TAWHAI: Oh, why do you torment me? I have looked on them all,
　And I am yours for ever.
WHANA:　　　　　　　　Then I will take you!
　Glad and proud will I take you, glad and proud
　From the reek of the village and the whare where love is stale.
　I will take you away from the repetition of life
　Meaningless, blind and endless in the Maori village
　Where the men are born for war and the women for childbirth
　And the back is bent at the cooking and the slender hands
　Lovelier than the toi-toi plumes waving in the moonlight
　Are stained and broken in the fields and only once
　In a hundred years of breeding for war and childbirth
　Does the swarming earth throw up such a flower as you,
　Of fire and grace and beauty to crown its labour
　And to show why women endured and men were valiant.
　Flower from the stubborn earth, fire from these stones,
　Aye, I will take you away to the flowers of the forest
　And the fire that leaps form the darkness and never grows cold.
TAWHAI: Yes, Whana, take me away.
FIRST WOMAN:　　　　　　　　He will take her now.
WHANA: I, Whana of the patu paiarehe,
　A chief among my people, who have dared to-night
　The steam and glare of your fires and your warrior's weapons
　And the wise old man with the gourd—who have dared you all
　For the love of this woman Tawhai—I take her now
　To be mine for ever in the forest. Throw down the gourd,
　Old man, throw down the gourd. You are wise in enchantment,
　But I have the voice of love.
SECOND WOMAN:　　　　She is gone for ever.
TAWHAI: I am yours for ever, Whana.
WERA:　　　　　　　　No, Tawhai!
RUARANGI: My wife whom I love, Tawhai my wife whom I love,
　　stay.
NUKUROA: Stay with your husband, my daughter.
TIKI:　　　　　　　　　　　　　Tawhai!
KOURA: Stay with your people, Tawhai.
TAWHAI:　　　　　　　Eh, the voices!
　So many voices of my people. And you, Te Kawau—
　Will you let me go? Why do you hand me the gourd?
TE KAWAU: Take the gourd, my child.
TAWHAI:　　　　　　　　No! Never!
　I do not want it, Te Kawau. I do not want it.
TE KAWAU: Hold it, Tawhai. If I speak to you one word,
　One syllable of folly, throw it to the ground.

The Golden Lover

FIRST WOMAN: She has taken the gourd of oil from old Te Kawau!
TE KAWAU: Eh, I am sorry for you, for I speak the thought,
 The secret truth of your heart. I, the cormorant!
 I have seen it all, Tawhai, all this is hidden
 In those depths more lovely than water where your spirit lives
 And truth, though it hides, abides. The golden lover!
 Oh the wild hours in the night, the midnight torrent
 Of stars and flowers and fire when your body tosses
 Like foam on the rushing waters. Oh the long deep calm
 When you rest as the spirits rest who live in the river,
 Calm on the silver sand, while life above you
 Flows and sings as it flows, the shining current
 With stars and trees reflected, unreal and tranquil.
 Eh, and the warm turning to the golden lover
 Whose body is a fire for a woman chilled with wonder.
 The fire that leaps from the darkness and never grows cold,
 The flower that blooms in the forest and never grows old,
 The hands that are never coarsened, the body of dawn
 That never is gross with day or haggard with dusk—
 Aye, Tawhai, I know it. I who am old
 And know the winding river from the snow to the sea.
TAWHAI: I am afraid of you. I am afraid.
TE KAWAU: Raise the gourd in the air, lift it up high.
SECOND WOMAN: She is lifting the gourd.
WHANA: O Tawhai, Tawhai.
TE KAWAU: Dreams, Tawhai, dreams.
 The golden dream. It is not Te Kawau you fear,
 Not me, but the truth. And truth is a bitter fruit
 For a girl in love.
TAWHAI: Three nights I have lived my dream.
 When my golden lover came I was woman awake,
 Not a girl asleep. And there is my lover now,
 No dream, but a man in splendour.
TE KAWAU: Yes, Tawhai, a man.
 Golden in the firelight, but no fire burns for ever.
 Now dream no more, you who are woman awake.
 Know you are woman. Not a flower of the forest nor a fire,
 But a woman of the Maori here among your people.
 The golden lover—what is that but the god of a dream?—
 A dream that will break as the day breaks on Pirongia.
 You know, and he knows too, it is only a dream,
 A love like another love, the dream of a night
 To fade with the dawn, turn ugly or nothing in a year,
 Or die at the best to the little embers of laughter.
 Will you who are woman here, loved by your people,
 A light that fills their eyes with the dance of the sun,
 Go to the forest to be nothing? Will you who are safe
 With mother and husband and a warm nest in the whare
 For the children not yet born, go out to the forest

To wander cold in the mist when your lover leaves you,
To fill the valleys of Pirongia with you lamentation
And die deserted, or at last come creeping back
To your people who want you no longer?
TAWHAI: Alas, I am lost.
WERA: O Tawhai, my daughter!
RUARANGI: Tawhai, my wife!
TIKI: Tawhai!
TE KAWAU: The gourd of oil, Tawhai. The gourd of oil.
The choice is your own. You can go with this Whana if you wish.
But know, as deep in your heart you have always known,
You are a woman of the Maori. The fields are for you,
That coarsen the hands; and the bending at the cooking-fire
That crooks that back; and childbirth and age are for you;
And if you are lucky, though you lose your golden lover,
You will laugh and not be bitter.
TAWHAI: You are wise, Te Kawau.
But never will I forget this man of the mist
Who struck at my heart like a golden hawk from the sky.
TE KAWAU: Aye, cherish your dream. It is true while it lasts.
I, too, although I am old, have sent my mind,
The flying shag, into a far country
Where the birds sing and the flowers are white or red
In a golden light that never goes out of the sky.
But that is a long journey. Our village is here.
And here is where you belong, in the Maori village
Where nothing happens that has not happened before
And the beasts or gods that prowl the fringe of your dreams
With promise of inhuman joy, impossible love,
Remain a dream, and do not come to torment you
Before all your tribe on a night at the gates of the pa.
Tawhai, woman of the Maori, lift the gourd,
Cover your body with the oil; come home to your people;
Come home to life!
TAWHAI: Alas, what have you done?
WHANA: Tawhai, Tawhai, you cannot do this thing.
Put down the gourd!
FIRST WOMAN: Tawhai is lifting the gourd!
SECOND WOMAN: She tips the bowl, the oil splashes in her hair,
It runs down her face, her shoulders, all over her body.
(*The Maoris cry out.*)
TAWHAI: Now! It is done. You have made be betray my love,
And I am sick and ashamed. Let me go home.
WHANA: Tawhai! Tawhai!
TAWHAI: I am ashamed before you.
WHANA: O lost, lost, lost! She, the white heron,
O lost for ever with all the gleam of her body
And her wild heart in the night. By your own hands
And your own will, Tawhai my flower and my fire.

The Golden Lover

The days will be long in the forest, and long the nights,
And cold the mist on Pirongia. If I had thought—
If I had said—and now, too late for ever.
You will wake in the night, Tawhai, and turn to me
For the blaze of my love, and your hands will be filled with ashes.
TAWHAI: Never again the love sweeter than the summer
And the fire that leaped from the darkness. All darkness now.
O lost, lost for ever, my golden lover.
WHANA: Lost, Tawhai, lost!
FIRST WOMAN: Look, he has gone!
(*The Maoris cry out.*)
SECOND WOMAN: Tawhai will weep for this. How lovely he was,
And now he is gone for ever.
TAWHAI: Gone, gone.
O Whana, my golden lover, what have I done
To you, and to me?
TE KAWAU: It is sad when the dreamer awakes.
TAWHAI: I will hate you all my life.
WERA: Tawhai, my daughter,
Come to my arms and weep.
KOURA: Weep; yes, weep.
TAWHAI: Ach, how I hate you all. I will not weep.
RUARANGI: Weep on my shoulder, Tawhai.
TAWHAI: You, you fat snail!
It is all your fault, Ruarangi, and now I am left
With a thing like you. If you dare, if you dare to touch me
I will kill you. There!
NUKUROA: Ruarangi, ignore this woman.
My daughter is wild as always. She will soon recover
And smile upon you.
TAWHAI: Truly I shall smile upon him
If the child is born with red hair.
RUARANGI: You are still bewitched.
NUKUROA: All women have a devil in their tongues.
TIKI: You are hard on Tawhai.
TAWHAI: What, Tiki here?
RUARANGI: Ach, there is always Tiki.
Go away, you fly!
TAWHAI: Of course. There is always Tiki.
What a pity his hair is so black.
TIKI: I would set it on fire
If that would please you, Tawhai.
TAWHAI: Of course it would please me.
I have set the village on fire these last few days
And it greatly pleased me.
NUKUROA: Ruarangi, you had better come fishing.
RUARANGI: No, I shall go and sit down.
TAWHAI: My golden husband!

Glossary

and guide to pronunciation

In Maori words of two syllables the accent generally falls on the first: e.g., Táwhai. In a compound word there is a secondary accent on the beginning of the second portion of the word: e.g., Rúarángi.

Each vowel has a long and a short value: e.g. a can be long as in the English "father" or short as in "cat"; long e is pronounced as a in the English "play", short e as in "pet"; long i as in "keep", short i as in "skin"; long o as in "note", short o as in "block"; long u as in "cool", short u as in "pull". The diphthong ai is sounded as in "why"; au as in "cow"; oi as in "boy". In ordinary New Zealand speech these sounds are considerably modified and it is best in reading or performance to follow popular usage. A rough guide to pronunciation of the Maori words used in the play is:

Hakarimata	hack-uh-ree-mat-uh
kahawai (type of fish)	car-why
Karewa	car-ée-wuh
Kawhia	car-fee-uh. "Wh" is sometimes pronounced "f" in Maori and this township has adopted the latter usage.
kiwi	keé-wee
kotuku (the white heron)	ko-too-koo
Koura	koo-ruh
kowhai (type of flowering tree)	ko-why, but usually pronounced ko-eye
kumara (sweet potato)	koo-muh-ruh
mere (battle-axe)	merray; "merry" is near enough
Nukuroa	noo-koo-ro-uh
pa (village)	par
patu-paiarehe (the people of the mist)	par-too py-uh fay-he
Pirongia	pee-rong-yuh
Pukearuhe	pooky-árrowy (oo as in "book")
rata (parasitic vine)	rah-tuh
raupo (bulrushes)	fow-po
Raurika	row-reek-uh
rimu (type of tree)	ree-moo (oo sound short)
Ruarangi	roo-uh-rangy (g hard as in "hang")
tapu (taboo)	tar-poo (oo sound short)

Glossary

Tawhai	tar-why
Teina	tay-nuh
Te Kawau	The Te should perhaps be tay but it would be much shortened in speech; and "tea", said swiftly, would be near enough. Kawau, ka-wow.
Tiki	tee-kee
tohunga (witch-doctor)	to-hung-uh (o as in "note")
toi-toi (type of pampas grass)	toy-toy
totara (type of tree)	to-tuh-ruh (o as in "note")
tui (a bird)	too-ee (the ee sound short)
urukehu (red-haired)	oo-roo-kay-hoo
Waipa	why-par
Wera	way-ruh. Actually the English word "wearer" is just about right.
Whana	whon-uh (more-or-less rhyming with "honour")
whare (hut)	whorry (rhyming with "lorry")

—D.S.

Introduction to
The Golden Lover
by Douglas Stewart

As everybody knows who has written anything from a quatrain to a three-decker novel, sometimes the completed work seems to be "given" to you and sometimes you have to fight for it. The struggle comes when you are trying to force the thing to go in a different direction from the way it wants to go itself, or the way your subconscious mind wants it to go; or it will come when you really don't know *what* you want to say and are clawing at the air to find it. The "given" work just comes of itself, and all you have to do is to write it down. There is no saying which process gives the best results: it depends, anyhow, on whether you win the fight. If you don't, the work will be flawed; if you do, you often get an added depth and weight out of the struggle. But I don't think that is necessarily or invariably the case; and, lighter or not, the "given" work, besides being an extraordinary pleasure to write, is at least likely to be freer from flaws than a play or a poem you have had to fight for.

At any rate, *The Golden Lover* was one of those "given" works. I never enjoyed writing anything in my life so much. To be sitting alone in your flat at King's Cross, rocking with laughter at your own jokes—and surely one is entitled to do that—is a most rare and rewarding experience in what Ezra Pound has rather harshly called "this damned profession of writing"; and if it is pleasing to laugh at your own jokes it is also pleasing to have the hope of making other people laugh at them too. Writers, if they are to be regarded "seriously" are generally expected to harass and torment their audiences, or to lead them into high and remote regions of complexity, but there is really a great deal to be said for amusing them, charming them, adding something to the beauty and gaiety of life if you can do it. If we are seers and visionaries and sociologists we are also, traditionally, entertainers. And beauty and gaiety are truths just as valid as their opposites.

The only other occasion when a long work came to me quite so readily as *The Golden Lover* was when I was writing the ballad sequence, *Glencoe*. *Glencoe* was quite fantastic. I wrote the whole book in five days, dashing it down on my typewriter in the midst of mundane affairs at the *Bulletin* office; and—though it really was the most complicated jigsaw of people and events to fit together in one piece—

Introduction to *The Golden Lover*

it seemed that all I had to do was to take down the ballads as they came; and I knew exactly which piece of the jigsaw had to be composed and fitted in next. After one ballad was finished, I used to go for a stroll to Circular Quay, take a breath of fresh air, and come back and write the next bit. I have always had a suspicion that one of my ancestors (to whom the remnant of the MacDonalds fled for refuge after the massacre) wrote it for me; or else it was because I had spent a year trying to make a play of its unmanageable groups of characters and episodes and, all the while that was going on, it was sorting itself out in my subconscious mind into the sequence of ballads.

But there wasn't any long period of study before *The Golden Lover* arrived. In fact there wasn't any study at all. After *The Fire on the Snow* and *Ned Kelly* I had made up my mind that I would confine myself chiefly to heroic and mythological themes that had some bearing on our lives in this part of the world, and I was looking through James Cowan's charming little *Fairy Folk Tales of the Maori* in search of the well-known story of Hinemoa and Tutanekai (which isn't in that book; but it is the Maori equivalent to the Hero and Leander legend) when I came across the chapter which Cowan calls "Whanawhana of the Bush": the legend of *The Golden Lover*. The whole play thereupon flashed into my mind complete. So it seems that, when you are lucky or when you are ready for it, you can see a long and quite complex work in one piece just as you would see a bird or a tree for a lyric.

Looking into Cowan's book now, to see how much I stole from him, I am pleased to discover that I really invented quite a lot: Nukuroa, Wera, Koura, the other women, Tiki, the Dog, none of them is in Cowan. There is nothing of the life of the village. The *tohunga* is mentioned but not described as a character; and I see that there is a considerable difference in the plot, for Tawhai in Cowan is much more distressed at her ravishment than she is in the play, and actually joins Ruarangi in calling in the *tohunga* to put an end to her love affair. All the same, the outline of the thing is there in Cowan; and so is Tawhai's wonderful phrase about her will being "as water" and her stratagem of returning to her husband each morning so that she could keep both husband and lover; which—the phrase and the stratagem together—so enchanted me at the time with their total and delightful femininity that they were, more than anything else, the reason why I wrote the play. In Cowan, Ruarangi goes out and finds his wife in the forest after her first night with Whanawhana on the mountain-top, and learns that Whanawhana

> had cast a most powerful spell upon her: the effect of this was that although she would be returned to her husband in the daytime, by night she must become again the bride of the fairy.
>
> The husband and wife returned to their home, but as the evening approached the thick fogs and mists rolled down from the mountains and all in a moment Tawhai-tu vanished from Ruarangi's gaze. The *patupaiarehe* had carried her off again.
>
> In the morning Tawhai-tu was returned to her husband in the same miraculous manner. "Alas", she said, "I have slept once more with the

> *patu-paiarehe.* His spell is upon me—my will is as the water of yonder river before his incantations and his fairy *mana."* And that evening Ruarangi found himself powerless to hold his wife with him: she vanished in a breath with the cloudy coming of her fairy lord: and as before, in the morning, she stood weeping on the threshold of the house on the Waipa bank.

Since this little scene, more than anything else, sparked the play off, and since we are all in these post-Freudian days expected to investigate the profound personal and psychological necessities that motivate a work of art, I suppose I had better admit that it was some natural interest in the behaviour of women that operated at this point; but there were also some other cogent reasons for the appeal of the story. One obvious reason was that I had not very long left New Zealand for Australia and, if I do not think I was suffering from "nostalgia", as is the common explanation for this kind of reminiscent writing—I have always liked Australia very much indeed—New Zealand had at least clarified in my mind and it was wonderful to have a theme in which I could express the image which it had formed. It was wonderful, too, for anybody faced with the problem of the poetic drama in the modern world—how do you get a theme which will let you write poetry?—to have all that New Zealand earth, which I knew so well, legitimately part of the play. The bush I described in it was not, in fact, that of Pirongia—we used to see that dark-green volcanic hump in the distance as we drove to beach holidays at Kawhia, a hundred miles or so away from my own territory—but all New Zealand bush is much the same anywhere. Nukuroa's speech about the *kahawai* ("salmon" in Australia) shoaling at Kawhia came direct from those beach holidays.

Still another reason was the one I have mentioned: my belief, which I still hold, that we should in general (if an ancestor doesn't come along and drag one off to Glencoe) write about our own part of the world. It is a question of what is significant to us; and, besides, our countries are new in the world's literature and fresh to write about.

Finally, there was the fact that I had always been fascinated—and still am—by the mystery of those light-skinned, red-haired strangers among the Maoris, to whose tribe Whana belonged and whom, still haunting if they didn't seem to be fairies, we used occasionally to meet in New Zealand. It may have been the late Judge F.O.V. Acheson who first aroused my interest in them: he wrote a book, *Plume of the Arawas,* which I read in my boyhood and in which he advanced the theory, if I remember rightly, that they were the descendants of Norwegian sailors, perhaps Vikings. If Thor Heyerdahl is right, they are the pre-Inca people (possibly of European origin?) who migrated from Peru to Easter Island and from there spread throughout Polynesia; to become, when they were conquered by the brown-skinned invaders whom Heyerdahl traces to North America, the people-of-the-mist, the outcasts, the fairies. There is, incidentally, another delightful New Zealand legend about a Maori youth who was carried off, much against his will, by the *patu-*

Introduction to *The Golden Lover*

paiarehe women. How these people got to New Zealand, except by inter-marriage with the Maoris, I don't know. There are records of pre-Maori inhabitants but not, so far as I know, of red-haired ones. Maybe they did get there; maybe the legends originated in Polynesia. At any rate they are a most interesting people.

But when you have said "finally" in discussing the origins of a work of art you have never really reached finality. For this play is not merely a comedy of love, or an evocation of New Zealand, or the dramatization of a Maori legend; it also seeks to express what I must call a view or a vision of life. It is a mistake to interpret it merely on a realistic level. If you do, as sometimes people have done, you can almost find a "moral" in it: that wives should not be unfaithful; or that passionate love doesn't last; or something equally obvious. I was not concerned with such matters. You can be disappointed, on the realistic level, that Tawhai does not finally choose to go off with her lover. Well, on that level, all I can say is that I was following the Maori legend and that Tawhai lacks something of the stature for great love. But symbolism and realism are inextricably entwined in the play and on its deeper, symbolic level, Tawhai's choice is not between her husband and her lover but between the life of the earth and the life of the sky—the immortal splendour which we can perceive or realize here only in flashes. Ruarangi and Wera, the good fat people, Nukuroa with his dog and his fishing, are the earth; Whana is, ultimately, not real, not human, a fairy, a symbol of the spirit. "Come home to life", says the *tohunga* to Tawhai at the end. It is a play about the acceptance of life.

The play was originally written for radio but has sometimes been put on the stage. Anybody who wants to do that with it had better cut scene 2 at Wera's line "You husband will want his dinner." If the scene is played in full the next scene becomes repetitive and even appears, disconcertingly, to go backwards.

The Playwright in Australia*

by Douglas Stewart

I suppose no writer in a democracy would readily admit that literature must serve the purposes of the nation. We all know it is for the world; for some mysterious end beyond the world in its visionary aspects; and the dangers in defining any other purpose for it are too alarming to face with composure ... corruption into serving one of the totalitarian ideologies or, at best, into mere tub-thumping patriotism.

Nevertheless, when all the dangers have been recognized, it is of course a fact that literature does serve, even in a sense create, the nation. Nothing remains of Greece but its sculpture, philosophies, and its plays: it is to these we turn to find out what the nation was. It is to Shakespeare that we must turn to find out what was Elizabethan England—or, rather, eternal England.

The interest, the great excitement of living in a new country such as Australia, where a new nation is being formed out of the old stock, is that all this work of creation is still to do. There is no Euripides, there is no Shakespeare; there is no Aristophanes, there is not, as yet, even a Wycherley or a Sheridan. It is all still to be done.

How, exactly, does the playwright help to "create" the nation? I think it is likely that, simply because his works are more clearly seen, because he makes living figures walk across the stage, he does more to create it than any other kind of artist in stone or paint or words. It is not enough to say that the plays are what is left when the nation vanishes; for they must also, if they are not a mere monument or a mere historical record, have "created" the nation while it was in being; they must somehow have formed the minds and shaped the lives of the audiences who saw them.

The playwright, I think, creates the myths by which the people live: the heroic, gigantic, legendary figures, fathers of the race, ancestors spiritual or actual, to which the living man can point and say, "That is what I am made of; that is what makes us different from other people; that is what I believe in; those are my gods and my devils." If you were a Greek you needed to know about the valour of Achilles and the crimes of Oedipus; if you are English, you must know the dreadful folly of Macbeth, the darkness and splendour of the kings, the enormous substantiality of Falstaff, gross, rich, and stable as the earth itself. In Australia—

Australian Theatre Year I (1955–56), pp. 9, 27 (issued by the Australian Elizabethan Trust as *The First Year*).

The theme that principally obsessed both the Greek and Elizabethan playwrights was the killing of the king. It had a twofold significance, at once religious and national. It was a crime against the divinity of kings, and it was a crime against society, the order of the State, the security and welfare of the people.

The problem that has most interested me in the Australian situation is, where do you find a theme of similar significance?

It is easy enough to find the ancestral heroes. Surely, increasingly as time goes by, they will be recognized in the voyagers, explorers, and pioneers who first broke through that wall of silence and sunlight beyond which the continent lay undiscovered for so many, many years. They are already, in fact, taking on a mythological status and stature in such poems as Kenneth Slessor's "Five Visions of Captain Cook", Robert D. FitzGerald's "Heemskerck Shoals" and Francis Webb's "Leichhardt".

But the significant crime against divinity and society, the traditional basis for tragedy, must obviously—in the absence of kings from our soil and in the growth of modern democracy—be found itself in more democratic circumstances: in mutiny on sea or land, which still has a smack of something sacriligious about it; in the rebellion of the bushrangers against society; in the dispossession of the Aborigines; perhaps, thinking of the convicts and completely reversing the theme, in the State's crime against humanity. That is where our tragic mythology lies: a set of problems to be examined from every angle until their significance is clarified and assimilated.

But in new countries time, as it were, telescopes. If the ballad is the most primitive form of poetry, we passed through and out of that period in, broadly, the first century of our existence. Modern Australian poetry, though it may be different in tone, is not expected to be any less sophisticated than poetry anywhere in the world. And, similarly, if we are still in that most stimulating age where our national myths need to find embodiment in the poetic drama, so are we, simultaneously, in the modern world where any kind of play that unselfconsciously expresses the spirit of the nation can, and should, be written: the play of the soil, the comedy of manners.

The play of the soil, after the poetic drama, is what I am myself most anxious to see; for, though of course, I would welcome a city comedy, it seems to me that the kind of distillation of the earth which we get in the plays of Synge and Chekhov is what is most grievously overdue in Australia.

Why has the drama, with a few gallant exceptions, lagged so far behind the other arts in Australia? I think there are two reasons: first, that, at least for the poetic drama, some years needed to elapse before they mythological figures could be seen in their proper stature against the mists of time (there are still, I am told a few people who think of Ned Kelly as a man rather than as a myth); and, secondly, simply that there was no theatre out of which the Australian playwright could make a living. Energy that might have gone into the drama has gone into the novel, the biography, the short story, and the narrative poem. Now, perhaps, it will come to the stage.

Ted Roberts

Mark Lee (Kevin) and Vincent Ball (Jim) in a scene from the 1974 A.B.C. television production of *Lindsay's Boy*. Photograph by courtesy of the Australian Broadcasting Commission.

Lindsay's Boy

Lindsay's Boy was first broadcast on A.B.C. television on 4 July 1974, with the following cast:

JIM LINDSAY	Vincent Ball
KEVIN LINDSAY	Mark Lee
DENISE	Jenny Lee
KAREN	Julieanne Newbould
MICK NELSON	Chris King
AUNTY MAY	Joan Bruce
UNCLE SID	David Curtis
BROTHER ERNEST	Robert Quilter
PRIEST	Ambrose Foster
COCKY	George Foster
TOD	Gordon Piper
JACK	Al Taylor
PORKY	Barry Lovett
SPIELER	Terry Redell
SOLDIER ONE	Doug Wiggins
SOLDIER TWO	Bill Ayres
SPINNER	Ernest Butchard
CONTROLLER	Ray Marshal

Producer: Frank Arnold.

Television production terms:

B/G	Background
Ext.	Exterior
Int.	Interior
OOS	Out of sight
POV	Point of view
SFX	Sound effects
V/O	Voice over

1. Ext. Waverley Cemetery
Priest/Gravediggers/Jim Lindsay/Kevin/May/Sid

(*A bleak, windy day, the grey sea stretching away, rough and blustery under a sky of scudding grey clouds. The monotonous drone of the priest's voice competes with the sigh of the wind.*)

PRIEST (OOS): I am the resurrection and the Life. He who believes in Me though he is dead will live on; and whoever has life and has faith in Me, to all eternity will not die.

(*Back from the cliffs, the headstones are still wet from the recent rain, forlorn and lonely. The priest continues to read the prayer as the gravediggers lower a coffin into an open grave. There are only four mourners around the grave: JIM LINDSAY, his son KEVIN, his wife's sister MAY, and her husband SID. JIM LINDSAY wears A.I.F. jungle greens, stained by rain, and carries a slouch hat. With him, but a little apart, KEVIN wears his school uniform, a long-trousered suit bearing the pocket badge of a Catholic High School. He is about fifteen. Both of them appear preoccupied, probably still stunned by the loss of wife and mother, oblivious to everything but the disappearing coffin. The other two mourners, MAY and SID, are both in their late forties, comfortable, suburban-looking, saddened but also a little embarrassed by the occasion. They stand under an umbrella, though it is not raining.*)

PRIEST: Our father, which art in heaven ... (*etc.*)

(*JIM staring at the coffin as the gravediggers begin the terrible job of hurling in the sods, collapsing the walls of the grave. He rubs his open palm hard, three times, against his thigh. It's a gesture common with him in times of strain. He looks away, sees KEVIN staring at him, expressionless.*)

2. Ext. Gates of Waverley Cemetery
Kevin/Jim/Priest/May/Sid

(*KEVIN kicks a smooth river-pebble and it rattles away along the path. JIM shakes hands with the priest, who nods to SID and MAY, leaves. For a moment the family stands silent, watching the departing priest, then they turn awkwardly to each other.*)

MAY: Will you come back?

(*JIM hesitates.*)

JIM: No. I think ... I better get back to camp.

MAY: They gave you till tomorrow.

JIM: I better get back.

(*Sees KEVIN staring at him. If the boy is showing any expression at all, it could be regarded as almost hostile. He looks away from his father.*)

You'll go with your Uncle and Auntie.

(*The boy makes no reply.*)

I've got to go.

(*The boy nods, slightly.*)

Don't give them any trouble.
(KEVIN *looks away again.*)
MAY: He'll be all right.
JIM: Look after your mother's ... Look after the grave.
(KEVIN *looks up at him quickly, tears coming. JIM reaches out, squeezes the boy's shoulder. Then abruptly turns away, strides off towards the gate.* SFX *of distant thunder. The day seems to darken.* KEVIN *stands watching his father walk out through the gate, without looking back. The boy begins to rock back and forward, very slightly, as rain begins to fall, gradually becoming heavier. His hair is plastered down by the rain. It runs down his face, and he blinks it back from his eyes, staring after his father, still rocking gently. Main titles over*: LINDSAY'S BOY.)

3. Ext. Jungle

(*Tropical rain falling vertically in sheets, unbelievably constant and heavy. The undergrowth streaming water, the earth a churned mess of mud. A group of perhaps five or six soldiers in jungle greens covered by ponchos, carrying rifles, struggle up a muddy slippery trail marked by the passage of previous boots, and running with rivulets of water. They slide and struggle to the top of a small clearing by the trail, and throw themselves down, exhausted, trying to find some shelter under their ponchos. One of them is* JIM LINDSAY, *who drags himself against a palm tree, struggles to take a letter from under the poncho, begins to read, trying to protect the letter beneath the brim of his slouch hat.* MAY's *voice is heard over as he reads.*)
MAY: It's not as though it's serious trouble and Sid and me don't want you to start worrying as everyone understands about the boy's mother being passed away and you up there and all and it's only little things like pinching things from shops and scaling trams and fights and things. Only I thought you had better know not that we want you to worry you've got enough on your mind ...
(*The letter is becoming saturated with the rain.* JIM *holds it, soggy now and drooping. He stares off into the jungle. Remainder main titles over.*)

4. Int. Brother Ernest's office
Brother Ernest/Kevin

(*The office is small, book-lined, and contains an inordinate number of religious pictures and statues.* BROTHER ERNEST *is a smooth-faced, young-looking fifty, fairly stout. He is relaxed, leaning back from his desk, gently swivelling his chair from side to side. He is smiling, but it's a humourless smile, and he gives the impression of being a man accustomed to being feared, and not*

unhappy about it. He is watching KEVIN, *who stands opposite him, silent. After a long moment, broken only by the creak of the chair,* KEVIN *speaks. His voice is almost inaudible.*)
KEVIN: I didn't take it.
(*The chair swings a couple of times more.*)
ERNEST: I beg your pardon?
(KEVIN'S *voice breaks a little.*)
KEVIN: I didn't take ...
ERNEST: Speak up, Lindsay. Let's hear you.
KEVIN: The ... the money.
(BROTHER ERNEST *stops swinging. Considers this, nodding.*)
ERNEST: You didn't take it.
(KEVIN *says nothing.*)
But you did ... er ... handle the purse.
(KEVIN *nods.*)
Speak up, Lindsay. Speak up.
(KEVIN *nods again, makes some sort of croaking sound.*)
Yes. You handled the purse.
(*He reaches out, takes a small wallet-type change purse from the desk, opens it, looks it over, very casual. He's enjoying the situation.*)
Who else handled the purse?
KEVIN: Muzza. M ... Michael Nelson, Brar.
ERNEST: Just you and ... Muzza. No one else, Lindsay?
KEVIN: No, Brar.
(BROTHER ERNEST *begins to swing again, looking at the purse.*)
ERNEST: Turn out your pockets, Lindsay.
(KEVIN *looks shocked, frightened.*)
KEVIN: It was empty when we found it.
ERNEST: Turn out your pockets.
KEVIN: I didn't take anything.
ERNEST: Then you won't mind displaying the contents of your pockets. Will you?
(KEVIN *stares at him. He is frightened and angry, near to tears. His hand rubs up and down the leg of his pants, in a gesture reminiscent of his father's at the graveside.* BROTHER ERNEST *smiles at the gesture.*)
You seem nervous, Lindsay.
(KEVIN *breaks.*)
KEVIN: You bastard.
(*He almost sobs it out, turns and tries to hurry from the room. Gets to the door, can't open it, fumbles with the door handle.* BROTHER ERNEST's *expression barely changes.*)
ERNEST: Lindsay!
(*He gets up, strides to the door, takes the handle.*)
I believe your father is in New Guinea.
(KEVIN *looks up at him, fearful, pleading.*)
In view of this ...
(*He pulls open the door.*)

If the money is placed on my desk before the last period, the matter will be ...
KEVIN: I didn't take it!
(*Pushes hard past the brother and runs from the room. BROTHER ERNEST recovers. He stands at the door a moment, shrugs, returns to his desk. He picks up the purse, holds it, shakes his head. More in sorrow than in anger, he would like us to think.*)

5. Int./Ext. Army pup-tent

(JIM LINDSAY *propped on his elbow, reading a letter in the gloom of the tent. Rain thunders down on the canvas, and the tent leaks in a number of places.*)
MAY (V/O): Not having any of our own, I suppose. He just seems to be always in trouble, Jim, if it's not at school it's setting fire to the paddock on the corner and the police coming and the fire brigade, and pinching fruit from Mitchell's shop, only specks, I know, but old Mitchell screamed like a pig.

6. Int. Brother Ernest's office
Brother Ernest/Kevin

(BROTHER ERNEST *is no longer smiling. He is seated in his swivel chair, hands on the desk, looking up at* KEVIN *without emotion.*)
ERNEST: You do not seem to be aware, Lindsay, that your country is at war.
(KEVIN *has eyes downcast, looks up at him, away again.*)
In times like this ... though God has seen fit to spare us the full ..: in times like this ...
(*He's not too sure what he's trying to say. Becomes a little angry with himself, and therefore with* KEVIN.)
The school is short staffed, Lindsay. Very short staffed. No one has the time or patience left to deal with recalcitrance such as yours.
(*He gets up, paces.*)
Disobedience, petty theft ...
KEVIN: I never stole anything!
ERNEST: Continued revolt, unexplained absences.
(*He turns on* KEVIN *with the greatest accusation of all.*)
Abuse of your teachers! Teachers who have done everything to make allowance for your ... for your ... exceptional circumstances.
(*He sits, heavily, apparently weary.*)
KEVIN: I never asked anyone ...
ERNEST: In the ... your home situation ... if it was any different ... I'm afraid I'd have no hesitation in expelling you from the College.
(KEVIN *jerks, flinches at the implied threat, but makes no reply.* BROTHER ERNEST *hardens, angry at his failure to penetrate.*)

I have spoken to your aunt. She informs me that your father has applied for compassionate leave. Because of you, Lindsay. Because of you.
(KEVIN *looks up slowly, meets his gaze. A long moment.*)
I trust that pleases you.
(*No flicker of expression on* KEVIN's *face.*)

7. Int. Kevin's room at May's
Kevin/May

(*The room is very dark, the only light coming from a window over which a holland blind has been pulled. The blind flaps occasionally in a gentle breeze, allowing flashes of sunlight to enter. One flash of light illuminates* KEVIN *who is lying on his back on the narrow bed, fully dressed in his school suit, hands behind his head, staring at the ceiling. Outside, distantly, we can hear the call of a clothes prop seller as he makes his rounds.*)
SELLER (OOS): Proooooops! Closprooooops!
(KEVIN *closes his eyes.*)
MAY (OOS): Kevin! Are you in there?
(*The call comes from out in the hall, but the door opens almost immediately, and* AUNTIE MAY *puts her head in the door. She is hatted and ready to go out. She peers through the gloom.*)
Good heavens, boy! Aren't you dressed yet?
KEVIN: Yes.
MAY: Well, what are you doing ... oh, Kevin, you'll get all crushed. Oh, what a boy ...
(*The blind flaps, she sees him clearly for the first time.*)
In your school uniform, too. What will your father think.
KEVIN: (*Quietly*) I don't want to go
(MAY *stares at him.*)
MAY: You don't want to ... your father's coming back from the war, boy!
KEVIN: I don't want to go.
(MAY *looks indignant.*)
MAY: And what would you want me to tell him? Why his son wouldn't come and welcome him back?
(KEVIN *stares at her for a long moment, then swings his legs off the bed.*)
KEVIN: All right. I'll come.
MAY: Good of you.

8. Ext. Central Railway
Jim/Sid/May/Kevin

(*A train unloading in* B/G. *The bustle and noise of the steam train area.* JIM LINDSAY, *with his kitbag and gear, just off the train, suffers the embrace of* AUNTIE MAY, *turns and shakes hands with* SID. SID *is awkward and embarrassed.*)

SID: Good to see yer.
  (KEVIN *is standing back, face unreadable, watching.*)
JIM: Thanks, Sid.
MAY: Kevin, come and say hello to your Dad.
  (KEVIN *moves forward slowly.* JIM *hesitates, holds out his hand.* KEVIN *takes it slowly.*)
KEVIN: Hello, Dad.
  (JIM *nods, at a loss for words.*)
  Welcome home.
JIM: Thanks. Thanks ... Kevin.
  (*He lets go the boy's hand. They stand awkwardly for a moment.*)
SID: How long you got, Jim?
  (JIM *turns to him with relief.*)
JIM: Bit of luck, I'm back for good. They reckon it's nearly over.
  (*He turns back to* KEVIN.)
  Couple of weeks, we might be able to go home. To your ... to your Mum's place.
  (KEVIN *stares at him for a minute.*)
KEVIN: I hope so.

9. Stock footage sequence

(*Clips from newsreels of end of Pacific War celebrations.* INTERCUT *as follows to establish time lapse.*)

10. Ext. Randwick Marist Brothers College

(*A group of boys pulling down the sandbags from the school windows. Skylarking, throwing the sand about at each other.*)

11. Stock footage

(*Newsreels of people dancing in the street.*)

12. Ext. Barracks

(JIM *lines up with men outside* QM *store; they are carrying their gear. One man walks out in an oversize, badly cut suit. Catcalls from the waiting men.*)
SOLDIER ONE: Gawd! Ain't she pretty!
SOLDIER TWO: Good on yer, Nugget!

13. Stock footage
(*Revelry. Servicemen on lamp posts in Martin Place. People kissing.*)

14. Ext. Outside May and Sid's place
Kevin/Jim/Sid/May

(KEVIN *walks out through the front door, carrying a battered suitcase.* JIM *follows, with another case, and followed by* SID *and* MAY. *They stop on the verandah,* JIM *puts the cases down.*)
MAY: You know you're welcome to stay, Jim. As long as you like.
JIM: Thanks, May. You've done enough. It's time we started to look after ourselves.
SID: I suppose you want to get off by yourselves.
MAY: Two men with no one to cook or clean for you. I dunno how ...
JIM: We'll be all right, May. You've got your own family to look after.
MAY: What? This lazy big good-for-nothing? Huh. Well, if you've made up your minds.
(JIM *leans forward, pecks her on the cheek.*)
JIM: Thanks, May. You've been ...
(*Doesn't know what to say. She brushes it aside, turns to* KEVIN.)
MAY: And you, young feller. You try and turn over a new leaf. You got your father back now.
(KEVIN *nods, avoiding her eyes.*)
All right, then. You better give your Auntie a kiss.
(KEVIN *walks towards he slowly, as though reluctant. He kisses her on the cheek, then she suddenly throws her arms around him, near tears, and hugs him. He wraps his arms around her, the affection they've hidden coming at last.*)
Oh, you're a terrible boy.
(*And she is crying.*)

15. Stock footage
(*The aftermath of the celebrations. Martin Place covered with twisted, dirty streamers, balloons blowing about, a few drunks sleeping in the G.P.O. arches. The Cenotaph.*)

16. Ext. Jim's house, Coogee.
Kevin/Jim

(*The house is small, a semi-detached cottage, about forty years old today. The garden is overgrown and the paint peeling away.* KEVIN *and* JIM *stand outside, looking at it, in silence.*)
JIM: Doesn't look too good.
KEVIN: I ... I meant to do the garden.
(JIM *nods. Silence again.*)
JIM: Well, better go in. See what it's like.
(*Neither makes a move for a moment, then* JIM *squares his shoulders, and with something of an effort, moves towards the door, carrying one of the cases.* KEVIN *hesitates, follows.*)

Lindsay's Boy 231

17. Int. Kitchen, Jim's house.
Kevin/Jim

(JIM *enters the room, stops, looks around silently.* KEVIN *stands in the doorway behind him.*)

KEVIN: Auntie May came down. Cleaned up a couple of times.

(JIM *nods. Camera pans around, and we see the kitchen from his POV A big, deal-topped table and six chairs dominate the centre of the room. There is a dresser with a collection of china, much of it odd. A Silent Knight gas refrigerator, sink, Early Kooka gas stove. An old calendar hanging on the wall, 1943 vintage. Camera rests on the calendar, the local grocer's.* JIM *moves to it, stares at it for a long moment, then pulls it off the wall.* KEVIN *just watches.*)

JIM: Two years.

(*He tosses the calendar on to the sink, walks away.* KEVIN *picks up the calendar, looks at it, then rolls it, carries it with him.*)

Well, I suppose we better clean it up.

KEVIN: Will I ... can I have my old room again?

(JIM *looks at him, impatiently.*)

JIM: Why the hell wouldn't you? There's two bedrooms. And only the two of us.

(KEVIN *is diffident, upset by* JIM'S *shortness.*)

KEVIN: I just thought you might ...

(*He breaks off, doesn't know how to finish.*)

JIM: I'll use our ... my old room.

(KEVIN *has no reply, but can't let it go.* JIM *gets angry.*)

It's been two years! Just because ... I can't ... Well, it's been two years.

(KEVIN *nods, quickly, wanting to get it over.*)

KEVIN: I'll start on my room.

JIM: No. We'll do the kitchen first. Then I'll go and get in some food.

(KEVIN *nods, unsure where to start.*)

Well, get into some old duds. See if you can find the broom.

(KEVIN *nods and exits quickly.* JIM *looks about again. Goes to the dresser, opens it, looks in at the china stacked there. He lifts out a willow pattern cup, stares at it, trying to remember.* KEVIN *appears behind him, half changed, shoving his shirt into his pants.*)

KEVIN: I was going ...

(JIM *starts, wheels round, the cup in his hand.*)

JIM: Oh. Uh ... I was just looking ... can't remember this stuff.

(KEVIN *looks at the cup, at* JIM.)

KEVIN: You gave it to Mum. For her birthday. Before you ... went away.

(*It's both a challenge and a recrimination.* JIM *puts the cup down on the table.*)

18. Int. Kitchen, Jim's house
Kevin/Jim

(It is several hours later. The kitchen has been tidied, the cup still on the table. KEVIN is dragging out a couple of pots from the cupboards. SFX the front door slams. KEVIN begins to whistle quietly through his teeth, fills one of the pots with water. JIM enters, carrying a cardboard carton of parcels of meat and vegetables; under his other arm, two newspaper-wrapped bottles of beer. He drops everything on the table.)

JIM: Had a couple of beers.

(By way of explanation for his lateness.)

KEVIN: It's all right. I thought I'd get ready.

(He starts to unwrap a parcel of meat. It contains about a dozen chops. JIM pulls the top off a beer bottle, takes a glass from the dresser. He hesitates, looks around at KEVIN, doubtful.)

JIM: I don't suppose you'd ...

KEVIN: No. No thanks.

(JIM nods, pours himself a beer as KEVIN sets the chops up on the griller.)

JIM: I should have got some lemonade or something.

KEVIN: No, I'm all right.

(JIM has a big swig of beer.)

JIM: I should of got something.

KEVIN: No. It's all right.

(Lighting the gas, getting the chops on. He hesitates, looking at the vegetables, worried.)

Do you put the vegetables on before the chops, or what?

(JIM thinks, sipping his beer.)

JIM: Doesn't matter, I don't think. You just turn the gas down.

KEVIN: What on?

(JIM shrugs, doubtful.)

JIM: The chops, I think.

KEVIN: Aw.

(He turns the flame over the griller down very low. Too low. Returns to the table where JIM is now sitting, drinking. KEVIN empties out some potatoes, looks at them.)

JIM: Look, I'll just duck up and get you something.

(KEVIN takes the potatoes to the sink.)

KEVIN: What?

JIM: To drink. Should have got something.

KEVIN: I'm not thirsty. I'm all right.

(He washes the potatoes briefly and sketchily, drops them into a pot full to the brim with water. Hesitates.)

Three each?

(JIM nods.)

JIM: Sounds all right.

KEVIN: You want peas or something?

JIM: No. That's great. Great.

(KEVIN *puts them on the stove, lights the gas. He stands looking at* JIM.)
My turn tomorrow.
KEVIN: O.K.
(JIM *grins at him.*)
JIM: Didn't put up much of an argument.
KEVIN: No.
(JIM *starts to pour another beer for himself, finds the bottle empty. He opens the second bottle.*)

19. Int. Kitchen, Jim's house
Kevin/Jim

(*Twenty minutes later. Both beer bottles are now standing empty on the sink.* JIM's *glass is half full.* KEVIN *is sitting opposite him at the table, which is minimally set at two places, no table cloth, just knives and forks, salt and pepper, tomato sauce. They are each confronted by a plate of boiled potatoes, which they are eating.* KEVIN *glances at the stove, starts to get up.*)

JIM: Might as well finish your spuds.
(KEVIN *sits again.*)
KEVIN: I guess I had the gas too low. On the chops.
JIM: Must have been.
KEVIN: I'll see how they're going.
(*Gets up quickly, has a look at the chops. Turns doubtfully with the griller in his hand.*)
I think they're done. They're burnt a bit.
JIM: Well, let's have a go at 'em, eh?
(KEVIN *brings them over, doles out four of the six on to his father's plate.*)
Look all right ... Here, no. Fair's fair. Half each.
(*And puts one of them on* KEVIN's *plate.*)
KEVIN: O.K.
(*He puts the others on his plate, replaces the griller and sits.* JIM *has started on one chop, stops, examines it, handling it gingerly.*)
JIM: Could have done with a bit more.
(KEVIN *looks at him disappointedly.*)
Mind you, they're O.K. No trouble ...
(KEVIN *cuts his.*)
KEVIN: They're raw. Aren't they?
JIM: Well ... no. No, they're fine. Don't want all the good cooked out of 'em.
(*He starts to eat, trying to disguise his distaste for the blood-red chops, and nearly gagging. He washes a mouthful down desperately with a glass of beer.* KEVIN *is watching him, his own food untouched.* JIM *grins, picks up another piece, hesitates, puts it in his mouth and chews. It is very hard going, and* KEVIN *is having just as much trouble with his own food. Finally* JIM *puts down his knife and fork, trying to be bright and cheerful.*)

Listen, this is mad. First night back in the old house and we're sitting here! Should be out celebrating. What about a feed at the Greeks? How's that sound?
KEVIN: All right.
JIM: Well, you don't sound very flaming enthusiastic.
KEVIN: No. It's all right. I'd like it.
(*Still without enthusiasm.* JIM *shoves his plate away.*)
JIM: Yeah. You're breaking your neck.
(*Staring at the boy with some hostility. He swills off the last of his beer.* KEVIN *pushes his plate away slowly.*)
KEVIN: I'm not very hungry.
JIM: What's that supposed to mean?
KEVIN: Nothing. I ... I might stay and wash these things ...
(JIM *stares at him angrily, then slowly relaxes, shrugs.*)
JIM: Aw, it doesn't matter. I'm not hungry myself.
(KEVIN *gets up, collects the unemptied plates.*)
KEVIN: I'm sorry about the chops.
(JIM *feels a bit remorseful.*)
JIM: Aw, that's all right mate. I should have cooked 'em anyway.
(*He grins.*)
Not that they'd have been much better. Might have to get ourselves a few lessons from Auntie May.
(KEVIN *smiles back at him. Starts to scrape and stack the few plates.*)
Look, leave those. Tomorrow'll do.
KEVIN: No, it's O.K. You sit down. I'll do them.
(JIM *shrugs, puts his empty glass on the sink, moves away. And immediately finds himself at a loss for something to do. He moves to one end of the room, looking about. Plunges his hands into his pockets, watches* KEVIN *busy at the sink. He feels for the breast pocket of his shirt, for smokes, then realizes that there are no breast pockets in civvies. He grins, amused.*)
JIM: Funny.
(KEVIN *looks a question.*)
Feeling for pockets in my shirt. Sort of used to my uniform. Take a while, I suppose.
(KEVIN *half smiles, goes back to washing up.* JIM *finds his "makings" and rolls a smoke, still standing.* KEVIN *is thinking, appears troubled.*)
KEVIN: Uh ... Dad?
(*Finds it a little hard to use the word; and it jars a bit on* JIM.)
You don't have to stick around.
JIM: Eh?
KEVIN: I mean ... If you want to go out. I've got some school work ...
JIM: Well?
KEVIN: Well, if you want to go out. I can do it.
JIM: Can't you do it while I'm here?
(*A bit aggressive.* KEVIN's *sorry he started it.*)
KEVIN: Yeah. It's just ...

JIM: You think I should go out.
   (KEVIN *looks beaten.*)
KEVIN: It doesn't matter. I'm sorry.
JIM: Aw, no ... I'm ... I'm a bit restless, I suppose.
   (*He moves about the kitchen as* KEVIN *goes back to washing up.* JIM *is edgy, feels caged. He moves about, looking at things as though he's trying to remember them. He picks up a piece of the paper the beer came in, spreads it out, starts to read it for a few seconds, then screws it up impatiently, throws it aside.*)
   Look. I might.
   (KEVIN *turns, questioning.*)
   Go out for a while.
KEVIN: All right.
JIM: I mean ... well, there's nothing for me to do ...
KEVIN: No, I'll look after this.
JIM: Not used to it, you know. Being in the house.
   (KEVIN *nods. He doesn't need any explanations.*)
   (*He glances at his watch, grins, unconvincingly.*)
   I'll go out for a while. Have a walk.
   (*He glances at his watch, grins, unconvincingly.*)
   Pubs are shut.
   (KEVIN *nods again.* JIM *is getting angry at feeling he has to explain, knowing he doesn't really.*)
   Well, I'll only be a while.
   (KEVIN *looks at him, surprised at the slight trace of anger.*)
   You ought to be able to look after yourself for half an hour.
   (KEVIN *nods again, still surprised.* JIM *stubs out his cigarette, hard. He moves to the door.*)
   'Bout half an hour.
KEVIN: O.K.
   (JIM *goes out.* KEVIN *stares after him for a moment, then goes back to the washing up, but does it absently, thinking. He starts at his father's voice behind him.*)
JIM: You'll be all right.
   (KEVIN *turns.*)
KEVIN: Yeah. Of course.
   (JIM *nods, almost reluctant to go, just as reluctant to stay.*)
JIM: All right. See you.
   (*He turns away.*)
KEVIN: See you.
   (JIM *exits.*)

20. Int. Kevin's room
Kevin

   (KEVIN *sits alone on the edge of his bed, staring into space, then gets up suddenly, picks up the calendar, unrolls it and hangs it up, stands staring at it. He turns away, digs out his schoolcase from under the bed, takes out some books, settles himself with a chair at the chest of drawers, which he uses as a desk. He searches among the books, extracts a copy of a maths text-book and an exercise book, starts to do his homework. After a few moments he stops work, staring into space, thinking.)*

21. Ext. Outside Jim's house
Jim

(It is very much later, the street dark. JIM moves along the street towards the house. As he reaches the front gate, pushes it open, he stumbles, nearly falls, supports himself on the gate. He is either sick or drunk. After a moment, he hauls himself upright, makes unsteady progress towards the door.)

22. Int. Kevin's bedroom
Kevin/Jim

(KEVIN is slumped over his makeshift desk, his head pillowed on his arms among his text-books, sound asleep. SFX the front door slamming. KEVIN starts awake, takes a moment or two to orientate himself. Off, SFX of JIM making his way unsteadily down the hall. KEVIN half rises, waiting, listening. The door bursts open, JIM stands there, swaying a little. His voice is slightly blurred.)
JIM: Bit longer'n I thought. Thought you'd be in bed.
KEVIN: No. I ... I fell asleep. Studying.
(JIM nods. He leans against the door frame.)
JIM: Couple of old mates. Met 'em down the Bay. Few drinks.
KEVIN: I thought the pubs were closed.
(JIM grins at him.)
JIM: Not to these blokes.
(He suddenly shivers violently. KEVIN looks disgusted.)
KEVIN: You better go to bed.
(JIM nods weakly. Makes no move. After a moment he pushes himself away from the door.)
JIM: Yeah. Better.
(His glance falls on the calendar. He stares at it for a moment.)
It's no good.
(He shivers violently again. An attack of malaria is coming on.)
It's no good trying ... to hang on to things. When they're gone.
(KEVIN looks at the calendar, gets angry.)
KEVIN: It reminds me of Mum. She got it.
(JIM nods, shivering almost constantly now.)
JIM: I ... didn't mean ...
KEVIN: You've forgotten her, haven't you?
(KEVIN is very harsh, accusing.)
It's been two years, and you've forgotten her.
(JIM just stares at him, shaking, ill.)
You couldn't even remember the present you gave her.
JIM: It's been a long time ...

KEVIN: Two years!
   (JIM *has no answer.*)
   You couldn't wait to get out tonight, could you? Get out and get pissed with your mates.
JIM: I didn't ...
KEVIN: Well, you don't have to stay. I was all right. You can go back ...
   (JIM *is no longer interested, suffering the full weight of an attack. He staggers towards* KEVIN'S *bed.*)
JIM: I've ... gotta ...
   (KEVIN *has broken off, staring at him, realizing something is very wrong, but unable to make himself move.*)
KEVIN: What ... what's up?
JIM: In my drawer ... inside ... some tablets ...
   (*He collapses on the bed, shivering uncontrollably.*)
KEVIN (*Panicky*): What's the matter?
JIM: Just ... the tablets.
   (KEVIN *backs to the door, horrified, as* JIM *drags the bedcovers up over him.* KEVIN *exits, hurriedly,* SFX *of him running up the hall.* JIM *drags the bedclothes around him, stretching out on the bed, trying to get warm.* KEVIN *appears in the doorway, holding the tablets.*)
KEVIN: I'll get some water.
   (JIM *makes no reply,* KEVIN *rushes off again.* JIM *curling himself up into a ball, trying to warm himself.* SFX KEVIN *hurrying back. He bursts into the room, carrying tablets and a glass of water, hurries to the bedside. With a great deal of difficulty, supporting his father, he manages to administer a dose of the atebrin.* JIM *collapses back on the bed again.*)
JIM: Blankets ...
   (KEVIN *looks around desperately, hurries out again.* JIM *shows no improvement.* KEVIN *returns, dragging double bed blankets from his father's bed, pulls them up and spreads them over* JIM. *He fusses with them, doubling them up, tucking them in. Finally, he's done all he can.* JIM *is shaking violently still, staring up at* KEVIN. KEVIN *stares back, helplessly, anxious and panicky.*)
KEVIN: I'll get a doctor.
   (JIM *shakes his head.*)
   I've got to.
   (JIM *shakes his head, adamant.*)
JIM: It'll pass.
   (KEVIN *undecided, stands hesitant.*)
   Stay.
   (KEVIN *nods slowly. He tucks the blankets in again, unnecessarily.* JIM *squints his eyes against the light.*)
JIM: Light ...
   (KEVIN *hurries and turns it off. Then he comes back, sits beside the bed in the semi-dark. After a long moment, he speaks softly.*)
KEVIN: I'm sorry.
   (*The only reply is a slight moan from* JIM.)

23. Int. Kevin's bedroom
Kevin/Jim

(*The morning light floods into the room. JIM is sitting up in the bed, still dressed in the clothes of the night before. KEVIN is in pyjamas, barefoot. He puts a tray in front of JIM with a bowl of corn flakes, toast, tea. JIM tries to eat some, KEVIN watching him.*)

KEVIN: About what I said. I didn't mean it.
(JIM *mouth full, looks at him, nods.*)
I suppose ... coming home ... I felt a bit ... you know.
(JIM *nods again.*)
Is that all right?
(*Meaning the breakfast. JIM grins.*)

JIM: Better than the chops.
(KEVIN *smiles back.*)

KEVIN: Bit easier too.
(*They lapse into silence as JIM continues to eat. After a few mouthfuls, he pushes the corn flakes away with an apologetic look.*)
It's O.K. Have your tea.
(JIM *begins to sip. Gratefully, enjoying it. Then he puts the cup down.*)

JIM: Kev, I haven't forgotten your mother.
(KEVIN *looks embarrassed.*)

KEVIN: There's no need.

JIM: No. Listen to me.
(KEVIN *nods.*)
It's two years since the accident. Since she was killed.
(KEVIN *looks away, remembering with pain.*)
And I'd been away, in the army for ... what ... nearly three years before that.
(KEVIN *nods slowly.*)

KEVIN: I was eleven.

JIM: Just about to go up to high school.
(KEVIN *looks at him, surprised he remembers that much.*)
I haven't forgotten. But ... look! For three years all I saw of your Mum was a photo. Snapshot I carried around in my wallet. You and her at the beach. Even that was, I dunno, a year old maybe when I enlisted.
(*He thinks back, remembering.*)
Well, it's not much to hang on to. You live in a world of blokes, of tents, a world of boredom ... and sometimes ... excitement. It's all strange, unreal. And you cling onto your snapshot, your occasional letter. You hang on. Then, one day, it all switches. Over there, that life is the real one. And it's the photo, the letters, that are unreal.
(KEVIN *takes the tray, a bit embarrassed.*)

KEVIN: I'll ... take this away. Do you feel all right now?
(JIM *nods.*)

JIM: It's passed. If I'd kept up my atebrin I wouldn't have had it.
(*He swings his legs unsteadily out of the bed. Looks down at the bed, which shows the signs of a restless night. Grins.*)
I'll change the sheets for you.
KEVIN: Doesn't matter.
(*He starts to move away.*)
JIM: Where'd you sleep?
KEVIN: In Mum's ... in your bed.
(*They are both painfully aware of the slip.* KEVIN *hurries out of the room with the tray.*)

24. Ext. Kevin's school

(*A boy stands in the middle of the quadrangle ringing a school bell as hard as he can. From the doorways, the boys surge out of the classrooms, carrying their bags, heading for the gates, and freedom, in a mad, jostling, good-humoured rush.* BROTHER ERNEST *watches the mob evacuation with slight distaste, sighs, and wearily retires to his office. The boys surge towards the gates.*)

25. Ext. Randwick street
Mick/Kevin

(KEVIN *walks down the hill towards Coogee, carrying his school case, deep in thought, alone. From behind,* MICK NELSON *calls, OOS.*)
MICK: Hey! Kev! Hang on!
(KEVIN *turns,* MICK *hurries to him, almost running. He is about the same age as* KEVIN, *but heavier built, rather untidy, cheerful in spite of everything.*)
Kept in. Bloody old Ernest took us for History.
(*He falls in beside* KEVIN *and they stroll on.*)
Wanted to know who broke the Treaty of Versailles ...
KEVIN: And you said it wasn't you.
(MICK's *face falls.*)
That's the corniest old ...
MICK: I hadn't heard it before. I've been saving it for months. Anyway, he forgot about it and I shot through.
(*He grabs* KEVIN *by the arm. They are opposite an open garage.*)
Here. In here. Got some smokes.
(*He drags* KEVIN *into the garage.*)
KEVIN: I don't want a smoke.
(MICK *ignores him, and* KEVIN *makes no attempt to leave.* MICK *pulls a paper bag from his pocket, takes out two cigarettes, a couple of matches and a piece of matchbox for striking them. He grins at* KEVIN.)
MICK: Me old man's got the fruit shop convinced he's an ex-serviceman. Got himself a ration.

(*He hands one to KEVIN and they light up, then start dragging off their school ties, shove them in their pockets. They make themselves comfortable sitting on their upturned suitcases. KEVIN takes a long, deep draw; then gags.*)

KEVIN: Gawd! What are they?
(*Looking at the cigarette.*)
MICK: "Signals". You get eleven in the packet. One free.
KEVIN: Ought to pay you for smoking 'em.
(*But they puff on. In silence for a moment.*)
MICK: What's it like, living with your old man again?
(*KEVIN looks at him, shrugs non-committally.*)
Wouldn't cook like your Aunty May, I'd bet.
KEVIN: I dunno. He hasn't cooked yet.
(MICK *looks unbelieving.*)
He was—pretty sick. Malaria.
MICK: Aw.
(*A silence as they savour their smokes. MICK takes a deep inhale, blows it out through his nose. It irritates him, and he expels breath through his nose to clear the smoke. KEVIN grins, amused.*)
You believe that stuff of Watson's?
KEVIN: What stuff?
MICK: Reckon he's been knocking off that sheila from the milkbar.
KEVIN: Watson's all bull.
MICK: On the beach, he said.
KEVIN (*disbelieving*): Aw.
MICK: Pie O'Grady said he did.
KEVIN: How would Pie know?
MICK: Said he watched 'em.
KEVIN (*disbelieving*): Aw.
MICK: Not that I believe him.
KEVIN: Pie'd tell you anything.
MICK: Yeah.
(*They are silent for a moment, thinking about it.*)
KEVIN: You don't believe Pie?
MICK: No. Tell you anything.
(*They are silent again. Both annoyed at the story, and the fear it might be true.*)
Just because a bloke's in the First Thirteen.
KEVIN: Who?
MICK: Watson. Thinks all the shielas are waiting to drop their pants for him.
KEVIN: He's not getting any.
(*Desperately hoping it's true.*)
MICK: Naw. All bull. Him and Pie.
(*Silence again. Then MICK, trying to be very casual, very Bogart, trickling out smoke.*)
I reckon I'm on to a bit.
(*It's like a bombshell. KEVIN tries to control it, but MICK is pleased with the involuntary reaction.*)
KEVIN: Aw ... you're getting like Watson.

Lindsay's Boy

MICK (*hurt*): No. Fair dinkum.
KEVIN: What do you mean "you *reckon* you're on to a bit"? You either are or you aren't.
(MICK *looks a bit uncomfortable.*)
MICK: I just haven't had the chance to ...
KEVIN (*scathing*): What? To ask her? "Please, do you mind if I give you ..."
MICK: I'm not gonna ask her! I'm not that stupid.
(KEVIN *lets that hang.* MICK *goes on hesitantly.*)
It's just—I haven't had a chance to get her alone.
KEVIN: But you're on to a bit.
MICK: I will be. Soon as I get the chance.
(*He tosses down the stub of his cigarette, stamps on it angrily.*)
I dunno why I'm wasting time here.
KEVIN: Naw. You could be knocking her off right now.
(MICK *gets up, hurt.*)
MICK: Gees, you're a disbelieving cow sometimes.
KEVIN: Aren't I.
MICK: All right. You want to see her?
KEVIN: See her? What do you mean, see her? You mean meet her?
(MICK *shakes his head.*)
MICK: I mean *see* her. I'm not taking a risk of getting me throat cut before I get started.

26. Ext. Outside Mick's house
Kevin/Mick/Karen
(*All we can see is* KEVIN, *sitting on the grass, back up against a paling fence, school case beside him.*)
KEVIN: I feel stupid.
MICK (OOS): You want to see her, don't you?
KEVIN: Gawd.
(*He starts to get up, when* MICK'S *voice hisses at him.*)
MICK: Look out!
(KEVIN *freezes. We cut to* MICK, *standing on the street side of the fence.*)
Here she comes.
(*His POV* KAREN *walking down the street towards him. She is carrying a school case, is in the uniform of a state school: skirt and blouse, bobby-sox and shoes. She's about sixteen, and pretty.* MICK *is getting nervous.*)
You don't make a noise.
(*Cut to* KEVIN *behind the fence, desperately trying to get a glimpse of the approaching* KAREN. *He can't see a thing, moves about trying to see. Whispers loudly.*)
KEVIN: I can't see.
MICK (OOS): Shut up.
(KAREN *approaching, still a fair distance away.* MICK *is getting decidedly nervous, leans back against the fence, hands in pockets.*)
(*softly*) Listen. She looks like she's in a hurry. I won't stop her today. You just grab a squiz as she goes past.

KEVIN (OOS): I'm not sitting here like a flaming Jap spy just to watch her go past. You stop her. Talk to her, lover boy.
(KAREN *getting closer and* MICK *sweating.*)
MICK: She's probably got to get home ...
KEVIN (OOS): You want me to tell Watson?
(MICK *reacts, is about to reply, realizes she's within hearing range. He kicks back savagely at the fence with his heel.* KAREN *continues to move towards him, draws level, is passing, as he tries to screw up courage. Finally he finds it. His voice comes out in a croak.*)
MICK: Hello.
(KAREN *looks at him, hesitates, smiles.*)
KAREN: Hello, Michael.
(MICK *is a bit taken aback. She is moving past.*)
MICK: Hey! How'd you know my name?
(KAREN *stops, turns back to face him.*)
KAREN: Oh. Sometimes I get the bus.
(MICK *looks bewildered.*)
MICK: Eh?
KAREN: Your cousin gets it.
MICK: Aw.
KAREN: We see you smoking in the garage.
(MICK *is embarrassed. They both stand.* MICK *looks away. Cut to* KEVIN *looking through a crack between the palings of the fence. His POV, the back of* MICK'S *legs. He moves along quietly to another position, trying to see.*)
(OOS) Well, I better be going.
MICK: Uh. I suppose you're in a hurry.
KAREN: Oh, no.
MICK(OOS): Oh.
(KEVIN *mutters to himself, still squirming to see.*)
KEVIN: Bloody dill! Ask her!
(*Cut to* MICK *facing* KAREN, *who's really making no attempt to go.*)
KAREN: Well. I'd better.
MICK: You ever go to the Grotto?
(*She nods.*)
KAREN: Uh-uh.
MICK: Good milk shakes.
(*Cut to* KEVIN *listening. He groans at this sally. Cut to* KAREN, *who reacts a little, then dismisses it. But* MICK *has heard the groan, reacts.*)
KAREN: I'll get going, then.
(MICK *is desperate, rushes the whole thing out in one breath.*)
MICK: Look, if you like I'll meet you at the Grotto and we'll go down on the beach.
(KAREN *looks bewildered.*)
KAREN: What?
(MICK *is in agony.*)
MICK: Tonight. I'll meet you at the Grotto. We'll go down on the beach.

Lindsay's Boy 243

(*Cut to* KEVIN, *hugging his knees in an ecstasy of amusement. He groans with delight.* KAREN'S *reaction. She looks hard at the fence.* MICK *knows she's on to them.*)

KAREN (*absently*): What would we go to the beach for? At night?
(MICK, *time running out, takes the plunge.*)
MICK: You know. A bit of ...
KAREN: There's someone behind the fence.
(*Very matter of fact.* KEVIN *freezes, the smile wiped from his face.*)
You've got someone behind the fence.
MICK (*trying innocence.*): Eh?
(KAREN *walks closer to the fence, peers through.*)
KAREN: It's your friend, isn't it?
(KEVIN *half to his feet, terribly embarrassed, not knowing how to carry it off.*)
Kevin. The one who smokes with you in the garage?
(MICK *is aghast, nods dumbly.* KEVIN *slowly appears, head and shoulders, over the fence, looking sick.*)
Hello.
KEVIN: Hello.
(MICK *doesn't look pleased.*)
MICK: This is my mate, Kevin.
KAREN: Hello.
(*They all three stand silent, awkward.*)
Well ...
MICK: (*hurriedly*): What about it? The Grotto?
(KAREN *looks at* KEVIN, *as if waiting for him to say he'll be there too.* KEVIN *says nothing. She is obviously disappointed.*
KAREN: All right.
(MICK *is both stunned and elated. Tends to swagger.*)
MICK: All right. Meet you there. 'Bout seven?
KAREN: All right. I better go. 'Bye. 'Bye, Kevin.
KEVIN: 'Bye.
(*She wanders off, slowly, along her way. The boys watch her.* KEVIN *silent,* MICK *very cock-a-hoop. He nudges* KEVIN.)
MICK: Get on to those legs. Talk about Betty Grable.
KEVIN: Bit skinny.
MICK: Reckon you could do better?
(*He's suddenly very much master of the situation.*)
Hear what she said? We're going down on the beach after.
KEVIN: I heard you say it.
MICK: Didn't hear her say no, did you?
(KEVIN *finds himself suddenly angry.*)
KEVIN: Gees you give me a pain sometimes.
(MICK *flares too.*)
MICK: You're shitty because I'm gonna get it and you're not. That's all.
KEVIN: Aw, you'll get your first one when you're married.
MICK: You want to bet?
KEVIN: I'm going home.

MICK: Sour grapes.

(KEVIN *tosses his bag over the fence, climbs over, picks it up, starts to walk off. He goes some distance before* MICK *calls after him.*)

Walk to school with you tomorrow?

(KEVIN *doesn't turn, calls back without much interest.*)

KEVIN: All right.

(MICK *watches him go.*)

27. Int. Kitchen, Jim's house
Jim/Kevin

(*Dinner is over, the dishes washed.* KEVIN *is at the sink, a tea towel around his waist as a pinafore, idly mopping down the sink. His thoughts are miles away. He begins to allow water to drip from the washrag, writes the letters K and A on the surface of the sink.* JIM *takes a stack of plates from the table, puts them away in the cupbaord, walks back to the sink, grabs a couple of wet ones to dry.* KEVIN *has finished water-writing the word Karen. As he becomes aware of* JIM *beside him, he quickly rubs it away with the cloth.* JIM *has noticed, grins.*)

JIM: Oh, yeah? Who's Karen?

(KEVIN *is mortified.*)

KEVIN: Oh, just a girl.

JIM: Didn't think it was a boy. Girl friend?

KEVIN (*hastily*): No.

JIM (*slightly disbelieving*): Uh, uh.

(KEVIN *pulls out the plug, grabs a couple of plates, begins to wipe. They work in silence for a moment.*)

No need to worry about it.

KEVIN: What about it?

(JIM *shrugs.*)

JIM: Girls. Karen.

KEVIN: I know.

(*He puts the plates away, doesn't really want to tell, but feels he has to.*)

I ... uh ... she's not my girl friend or anything. She's ... well ... Mick knows her.

JIM: Mick?

KEVIN: My mate.

(JIM *is a little puzzled, glances involuntarily at the sink where* KEVIN *was writing the name.* KEVIN *notices, is embarrassed.* JIM *turns away to spare him, grinning slightly. They finish the work,* KEVIN *picks up his school case, opens it, starts to take out homework books.*)

JIM: Homework?

KEVIN: French and Maths.

JIM: I thought ... (*he shrugs*) Might have gone to the flicks.

KEVIN: I've got a fair bit to do.

(JIM *nods, slightly disappointed. Standing, feeling restless and at a loss again.*)

JIM: Well—if you get finished we might go for a walk. Down the Bay. Milkshake or something. That place near the beach.

(KEVIN *looks up, this is the last thing he wants.*)

KEVIN: The Grotto? Uh ... I've got a lot. Homework.

(JIM *a little puzzled by the reaction, shrugs.*)

JIM: O.K.

(*He watches as* KEVIN *gets his books ready.*)

KEVIN: Bother you if I work here?

JIM: No.

(KEVIN *sits, opening a French book, stares at it for a while.* JIM *sits, takes out his "makings", begins to roll a cigarette.*)

You ... uh ... haven't got one yourself? A girl friend?

(KEVIN *hesitates.*)

KEVIN: No.

JIM: Well, plenty of time.

(KEVIN *looks a bit desperate.*)

KEVIN: Yeah. Plenty.

(JIM *reacts, a little surprised at the boy's vehemence.* KEVIN *suddenly slams his books closed.*)

I could do this in the morning. If you still want to go.

(JIM *more surprised.*)

JIM: Well, fine. Let's go.

28. Ext. Coogee Bay area
Mick/Karen

(MICK *and* KAREN *are strolling along the beach front, on the promenade side.* MICK *is not feeling too confident, having trouble keeping the conversation going, a bit nervous about how he's going to broach the subject of going down to the beach. They walk in silence, about two feet apart. Suddenly* KAREN *shoots a scornful look at him.*)

KAREN: You don't have to hold my hand if you don't want to.

(MICK *almost recoils.*)

MICK: Uh. Oh. I ... uh ... forgot.

(*He moves a bit closer, reaches out and takes her hand. They walk on, holding hands, but still a good foot of space between them, and no more comfortably.*)

KAREN: I won't bite.

MICK: No. I ... I forgot.

(KAREN *rolls her eyes to the sky, and they walk on in silence.*)

29. Ext. Outside milk bar
Jim/Kevin

(JIM *and* KEVIN *walk out from the milk bar, licking ice cream cones. They head off towards the promenade.* JIM *glances at* KEVIN, *smiling.*)

JIM: Haven't had an ice cream in five years. Or a milk shake, for that matter.

KEVIN: You don't mind—eating it in the street?

(JIM *looks surprised.*)

JIM: Why would I mind?

(KEVIN *shrugs, pleased. They walk on, their silence companionable.*)

30. Ext. The Promenade, Coogee
Karen/Mick/Jim/Kevin

(KAREN *and* MICK *walk along the promenade, no longer holding hands.* KAREN *suddenly stops, leans on the rail, looks down at the beach.* MICK *has gone on a step or two before he realizes, hurries back.* KAREN *ignores him. He leans on the rail beside her.*)

MICK: Good surf.

(KAREN *gives him a withering look.*)

KAREN: Is it?

(*And turns away, reacts, as she sees* KEVIN *and* JIM *walking up the few steps on to the promenade, some fifty yards away.*)
Oh! There's ...

(*She stops herself, but* MICK *has sighted* KEVIN.)

MICK: It's Kev. Must be his old man.

(KAREN *looks pleased, absently straightens her hair.* MICK *notices.*)

Might as well walk.

(*He takes her hand, but she pulls it away.* MICK *is turning away, stops, realizing she's going to wait for* KEVIN. *Cut to:* KEVIN *still has the ice cream, though* JIM *has finished his.* KEVIN *is in the act of licking it thoughtfully, making it last, when he catches sight of* KAREN *and* MICK. *He stops abruptly, ice cream to mouth.* JIM *glances at him.*)

JIM: What's up?

KEVIN: Uh ... nothing

(*He looks panicky, doesn't know what to do with the ice cream, suddenly jams the rest into his mouth, with some difficulty, and chews rapidly, to* JIM'S *amusement.*)

JIM: What ...

(KEVIN *is turning away, looking for escape, towards nearby steps back to the footpath.*)

KEVIN: Let's cross over the road.

(*And leads off quickly,* JIM *following, at a loss. Cut to* KAREN *watching* KEVIN *and* JIM *hurrying away. Her face falls, then hardens.* MICK *looks pleased.*)

MICK: Shot through.

(KAREN *glances at him, angry.*)

KAREN: Let's go down the beach.

(MICK *can hardly believe his ears.*)
MICK: Eh?
(KAREN *is already moving towards the steps, hurrying, and he scuttles after her. She reaches the stairway leading to the sand, stops, glancing across the road, where* KEVIN *and* JIM *are walking past. She slips off her shoes, throws one challenging glance at* KEVIN, *and runs down towards the sand.* MICK *reaches the steps, hesitates, not sure whether to call to* KEVIN *or not, decides against it, and follows her. Cut to:* KEVIN *stops, very agitated, staring across at the steps.* JIM *follows his gaze, sees nothing, looks at* KEVIN *puzzled.*)
JIM: What's up? You look—
KEVIN: Nothing.
(*He walks on.*)
Nothing.

31. Ext. Coogee Beach
Karen/Mick

(KAREN *hurries along the beach in her bare feet, almost running, with* MICK *hopping along behind, trying to drag off his shoes without stopping.*)
MICK: Hang on, Karen.
(KAREN *suddenly throws herself down on the sand, sits with her arms clasped around her knees, tight, staring out towards the sea.* MICK *drops down beside her, pulls off the second shoe, starts dragging off his very sandy socks, stuffs them carefully into the shoes.*)
Gees it feels crook walking ...
(KAREN *unwraps her knees, looks across at him, still angry.*)
KAREN: Are you just going to sit there?
(MICK *startled, hesitant. Then he pushes the shoes aside, leans over awkwardly, puts an arm around her and kisses her.* KAREN *allows herself to drop slowly backwards, and* MICK *follows, almost on top of her, still kissing.*)

32. Int. Kevin's bedroom
Kevin/Jim

(KEVIN *sits on the side of his bed, staring at the floor, his shirt off, pyjama pants on, one shoe in his hand, in the process of taking them off, frozen in melancholy thought. The whole world has crashed around him. The door opens gently and* JIM *puts his head in.*)
JIM: Not in bed yet?
(KEVIN *nods, uninterested.*)
Have a beer, maybe.
(KEVIN *nods again.* JIM *hesitates.*)

Nothing wrong?
(KEVIN shakes his head.)
KEVIN: No.
JIM: All right. You get to bed. Still got that homework in the morning.
(KEVIN nods, begins to pull off the other shoe and sock. JIM waits a beat, then withdraws, pulls the door closed. KEVIN stops undressing, sits motionless, staring again. SFX the front door opening and closing, as JIM leaves.)

33. Int. Kevin's bedroom
Kevin/Jim

(KEVIN is asleep in bed, lit by a faint light from the window. He is sleeping restlessly. SFX of the front door suddenly banging open, a muffled man's laughter, a loud "Shhhhh!" KEVIN stirs slightly. SFX of people in the hall, entering from the front door, shuffling about in the dark, the bang of the door as it closes again. KEVIN'S eyes flick open. He lies tense, listening. SFX footsteps down the hall. Then a man's voice, whispering loudly.)
MAN (OOS): Where's the flaming light, Jimbo?
JIM (OOS): Shhhh!
(KEVIN sits up, wide awake, listening. There are further sounds of footsteps, several people coming down the hall. Then right outside his door, a muffled giggle. A woman's. KEVIN reacts.)
(OOS, harshly) Shut up!
(Then, in a whisper.)
The kid's in there.
(A woman's voice replies, petulantly.)
WOMAN: Sorry.
(The footsteps pass by. KEVIN finally lies back, listening to the faint noises from the kitchen. After a few moments he rolls over, facing the wall, pulls the blankets up over his head. The door opens a little, JIM's face is visible as he looks in, closes the door gently.)

34. Int. Jim's kitchen
Jim/Kevin

(JIM is cooking at the stove, preparing breakfast. KEVIN enters from the bathroom, hair wet, tying his tie. He stops when he sees JIM.)
KEVIN: Oh. Didn't know you were up.
(JIM turns. He looks pretty dreadful, hungover. And a little nervous.)
JIM: Thought I'd give you a hand. Get you off early.
KEVIN: Oh, beaut. Still got that work to do.
JIM (quickly): Do that at school, won't you?

(KEVIN *nods.*)
KEVIN: Uh-uh.
(*He is feeling in his pockets.*)
Couldn't find a clean hanky. Can I get one from your drawer?
JIM: Sure ... oh. Hang on. I'll get you one.
(*A bit concerned, in a hurry to cut* KEVIN *off as the boy makes for the door.*)
KEVIN: I can get it.
JIM: No. I will. It's O.K. Know where they are.
(*He hurries out.* KEVIN *looks surprised, goes to the stove, shovels out some of the food cooking there, takes his plate to the table, starts to eat. Then he stops, hearing something off. Listens, brow furrowed. After a moment he calls out.*)
KEVIN: You call, Dad?
(*Immediately the sound of a door closing, off,* JIM *returning.* KEVIN *watches him enter.*)
Thought I heard you call.
JIM: Eh? No. Just ... talking to myself, I suppose.
(*Turns away to the stove.* KEVIN *resumes eating, but glances occasionally at his father, off towards the hall. He is puzzled, aware of something wrong.*)
Didn't wake you last night, did we?
KEVIN: Well ... I stirred a bit.
JIM: Couple of mates. Army. Brought 'em back for a drink.
(KEVIN *nods, goes on eating for a moment.*)
KEVIN: I thought I heard a ... a lady.
(*Slightest reaction from* JIM.)
JIM: Yeah. They had their better halves with 'em.
KEVIN: Oh.
JIM: Getting a bit late, isn't it?
(KEVIN *glances at the clock.*)
KEVIN: Suppose so.
(*He bolts another mouthful of breakfast, pushes his chair back.* JIM *takes his plate. It is becoming evident that he wants* KEVIN *on his way.* KEVIN *picks up his case, heads for the door.*)
See you later.
(JIM *puts the plate down.*)
JIM: I'll ... see you off.
(KEVIN *looks at him, surprised.* JIM *almost shepherds him into the hallway, then along the hall, past the boy's room, where the door stands open, then past his own room.* KEVIN *glances at the shut door of* JIM'S *room as they pass.* JIM *hurries him on and holds the door open for him to leave the house.* KEVIN *slips past him and out.*)
KEVIN: See you.
JIM: Yeah. Right.
(KEVIN *moves off,* JIM *closes the door.*)

35. Ext. Randwick street
Mick/Kevin

(MICK *carrying his school case, hurries, puffing slightly, up the hill towards the school. He is in high spirits, a grin on his face, and in spite of the speed of his walk and the stiffness of the gradient, he occasionally gives a light-hearted swing of his case at flowers and shrubs that project through the fences. He is approaching the open garage where the boys do their surreptitious smoking. MICK is completely absorbed in his own pleasant thoughts, and is hurrying past the garage, unaware of KEVIN sitting inside on his upturned case. He is nearly past before KEVIN calls.*)

KEVIN: Hey.

(MICK *props, returns, and sees KEVIN inside, looking rather morose.*)

MICK: What're you up to in there?

(KEVIN *just looks at him.* MICK *enters.*)

You're gonna be late ... Hey! Ask me how I went last night!

KEVIN: Don't give a stuff if I'm late or not.

MICK: Come on! Ask me.

KEVIN: Didn't do my French and Maths.

MICK: Are you gonna ask me?

(KEVIN *sits staring morosely at the floor.*)

KEVIN: Got any smokes?

MICK: No. Anyway, if you're not interested ... Arrr.

(*He pulls out his cache from an inside pocket, a paper bag with two cigarettes, a piece of match box, a couple of matches.*)

Saving 'em for after school.

(*They light up.* KEVIN *draws in the smoke as though he needs it, and it makes him cough a little.*)

MICK: Absolutely incredible, it was. Incredible.

(KEVIN *looks at him, expressionless.* MICK *feels he has to elucidate.*)

Last night. Incredible! Straight down the beach.

KEVIN: I'm going to wag it today.

MICK: Practically dragged me down there. Gees, talk about a hot shiela!

KEVIN: I'm not fronting up to Brother-bloody-Ernest again.

MICK: Pulls off her shoes, and straight down on to the sand. Gawd.

(KEVIN *lapses into silence, involved with his thoughts.*)

You should of seen her. Plops herself down on the sand, and it's on! Smooshed her once and next thing I've got me hand ...

KEVIN (*angry*): Shut up!

MICK: Half-way up her leg ...

KEVIN: Shut up!

(MICK *looks put out.*)

MICK: What's eating you? If I wanna talk ...

KEVIN: I don't want to hear.

(MICK *is getting angry too, but unsure, doesn't want to fight.*)

MICK: Well that's too bloody bad ...

KEVIN: You're a liar. A stupid, dirty, idiot liar.
(His voice is full of venom. The shock alone is enough to render MICK speechless.)
You never laid a finger on her. Her or any other shiela. You wouldn't have the guts and you wouldn't know how.
(He drops the cigarette, barely started, on the floor, and to add insult to injury, grinds it out with his heel. MICK gets slowly to his feet, pale and angry.)
MICK: I don't know what's the matter with you, and I don't care. I'm going, and you can shove it.
(He throws down his own smoke and grinds it out, turns towards the door, starts to go, then stops.)
I wasn't going to say I knocked her off. But I bloody will next time.
(He stalks out and disappears from sight. KEVIN sits morosely for a moment, then notices MICK'S cigarette is still smoking, though badly crushed. He picks it up, tries to straighten it as best he can, drags on it. And sits smoking in lonely silence.)

36. Ext. Outside Jim's house

(KEVIN hesitates at the gate, walks towards the front door. It is late afternoon, a group of school-kids in uniform, carrying their bags, skylarking as they wind their way past the house. KEVIN puts his key in the door, hesitates, then goes in.)

37. Int. Jim's house
Kevin/Jim/Denise

(KEVIN closes the door behind him in the dim hall, then walks towards the kitchen. As he passes his father's room, he stops, looks in. His POV. The room looks quite normal, bed made, tidy. Nothing out of place. KEVIN stares in for a few moments, then starts as he hears the murmur of voices from the kitchen. He turns towards it, then slowly walks, a little doubtful. As he passes his own room, he shoves his case in through the open door, continues on. JIM suddenly appears framed in the kitchen doorway. He is grinning a little nervously.)

JIM: G'day. Didn't hear you come in.
(KEVIN stops at the door.)
KEVIN: Dad.
(A sort of disinterested greeting. KEVIN is staring into the kitchen. His POV, DENISE standing at the stove, facing him a little nervously. She is a young, attractive girl, in her very early twenties. She is dressed in street clothes, but has a tea towel around her as a apron. JIM reacts.)
JIM: Oh. Kevin—this is Denise.
(DENISE offers a small smile.)
DENISE: Hello.

KEVIN: Hello.
JIM (*quickly*): Denise is a friend of mine. She ... she dropped in to fix us dinner. Just now. A while ago.
(*Slight reaction on* DENISE'S *face.*)
DENISE: I'm not a very good cook. It's just steak and things.
(KEVIN *is not showing much reaction.*)
KEVIN: Steak's fine.
JIM: Well, why don't you go and hang up your coat. Have an early tea. We thought we might ...
KEVIN (*abruptly*): All right.
(*He turns and walks off to his room, cutting* JIM *off short.* JIM *stands looking after him for a moment, then turns back to* DENISE. *She meets his gaze for a moment, then turns away to the stove.*)

38. Int. Kevin's bedroom

(KEVIN *stands at his wardrobe, slowly taking off his coat, deep in thought, looking troubled. He hangs up his coat, closes the wardrobe. Then he stares at the calendar for a long moment, before he moves to the door.*)

39. Int. Kitchen, Jim's house
Kevin/Denise/Jim
(KEVIN, DENISE *and* JIM *sitting at the kitchen table, eating their meal. There is a feeling of strain between them, and long silences develop often.*)
JIM: What sort of day did you have at school?
(KEVIN *hesitates, doesn't meet his eyes.*)
KEVIN: O.K.
JIM : Kev's at the Marist Brothers, up the road.
DENISE: What class are you in, Kevin?
KEVIN: Fifth year.
JIM: Doing his leaving. Aren't you, mate?
(KEVIN *doesn't reply.*)
Tell you what. Best feed we've had since ...
(KEVIN *looks at him sharply.*)
... quite a while.
(KEVIN *ignores him, turns to* DENISE.)
KEVIN: You must have known him a while. Cooking our meals.
(DENISE *looks confused.*)
Dad. You must have known him a long time.
JIM: No. I only met ...
KEVIN: Did you know my mother, too?
(*It's a challenge, and stops* JIM.)
DENISE: No. I only met your ... Dad ... a little while ago.
(KEVIN *stares at her, waiting for more.* DENISE *refuses to be rattled.*)

> The night before last, actually.

KEVIN: Actually.

JIM: Kevin!

KEVIN: I'm sorry. I didn't ...

JIM: Denise was silly enough to make a bet with me. She lost.

KEVIN: What was the bet?

(DENISE *loses her cool, looks away. It was apparently very personal.* JIM *comes to her rescue.*)

JIM: Doesn't matter what it was. The dinner was all right, wasn't it?

(KEVIN *nods, still watching* DENISE, *aware of her embarrassment.*)

KEVIN: Yes. Excuse me.

(*He pushes his plate away, pushes back his chair.*)

DENISE: I made pudding.

KEVIN: No thanks. I'm not hungry.

(*He pushes his chair into the table carefully, exits.* DENISE *avoids* JIM's *eyes, toys with her food. Then she pushes her plate away too.*)

40. Int. Living room, Jim's place
Kevin/Jim/Denise

(KEVIN *is sprawled on the lounge, a newspaper thrown beside him on the floor. He is listening to a radio serial of the period, probably* "Yes, What?" "Martin's Corner", *or* "Mrs 'Obbs". *The radio fairly loud.* JIM *walks into the room. He goes to the radio and turns it down a little.* KEVIN *looks up at him.*)

JIM: Uh ... I was thinking of taking Denise home ...

(KEVIN *shows his surprise.*)

KEVIN: Oh.

JIM: ... to change. Thought we might go to see a picture.

(*A pause.* DENISE *enters, stays back near the door.*)

Denise thought you might like to come.

(KEVIN *is taken off guard.*)

KEVIN: Uh ... no. No I ... I've got some homework.

JIM: Do it in the morning. Like yesterday's.

KEVIN: I didn't do yesterday's.

JIM: Oh. Well.

(*He glances at* DENISE. *He's tried.*)

Well—if you're sure.

(*A bit relieved.*)

We'll be off.

KEVIN: All right.

(JIM *hesitates, then moves towards the door.*)

JIM: Just get my coat.

(*He exits and* DENISE *and* KEVIN *are alone.* KEVIN *gets up, moves to the radio, fiddles with the dial.*)

DENISE: Kevin? I want to ...

(KEVIN *turns on her quickly, coldly.*)

KEVIN: How old are you?
(DENISE *taken aback*.)
DENISE: I ... I'm twenty-two.
(*He stares at her for a moment before he speaks*.)
KEVIN: Dad's forty-two.
(*Turns up the radio loud before she has a chance to reply, and moves back to the lounge, ignoring her. JIM re-enters immediately with his jacket on*..)
JIM: Right! You're sure ...
(*He sees DENISE looking hurt, KEVIN pointedly ignoring her*.)
Come on, Denise.
(*Shepherding her towards the door. Hesitates, looks back to KEVIN*.)
Don't ... stay up too late.
(KEVIN *doesn't answer. The radio is so loud he mightn't have heard*.)

41. Int. Kevin's bedroom

(*The room in darkness, KEVIN sleeping. We hear, barely noticeably, off, a soft groan, the movement of bed-springs. It is repeated, and KEVIN suddenly opens his eyes. He is immediately aware, and lies in the dark, listening. Faintly from the next room, his father's bedroom, can be heard the sounds of DENISE and JIM making love. KEVIN listens, tensing with horror as he becomes aware of what he is hearing. In the next room, DENISE moans, a little louder. KEVIN pulls the bedclothes over his head. After a moment he draws up his legs in a foetal position*.)

42. Int. Kevin's bedroom

(*The sun is streaming through the window. KEVIN throws his books into his school case, slams it shut. He is already dressed for school, runs a comb through his hair. He moves quickly, angrily. The hair won't stay in place, and with the comb in his hand, KEVIN leaves the room, heading for the bathroom*.)

43. Int. Jim's living room
Kevin/Jim

(KEVIN *hurries into the living room comb in hand, almost crashes into his father, who is passing through from the kitchen, carrying a tray. Both are surprised, look guilty*.)
KEVIN: Oh.
(*They stand in each other's way. KEVIN stares at the tray. On it are a teapot and two cups and saucers. He looks up at his father. JIM returns his gaze, says nothing. KEVIN steps around his father*.)

Going to wet my hair.
(He starts towards the kitchen, stops as JIM calls.)
JIM: Kevin!
  (KEVIN turns.)
  You're ... you're up early.
KEVIN: Yes. I'll ... be going in a minute.
JIM: You haven't had breakfast.
  (KEVIN glances at the tray again.)
KEVIN: No.
  (Turns away. JIM'S voice snaps out sharply.)
JIM: Kevin!
  (The boy hesitates.)
  You might as well know. I've ... I've asked Denise to ... stay for a while.
  (KEVIN turns and looks at him, expressionless.)
  I think ... well ... she can ...
  (He's not sure what she can do that's going to meet with approval, breaks off.)
KEVIN: Cook?
  (His voice is ironic and JIM shows his embarrassment. KEVIN looks pointedly at the tray again.)
  You used to do that for Mum.
JIM: Kevin ...
KEVIN: But you've probably forgotten.
  (He wheels back towards his room. JIM stands watching helplessly as KEVIN darts into his room, reappears immediately with his case, flees down the hall. The front door opens and slams closed. JIM stands, looks down at the tea things, very unhappy.)

44. Ext. Randwick Marist Brothers College
Brother Ernest/Kevin

(Boys hurrying into the school, SFX of a bell ringing for classes. BROTHER ERNEST stands near his office watching. He sees KEVIN hurrying towards his classroom, calls.)
ERNEST: Lindsay!
  (KEVIN reacts, walks hesitantly rowards the brother. ERNEST looks him over for a moment.)
  Not at school yesterday, Lindsay?
KEVIN: No, Brar.
  (He's in no mood to offer excuses. ERNEST just watches him for a few moments. The treatment. Then he slowly smiles. Not a pleasant smile, but the best he can do.)
ERNEST: And, I would venture, no note.
  (KEVIN doesn't reply.)
  Well, I suppose this once ... your father back from the wars. Making friends again. Eh? Eh, Lindsay?
  (KEVIN stares at him, answers flatly.)
KEVIN: Yes, Brar.

45. Ext. Randwick street
Kevin/Mick

(MICK *hurries down the street, almost runs a couple of paces, catches up with* KEVIN, *who is striding out, heading homewards, both boys carrying their cases.*)

MICK: Gawd, hang on. Like a Bondi tram.

(KEVIN *doesn't even glance at him. Keeps walking.* MICK *grabs him by the arm.*)

Guess what I got.

(*No answer.*)

Ardath. Packet of twenty.

(KEVIN *shakes the arm off, keeps going. They are at the garage, and* KEVIN *walks straight past. This time* MICK *grabs and holds his arm, making him stop.*)

Listen, Kev ...

KEVIN: Let go my arm.

(*He tries to shake off* MICK'S *grasp, but* MICK *holds on.*)

MICK: I'm sorry. About yesterday. I dunno what I did, but I'm sorry.

(KEVIN *stares at him for a long moment, coldly.*)

KEVIN: Why don't you get the bus occasionally, Muzza?

(MICK *is hurt. Takes a moment to reply.*)

MICK: Yeah. Why don't I?

(*He drops* KEVIN'S *arm—almost throws it—and turns away, stalks across the street to the bus stop.* KEVIN *walks on, trying to appear unconcerned.* MICK *watches him go, angry and hurt. The sound of a bus approaching in the distance. He turns his gaze from* KEVIN, *preparing for the arrival of the bus.* KEVIN *keeps walking. Behind,* SFX *of the bus stopping, starting off again, approaching, as* KEVIN *walks on. Close on a window of the bus as* MICK *drops into a window seat, looks out. His* POV KEVIN *turns sharply round a corner.* MICK *turns his head away.* KEVIN *walks along the street alone. Suddenly he stops, grabs hold of the fence, as though to steady himself, and drops his bag. For a moment his stomach heaves, and he has trouble stopping himself from being sick. He leans his head on his forearms, on top of the fence, and rests there, trembling.*)

46. Int. The Grotto Milk Bar
Kevin/Karen/Christina.

(CHRISTINA, *the Italian daughter of the Grotto's owner, puts a milk shake on the shaker, gives it a short run and hands it across to* KEVIN. *He pays, picks up his school case, tucks it under his arm with some difficulty, takes the milk shake can and glass and moves away to a corner table. He is almost seated before he sees* KAREN *sitting at the next table, smiling at him.*)

KAREN: Didn't you see me?

KEVIN: No.
> (*It looks as though he's going to change his mind about sitting there, but his case slides under his arm, he's forced to put it down. So he sits. He spends a few seconds arranging his case, pouring his shake, avoiding her eyes, but she watches him with great interest.*)

KAREN: You're late. Kept in?
> (*She is wearing casual clothes, has obviously been home to change. KEVIN swigs his shake, decides he's not going to be friendly.*)

KEVIN: Why? Make you happy if I was?
> (KAREN *a bit surprised, the smile hesitates, but remains.*)

KAREN: No. Why would it?
> (KEVIN *can't answer that, shrugs.*)
> Why don't you sit over here?
> (*Nothing coquettish, just a straight question. But it sets* KEVIN *back for a moment. He recovers, remains belligerent.*)

KEVIN: Aren't you worried Muzza'd see you?

KAREN: Who?

KEVIN: Mick.

KAREN: Oh, Michael.
> (*A little disparagingly. He mimics her tone a little.*)

KEVIN: Yes, Michael.

KAREN: Why should I care?
> (KEVIN *doesn't reply. Finds this a bit callous, considering.*)
> Well? Are you going to?
> (KEVIN *puzzled.*)
> Come and sit here?

KEVIN: Might as well, I suppose.
> (*He kicks his case across to the other table, picks up his shake, and crosses. As he puts the shake down he spills some, a little clumsy and unsure of himself.* KAREN *looks away, giving him a chance to collect himself.* KEVIN *begins to drink.*)

KAREN: You don't come here much.

KEVIN: No.

KAREN: Neither do I.

KEVIN: No?
> (*She laughs a little.*)

KAREN: You sounded as though you didn't believe me.
> (KEVIN *shrugs.*)

KEVIN: You came here the other night. With Mick.
> (*She shoots a quick, defensive glance at him.*)

KAREN: *He* asked me.
> (*They glare at each other a moment, and* KEVIN *is the first to drop his eyes.*)

KEVIN: Not that it matters.

KAREN: No.
> (*They sit in silence for a moment.* KAREN *finishes her shake, pushes it away.* KEVIN *looks at it, embarrassed. She notices.*)
> What's wrong?

KEVIN: I ... only had enough for one milk shake.
> (*She smiles, easy and friendly.*)

KAREN: I couldn't drink another one, anyway.
(*She stands.*)
I'll have to get home.
(KEVIN *looks a little panicky.*)
KEVIN: Uh ... look ...
(*She waits. He doesn't know how to start.*)
I've ... I've got to get back too. If you're going my way ...
KAREN: I live in Patton Street.
KEVIN: That's near my Aunt's place. I ... I've got to go up there ...
(*He tosses off the rest of his shake, rising at the same time. Grabs his bag.*)

47. Ext. Outside Karen's house
Karen/Kevin

(KAREN *stops at her gate, turns to* KEVIN.)
KAREN: I get the ten past eight bus. When I'm not late.
(KEVIN *half smiles.*)
KEVIN: Uh ... so do I. Or I will. When I'm not late.
(*She laughs, pleased. Then* KEVIN's *face clouds.*)
Look, Karen. I ... the other night ... When you ... went down the beach. With Mickey.
(KAREN'S *smile fades. She becomes very serious.*)
KAREN: Kevin? Do you *have* to ask me?
(KEVIN *looks torn.*)
KEVIN: I ... No. I ... don't suppose so. No. I'll ... see you. On the bus.
(*He turns and walks away quickly.* KAREN *almost makes a gesture to stop him, doesn't. She watches him a moment, then turns and goes into her house.*)

48. Int. Aunt May's kitchen
May/Kevin

(AUNT MAY *is buttering scones, setting them out, pouring tea.* KEVIN *sits at the table. She's trying to look as though she's not delighted to see him.*)
MAY: Shouldn't be eating this close to your tea-time. Why aren't you home, anyway? Father'll be looking everywhere for you.
KEVIN: I ... walked home with ... a friend. Lives near here.
(MAY *makes a long-suffering gesture, shakes her head.*)
MAY: Might have known you wouldn't just come to see your aunt.
(KEVIN *grins, takes a scone, begins to eat and drink. She watches him.*)
Well. Look like you're half starved. Not that you're wasting away, exactly.
(*He grins at her, mouth full.*)
Well, how's he coping, that father of yours?

(KEVIN *swallows the scone.*)
How's the cooking going?
(KEVIN *hesitates, avoiding her eyes.*)
KEVIN: It's ... all right. He's coping.
(MAY *doesn't entirely miss his hesitancy.*)

49. Int. Jim's kitchen
Jim/Denise/Kevin

(JIM *is sitting at the kitchen table with a glass of beer in front of him. He tops it up.* DENISE *moves an empty bottle to the sink, stands there.* JIM *looks as though he's been drinking quite a bit. Not drunk, but affected by beer.* KEVIN *stands in the doorway, tie and coat off, still in the rest of his uniform. He looks defensive.*)
JIM: And it's no good sticking out your lip. I've made up my mind.
KEVIN: I'm not sticking out my lip.
DENISE: Jim ...
JIM: What'd your Aunt May think if ...
KEVIN: She wouldn't mind. I could have my old room ...
JIM: And what would they think of me?
(*Glaring at the boy.* KEVIN *remains very cool.*)
KEVIN: I didn't think you'd mind.
JIM: Well, I bloody-well do mind. You'll stay here. In your own home.
DENISE: Jim, I think I should ...
(JIM *is angry, unreasonable.*)
JIM: Not gonna be dictated to by some prude of a kid.
DENISE: Jim, please.
JIM: Well, what's up with you? You want to go too?
(DENISE *doesn't answer.*)
Well? Do you?
(DENISE *looks at* KEVIN, *hesitant.*)
DENISE: No.
JIM: No.
(*He wheels back on* KEVIN.)
So make the best of it.
(*He picks up the bottle, sees it's empty, goes to the fridge.* KEVIN *watches him coldly. There's no more beer in the fridge.* JIM *slams the fridge door angrily, glares at* DENISE *and* KEVIN, *as though it's their fault.*)
No beer. I'm going out ...
(DENISE *jumps at the opportunity to end this.*)
DENISE: I'll just get my jacket.
JIM: No! No. I just ... want to ... go by myself.
(*He has calmed down.* DENISE *upset by this.*)
You ... you can stay and talk to the boy.
(KEVIN *steps aside as* JIM *makes for the door, glances at him.*)
Might be able to tell him some of the facts of life.
(*And exits, bumping against the door frame as he goes.* KEVIN

looks at DENISE. *She returns the look, very troubled. After a moment,* DENISE *wearily sits at the table.* KEVIN *watches her dispassionately. After a moment, she speaks.*)
DENISE: Do you want something to eat?
KEVIN: I had something at Aunty May's.
(DENISE *avoids his eyes.*)
DENISE: Did you tell her? About me.
KEVIN: No. I didn't say anything.
(*He turns to leave the room.*)
DENISE: Kevin? I ... I love him, too.
(*He turns on her, furious, near tears.*)
KEVIN: Bugger him! I hate him!
(*She flinches at his anger.*)

50. Ext. Outside sly grog shop
Jim/Cocky

(*The "shop" is surrounded by a high corrugated iron fence with a small, heavy gate, in a city lane.* JIM *hammers on the gate loudly. After a moment it partially opens, held by a heavy chain. The "cockatoo's" face appears in the opening.*)
COCKY: Yeah?
JIM: Want a drink. Let's in.
(*The cockatoo looks at him hard for a moment.*)
COCKY: You're the Spieler's mate, aren't ya?
JIM: Yeah. Here the other night.
(*The cockatoo unchains the gate, pulls it open, glancing down the lane.*)
COCKY: He's inside. Him an' Porky.
(JIM *slips in and the gate is slammed,* SFX *the rattle of the chain being fixed.*)

51. Ext. Yard of sly grog shop
Jim/Cocky

(JIM *waits for the cockatoo to fix the chain. The cockatoo turns, nods towards a door in a battered old house.*)
COCKY: Know where to go?
(JIM *nods, walks to the door, followed by the cockatoo.*)

52. Int. Sly grog shop
Jim/Spieler/Porky/Cocky

(*The interior is sleazy, a few battered chairs and tables, bare lights, a bar. There's an unused piano, a few pictures on the walls, very little other furniture. The people sitting at the tables look very ordinary. The types you'd find in any R.S.L. or Leagues Club today, except that they're all men. There is nothing foreboding or evil about the place. It's somewhere to get a drink after hours. JIM sees SPIELER and PORKY immediately. They're sitting at a table with a bottle of beer, merry, SPIELER watching happily as PORKY roars his head off at one of SPIELER's stories.)*

PORKY: Gees, Spieler, you'll be the death o' me. Honest ...

(*JIM reaches the table with the cockatoo.*)

COCKY: Spieler, Porky—mate o' yours.

(*SPIELER looks over his shoulder.*)

SPIELER: Jimbo!

(*PORKY gives a hoot of welcome. SPIELER gets up unsteadily, pushes out a chair, slaps JIM on the shoulder.*)

Put your bum down, mateybo! Put your bum down!

JIM (*grinning*): G'day, Spieler, Porky.

PORKY: G'day, Digger.

(*SPIELER shoves JIM down in the chair.*)

SPIELER: Get another bottle, Porky. Good to see yar, Jimbo. Got in all right.

COCKY: He's 'ere, isn't he?

SPIELER: Good on you, Cocky. You're a sweet old bastard.

(*COCKY goes to turn away, remembers something.*)

COCKY: You all staying for the game? Swy.

SPIELER: We'll be in it, Cock. What time?

JIM: I've come to drink.

(*SPIELER slaps him on the shoulder.*)

SPIELER: You'll be all right, mate.

COCKY: Starts at nine.

SPIELER: We'll be in it.

(*Grins at JIM.*)

SPIELER: After we get a few into us, eh?

(*PORKY returns with two bottles, and another glass. JIM grabs the glass, starts to pour. COCKY looks at the three of them, not very happy.*)

COCKY: All right. Just remember the rules, you blokes. No fightin', no singin'. Or you're out on your arse.

(*PORKY looks hurt.*)

PORKY: Cocky!

(*COCKY turns away, leaves. The three men fill their glasses. The SPIELER raises his glass.*)

SPIELER: Here we go again, Jimbo! The old Unit!

(*Offering a toast.*)

JIM: Stuff the Unit.

(*He throws the glassful down his throat at a swallow, reaches for the bottle again. He's going to do some steady drinking. PORKY looks at his effort with admiration.*)

PORKY: Me too! Stuff the Unit!

(*And pours his down in similar fashion. SPIELER shrugs.*)

SPIELER: Whatever you say. Stuff the unit!

(*And bombs down his drink. JIM starts to fill them up again. The room is filling up with drinkers as COCKY lets more men in, and the noise level is rising. Mostly conversation, a few laughs, nothing out of hand.)*

53. Int. Jim's living room
Denise/Kevin

(DENISE sitting in the living room, hands in lap, thinking. KEVIN walks in from the kitchen, as though to pass through.)
DENISE: Kevin.
  (He hesitates.)
  Sit down.
  (He doesn't move.)
  I want to talk to you. It's important.
  (He moves across and sits on the arm of a chair.)
KEVIN: What?
  (She takes a moment to start, picking her words, rather hesitant.)
DENISE: I think I know how you feel. About me being here.
KEVIN: Then why stay?
DENISE: I told you why.
  (KEVIN stares at her unrelenting.)
  Don't you know what it's like to love someone?
  (He says nothing, looks away.)
  I thought you might understand.
  (KEVIN turns on her angrily.)
KEVIN: You've only known him a couple of days.
  (She nods gently. And it makes him angry.)
  You expect me to be like him, don't you! You think you can make me forget my mother ...
  (He stops, fury welling up, and it's a moment before he can go on.)
  Well I won't. You think ... just because ... because you're a bit pretty ...
DENISE: Kevin. Please ...
  (She seems reluctant to say it.)
  I ... don't think I'll be here long.
  (KEVIN shows some surprise.)
KEVIN: But ...
DENISE: I think ... your father needed me. Needs me now. For a little while.
  (KEVIN can't cope, stares silently.)
  In a while ...
  (She shrugs.)
  He won't need me!
  (KEVIN resorts to anger.)
KEVIN: Then go. Go home now. While he's out.
  (She shakes her head, no..)
DENISE: Not as long as he wants me here.
KEVIN: He doesn't want you! You ... you're too young.
  (She looks at him with surprise at this turn.)
  You're not much older than me!

(She's got no answer. After a moment she changes tack.)
DENISE: Have you got a girl-friend?
(KEVIN looks at her quickly.)
KEVIN: It's none of your business.
DENISE: No. I'm sorry.
(Silence for a moment.)
KEVIN: Why?
DENISE: If you did ... you might understand. Maybe.
KEVIN: All right. I ... I have. But I still don't—
DENISE: Don't you ... don't you find it helps when things aren't going well ... just to talk to her?
KEVIN*(bitterly)*: Is that what you do with Dad? Just talk?
(It hits home. DENISE flushes. KEVIN gets up.)
I'm not going to stay here. I'm going out.
DENISE: Kevin? I hope you're not as cruel to her.
(She looks very hurt, and for a moment KEVIN is sorry. But steels himself.)

54. Int. Sly grog shop
Jim/Spieler/Porky/Spinner/Controller/Cocky/Gamblers

(A large area has been cleared, all the tables removed, although one or two men are still drinking at the bar. In the centre of the room a tarpaulin has been laid, and a noisy two-up game is in progress. The spinner stands in the middle with the kip and pennies, ready. The controller calls.)
CONTROLLER: Centre's set!
(JIM stands upright, from the centre of the ring, where he has laid his bet. As he backs away, he nearly falls. SPIELER catches him.)
SPIELER: Twenty quid! I thought you weren't gonna bet.
(JIM pulls away from him, says nothing.)
CONTROLLER: Come in Spinner!
(The coins fly up and fall. A cry rises from round the ring.)
GAMBLERS: And it's heads!
(SPIELER looks wryly at JIM. JIM ignores it, pulls out his wallet, looks in it. He's got nothing. He turns to SPIELER.)
SPIELER: Don't look at me, mate. I got enough for a couple more bottles.
PORKY: I'm flat.
(JIM looks about, sees COCKY.)
JIM: What about the house?
(PORKY looks worried.)
PORKY: You're not playing with the boys now, mate. These blokes ...
JIM: Will they?
(SPIELER shrugs.)
SPIELER: You're a mate of ours. They'll front you credit. Till tomorrow.
JIM: Tomorrow?

(SPIELER *nods.*)
SPIELER: If you can't pay tomorrow ...
JIM: Fix it for me, Spieler. Get us a hundred.
(SPIELER *looks at him long and hard, shrugs.*)
SPIELER: Your funeral, Jimbo.
(*And calls to the cockatoo.*)
Cocky!
(COCKY *places a bet himself, moves towards them as the controller calls.*)
CONTROLLER: Centre's set!
(JIM *wipes the palms of his hands on his trouser legs, nervously, as* COCKY *approaches.*)

55. Ext. Karen's porch
Karen/Kevin

(KAREN *stands in her doorway, facing* KEVIN, *who is using the same nervous gesture as his father.*)
KAREN: Out where?
KEVIN: Just for a walk. Down the Bay.
(KAREN *looks doubtful.* KEVIN *struggles to keep the plea from his voice.*)
I ... I want to talk to you.
(KAREN *realizes something's wrong.*)
KAREN: I'll just tell Mum.
(*She hurries inside.* KEVIN *waits, moving nervously.* KAREN *returns, with a cardigan, pulls the door closed.*)
It's all right.
(KEVIN *looks relieved, lets her walk past, follows her to the gate, hurries and opens it for her. She smiles at him.*)

56. Int. Sly grog shop
Jim/Spieler/Porky/Cocky/Gamblers

(JIM *standing watching the centre as the gamblers snatch up their winnings. His face shows he's lost again.* SPIELER *takes his arm.*)
SPIELER: Come on. You better come with us, Jimbo.
(JIM *pulls his arm away. He has a glass of beer, swigs at it.*)
JIM: 'Nother fifty. Get us another fifty.
(*He is getting slurred, fairly drunk.* SPIELER *is remarkably sober.*)
SPIELER: No chance, mate. You've done enough.
(JIM *gives him a dirty look, looks around, sees cockatoo.*)
JIM: Hey, Cocky. C'mere.
(*The cockatoo walks across.*)
SPIELER: Well, you're on your own. I'm taking Porky home.
(*He nods to where* PORKY *is leaning drunkenly on the bar.*)
JIM (*uninterested*): Good on you. Cocky? What about another fifty.

(COCKY *considers.*)
COCKY: You good for it?
JIM: You'll get it back.
(COCKY *shrugs.*)
COCKY: I know.
(*He digs for the money. SPIELER makes a last try.*)
SPIELER: Aw, come on, Jim. Cut your losses.
(*JIM holds his hand out for the money as COCKY counts it out.*)
JIM: Buzz off, Spieler.
(*COCKY grins at SPIELER, hands the last of the fifty to JIM. SPIELER stares at him, a bit hurt.*)
SPIELER: All right. I will. Mate.
(*And turns away. JIM is unaffected, already peeling off a bet, turning back to the game.*)

57. Ext. Promenade, Coogee
Kevin/Karen

(*KAREN and KEVIN walk hand in hand from the direction of the Grotto Milk Bar towards the Promenade. They reach the wall overlooking the beach, and KAREN takes her hand from KEVIN's, leans on the wall. KEVIN leans beside her.*)
KAREN: It's calm. Pretty.
KEVIN: Mm.
(*He rather hesitantly puts his arm around her shoulders, half expecting it to be pushed away. KAREN smiles at him, moves a little closer. Reassured, KEVIN holds her firmly, and they both stand in silence, looking at the sea.*)
KAREN: What are you going to do? About ... home?
(*KEVIN shrugs.*)
KEVIN: I don't know. I don't want to think about it now.
KAREN: Could you talk to your Auntie? She might be able ...
KEVIN: I don't want to talk about it.
KAREN: I thought you wanted to.
KEVIN: I want to ...
(*He grabs her, pulls her around, and kisses her, very roughly. She struggles against him. Finally he lets her move back a little.*)
KAREN: You were hurting me ...
KEVIN: I'm sorry.
(*He's getting agitated, grabs her again.*)
KAREN: Kevin!
(*He kisses her again, not quite so fiercely, but still rough. She suffers it for a while, finally has to break free.*)
I can't breathe ...
KEVIN: Come down to the beach.
KAREN: No.
KEVIN: Come on.
KAREN: No!
KEVIN: Come on!

KAREN: Kevin, no!
(By now he is trying to drag her towards the steps, shaking with his passion.)
KEVIN: Come on.
(She resists, beginning to get scared.)
KAREN: Kevin, please, stop it! I can't!
(He pulls her hard, grabs her, angry, frustrated.)
KEVIN: Why? Why not?
KAREN: I can't. I told Mum ...
KEVIN: You did for Muzza. You did for him!
(KAREN looks as though he's slapped her.)
KAREN: What? I didn't ...
KEVIN: Why not me? What's wrong with me? You let him!
(KAREN is getting wild, half frightened, half furious.)
KAREN: I didn't let him do anything! He kissed me ...
(KEVIN lets her go.)
KEVIN: Don't bloody lie! What's wrong with me? Eh?
(KAREN released, sobs, pushes away from him and starts to run. KEVIN makes a grab at her, misses, and suddenly deflates.)
Karen!
(She keeps running. He takes a step or two after her.)
Karen!
(She runs off into the dark. KEVIN stops. Staring after her. His shoulders fall and he stands looking as if he's lost everything in the world.)
KEVIN: Oh, God.

58. Int. Sly grog shop
Jim/Cocky/Tod

(The game is going on in B/G. JIM and COCKY stand at the bar. JIM is desperate.)
JIM: Another fifty, all right?
(COCKY grins.)
COCKY: No chance, mate. You're in for two hundred now.
JIM: Just a chance to get it back.
(COCKY shakes his head. JIM gets coldly angry, sobering up.)
JIM: Listen. You bastards think you hold all the cards, don't you?
(COCKY retains his good humour.)
COCKY: Don't cause yourself any trouble, matey.
JIM *(aggressively)*: Trouble. See who's gonna get trouble ...
(As he starts to speak, COCKY casually snaps his finger over his head. JIM breaks off at the gesture, and almost instantly a big man, TOD, is standing beside COCKY, grinning at JIM.)
COCKY: I think you've had enough tonight, Mr. Lindsay. Time you were tucked up in bed with mum.
JIM: Bastard.
(TOD puts his hand on JIM'S shoulder. JIM wrenches it away. TOD and COCKY find all this very funny.)

COCKY: I dunno. You blokes. You think you spend a couple of years in the army, you're tough guys.
(*He stops playing.*)
Show him the way out, Toddy.
(TOD *moves alongside* JIM.)
TOD: Come on, Digger.
(*Grinning at the name. Gives* JIM *a slight, gentle push.* JIM *braces himself, then realizes he's got no show.*)
JIM: All right.
(*He starts to move.*)
COCKY: Two hundred. Tomorrow.
(JIM *hesitates.*)
JIM: Tomorrow's Saturday. If you can wait ...
COCKY: Tomorrow.
(*Smiles at* JIM.)
Or you'd better expect visitors. You explain what I mean, Toddy. When you show our mate out.
(TOD *grins back, gives* JIM *another gentle push forward.* JIM *moves, looking worried, not a little frightened.*)

59. Int. Jim's house
Kevin/Denise

(*The hallway. The front door opens,* KEVIN *slips in quietly. He closes the door gently and moves slowly down the dim passageway. As he passes his father's door,* DENISE *calls softly from the bedroom.*)
DENISE: Kevin? Is that you?
(KEVIN *hesitates, decides against replying, hurries past. He turns into his own room.*)

60. Int. Kevin's room
Kevin/Denise/Jim

(KEVIN *flops on the edge of his bed, sits for a moment, then wrenches his shoes off, throws them in anger at the wardrobe.*)
KEVIN: Bitch! Bitch!
(*Then he throws himself backwards, on to the pillow, puts his arm up over his face to shield his eyes from the light. The door slowly opens,* DENISE *stands there, in a night-dress.*)
DENISE: Kevin? Is anything wrong?
(KEVIN *groans, twists away, impatiently.*)
KEVIN: Oh, God.
(*She doesn't know what to do, moves into the room a little hesitantly.*)
This is *my* room.
DENISE: Did you see your girl?
(*He stiffens a little, and she knows that he has.*)

I thought you might. Did it ... help? Talking about it?
(*He makes no reply. She moves to the bed, sits on the edge, half expecting him to complain.*)
I thought ... maybe ... you might feel different. About me. And your father.
(*She waits, but gets no reply.*)
I suppose I was hoping for a bit much.
(KEVIN *looks at her. She is staring at the floor, unhappy, and it spurs him to attack.*)

KEVIN: Why would I want to talk about it? It's none of my business. And I couldn't care less.

DENISE: I know you don't mean ...

KEVIN: You want to know what we talked about? Nothing! I took her down the beach and knocked her off!
(*Glaring at her. She reacts a little at the harshness of his voice.*)
Well? How does that affect you? You wanted to know, didn't you?

DENISE: Kevin ...

KEVIN: What? It's good enough for you and him. Why shouldn't I?
(*She is silent for a moment.*)

DENISE: I ... can't very well ... (*shrugs*) ... say anything to you. Not when ...
(*She stops, puts her hand on his shoulder, concerned.*)
Is that how you think of it? Of her? As "knocking her off"?
(*He glares at her angrily. Then the anger slowly evaporates. He looks away.*)

KEVIN: I didn't. She ... didn't let me.
(*All his humiliation and frustration in it.*)

DENISE: Kevin, she's very young. Sixteen?
(*He nods.*)

DENISE: At her age ...

KEVIN: She let him. She let Mick!
(*He's very near to tears. She tries to console him.*)

DENISE: Oh, Kevin.
(*He turns back.*)

KEVIN: She let him. My mate. She let him ...
(DENISE *touches his hair, brushing it back with her fingers, a light caress, soothing him.*)

DENISE: You musn't ... don't think about it. Don't torment yourself.
(*He stares up at her as she leans over him, and he relaxes, begins to tremble slightly. As she strokes his hair, he reaches up, slowly, almost fearfully, and places his hand on her breast.* DENISE *shows no reaction, just continues to stroke his hair. Then she slowly leans down and kisses him gently on the lips. For a long moment, neither of them move; then, at* KEVIN'S *first stirring, she sits up slowly, and gently takes his hand from her breast. She kisses it, places it down on the bed.*)
Go to sleep, Kevin.
(*She stands.*)

KEVIN: Denise ...

DENISE: Go to sleep.

(*She switches off the light and leaves the room. As she moves into the hall, the hall light flicks on. She starts and turns.* JIM *is standing at the open front door, leaning on it drunkenly, staring at her. His face has been bruised, his lip cut, by* TOD'S *"lesson".*)
Jim!
(*He lurches upright.*)
JIM: You're in the wrong room.
(*And stumbles towards her. She hurries to him and holds him. He's very drunk.*)

61. Int. Kitchen, Jim's house
Kevin/Jim

(KEVIN *stands in the doorway, in a casual shirt, shorts. He is watching* JIM *at the sink, dabbing at his bruised face with a cloth and hot water.* JIM *grimaces, pours out the water, turns and sees* KEVIN. *He grunts.* KEVIN *walks towards the sink.*)
KEVIN: Will I make you some tea?
(JIM *shakes his head, grimaces again at the pain caused.*)
JIM: Yeah. Please.
(KEVIN *starts to fill the kettle, watching his father surreptitiously.* JIM *sits at the table. He doesn't look well, has a hangover and is depressed.* KEVIN *goes through all the actions of making tea, and it's not till the kettle is on that he picks up enough courage to speak.*)
KEVIN: I ... Is Denise
JIM: She's gone. I ... She went last night. Won't be back.
(KEVIN *looks away. They both avoid each other's eyes.* KEVIN *finds the cloth at the sink, tosses it into the rubbish bin. He is hesitant about bringing up the subject.*)
KEVIN: Did you ... was there some trouble? At the pub?
JIM: No.
(*Intending to end it there, but sees* KEVIN *is hurt by his abruptness.*)
I ... went to a gambling place.
(KEVIN *looks at him quickly.* JIM *shrugs.*)
Lost some money. Couldn't pay.
(*He glances at the clock, gets up.*)
Look. I can do that. Why don't you get off to the beach?
KEVIN: I thought I'd have a cup ...
(JIM *digs in his pockets.*)
JIM: Why don't you get a milk shake?
(*He can't find any money, but* KEVIN *gets the message.*)
KEVIN: I've got money. All right.
(*He moves to the door.* JIM *calls after him.*)
JIM: You could have your lunch there. Pies or something.
(KEVIN *looks at him, feeling he's being got rid of.*)
KEVIN: All right. I will.
(*And leaves.* JIM *looks after him, unhappily. Glances at the clock*

again. SFX *the front door opens and closes, he starts a little, realizes it's only* KEVIN *going, relaxes. He finds the water is boiling, pours it into the pot for tea. Is putting the kettle back on the stove, thinks of something. He pulls the belt from his pants, looks at it for a moment, wraps one end of it round his fist, the buckle hanging free, swings it and lets the buckle thud into the palm of his hand. Then he re-threads it through his belt loops, carefully leaving it out of each second loop, does up the belt. Then very quickly he undoes the buckle, wrenches the belt out of the few loops holding it, wraps it around his fist. Satisfied, he starts to re-thread it as before.*)

62. Ext. Coogee Promenade
Kevin/Mick

(KEVIN *stands on the Promenade, looking down at the beach. He sees* MICK, *lying on the sand, looking up at him. They hold each other's eyes for a beat, making no signs of recognition. Then* KEVIN *turns his back, faces away from the beach. He moves away towards the footpath.* MICK *lowers himself back on to the sand, sunbakes, eyes closed.*)

63. Ext. Back yard of Jim's house
Jim/Cocky/Tod/Jack/Kevin/Porky/Spieler

(JIM *stands at the back door, looking out at* COCKY, TOD, *and another tough,* JACK. JIM *now seems quite calm.*)
JIM: I haven't got it.
(COCKY *nods, smiling.*)
COCKY: Kind of expected you wouldn't. Why I brought the boys.
(JIM *watches as* JACK *moves away to the back gate, props a length of wood against it, so it can't be opened.*)
JIM (*calmly*): I've got fifty quid left of my deferred pay.
COCKY: Not enough, mate. Is it?
(JIM *shakes his head slowly.* COCKY *shakes his in unison, mock-sadly.*)
No. I dunno. You blokes.
(*He sighs.*)
We can't let it go, mate. Y'know that.
(JIM *pulls the back door closed behind him, moves down a step.* JACK *and* TOD *move slightly out on either side of* COCKY.)
Two hundred quid is a lot o' money, mate.
(*He grins.*)
We're prepared to go to a lot of trouble to get it back.
(TOD *has been moving warily closer.* JIM *suddenly pulls off his belt and winds it onto his fist.* TOD *stops short, glances at* COCKY. COCKY *looks pained.*)
You know you've only got yourself to blame for this, mate. Bit unfair taking it out on poor old Toddy.

(JIM *suddenly becomes aware of a movement on his side, manages to half-turn as* JACK *barrels into him, grabbing the belt.* JIM *is beaten before he starts.* JACK *swings the belt, and* JIM, *already off balance, sprawls flying into the yard, and* TODDY *bounces on him, driving his heel into the small of* JIM'S *back, bringing a cry of pain from* JIM, *and driving him to the ground. Then* JACK *and* TODDY *start to work him over, as* COCKY *watches dispassionately. The two men use their fists, pulling* JIM *up as he slumps to the ground, or kicking him up for variety. Then they hold him against the fence, battered and bleeding, and look to* COCKY.)

TOD: 'Nough, Cock?

(COCKY *looks at* JIM, *who looks back at him, pleading.*)

COCKY: Two hundred quid? You reckon that's two hundred quid's worth, Toddy?

(TOD *shrugs.*)

JIM: You ... bastard.

(TOD *hits him again, and* JACK *moves in again.* JIM *groans with pain. The back door of the house flies open, and* KEVIN *is standing there.* KEVIN'S *face registers his shock, fear.*)

KEVIN: Dad!

(*The four men turn,* JIM *being held up by* JACK.)

JIM: Kev ...

(KEVIN *rushes at* JACK *in fury, swinging his fists.*)

JACK: Here!

KEVIN: Let him go! Let him go!

(TOD *swipes at* KEVIN, *knocking him aside.* COCKY *grabs him and hangs on to him.*)

COCKY: Come on, finish it off.

(KEVIN *struggles to free himself as* JACK *and* TOD *return their attentions to* JIM. *They no sooner get the first blows in, than the back gate is smashed with a splintering crash and* PORKY *appears amid the wreckage.* COCKY *shoves* KEVIN *cruelly away and the boy slams against the fence and falls heavily.* PORKY *lumbers heavily into the yard,* COCKY *backs away from him.* PORKY *sees* JIM, *battered, held up by* JACK.)

PORKY: You bastards.

(*He moves towards them.*)

TOD: Get him!

(JACK *drops* JIM, *moves forward towards* PORKY. *There is a sudden sound of splintering wood, and* TOD *turns quickly to see* SPIELER *with a paling he's ripped from the fence. The paling shatters over* TOD'S *head, and he drops like a pole-axed bull.* JACK *looks back, frightened now, as* SPIELER *pulls another paling from the fence.* SPIELER *has no chance to use it, as* PORKY *grabs* JACK *and hammers him to the ground.* COCKY *is out of the gate and running as fast as he can.* KEVIN *drops beside his father, turns him over.* JIM'S *face is a mess, he's unconscious.*)

64. Int. Jim's bedroom
Kevin/Jim/Denise

(JIM *is lying on his bed, opens his eyes painfully. His face is washed, sticking-plastered, and he's been changed into pyjamas. He groans, sits up.* KEVIN *is standing on the other side of the room, moves into view.*)

KEVIN: Porky says you've got to stay in bed.

(JIM *swings his legs over the edge, it hurts, and he feels his chest.*)

JIM: Bugger Porky. Gawd!

(*He opens his pyjama shirt, looks at his chest. It is liberally daubed with a red dye.*)

Porky didn't do that.

(*Feels his face, touches the sticking-plaster.*)

Or this.

(KEVIN *hesitates.*)

KEVIN: I ... got Denise.

(JIM *looks at him hard, for a long moment, and* KEVIN *meets his gaze.* JIM *looks away.*)

JIM: Where is she?

KEVIN: Outside.

(DENISE'S *voice is heard from the doorway.*)

DENISE: I'm here. I was just going.

(JIM *turns and looks at her.* KEVIN *hesitates, walks to the door.*)

KEVIN: I'll be outside.

(*He leaves.* DENISE *doesn't move from the doorway, stands staring back at* JIM.)

65. Int. Jim's kitchen

(KEVIN *walks slowly into the kitchen, stands inside the door, looking at the kitchen table. It is a few moments before he registers that there is something on the table. He investigates. It is* JIM's *belt, and under it a pile of ten pound notes. He picks them up, wondering, then suddenly, realizing, hurries to the back door, which is open.*)

66. Ext. Jim's back yard

(KEVIN *looking out the back door. His POV the empty yard. The gate has been placed back in position, propped up in its frame. There is no sign of* PORKY *or* SPIELER. KEVIN *turns back inside.*)

67. Int. Jim's kitchen

(KEVIN *slowly closes the door, walks back into the kitchen, picks up the money again.* SFX *the front door closes. He hurries to the end of the hall, looks up the passageway to the front door, which is closed. Then he hurries up the passage to his father's bedroom.*)

68. Int. Jim's bedroom
Kevin/Jim

(KEVIN *stops at his father's door, looks in.* JIM *is sitting on the side of the bed. He looks up at* KEVIN.)
KEVIN: Where's ... Denise?
(JIM *gets up, pulling off his pyjama shirt.*)
JIM: She's ... gone.
(*He picks up a shirt, climbs into it.* KEVIN *watches, upset.*)
KEVIN: Dad. I wish ...
(*Then blurts it out.*)
Dad, I'm sorry. For everything. If you want her to stay ...
(JIM *turns to him.* KEVIN *breaks off, unable to continue.* JIM *turns away, does up the shirt, thinking over what he's going to say.*)
JIM: I ... know what you mean. I think, maybe, you and I have got some catching up to do. First.
(*Then he turns and grins at the boy.*)
O.K.?
(KEVIN *nods, smiles back.* JIM *reaches for his trousers.*)
There's still plenty of sun left. Why don't you use it?

69. Ext. Coogee Beach
Mick/Kevin

(MICK *lies stretched out like a lizard on the sand. A pair of bare feet appear beside him. He looks up.* KEVIN *is standing there, looking down.*)
KEVIN: Mick.
(MICK *rolls over on his side.*)
MICK: G'day.
(KEVIN *drops his shorts, pulls off his shirt and sits on the sand beside* MICK.)
KEVIN: Good surf.
(MICK *nods, rolls over on his belly. Both boys stretch out on their stomachs, letting the sun beat down on them. After a moment,* MICK *murmurs lazily.*)
MICK: Great day.
(KEVIN *nods, drowsy.*)
KEVIN: Yeah. Great.
(*They lie, soaking up the sun.*)

Roberts on *Lindsay's Boy**

As an inordinately lazy professional writer for television, I never fail to succumb to the temptation to leave the correction of even the most obvious script faults to a second, later draft. The first writing is a thing of pleasure. Rewriting is just work. Should the producer fail to find the faults that exist in the first draft, all the better. They stay. I find it easy enough to convince myself I'm being hyper-critical of my own work, and that everyone else can see the underlying genius I am too modest to admit. Naturally, of course, the faults that were obvious to me in the script become just as obvious to the viewer in the production, and I come to bitterly regret my laziness in not correcting them.

More often than not, this situation is negated by a careful and wily script editor working on the principle that all writers are not only lazy but narcissistic and have to be bullied into changing their deathless dialogue or their skilful directions. But *Lindsay's Boy*, through unusual circumstances, was never edited, and was produced in its first draft form, warts and all, as it is printed here. It abounds in faults that I assure myself would have been corrected if someone had made me rewrite. The pace in a couple of scenes is slow to the point of tedium, the characters at times become laconic to the point of obscurity, and some intended humour is completely unfunny.

Yet, in spite of its faults, *Lindsay's Boy* is the play I like best of all that I've written. I feel no need to defend it, and I feel none of the usual embarrassment when someone mentions it either with praise or disapproval. A trilogy of plays, "Three Men of the City", written about the same time, brought me more critical approval, a B.B.C. sale, and a Writers' Guild Award, but *Lindsay's Boy* brought the satisfaction of doing something that, good or bad, was honestly felt. I suppose that, in a medium which encourages as much hack writing as good writing, is something to be pleased about.

---

* Both this and the following piece were written for this anthology, 1975.

Roberts on Writing for Television

That I am and always have been a one-medium writer, and that my medium is television, has sometimes been levelled at me as an accusation of being involved in something a little seedy. There seems to be a tendency among some to equate the television scriptwriter with the pulp novelist, the women's magazine short story writer, and the pornographer. Fill the page, take the money and run.

But television drama need not be pulp any more than all novels need be Dirty Dick Westerns or Quivering Heart romances.

In this country, certainly, where almost every economic condition mitigates against quality in the medium, there is a constant stream of excellent writing for television from a small group of writers who believe in their medium, who see no sin in its popularity, and who would prefer to present their work once to a living room audience of perhaps three million than to watch it die by degrees in near-empty theatres.

The playwright and the novelist will blame television for the decline of those media, and will be largely correct in doing so. But the fact is there and will apparently remain. Television appears certain to attract larger and larger audiences. Cable TV, casettes, satellites, and all the new and forthcoming hardware of science will expand both the audiences and the volume of writing the medium will consume. The stage, the cinema, and the novel may well suffer further losses.

This is not the gloating of someone who thinks he's backed the right contestant. I believe it is a simple acceptance of a very apparent trend. And while the falling off in one medium can never be fully replaced by growth in another, we must accept the fact that every effort must be made, every opportunity taken to prepare the conditions, the soil from which good television writing may continue to spring. Or all good writing might very well die.

The screen in the living room consumes an incredible number of hours of drama writing, and quantity does not necessarily breed quality. But it does provide opportunity, both to financially support writers and to provide them with audiences. And only the dreamer can deny the necessity of these.

There is a strong basis of good television writing already existent in this country on which to build. It is subject to a lack of support from the controllers of commercial channels, to an often vicious and unreasonable assault from some of Australia's notoriously bitchy critics, and to an unequal struggle against cheaply purchased imported drama.

That Australian television writing continues to maintain and lift its standards in at least some areas is as remarkable as it is praiseworthy.

Perhaps I tend to protest too much, but I feel no shame in being a one-medium television writer. And I'm very proud of the company I keep.

Select Bibliography

CONTEMPORARY AUSTRALIAN PLAYS

Published by Angus and Robertson, Sydney:

Michael Boddy and Robert Ellis, *The Legend of King O'Malley*, 1974.
Barry Oakley, *The Feet of Daniel Mannix*, 1975.
Alexander Buzo, *Tom*, 1975.

Published by Currency Press, Sydney (later Currency Methuen):

Alexander Buzo, *Macquarie*, 1971.
James Searle, *The Lucky Streak*, 1972.
Dorothy Hewett, *The Chapel Perilous*, 1972.
David Williamson, *The Removalists*, 1972.
Jack Hibberd, *A Stretch of the Imagination*, 1973.
Jim McNeil, *The Chocolate Frog and The Old Familiar Juice*, 1973.
David Williamson, *Don's Party*, 1973.
John Romeril, *I Don't Know Who To Feel Sorry For*, 1973.
Alexander Buzo, *Three Plays*, 1973.
Peter Kenna, *A Hard God*, 1974.
Alexander Buzo, *Coralie Lansdowne Says No*, 1974.
Ron Blair, *President Wilson in Paris*, 1974.
Jim McNeil, *How Does Your Garden Grow*, 1974.
David Williamson, *Three Plays*, 1974.
Barry Oakley, *Bedfellows*, 1975.
John Romeril, *The Floating World*, 1975.
David Williamson, *The Department*, 1975.
Colin Free, William Leonard Marshall, Geoffrey Maslen, Louis Nowra, ed. Alrene Sykes, *Five Plays for Radio*, 1975.
Ron Blair, *The Christian Brother*, and Barry Oakley, *A Lesson in English*, 1976.
Dorothy Hewett, *The Tatty Hollow Story and Bon Bons and Roses for Dolly*, 1976.
Edward Geoghegan, *The Currency Lass*, ed. Roger Covell, 1976.
Jennifer Compton, *Crossfire*, 1976.

Dorothy Hewett, *This Old Man Comes Rolling Home*, 1976.
Alexander Buzo, *Norm and Ahmed*, and Louis Esson, *The Woman Tamer*, 1976.
Peter Kenna, *Three Plays*, 1976.
Richard Bradshaw, *Bananas*, and Joseph Musaphia, *The Guerilla*, 1976.
Ric Throssell, *For Valour*, 1976.
Mary Gage, *The New Life*, and Jill Shearer, *The Foreman*, 1976.
Alma De Groen, *Going Home*, 1976.
Alexander Buzo, *Martello Towers*, 1976.
Steele Rudd, *On Our Selection*, ed. Helen Van Der Poorten, 1976.

Published by Eyre and Spottiswoode, London (and later Sun Books, Melbourne):
Patrick White, *Four Plays*, 1965.

Published by Heinemann Educational, Melbourne:
Bill Reed, *Burke's Company*, 1969.
Alan Hopgood, *And the Big Men Fly*, 1969.

Published by Methuen, London:
Rodney Milgate, *A Refined Look at Existence*, 1968.

Published by Penguin, Harmondsworth and Melbourne:
Alan Seymour, Douglas Stewart, Hal Porter, *Three Australian Plays*, 1963.
Alexander Buzo, Jack Hibberd, John Romeril, *Plays*, 1970.
Jack Hibberd, *Dimboola*, and John Powers, *The Last of the Knucklemen*, 1974.
Kenneth Cook, *Stockade*, and Thomas Keneally, *Halloran's Little Boat*, 1975.

Published by University of Queensland Press, St. Lucia:
Ray Mathew, *A Spring Song*, 1961.
David Ireland, *Image in the Clay*, 1964.
Summer Locke-Elliott, Ray Mathew, Jack McKinney, ed. Eunice Hanger, *Three Australian Plays* (*Khaki, Bush and Bigotry*), 1968.
Eunice Hanger, ed., *6 One-Act Plays*, 1970.
Barbara Stellmach, *Four Australian Plays*, 1973.
Paul Sherman, *Melba*, 1976.

CRITICAL MATERIAL

Brisbane, Katharine. Chapter on Australian drama in Geoffrey Dutton, ed., *The Literature of Australia*. Ringwood: Penguin Books, rev. ed., 1976.
Burrows, J.F. "An Approach to the Plays of Douglas Stewart". *Southerly* 23 (1963): 94–108.

Davison, P.H. "Three Australian Plays: National Myths Under Criticism". *Southerly* 23 (1963): 110-27.
Duncan, Catherine. "A French Production of Alan Seymour's *The One Day of the Year*". *Meanjin Quarterly* 25 (1966): 229-37.
Gostand, Reba. "Perilous Journey to the Chapel", in Leon Cantrell, ed., *Bards, Bohemians, and Bookmen*. St. Lucia: University of Queensland Press, 1976.
Kiernan, Brian. "The Games People Play: The Development of David Williamson". *Southerly* 35 (1975): 315-29.
Oliver, Harold. "Douglas Stewart and the Art of the Radio Play". *The Texas Quarterly* 5 (Summer 1962): 193-203.
Palmer, Vance. *Louis Esson and the Australian Theatre*. Melbourne: Georgian House, 1948.
Phillips, A.A. "Assaying the New Drama". *Meanjin Quarterly* 32 (1973): 189-95.
Rees, Leslie, *The Making of Australian Drama*. Sydney: Angus and Robertson, 1973.
Semmler, Clement. *Douglas Stewart*. New York: Twayne Publishers, 1974.
Seymour, Alan. "Emu Rising: Lawler to Williamson". *London Magazine* 15 (1976): 102-08.
———. "One Image of Australia". *Meanjin Quarterly* 26 (1967): 223-29.
Sykes, Alrene. "Alan Seymour". *Australian Literary Studies* 6 (1974): 277-87.
———. "Australian Bards and British Reviewers". *Australian Literary Studies* 7 (1975): 39-49.
———. "Jack Hibberd", in Leon Cantrell, ed., *Bards, Bohemians, and Bookmen*. St. Lucia: University of Queensland Press, 1976.
Williams, Margaret. "Snakes and Ladders: New Australian Drama". *Meanjin Quarterly* 31 (1972): 178-82.
———. "Mask and Cage: Stereotype in Recent Drama". *Meanjin Quarterly* 31 (1972): 308-13.
———. "Australian Drama—A Postscript: Some Comments on Recent Criticism". *Meanjin Quarterly*, 31 (1972); 444-48.
Williamson, David. "The Removalists: A Conjunction of Limitations". *Meanjin Quarterly* 33 (1974): 413-17.

Theatre-Australia is a periodical devoted to theatre in Australia; the first issue appeared August/September 1976.

Southerly 35 (Vol. 4, 1975) contains several articles on recent Australian drama. For further critical material, see the annual bibliographies published in *Australian Literary Studies*.